CALVINUS SINCERIORIS RELIGIONIS VINDEX

Habent sua fata libelli

Volume XXXVI
of
Sixteenth Century Essays & Studies

Charles G. Nauert, Jr., and Raymond A. Mentzer
General Editors

Composed at Truman State University, Kirksville, Missouri 63501 USA. Manufactured by Edwards Brothers, Ann Arbor, Michigan. Text is set in Minion 10/12.

CALVINUS SINCERIORIS RELIGIONIS VINDEX

Calvin as Protector of the Purer Religion

EDITED BY

WILHELM H. NEUSER

AND

BRIAN G. ARMSTRONG

VOLUME XXXVI
SIXTEENTH CENTURY ESSAYS & STUDIES

Copyright© 1997. All rights reserved.
Sixteenth Century Journal Publishers, Inc.
Kirksville, Missouri 63501-4221 USA
escj@truman.edu

This book has been brought to publication
with the generous support of
Truman State University, Kirksville, Missouri

Library of Congress Cataloging-in-Publication Data

International Congress on Calvin Research (1994 : Edinburgh, Scotland)
  Calvinus sincerioris religionis vindex = Calvin as protector of the purer
religion : die Referate des Congrès international des recherches calviniennes.
International Congress on Calvin Research. Internationalen Kongresses für
Calvinforschung, vom 13. bis 16. September in Edinburgh / herausgegeben
von Wilhelm H. Neuser & unter Mitwirkung von Brian G. Armstrong.
    p.   cm. — (Sixteenth century essays and studies ; v. 36)
  English, French, and German.
  Includes bibliographical references.
  ISBN 0-940474-40-9 (alk. paper; casebound)
  ISBN 0-940474-42-5 (alk.paper; paperback)
  1. Calvin, Jean, 1509–1564—Congresses. 2. Reformed Church—Doc-
trines—History—16th century—Congresses. 3. Theology, Doctrinal—His-
tory—16th century—Congresses. I. Neuser, Wilhem. H. II. Armstrong,
Brian G. III. Title. IV. Series.
BX9418.I67   1997   97-10433
284'.2'092—dc21   CIP

∞ The paper in this publication meets the minimum requirements of the American National Standard
for Permanence of Paper for Printed Library Materials ANSI Z39.48, 1984.

Contents

Abbreviations Used in This Work

A.E.G. RC — The Registers of the Council of State, in the Genevan State Archives

A.E.G., RConsistoire — The Registers of the Consistory, in the Genevan State Archives. See also *RConsistoire*, below.

Barth, *CD* — Karl Barth, *Church Dogmatics*, 4 vols. in 11, edited by G. T. Thomson; translated by G. Bromiley (Edinburgh: T. & T. Clark, 1936–1962).

Calvini Opera — *Commentaires de Jehan Calvin sur le livre des Pseaumes* [1557], Bd. 2 (Paris, 1859), 271–72. *Calvini opera quae supersunt omnia,* 59 Bde. (Brunschwig-Berlin, 1863–1900)

CO — *Ioannis Calvini Opera Quae Supersunt Omnia ...*, 59 vols., ed. Guilielmus Baum, Eduardus Cunitz, and Eduardus Reuss (Brunsvigae & Berolinae: C. A. Schwetsche & M. Bruhm, 1834–1900. [These are vols. 29–87 of *Corpus Reformatorum*.]

CTJ — *Calvin Theological Journal*

CTS — Calvin Translation Society

Institutes — John Calvin, *Institutes of the Christian Religion*, ed. John T. McNeill, H. P. Van Dusen, trans. F. L. Battles, J. Baillie, Library of Christian Classics (Philadelphia: Westminster Press, 1960)

Migne — *Patrologia Latina*, ed. J. P. Migne (Paris: Migne, 1844–1864)

NCE — *New Catholic Encyclopedia.*

NRSV — Bible. English. New Revised Standard, 1994 [The New Oxford Annotated Bible Containing the Old and New Testaments, ed. Bruce M. Metzger, Roland E. Murphy] (New York: Oxford University Press, 1994)

OS — *Joannis Calvini Opera Selecta*, 5 vols., ed. Petrus Barth and Guilelmus Niesel (Monachii in Aeddibus: Chr. Kaiser, 1926–1962).

PL — *Patrologia Latina*, ed. J. P. Migne (Paris: Migne, 1844–1864)

R.C. — A.E.G. Registres du Counsiel, Genève

RConsistoire   *Registres du consistoire de Genève au temps de Calvin: Tome I, 1542–1544,* ed. Thomas A. Lambert and Isabella M. Watt (Geneva: Droz, 1996),

SC   *Supplementa Calviniana = Sermons Inédits [de Jean Calvin],* J. I. McCord, moderator. Erwin Mülhaupt, ed., (Neukirchen-Vluyn, Verlag des Erziehungsvereins, 1994)

STC   *A Short-Title Catalogue of Books Printed in England, Scotland & Ireland and of English Books Printed Abroad, 1475–1640.* Ed. A. W. Pollard and G. R. Redgrave. London: The Bibliographical Society, 1926

WA   Martin Luther, *Werke. Kritische Gesamtausgabe* [Weimar Ausgabe]. 107 vols. Weimar, 1883.

ZKG   *Zeitschrift für Kirchengeschichte*

Vorwort

W. H. Neuser

THE CONGRESS MET IN AUGUST 1994 at the places where the famous Calvin scholar John Knox held forth. I refer to Edinburgh and St. Andrews, the latter being where the Congress participants visited and where at the University one of the lectures was held and discussed.

The Congress was delighted to accept the invitation from the New College of the University of Edinburgh. The hearty reception and the friendly greetings of those involved are worthy to be mentioned here: The gracious welcome from the dean of the College and from the principal of New College; the invitation of the minister and the kirk session to hold the opening service in St. Giles Cathedral; the greetings of the moderator of the General Assembly of the Church of Scotland, the Right Reverend James A. Simpson; and not least, the impressive organ music by the church organist, as well as the marvelous choir performance. Additionally, the lord provost of the city of Edinburgh, the Right Honorable Norman Irons, and the principal-designate of the University of Edinburgh, Professor Stewart Sutherland, hosted the reception after the service in the city chambers. In St. Andrews the Congress also found a gracious reception and host, with a wonderful banquet. At the University library a special exhibition of Reformation texts had been prepared to the delight of the attendees, and we thank the library staff for this exhibit. Also, the Congress was welcomed by the Reformation Institute and its director, Dr. Andrew Pettegree. To all of the foregoing we offer our heartfelt thanks.

Similarly, we offer thanks to the institutions of the United Kingdom which supported the Congress financially:

- The British Academy
- The Senate of New College, Edinburgh
- The Hope Trust, Edinburgh
- The Senate of Trinity College, Glasgow
- The Scottish Reformation History Society
- The Principal and Senate of the University of St. Andrews

Particularly, we give special mention to the host institution, New College, and its faculty, especially David F. Wright, who shouldered the burden of the local arrangements.

Without the support of the Dutch, German and Swiss churches and institutions the Congress could not have been prepared and held. It made possible the meeting of the Präsidium in 1992, the translation of the lectures into the conference languages, the travel expenses of the lecturers, the printing of the proceedings, and other of the expenses. We offer our grateful thanks.

In addition, the Präsidium offers its thanks to the following:
- Deputaten Hulpverlening van de Christelijke Gereformeerde Kerken
- Evangelische Kirche in Hessen-Nassau
- Evangelische Kirche von Kurhessen-Waldeck
- Evangelische Kirche der Union
- Evangelische Kirche von Westfalen
- Evangelisches Diasporawerk Steinfurt
- Gereformeerde Bond in de Nederlandse Hervormde (Geref.) Kerken
- Kirchenkreis Tecklenburg
- Lippische Landeskirche
- Stichting Het Nederlands Protestants Convent
- Stichting Zonnenweelde
- Vereinigte Evangelische Mission Wuppertal

Now these lectures and seminars are prepared for the public; they are designed to give new impulses to Calvin research throughout the world. We are sorry not to be able to provide a short summary of the contents of the papers and seminars, but we trust the table of contents is complete enough to indicate the main ideas. In any case, surely the harvest of these papers and seminars will be reflected in future publications of the participants.

Opening Remarks

The Right Reverend James A. Simpson
Moderator of the Church of Scotland

IT GIVES ME TREMENDOUS PLEASURE on behalf of the Church of Scotland to welcome you at the commencement of this Sixth International Congress on Calvin Research. I hope that in every way you will have a most profitable conference here in this lovely city of Edinburgh. I once heard Edinburgh University described as the theological center of the Old World. Princeton was described as the theological center of the New World, and Glasgow University, my own Alma Mater, as the theological center of the Underworld. I would strongly refute the third of these suggestions, for it was in Trinity College, Glasgow, that I was first introduced to Calvin's *Institutes*. What better theological foundation could anyone have?

The poet Ben Jonson once said of Shakespeare, "He is not of an age, but for all time." I believe the same could be said of John Calvin. I personally would like to see posted on the walls of every theological college and every church vestry Calvin's statement about the task of the theologian. "The theological task," he said, "is not to divert the ears with chatter, but to strengthen consciences by teaching things true, sure and profitable." For Calvin, "talking the talk" of religion was not sufficient; we must also "walk the walk." How relevant also for the church today is the underlying principle that governed his interpretation of the Bible. "The meaning of many statements in Scripture," Calvin said, "depends on their context." The narrow, shallow biblicism of today is not the *sola scriptura* of the Reformers. I rejoice that John Calvin continues to be studied in our day.

It is surely also appropriate that the opening act of worship of your congress should be held in this church where John Knox, one of Calvin's distinguished students, once ministered. God bless you in your deliberations this week.

Address of Prof. Dr. W. H. Neuser

Secretary of the International Congress for Calvin Research

Most Esteemed Moderator of the General Assembly of the Church of
  Scotland
Most esteemed Lord Provost of the City of Edinburgh
Spectabilis and honored Colleagues of the Faculty of Divinity at New
  College
Worthy participants of the Congress who have not shied away from a
  long journey, some coming from halfway around the world
Dear members of the participants' families and guests
Dear members of the Congregation

In the name of the Präsidium I wish to thank the highly esteemed faculty for
the invitation and for the accommodations in the famous Old College. We are
delighted to hold there the Sixth International Congress.

Mentioning the Sixth International Congress invites us to give a brief resume.
The first two Congresses met in Amsterdam at the Free University. In 1982 we met
in Geneva, the so-called city of Calvin. Four years later we met in Debrecen,
known as "the Hungarian Geneva." In 1990 we left Europe in order to justify our
name as an International Congress, and we met in the heartland of America in
Grand Rapids. The grateful memory of this latest meeting at the Calvin Theological Seminary is still with us. Now we are in the city of John Knox. We have always
been associated with churches of the Reformed faith, which have a special affinity
with John Calvin and his work. But this aspect should not conceal the fact that we
are a scientific, scholarly Congress which brings together Protestant and Catholic
scholars, and indeed scholars from all denominations and persuasions. We are
proud that they all seek to gain a critical understanding of Calvin and his work.

CALVIN AND JOHN KNOX

THESE TWO MEN have, at the very least, one thing in common: both have been
viewed conservatively by their contemporaries and even today. John Knox was
evaluated in an entirely different way in his time. In 1559 François de Morel wrote
to Calvin: "John Knox has been for some time in Dieppe. He is now currying favor
in Scotland. He has dared to confess the most evil and pestilential teaching that
women are unworthy to govern, and that Christians are permitted to take up
weapons to defend themselves against such tyrants. I fear that he will be called to

the Pastoral Office by the people of Dieppe." At the same time, the congregation of Dieppe sent a letter to Calvin, writing that "John Knox is a unique organ of the Holy Spirit who, according to the grace which the Lord has poured upon him superabundantly, works to promote the Glory of Christ." One cannot speak more contradictorily about Knox.

As is well known, Calvin is criticized generally on the point of church discipline—in the next few days we shall discuss the latest, surprising findings on this theme. His polemic writings inspired fear—we will hear two lectures on this theme. He is blamed as the "father of capitalism" —we will discuss the validity of this charge. By these words I have mentioned only the best known controversies. In the other lectures and seminars we will look for solutions to many general or specific problems, or just hear about new research findings. I have the impression that we stand at the doorway of a gripping Congress.

With this festive service we open the Congress. The Präsidium has asked David Wright, himself a member of the Präsidium, an internationally recognized scholar, and Senior Lecturer in Ecclesiastical History at New College, to give the opening address.

Autoren

Prof. **Akira Demura,** Nagamachi 2-19-18, Takhaku-ku, Sendai, Miyagi 982 Japan

Dr. **Max Engammare,** Ave. Blanc 12, CH-1202 Genève, Switzerland

Prof. Dr. **Hans-Helmut Eßer,** Schloßstrasse, 15, D-48612 Horstmar, Germany

Dr. **Francis Higman,** Institut d'Histoire de la Réformation, Bibliothèque Publique et Universitaire, Ch-1211 Genève, Switzerland

Prof. **Douglas F. Kelly,** Reformed Theological Seminary, 2101 Carmel Road, Charlotte, NC 28226, USA

Prof. **Robert Kingdon,** 4 Rosewood Circle, Madison, WI 53711, USA

Mr. **Anthony N. S. Lane,** London Bible College, Green Lane, Northwood, Middlesex HA6 20W, United Kingdom

Prof. Dr. **Sou-Young Lee,** Presbyterian College and Theological Seminary, 353 Kwangjang-dong, Kwangjin-ku, Seoul, Korea

Bischof Dr. **Márkus Mihály,** Kocsi u. 15, H-2890 Tata, Hungary

Prof. Dr. **Olivier Millet,** 130 Ave. des Versailles, F-75016, Paris, France

Prof. **Richard Muller,** Calvin Theological Seminary, 3233 Burton Street, S.E., Grand Rapids, MI 49516, USA

Prof. Dr. **Wilhelm Neuser,** Lehmbrock 17, D-48346 Ostbevern, Germany

Prof. **Charles Partee,** Pittsburgh Theological Seminary, 616 N. Highland Avenue, Pittsburgh, PA 15205, USA

Dr. **Andrew D. M. Pettegree,** Dept. of Modern History, University of St. Andrews, Fife Ky16 9AL, United Kingdom

Prof. Dr. **Hans Scholl,** Scheuermassweg 11, Ch-3043 Vettlingen, Switzerland

Dr. **Jan J. Steenkamp,** Poort, Postbus 15622, Lynn East 0039, South Africa

Prof. **David Steinmetz,** The Divinity School, Duke University, Durham, NC 27706, USA

Dr. **Peter Wilcox,** St. Columba House, Peterborough Close, United Kingdom

Prof. **David Wright,** Ecclesiastical History, New College, University of Edinburgh, Edinburgh, Scotland, United Kingdom

Dr. **Annette Zillenbiller,** Am Alten Weg 33, D-55127, Mainz, Germany

Lectures

Calvin's Accommodating God

David F. Wright

I. CORRECTING CARICATURES

"Striving after clarity in the concept we should entertain of God" is "a fundamental mark of the Calvinistic mind."[1] Such is the judgment of Brian Gerrish of the University of Chicago in the published version of his Cunningham Lectures, delivered in New College Edinburgh in 1990, on the eucharistic theology of John Calvin. The lectures painted a portrait of Calvin's God that many Scots would find almost unrecognizable. For they have been reared on, and are still repeatedly fed by some of the media, a fearful caricature of the Calvinist deity: an arbitrary heartless despot, disposing of the destinies of human beings in this life and the next with capricious cruelty—the kind of God tailor-made by and for the tyrant of Geneva, John Calvin himself, for whom dispatching awkward dissidents to the funeral pyre was all in a day's work.

How it has come about that otherwise responsible echelons of Scottish cultural life should harbor such ill-informed prejudice against Calvin and his God it is not my task to investigate—although some careful research would not be wasted labor. If this address has any apologetic value, it will derive from exposition rather than direct confrontation of false images.

1. The Parent-God

For Brian Gerrish the key to Calvin's theology is the fatherly generosity—and the motherly care—of the God who is the fount of all goodness to his children. "Not the divine despot, but the Parent-God, who is goodness itself, was the object of Calvin's piety and therefore the main theme of his doctrine of God."[2] Gerrish bids us listen to Calvin's commentary on Isaiah 49:15: "Can a woman forget her sucking child?"

> By an apt comparison, [God] shows how strong is the concern he bears for his own. He compares himself to a mother, whose love for her baby is

---

[1] B. A. Gerrish, *Grace and Gratitude: The Eucharistic Theology of John Calvin* (Minneapolis: Fortress; Edinburgh: T. & T. Clark, 1993), 81. This published version of my paper has benefited from responses by members of the Congress, even at points of which I was not fully persuaded.

[2] Ibid., 41. For another recent work that orders its account of Calvin's theology around the themes of father, adoption, and children, see R. C. Zachman, *The Assurance of Faith: Conscience in the Theology of Martin Luther and John Calvin* (Minneapolis: Fortress, 1993).

3

so engrossed and anxious as to leave a father's love a long way behind.... To express his burning affection, he preferred to compare himself to a mother, and he does not call them just "children" but his "baby" (*foetum*), since affection for a baby is normally stronger. The affection a mother feels for her baby is amazing. She fondles it in her lap, feeds it at her breast, and watches so anxiously over it that she passes sleepless nights, continually wearing herself out and forgetting about herself.... The affection which God bears towards us is far stronger and warmer than the love of all mothers.... Men and women, though perverse and addicted to self-love, take care of their children. What of God, who is goodness itself? Will he be able to cast aside his fatherly affection? By no means.[3]

2. The God Who Prattles

A closely related image is used by Calvin in a sentence in the *Institutes* of 1539 that in recent years has become more widely quoted than anything else Calvin wrote. He is astounded that anyone should imagine that God has a body just because Scripture speaks of his hands, ears, eyes, and feet.

Who even of slight intelligence does not understand that God is accustomed to prattle, as it were, with us, like nurses with babies? Such forms of speaking do not so much give a crystal-clear picture of what God is like as accommodate the knowledge of him to our slender capacity. That this may be done, it is necessary for a descent to be made far below his majesty.[4]

"Prattle" is my attempt to translate the Latin verb *balbutio*, which by Calvin's time had a long history of usage in such a context. It is an onomatopoeic term for "stammer, stutter, babble," that is, to speak indistinctly or obscurely.[5] In this passage it is sometimes translated "lisp," which means "to speak with imperfect pronunciation,: chiefly of the letter "s." It is perhaps too readily assumed that Calvin intended it here to denote only lucid simplicity, of an adult engaging in repetitive baby talk. But however we translate the verb—stammer, lisp, prattle—the implication of indistinctness is also present, and the context confirms this. God's babbling to us conveys not a pristine (*ad liquidum*) picture of what he is like but only

---

[3]Gerrish, *Grace and Gratitude,* 40–41, slightly altered; *CO* 37:204–5 (English translation, *CTS* 4:30–31).
   [4]*Institutes,*1.13.1 (*OS* 3:109; cf. McNeill-Battles 1.121).
   [5]Cf. today in French, Joseph De Finance, *En balbutiant l'indicible* (Rome: Editrice Pontificia Università Gregoriana, 1992), picking up Thomas Aquinas' use of the Latin verb.

So even if it lang. or something behind C's use, he doesn't let go of personal O

that knowledge which is adapted to our slender capacity. Divine accommodation, it seems, both reveals and conceals. Its double-edged force is nicely caught by the verb *balbutire.*

II. Previous Investigations of *Accommodatio*

The term accommodation refers to the process by which God reduces or adjusts to human capacities what he wills to reveal of the infinite mysteries of his being, which by their very nature are beyond the powers of the mind of man to grasp.[6]

Thus runs the much-quoted definition by Edward Dowey of Princeton, the honored doyen of American Calvin scholars. It is rather too systematic and, dare I say, highfalutin to be wholly satisfactory, but I leave the reader to determine the issue in the light of the rest of this paper.

Accommodation was not an invention of John Calvin's. It had enjoyed a long vogue in Jewish and Christian thought, which has recently been surveyed for the first time, albeit rather leadenly, by an American Jewish scholar Stephen Benin.[7] He demonstrates the remarkable versatility of this concept (or device, or procedure)

which permeates Christian and Jewish thought, finds expression in exegetical, legal, homiletical, and philosophical sources from the first through the sixteenth centuries, and conceivably enters the mainstream of post-Enlightenment thought as a possibly undetected element in the rise of historicism.[8]

But neither the antecedents of Calvin's usage nor its subsequent influence concern us on this occasion.[9] Our aim is to attempt to place it within the body of his theology, to ascertain its functional importance, particularly in relation to his understanding of God.

---

[6]Edward A. Dowey, Jr., *The Knowledge of God in Calvin's Theology* (New York: Columbia University Press, 1952), 3.

[7]Stephen D. Benin, *The Footprints of God: Divine Accommodation in Jewish and Christian Thought*, SUNY Series in Judaica: Hermeneutics, Mysticism, and Religion (Albany: State University of New York Press, 1993).

[8] Ibid., xiii; cf. xix, "As extraordinary as the story of accommodation is, perhaps equally remarkable is the almost complete lack of scholarly attention its history and career have received."

[9] I have considered the sources in David F. Wright, "Calvin's Accommodation Revisited," in Peter De Klerk, ed., *Calvin as Exegete: Papers and Responses Presented at the Ninth Colloquium on Calvin and Calvin Studies, May 20, 21 and 22, 1993* (Grand Rapids: Calvin Studies Society, 1995), 171–90 (with response by E. David Willis-Watkins, 191–93).

In addressing these questions in Calvin, we are dealing with someone who used accommodation extensively—in Benin's analysis, second only in Christian writers to John Chrysostom, the "father of accommodation" as he styles him.[10] (We may note in passing that the two employ different dominant vocabularies—Chrysostom that of condescension, chiefly the Greek *sunkatabaino*, etc.; Calvin that of adjustment and adaptation, *accommodo* and *attempero*).[11] Given its pervasiveness in Calvin's vast corpus, it is astonishing that accommodation passed almost wholly unnoticed in Calvin studies until a little more than a generation ago. The first chapter-length discussion, by Edward Dowey, was published in 1952.[12] The heavily used work by François Wendel, *Calvin: The Origins and Development of His Religious Thought*, published in French in 1950 and in English translation in 1963 and still staple fare for students in Britain after three decades, cites Calvin's use in *Institutes* 2:16:2, but draws no attention to accommodation as a distinctive element in his thought.[13] It is my impression that German-speaking Calvin scholarship has been slow to take accommodation to its bosom.[14] It is conspicuously absent from Hans Joachim Kraus's almost standard listing of "Calvins exegetische Prinzipien" of 1968, influential since 1977 in an English version,[15] while on the contrary H. Jackson Forstman went overboard in describing it in 1962 as "perhaps [Calvin's] most widely used exegetical tool."[16] For a British

---

[10]Benin, *Footprints*, xix; he used it "seemingly without end." Benin's treatment (see esp. 56–71) is based on a narrow selection of Chrysostom's works. See the discussion in my paper referred to in n. 9 above, which engages with the important study by O. Millet, *Calvin et la dynamique de la parole. Étude de rhétorique réformée*, Bibliothèque littéraire de la Renaissance, ser. 3:28 (Geneva, Slatkine, 1992).

[11]But the contrast is not absolute: Cf. from the newly published *Sermons on the Acts of the Apostles*, ed. W. Balke and W. H.T. Moehn, *SC* 8:334: "Dieu, congnoissant nostre infirmité, condescend bien à nous. Il sçait que nous ne pourrons pas parvenir jusques à ceste haultesse de sa majesté. Et pour ceste cause il se faict comme petit, afin que nous le contemplyons en tant qu'il nous est utile."

[12]Dowey, *Knowledge of God*, 3–7.

[13]François Wendel, *Calvin: The Origins and Development of His Religious Thought* (London: Collins, 1963), 229–30.

[14]But there is an excellent full treatment in R. Hedtke, *Erziehung durch die Kirche bei Calvin* (Heidelberg: Quelle & Meyer, 1969), although this work itself seems not to have enjoyed wide currency. Accommodation barely features in A. Ganoczy and S. Scheld, *Die Hermeneutik Calvins* (Wiesbaden: F. Steiner, 1983), 97, nn. 51–52, but neither Ford Lewis Battles nor Dowey is mentioned—nor has it an entry in *TRE*. After completing this paper I learned of the attention devoted to accommodation in Calvin by the Dutch theologian Klaas Schilder (1890–1952) in his inaugural dissertation at Erlangen, *Zur Begriffsgeschichte des "Paradoxon," mit besonderer Berücksichtigung Calvins und das nach-kierkegaardschen "Paradoxon"*(Kampen: J. H. Kok, 1933), 419–47: "Calvins Weg von der Transzendenz Gottes zu der 'accommodatio' Gottes"; "Calvins Rückweg von der accommodatio Gottes zu der Transzendz Gottes." See further Jacobus de Jong, *Accommodatio Dei: A Theme in K. Schilder's Theology of Revelation* (Kampen: Dissertatie-Uitgeverij Mondiss, 1990). There is a useful discussion in Peter Opitz, *Calvins Theologische Hermeneutik* (Neukirchen-Vluyn: Neukirchener Verlag, 1994).

[15]Hans J. Kraus, "Calvins exegetische Prinzipien," *ZKG* 79 (1968): 329–41; Hans Joachim Kraus, "Calvin's Exegetical Principles," *Interpretation* 31 (1977): 8–18.

[16]H. Jackson Forstman, *Word and Spirit: Calvin's Doctrine of Biblical Authority* (Stanford: Stanford University Press, 1962), 13. The discussion in Benin, *Footprints*, 187–92, 277 n. 54, of Calvin on accommodation is heavily dependent on Forstman, backed up by F. L. Battles (see n. 17).

scholar the truth can lie only somewhere between this German indifference and American exaggeration.

III. Accommodation and the Problems of Scripture

According to the best-known study of the subject, "Accommodation begins as an apologetical tool against hostile critics of Scripture; it ends as a pastoral instrument for the edification of believers."[17] Beyond doubt the apologetic appeal to accommodation is prominent in Calvin. He has recourse to it repeatedly in coming to terms with difficulties of all kinds that he encounters in the Bible. These range from anthropomorphic or anthropopathic depictions of God's being or words or actions to sundry aspects of the Mosaic legislation in the Pentateuch, and to features of Israelite history that have challenged exegetes in every age, such as military campaigns and punitive measures undertaken at God's command. Indeed, we can almost formulate a general rule for Calvin's handling of these problems. Whereas early church Fathers like Origen and Augustine decreed that, whenever one found something in Scripture that was patently unworthy of God if taken literally, a resort to allegorical interpretation was indicated, Calvin's response in such situations was to invoke divine accommodation. The comparison may seem a strange one, for allegory was an unthinkable escape route for Calvin. Yet there may prove to be an uncanny similarity between allegory in the Fathers and accommodation as Calvin applies the latter.

1. *Ezekiel 20: 8–9*

This apologetic use of accommodation is so widespread in Calvin's biblical expositions that it needs no demonstration. Some illustrations may nevertheless be helpful. In Ezekiel 20:8–9, God declares through the prophet, "I determined to pour forth my burning fury (*excandescentiam*) upon them, to vent my anger on them in the midst of the land of Egypt. But I acted for the sake of my name, lest it be profaned in the eyes of the heathen...." Calvin's lecture comments as follows:

> Here God indicates that he would have been inflamed with anger had he not, out of regard for his name, withdrawn his hand, as it were, from the vengeance for which it was prepared and armed. We know that this is not strictly applicable to God; this way of speaking is used by transference (*translatitiae*), because in the first place God is not affected by anger and secondly he does not decide anything that he subsequently retracts. Since

[17]Ford Lewis Battles, "God Was Accommodating Himself to Human Capacity," *Interpretation* 31 (1977): 19–38, at 26; reprinted in Donald K. McKim, ed., *Readings in Calvin's Theology* (Grand Rapids: Baker, 1984), 21–42; and also in Richard Gamble, ed., *Articles on Calvin and Calvinism* (New York and London: Garland, 1992), 6:13–32.

these experiences are alien to God, he accommodates them to himself by means of analogy (*similitudinem*). As often as the Holy Spirit uses these forms of expression, let us learn that they apply to the matter in hand rather than to the person of God. "God determined to pour out his anger"; that is to say, by their offences the Israelites had so deserved it that punishment must be exacted from them. So the prophet simply means that the people's wickedness had reached its peak, and accordingly God's retribution would have been timely, if he had not been restrained for some other reason.[18]

Calvin routinely invokes divine accommodation with reference to the two kinds of problems found in these verses in Ezekiel. First is the attribution to God of improper emotions or experiences or actions. In this instance Calvin's clarification approximates to a recognition of the analogical character of human language about God, even when used, so to speak, by God himself. In such cases the accommodation involved is correlative to human beings simply as human beings. It was necessary in paradise, before the Fall.

2. *Psalm 78:65*

On other occasions, however, it is justified by Calvin in terms of the sinfulness of those addressed, particularly their blindness, insensitivity, sluggish unresponsiveness, torpidity—their spiritual and moral deadness. So when the Psalmist depicts God as waking up out of drunkenness, Calvin's comment is remarkably sharp:

> The analogy of a drunk man, although very harsh, is used deliberately, because it is accommodated to the people's insensitivity (*stuporem*). Had they been of a pure and refined (*defaecata*) understanding, God would not have thus transformed himself or assumed a guise (*personam*) alien to him. It was the drunkenness of the people, that is their unresponsiveness (*socordia*), which drove him to compare himself to a drunk, and to their great shame. As far as God is concerned, the likeness detracts not a whit from his glory.[19]

Notice in particular two things: the responsibility for the use of the image is left with God—he is the agent of accommodation; secondly it is the human trait—the Israelites' spiritual drunkenness—that provokes the self-ascription to God.

---

[18] *CO* 40:478–79; the rendering in *CTS* 2:293 is inadequate at several points.
[19] *CO* 31:742; cf. *CTS* 3:274, on Ps. 78:65.

3. *Zephaniah 3:17*

Calvin is alert to divine accommodation not only when darker emotions such as anger are ascribed to God. In Zephaniah 3:17 he finds God quietly cherishing Jerusalem—his church—with the love of a husband for his wife.

> We see how God lowers (*demittat*) himself to us. For if we consider whether such expressions are appropriate to God's nature, we must say bluntly that nothing is more improper. It is utterly unseemly that God be depicted to us like a husband wholly consumed with love for his wife. But from this ... we grasp more clearly the greatness of God's indulgence towards us, who thus lowers himself for our sake and transforms himself, as it were, assuming incongruous guises (*alienas personas*). Let each of us delve into our own self (*descendat ... in se*) and recognize how deep-rooted is unbelief, when God cannot serve our good and amend this evil ... without in some sense departing from himself to come nearer to us.[20]

Here accommodation does indeed begin in apologetic and end in pedagogy. The passage is a fine illustration of Calvin's humanist sensitivity to language, together with that pastoral inquisitiveness which repeatedly penetrates behind the words of Scripture in quest of motivations, divine and human. In this case yet again, a misleading portrayal of God proves nevertheless in his grace an unveiling of his heart.

4. *Institutes 1:17:13*

The second aspect of accommodation we noted in Ezekiel 20 centered on an apparent change of mind on God's part. This too is found pervasively in Calvin's writings, for example, whenever God is said to repent. This usage provokes an important discussion of accommodation in the *Institutes*: "The rationale of accommodation is this, that God represents himself to us not such as he is in himself but such as he is sensed (*sentitur*) by us." Divine repentance, then, implies no reversal of plan or alteration of will, but speaks only of the apparently changing actions of God as seen from a human perspective.[21]

5. *Summary*

Calvin's position has been summed up as follows by Paul Helm of King's College, London:

> Given that God, the eternal God, has not only decreed the course of history but has himself acted in history, such actions can only be fully

---

[20] CO 44:72–73.   [21] *Institutes* 1.17.13 (*OS* 3:217–18; McNeill-Battles 1:277).

understood and, more particularly, can only be responded to, when they
are taken to be the actions of a person who is himself in time and who
therefore appears to change or vary in his action. More than this, if men
and women who are themselves in time are to respond to God he *must*
represent himself to them as one to whom response is possible, as one
who acts and reacts in time. Only on such an understanding of divine
activity is the divine-human interaction which is at the heart of biblical
religion possible.[22]

We begin to glimpse something of the extensive ramifications of accommodation in Calvin's thought. It enabled him to conceptualize not only how God
could communicate with that wholly other order of being that is humankind and
interact with it, person to persons, as it were, but also how God could genuinely
reveal himself in human discourse that was never quite adequate for the job. God's
accommodation to human beings, and to sinners in their perversity, is a revealing
of himself that is at the same time a veiling of himself, because the mode of that
revelation—always an accommodated mode—is tailored to the character of its
recipients, who are not only human but frequently blind and stubborn.

IV. Accommodation to Barbarity

We have not yet plumbed the full depths of accommodation in Calvin. Its apologetic force is most plainly exposed when he deals with numerous features of the
early history of Israel, especially in the Pentateuch. This is accommodation not
merely to humanity qua humanity, or to sinful humanity, but to barbarity, the
crudity and cruelty of a primitive stage of human history.[23] Calvin's sense of historical development enabled him to identify among the laws of Moses divine concessions to a raw, uncivilized nation that would not have been tameable at all
unless God had authorized things of which he undoubtedly (so Calvin believes)
disapproves and did at the time disapprove.[24]

[22]Paul Helm, "John Calvin on Divine Accommodation," an unpublished paper read to the Calvin
Group of the Rutherford Fellowship, Edinburgh, March 1992. The paper is valuable in warning against
reductionist understandings of accommodation in Calvin as solely pedagogical or as an anticipation of
post-Kantian theological agnosticism, as though God were unknowable.

[23]See David F. Wright, "Accommodation and Barbarity in John Calvin's Old Testament Commentaries," in A. G. Auld, ed., *Understanding Poets and Prophets: Essays in Honour of George Wishart
Anderson. JSOT* Suppl. 152 (Sheffield: Sheffield Academic Press, 1993), 413–27.

[24]Fuller documentation is given in David F. Wright, "Calvin's Pentateuchal Criticism: Equity,
Hardness of Heart, and Divine Accommodation in the Mosaic Harmony Commentary," *CTJ* 21
(1986): 33–50; reprinted in Gamble, *Articles*, 6:213–30.

1. *Slavery*

Let us take as an example what the Pentateuch enacted concerning slavery. Calvin deprecated any of the Israelites becoming slaves, even for a limited period as Leviticus provided, because slavery infringed God's sovereign rights over them as his redeemed servants. God had to be satisfied with a token of his ownership of them, by allowing them by way of concession (*per indulgentiam*) to be enslaved for a fixed six-year period. "God simply chose to apply this remedy, to prevent slavery extinguishing altogether the recollection of his grace, although he permitted it to be smothered."[25]

2. *Separation of Wife from Husband*

Far more terrible, in Calvin's estimation, was the stipulation in Exodus that, if, within the six-year span, a male slave married a fellow slave and had children, he could be freed in the seventh year only if he left his wife and children behind with his master. This was a monstrous flouting of nature, that the bond of slavery could be dissolved only by this impious violation of marriage. "There was gross barbarity in this forced separation." This scandal had to be ranked among the others that God tolerated in Israel on account of the people's irremediable hardness of heart.[26]

3. *Selling One's Own Children into Slavery*

The same chapter of Exodus proceeds to specify what should happen in the case of an Israelite woman sold into slavery by her father. The passage revealed to Calvin how many perversities God had to tolerate in such a people. It was an act of gross barbarity that fathers should sell their children for the relief of poverty. Calvin discerns some redeeming features in the detailed provisions that follow, and adds this comment: "God showed, as far as the people's hardness could take it, that chastity pleased him."[27] God's revelation of the law of chastity had to limit itself to what this recalcitrant folk would bear.

These are by no means the starkest instances of God's limiting the demands of holiness and justice in recognition of the intractability of primitive Israel, as Calvin reads the history. What picture of his accommodating God emerges from these expositions? It is of a God incapable of implementing the perfection of his law because he knows that the people could not or would not take it. Everywhere Calvin finds God making concessions to their hardness of heart—a general

[25] *CO* 24:704, on Lev. 25:42; cf. *CTS* 3:165.
[26] *CO* 24:701, on Exod. 21: 1–6; *CTS* 3:160.
[27] CO 24:650, on Exod. 21:7–11; *CTS* 3:80–81.

hermeneutical key he fashions from Jesus' words in the Gospel about Moses' permission of divorce (Matt. 19:8).

V. Saving the Old Testament

Yet Calvin saves both God from appearing ineffectual and incompetent and the law of Moses from seeming inferior to what God intended by insisting throughout that it was God who was sovereign in accommodation. He may have seemed at the mercy of those ungovernable Israelites, but in reality he was always in control. It is important to emphasize this point, lest we falsely modernize Calvin in terms of nineteenth-century liberalism. The Old Testament is not, in Calvin's understanding, the all-too-imperfect product of Israelite religion, preserving at best its primitive and limited apprehensions of divinity. Not even the most breathtaking of Calvin's appeals to divine accommodation is inconsistent with this judgment of T. H. L. Parker: "For Calvin the Bible, the whole Bible and every nook and cranny of the Bible, is the Word of God as completely as if God himself had spoken the actual words."[28]

1. *The Mosaic Law*

Calvin evaluates the different elements of the Mosaic law by reference to the absolutes of "equity" (*aequitas*) or the natural law (*ius gentium*), which for him are perfectly set forth in the Decalogue. It is by this touchstone that he assesses the sundry detailed enactments of the Pentateuch, and finds many of them wanting the perfection of God's law. This basis of evaluation means that Calvin's judgments are not arbitrary, but the result is that laws issued in God's name in fact obscure his will as much as they reveal it. Only in a few contexts is any explicit clue given in the biblical text that God is choosing to make do with something less than his perfect will. Theodicy is the task—to justify breaches of God's justice and goodness—and accommodation to a raw and refractory people is the divine mode of acting that achieves it.

2. *The Sacrificial and Ritual Order*

This "negative accommodation," as it has been labelled,[29] recalls the arguments found in several of the Fathers in their polemic against Jews and Judaism. The sacrificial and ritual order of the Old Testament was no longer to be observed because it had never been more than a concession to Israel's blindness and depravity. This line of reasoning could also be useful to rescue the Old Testament

---

[28]Thomas H. L. Parker, *Calvin's Old Testament Commentaries* (Edinburgh: T. & T. Clark, 1986), 66.
[29] Benin, *Footprints*, xv-xvi.

dispensation from radical dualists, like the gnostics and Manichaeans, who assigned it to another malign or incompetent deity. In Calvin's hands accommodation has become a pattern of divine interaction with Israel which assisted him in holding together two such diverse economies as the work of one and the same God. Calvin is quite clear that the whole system of tabernacle and temple, of priesthood and sacrifice was an accommodation to an Israel that in the *Institutes* he describes more as infantile—the childhood of the church[30]—but in the commentaries rather as primitive and barbaric. The Reformed tradition of biblical theology, of which Calvin is the chief originator, is distinguished from, say, the Lutheran or Anglican by, inter alia, the significance it assigns to the Old Testament. It is worth noting that in Calvin this is achieved without either an excessively Christocentric reading (more characteristic of Luther) or a levelling-out treatment that flattens the differences between the two Testaments. Calvin succeeds—if that is the right word—in regarding the whole Old Testament as the oracles of God while handling it with a remarkable measure of historical distance.

VI. The Single Will of God

Before attempting to draw together some general considerations, I wish to highlight Calvin's use of accommodation to resolve problems internal to his own distinctive theology.

1. *Revelation 3:5, etc.*

In his treatise on *The Eternal Predestination of God*, he comments on a threat in the Apocalypse of John that sinners would be blotted out of the book of life. Calvin has to counter a hostile objection: According to his teaching if these sinners were reprobate, they had never been in the book, and if they were elect, then election became insecure if they could be erased from it.

> The monk (George the Sicilian) drivels on as though God never accommodated himself to our capacity. It is surely base ingratitude to reproach God thus when he is so indulgent to us as to prattle (*balbutiat*) for our sake. This reasoning will contrive for us a God with a body just because Scripture ascribes to him ears and eyes and feet and hands. The meaning is simple. The ones deleted from the book of life are those who were regarded for a time as God's sons and daughters but afterwards went where they really belonged.[31]

---

[30] Cf. *Institutes* 1:11:3, 2:11:2 (*OS* 3:91, 424; McNeill-Battles 1.102, 451); cf. Parker, *Calvin's Old Testament Commentaries*, esp. 63–69, 83–90.

[31] *CO* 8:338–39; tr. J. K. S. Reid (London: James Clarke, 1961), 151–52; Calvin alludes to Revelation 3:5, 22:18–19.

Proof texts are ready to hand; in particular, "what John expresses bluntly (*crasse*), the prophet Ezekiel put more precisely (*subtilius*): 'They will not be in the hidden sanctum of my people, nor will they be written in the register (*catalogo*) of Israel.'" But when we turn to the lecture on Ezekiel 13:9, the language is not precise enough; the future tense of "they will not be written" raises the rejoinder, surely all the writing in the book of life was done before the foundation of the world? Yes, indeed, says Calvin, but,

> Ezekiel here accommodates his language to the usual custom of human beings. The language of the Psalms is cruder: "let them be blotted out of the book of life" (69:28).... For a time they seemed to belong to the ranks of the godly. Hence a change is here depicted to us, but in deference to the limitations and rawness of our minds.[32]

The issue is partly the one we noted above, of containing within time-bound human discourse the transactions of the eternal God. But the problematic element is undoubtedly compounded by Calvin's doctrine of election, as is further evident from his treatment of Jesus' plaint over Jerusalem, "How often would I have gathered your children together, like a hen gathering her chicks under her wings, but you refused" (Matt. 23:27).

> It is a wonderful and incomparable proof of his love that God did not mind condescending to endearments to win rebels to his service.... Whenever the Word of God is set before us, he bares his breast to us with motherly kindness, and not content with that, condescends to the humble affection of a hen fostering her chicks.... When he assumes a mother's role, he comes a great way down from his glory; how much further when he takes the guise of a hen, and deigns to treat us as his chicks![33]

Calvin has "an easy answer" to those critics ("sophists") who seize here on an undermining of God's secret predestination. We have here no statement of his "hidden plan" (*consilium*) but of his will (*voluntas*).

> If anyone objects that it is absurd to imagine a twofold (*bifariam*) will in God, I respond that this is exactly my belief also. God's will is one and undivided, but because our minds cannot plumb the deep abyss of his secret election, to meet our inadequacy God's will is set before us as twofold. I am amazed at the obstinate attitudes of those who meet anthropo-

---

[32]*CO* 40:280–81; cf. *CTS* 2:17, but it is partly inaccurate.
[33]*CO* 45:642; tr. A. W. Morrison, *Calvin's Commentaries. A Harmony of the Gospels Matthew, Mark and Luke*, vol. 3 (Edinburgh: St. Andrew Press, 1972), 68, here slightly altered.

pathia frequently in Scripture unperturbed, and only reject it in this case.[34]

The standard terminology of accommodation may be missing, but the message is clear.

2. *Zephaniah 3:7*

When Calvin addresses the same issue in commenting on a verse in Zephaniah that apparently envisages the thwarting of God's expectation, the theme of accommodation is once again explicit.

I have already said that God speaks here in a human fashion and inaccurately (*improprie*). Hence we should not enter or penetrate into the hidden purpose of God.... [Calvin fastens on the folly of those who never see beyond "everyday ways of speaking"—"God says he wants all to be saved"—and claim that either there is no real election or else God's will is two-sided].... What is more absurd than to conclude that God's will is twofold just because he speaks to us in a manner incompatible with his incomprehensible majesty? God's will is indeed one and unitary (*simplex*), but manifold (*multiplex*) to human perception.... The Lord accommodates himself to the level of our competence (*ingenii*), as this passage teaches with crystal clarity. If we accept what the fanatics intend, God will surely be like a human being, optimistic but realizing subsequently that he was deceived. What could be more foreign to his glory?[35]

VII. NOT MERELY PEDAGOGY

We have by now, I reckon, examined sufficient examples of divine accommodation in action to regard the view that it affects only the form and not the substance of revelation as wholly inadequate.[36] This judgment overlaps with, but is not fully coterminous with, another one, that accommodation is no more than a matter of pedagogics.

---

[34] *CO* 45, 643–44; Morrison, *Calvin's Commentaries*, 69.

[35] *CO* 44.56; cf. *CTS* 4:276–77. Calvin is commenting on Zeph. 3:7, which he translates, "I [God] said, 'You will certainly fear me, you will accept instruction....' Truly they have made haste, they have corrupted all their doings."

[36] So A. G. Baxter, "What Did Calvin Teach about Accommodation?" *Evangel* 6:1 (Spring 1988): 20–22, at p. 21; C. M. Ashley, "John Calvin's Utilization of the Principle of Accommodation and Its Continuing Significance for an Understanding of Biblical Language" (dissertation, Southwestern Baptist Theological Seminary, Fort Worth, Texas, 1972), 29.

1. Not Rhetoric Alone

This latter, inadequate, viewpoint has been fostered by tracing the roots of Calvin's accommodation to the categories of classical Roman rhetoric.[37] The main reason why this cannot be the case is simply that there is no close equivalent in Roman rhetorical theory to Calvin's (or for that matter, the leading Fathers') use of accommodation. The rhetoricians certainly worked with criteria of aptness (aptum) and propriety (decorum), whereby an orator adjusted what he said and how he said it to his audience, the occasion, his subject matter and intention, and so on. Quite apart from the absence of distinctive terminology, this is light years away from the range and depth of Calvin's applications of accommodation.[38] Let this be my modest corrective, in the opening address of this Congress, to the fashionable recent tendency to explain too much of Calvin in terms of the rhetorical tradition.

2. God's Self-revelation

What the pedagogical-rhetorical approach has done has been to restrict the question of accommodation too narrowly to the question of Scripture.[39] This is to mistake the immediate for the ultimate, the medium for the source, or at least to collapse the two into one. For while it is not difficult to find in Calvin occurrences of the tell-tale verbs of accommodation with "Scripture" or "the prophet" or "Moses" as their subjects,[40] characteristically for Calvin it is God who accommodates himself and his word and will. Dowey's definition is quite to the point: "the

---

[37]Propounded by Battles, "God was Accommodating," and propagated by others; see e.g. J. B. Rogers and Donald K. McKim, *The Authority and Interpretation of the Bible* (San Francisco: Harper & Row, 1979), 98: "The concept of 'accommodation' … Calvin learned from the Latin rhetoricians and jurists."

[38]I dealt with this matter in detail in David F.Wright, "Calvin's Accommodation Revisited," 172–76, where I also consider the important contribution of Millet, *Calvin et la dynamique;* W. de Greef "*De Ware Uitleg*," *Hervormers en hun verklaring von de Bijbel* (Leyden: J. J. Groen en Zoon, 1995), 199–200, again emphasizes the rhetorical roots of the concept in Calvin. He refers to the uses in Quintilian listed in Eckart Zundel, *Clavis Quintiliana* (Darmstadt, Wissenschaftliche Buchgesellschaft, 1989), 1, but such a listing has long been available in E. Bonnellus, *Lexicon Quintilianeum* (1834; reprint: Hildesheim: Georg Olms Verlagsbuchhandlung, 1962), 10–11. After reviewing Quintilian's uses, I see no reason to revise my judgment in "Calvin's Accomodation Revisited," 184–85 n. 16, that Quintilian and similar rhetorical resources provided no recognizable category of *accommodatio.*

[39]Cf. Benin, *Footprints*; for Calvin, this meant that Scripture was accommodated to the human level.… Scripture itself therefore is an accommodation to human capacity.… This exposition implies that Scripture itself is an accommodation.… Calvin understood all of Scripture through the lens of accommodation" (pp. 189,191,192). The perspectives of Ashley and of Rogers and McKim incline them in the same direction.

[40]For an interesting example see his comment on Ezekiel 3:11 (*CO* 40, 83): "he accommodated his speech to his disciples, because he was dealing with a people who were not only crude and dense, but also obstinate. Their language had degenerated as well as the purity of their faith'; tr. David Foxgrover and Donald Martin, *Calvin's Old Testament Commentaries* 18, *Ezekiel I* (Grand Rapids: Eerdmans; Carlisle: Paternoster, 1994), 83.

process by which God reduces or adjusts to human capacities what he wills to reveal...." Although Calvin's theory of accommodation is offered as a set of explanations of what is accessible to us now only in Scripture, in Calvin's mind Scripture is what it is because of God's acting and speaking: "We cannot comprehend God except insofar as he accommodates himself to the meagre measure of our understanding."[41] All God's self-revelation is attempered to human, and even sinful human capacities, using human languages, expressed in the forms and patterns of human life and society, and so on. That this is the case, so Calvin believes, belongs not to the limitations and distortions of ancient Near Eastern or Graeco-Roman religious cultures, but to the gracious purpose of God. This does not of course exclude the miraculous and supernatural. But even when Calvin comes to speak of Ezekiel's visions, he sees them as expressive of God's considerate indulgence: "God usually accommodated visions to the pattern of the law in order to hold the people to its simplicity."[42] The vision of the wheel within wheels was in this form a concession to human weakness, but God wanted to depict, even by an inappropriate figure, the revolutionary character of events. "So thereby God both corrected an error and made a real concession to human naivete."[43]

[margin handwritten note: Ezek's vision]

VIII. Condescension to Humanity

1. In Christ

The appearance of the likeness of a human being in the vision in Ezekiel 1 sparks Calvin off on a lengthy, wide-ranging review of different divine manifestations in human form. He endorses the common patristic interpretation, that such appearances were a prelude to the incarnation itself. The prophet saw God only in the person of Christ, for it is only in Christ that God takes on human visibility, on this occasion in appearance only, not in substance. And Christ appeared thus in human form "only to accommodate himself to the prophet's capacity."[44] This reminds us of the familiar statement in the *Institutes* in a section added in the final 1559 edition:

> Irenaeus writes that the Father, himself immeasurable, is measured in the Son, for he has accommodated himself to our level, lest he swallow up our minds in the immensity of his glory.[45]

---

[41]On Ezekiel 9:3–4, see CO 40.196; Foxgrover and Martin, *Calvin's Old Testament Commentaries*, 216.

[42]CO 40.217; Foxgrover and Martin, *Calvin's Old Testament Commentaries*, 241.

[43]CO 40.214; Foxgrover and Martin, *Calvin's Old Testament Commentaries*, 238.

[44]CO 40.53, 55; Foxgrover and Martin, *Calvin's Old Testament Commentaries*, 49, 51.

[45]*Institutes* 2:6:4 (*OS* 3:326; McNeill-Battles 1:347).

And more movingly in his commentary on 1 Peter:

> All thinking about God apart from Christ is a vast abyss which immediately swallows up all our perceptions.... In Christ, God, as it were, makes himself small, in order to lower himself to our capacity, and Christ alone sets our consciences at rest that we may come to God in intimate confidence (*familiariter*).[46]

2. Familiariter

Familiariter is a favorite word of Calvin's but not easy to translate satisfactorily into English; neither "familiarly" nor "intimately" quite preserves the note of confidence of access alongside closeness of personal relationship. It is an adverb he uses fairly frequently in the Pentateuch commentary to characterize the fellowship God enjoyed with his people through some of the offerings and sacrifices. The loaves set before the Lord in Leviticus 24 betokened "no symbol of God's routine favor, since he descended *familiariter* to them as though he were their table companion. The loaves were called 'the breads of faces' (i.e. shewbread) because they were placed before God's sight, and therein he displayed his special favor, as if coming to eat with them."[47]

3. Limitation

Condescension is the hallmark of all the dealings that God the transcendent has had with humanity. That is why the motif, or cluster of motifs, of divine accommodation takes us to the heart of Calvin's theology. He presents it in diverse forms as God's way of coping, in his self-disclosure and redeeming work, with the finite capacities and perverse propensities of humanity. "Revelation (is) God's persuasive accommodation ... and the story of this accommodation is the history of the economy of his covenantal purpose."[48] Adaptation and flexibility are its keynotes, in response to changing eras and cultures and languages. Yet God remains in control throughout, but at the cost of self-limitation, sometimes to such an extent that the true knowledge of God and his will is largely veiled. That is why there is an uncanny similarity at times, as I said earlier, between allegory and accommodation. Too often in the Pentateuch Calvin claims that what Moses in the name of God instructed or allowed the Israelites was a travesty of God's per-

---

[46]*CO* 55:226–27; cf. tr. W. B. Johnston, *Calvin's New Testament Commentaries: Hebrews...* (1963), 250, on 1 Pet. 1:20.

[47]*CO* 24:488; cf. CTS 2: 291; on Lev. 24:5–9.

[48] E. D. Willis, "Rhetoric and Responsibility in Calvin's Theology," in A. J. McKelway and Willis, eds., *The Context of Contemporary Theology. Essays in Honor of Paul Lehmann* (Atlanta: John Knox Press, 1974), 43–63, at 53.

fect law. The real truth was as much masked as exposed by the text. Prattling to babes expresses only an accommodated message.

IX. Revealed and Hidden

The importance of accommodation for Calvin is further corroborated by its appearance in tandem with the most problematic aspect of his theology—God's hidden purpose of election, and the misleading impression we are given that his will is two-sided. We may single this out as peculiarly difficult, and no doubt correctly. I do not share the opinion of some that predestination is but an ancillary or auxiliary doctrine in Calvin, conscripted to explain why some believe the gospel and others do not. Predestination is woven inextricably into the warp and woof of all Calvin's theologizing. But against the backcloth of divine accommodation it is not so exceptional a problem. Susan Schreiner has shown how, in wrestling with the book of Job, Calvin struggled with a concept of a twofold divine justice, hidden and revealed.[49] The revealed God is always still for Calvin the partly hidden God, for all knowledge of God is accommodated knowledge—which means knowledge tailored to our measure and hence knowledge curtailed. We must make do with the prattling of God until hereafter he speaks to us face to face.

X. The Quest for an Integrated Portrait of Calvin's God

The God who prattles to us and with us, as babies and infant children—is he a different God from the hectoring, scolding, chastising God? Well, the prattling God may not be compatible with the vulgar gross caricature of Calvin's deity. Yet there may be a deeper challenge here for Calvin scholars—to strive after a rounded, integrated grasp of Calvin's understanding of God, his theology. I think that Gerrish's attractive presentation is in the end a little one-sided—but it is an important corrective. And if the accommodating God who treats us as a father or mother condescends to baby talk to communicate with us, then for Calvin discipline and chastening are also essential elements of a parent's responsibility towards his or her children. What we dare not do, if the argument of this address has any substance, is paint a portrait of Calvin's God that ignores the kindly considerateness of the one who lowers himself to our level, to speak and to save and to bless.

---

[49]Susan Schreiner, "Exegesis and Double Justice in Calvin's Sermons on Job," *Church History* 58 (1989): 322–38.

A New View of Calvin in the Light of the Registers of the Geneva Consistory

Robert M. Kingdon

THIS PAPER IS A BY-PRODUCT OF A PROJECT in which I have been involved for a number of years, a study of the Consistory that John Calvin persuaded the city of Geneva to establish in 1541, in order to control the behavior of the entire population, to make sure that everyone not only accepted the Reformed version of Christian doctrine but also behaved in a Christian way. An unusually detailed and complete set of registers, now deposited in the Geneva State Archives, record the decisions of this body. Because they are in extremely bad handwritings, however, they have never been extensively used. I assembled a group of scholars who transcribed into readable form the entire twenty-one volumes of registers kept by this body from 1542, the date of the first surviving register, to 1564, the date of Calvin's death.[1] Two of these scholars have published an annotated critical edition of the first volume of these registers.[2] We have used these materials in a preliminary way for a variety of studies, some already published, others soon to appear.[3]

In this paper I report on what these registers reveal of John Calvin himself. This should provide a fresh and suggestive view of Calvin, not as a theologian or teacher, but as a pastor who dealt with the personal needs of the congregation for which he was responsible.

I. The Consistory

Let me begin by describing the Consistory and how it operated. It was composed of about two dozen members. Its presiding officer was one of the four syndics, or magistrates, who were elected each year to be the chief executives of the Genevan

---

[1]They include Jeffrey Watt, of the University of Mississippi; his wife, Isabella; Glenn S. Sunshine of Connecticut Central State University; David Wegener, formerly of the University of Wisconsin-Madison; Thomas Lambert, of the University of Wisconsin-Madison; Mme. Gabriella Cahier of Geneva. Grants from the H. H. Meeter Center for Calvin Studies at Calvin College and Seminary and from the Graduate School of the University of Wisconsin-Madison made our work possible.

[2]Thomas Lambert and Isabella Watt, eds., *Registres du Consistoire de Genève au temps de Calvin.* vol. 1, *1542–1544,* Travaux d'Humanisme et Renaissance, no. 305 (Geneva: Droz, 1996) [hereafter *RConsistorie*].

[3]See, inter alia, Robert M. Kingdon, *Adultery and Divorce in Calvin's Geneva* (Cambridge, Mass.: Harvard University Press, 1995); idem, "Calvin and the Establishment of Consistory Discipline in Geneva: The Institution and the Men Who Directed It," *Nederlandsche Archief voor Kerkgeschiedenis* 70 (1990):158–72; Jeffrey Watt, "Women and the Consistory in Calvin's Geneva," *Sixteenth Century Journal* 24 (1993): 429–39.

government. At these same annual elections a group of twelve laymen were also chosen to be elders, commissioned to the Consistory. These elders could be re-elected, and often were, for terms of several consecutive years. They were chosen to represent the three elected councils that governed Geneva: two from the Small Council, Geneva's real executive body; four from the Council of Sixty, which handled select problems, including some foreign policy decisions; six from the Council of Two Hundred, which handled other matters of policy and also appeals from decisions of the Small Council in criminal cases. These elders were also selected so that they would represent the different neighborhoods into which Geneva was divided for administrative purposes. The remaining members of the Consistory were the pastors of the city, headed by John Calvin as their moderator. At the height of Calvin's career there were about twelve of these pastors, so membership in the Consistory was fairly balanced between laymen and clergymen. Also attached to the Consistory were two additional officers: one was a secretary, usually a professional notary, who kept registers of its weekly meetings; the other was a summoner, who arranged for the appearance of the people to whom the Consistory wished to speak.

The Consistory met once a week, on Thursdays, in sessions that by the time of Calvin's death lasted for several hours. The elders and the officers of the Consistory were paid small sums of money for each session they attended. The pastors, as salaried servants of the state, were not paid for attendance, since it was regarded as a regular part of their work. The people summoned before the Consistory came from every walk of life in Geneva. They included noblemen, sometimes refugees, who happened to be living in the city. They included urban patricians, merchants and professional men, members of the elite who actually governed the city. They included skilled artisans, journeymen, and domestic servants. A high percentage of those summoned, a majority in some categories, were women. A certain number of them were illiterate. The Consistory cases thus cover a genuine cross-section of the entire population of Geneva. They supply us with fascinating and detailed information on the behavior and ideas of these people, many of whom were of types who often leave no other historical record.

A typical entry in the Consistory registers begins with the name of the person summoned, a brief description of the charge against this person, a somewhat longer summary of answers provided by the accused, and a short statement of Consistory's decision in the matter. The average entry is only one short paragraph. It was not uncommon, however, for entries to require more space, sometimes to run for pages, sometimes to involve appearances at several sessions. The final decision of the Consistory was usually to administer a "remonstrance," or "admonition," a kind of public scolding. If the party summoned accepted this scolding in a good spirit, displaying true repentance without protest or complaint, the matter was concluded. If the case involved several people (for example some sort of public quarrel) within a family, among business partners, or between neighbors, the scolding might be followed by a formal reconciliation. In serious cases this reconciliation would itself become a kind of public ceremony. These scoldings and reconciliations brought most cases to an end.

Our knowledge of the operations of the Consistory has been distorted considerably by the concentration of past historians on a few spectacular cases of people who protested vehemently and were punished severely. They give the impression that the Consistory was a kind of inquisitorial court. But protests were in fact the exception. The Consistory was closer to an obligatory counseling service than to a court. This power to admonish and reconcile was the only power that everyone from the beginning agreed the Consistory possessed. This is a point that was made emphatically by François Bonivard, who wrote the first historical analysis of the Genevan constitution as it had taken shape after the Reformation.[4] And Bonivard was in a position to know from personal experience. He had been summoned before the Consistory a number of times, beginning in its earliest years of operation. To a noble man of the world like Bonivard, to be sure, a remonstrance may not have seemed like a great ordeal. To many ordinary Genevans, however, it was clearly frightening, so frightening that some left the city rather than obey a summons to appear before the Consistory.

Before long the Consistory also claimed a right to excommunicate those whose sins were serious or who were stubborn about accepting correction. Excommunication was a very serious penalty, which could lead to ostracism and even banishment from the city.[5] The Consistory claimed further that its right to excommunicate was absolute, and could not be reversed or vacated on appeal. The Consistory had to fight rather strenuously for this right, but finally won it decisively in 1555, when the Libertine followers of Ami Perrin, who had opposed consistorial excommunication, were deprived of all power in a brutal crackdown by the faction that supported Calvin. The Consistory also claimed from its beginning the right to refer cases to the Small Council, Geneva's true executive, for further investigation and, if appropriate, a formal trial and punishment. In early years these referrals were sometimes considered but often ignored, sometimes even dismissed as frivolous. In later years they were usually but not always considered. These additional steps, however, do not concern me here. It is upon the

---

[4]François Bonivard, *De l'ancienne et nouvelle police de Genève et source d'icelles* (Geneva, 1847), 119–20.

[5]Emile Rivoire and Victor van Berchem, *Les sources du droit du canton de Genève*, 4 vols. (Aarau: Sauerländer, 1927–1935), 3:50–51 (12 November 1557), and 100–101 (1 February 1560).

practice of admonition or remonstrance that I want to concentrate. For this brings us to Calvin's most important personal contribution.

II. Remonstrances

One of Calvin's earliest biographers noted that Calvin made a point of regularly attending sessions of the Consistory and claimed that Calvin "made all the remonstrances."[6] This is clearly an exaggeration, but it does contain an important kernel of the truth. The registers often do not reveal the name of the person who administered the final scolding; they simply announce that it had in fact been delivered. This is in keeping with the general view of all Genevans, including Calvin himself, that decisions of this sort should always be collective, should never be identified with any individual. In a number of cases, however, the name of the person who administered the scolding is supplied. It is almost always a minister instead of a lay elder. And more often than not, that minister is John Calvin. When Calvin did speak, however, he frequently insisted that he was not speaking for himself; he was speaking for the Consistory as a body.

Just as the registers disappointingly fail to identify the person who administered the remonstrances, so are they teasingly brief in their descriptions of the remonstrances. I keep hoping to find a complete text of a remonstrance, but so far have had no such luck. Some of the entries do say enough, however, to give us some general notion of their content. They often contain Biblical references. In one not atypical case, for example, Calvin administered to Benoite Ameaux, a woman accused of defending the practice of adultery, "beautiful admonitions taken from Holy Scriptures."[7] These references help confirm my impression from other sources that a very real determinant of Calvin's power in Geneva is found in his use of the Bible. He clearly knew the Bible very well. He could produce on-the-spot quotations from the Word of God that seemed to his listeners to be particularly appropriate for whatever topic was under discussion. He was also skillful in defending his use of those quotations, persuading his listeners that he really understood their meaning better than anyone in the audience.

Let me now make my argument more concrete by providing specific examples of remonstrances administered by Calvin during Consistory sessions. I take this series from a register beginning in 1548. At that time a new secretary took over, and during his first months in office he provided somewhat fuller accounts of these scoldings than other secretaries. Here are three, all from the session of 23 February: (1) Pierre Tornier, probably a peasant, was referred to the Consistory by

---

[6]Nicolas Colladon, *Vie de Calvin*, in *CO* 21: col. 66.
[7]*RConsistoire*, 1:305 (17 January 1544).

the officer responsible for governing the village of Peney[8] on charges that he had committed fornication with a girl. He had already been punished in Peney in the manner required by the ordinances. That probably meant he had been imprisoned for a few days on bread and water. He now appeared in order to show repentance for the sin and scandal he had committed. Calvin administered to him remonstrances "that the Christian should not fornicate, but rather remain chaste in body and spirit." Tornier then showed signs of repentance and was sent home.[9] (2) Jean Frochet, obviously a fairly young man, was referred to the Consistory by the presiding syndic on word that instead of working at his job as a tailor he was spending his time wandering around with dissolute truants. Calvin told him "that a young man should remain chaste and modest, serving his father and mother, not drinking with bums." He advised Frochet to get back to work and "live in a Christian way with his father and mother." (3) Françoise de Calegny was an immigrant from Burgundy who was summoned on the charge of misbehavior with a dog. After her baby died she had developed a fever that created considerable pain in her breasts. To relieve the pain she had nursed a small dog. Calvin told her that "it was a scandal and beyond all good manners to give what belongs to infants instead to dogs, and several other Christian remonstrances." She begged pardon of the Consistory, said she hoped never to return before the Consistory, and showed signs of repentance.[10]

Here is another case, from the following week, 1 March 1548: Marquet, a hatmaker, and his wife were summoned because of a domestic quarrel. He had beaten her with a whip, because she had disobeyed his order not to spend time with another woman, the wife of a man named Phocasse. His wife denied ever having heard the order and complained he had beaten her so severely that she was sick. He replied that he had gone to the Phocasse home one evening to find his wife and someone had thrown water on his head. Calvin admonished him that "a Christian man should not treat his wife in this way." He also warned her that she should "not visit the wife of Phocasse if that was against her husband's wish."[11]

Here is yet another case, from the week of 8 March 1548: Claude, widow of André Dhatena, was summoned because she had committed fornication with a young man, who had then skipped town. She had already been convicted in a court and had been punished with imprisonment for eight days. Calvin in his remonstrance pointed out that God expected "a woman who had fornicated to

---

[8]Peney had remained under Geneva's control in the political changes that began the Reformation.

[9]A. E. G., RConsistoire, vol. 4, fol. 3 (23 February 1548). Cf. A. E. G., Registres du Conseil (hereafter RC), vol. 43, fol. 22 (20 February 1548).

[10]A. E. G., RConsistoire, vol. 4, fol. 3 (23 February 1548).

[11]A. E. G., RConsistoire, vol. 4, fol. 5v (1 March 1548).

repent in a Christian way of her sin." She was dismissed in peace, with a parting warning not to allow herself to be seduced so unhappily.[12]

Here are two more cases, involving insults to ministers: (1) Baltasar Shet [Sept] was summoned on 12 April 1548 and charged with mocking the minister Abel Poupin, laughing when Poupin in a sermon spoke of the "terrible trumpet of the judgment of God." Calvin told him that it was "infamous for a young person to mock the Word of God in this way." Sept protested that he had not intended to mock either the preacher or the Word of God. He admitted, however, that he had indeed laughed at Poupin. He begged pardon of God and of the government.[13]

(2) Jean le Bragart was summoned on 17 May 1548 for insulting the minister Jean Ferron while drunk. When Ferron did not respond to le Bragart's calls, le Bragart said it was time for Ferron to leave town, to go some place else, advancing an argument that seems to me rather ingenious, particularly from a drunk. Paraphrasing the final verses of the Gospel of Matthew, the command of Jesus to his disciples to go and preach throughout the world, he told Ferron it was time for him to move on and convert some other community. In his Christian remonstrance, Calvin scolded le Bragart for "perverting this passage" of Scripture. Le Bragart was then asked if he was engaged to a girl named Lemaz Grisa. He said that he was not, but that he had called to Ferron to find out if it was time for him to marry his girlfriend. Ferron said he would not reply while le Bragart was drunk. There followed a further inquiry into suspicions of sexual irregularities between le Bragart and Grisa.[14]

These cases provide a fairly typical sample of cases heard before the Consistory, a far more typical sample than that derived from a few of the more notorious cases cited by such previous commentators as Walther Köhler.[15] They often involve charges of sexual irregularity or disrespect for authority. They reach a climax in Calvin's scolding before the Consistory. The accused accepts the scolding and is dismissed in peace, and that is the end of the matter. Only rarely do these people get into further trouble and return. The appearance before the Consistory and the scolding normally seem to have been salutary, to have effectively persuaded these people to improve their lives. This effectiveness provides convincing testimony to the power of the remonstrance as a sanction. It reminds us of the central role of public shaming in maintaining social discipline in sixteenth-century communities. Calvin clearly developed considerable skill in the use of the

---

[12]A. E. G., RConsistoire, vol. 4, fol. 7 (8 March 1548).

[13]A. E. G., RConsistoire, vol. 4, fol. 20 v (12 April 1548).

[14]A. E. G., RConsistoire, vol. 4, fol. 29 v (17 May 1548).

[15] Walther Köhler, *Zürcher Ehegericht und Genfer Konsistorium*, vol. 2 [vol. 10 in the *Quellen und Abhandlungen zur Schweizerischen Reformationsgeschichte*] (Leipzig, 1942), chap. 14, "Johann Calvin und Genf," pp. 505–652. This detailed study did not use the original registers of the Consistory but rather a set of extracts prepared by Frédéric-Auguste Cramer in 1853.

remonstrance. The fact that he was so often asked to administer the remonstrance demonstrates the respect of his colleagues on the Consistory for his skills in this kind of exercise.

When a remonstrance ended a hearing that was usually the conclusion of a case. The remonstrance often followed the administration of secular punishment, as in the two fornication cases reported above. The remonstrance seems to have carried with it an act of public forgiving, and it signaled the formal integration of the accused back into the Christian community. It can be compared to the absolution administered by a priest to a forgiven sinner in the Catholic confessional, and no doubt filled a similar psychological function.

Calvin's admonitions did not always take the form of concluding remonstrances. Occasionally the registers reveal that Calvin interjected an admonition not at the end of a hearing but towards its beginning, as a way of elaborating a charge. Let me once more provide examples: In the early months of the Consistory's first year of operation, a woman named Janne Pertennaz was repeatedly summoned to be cross-examined on her religious beliefs. She had obviously remained Catholic and was quite stubborn and vocal about her objections to the Reformed religion. At her second appearance, to face charges that grew from a conversation she had had with a German visitor in which she told him that no one in Geneva dared to pray to the Virgin Mary any longer, the questioning began after Calvin administered "admonitions from the Word of God." Whatever they were they did no good. Mme. Pertennaz made her Catholic convictions very clear in the course of the cross-examination and was excommunicated as a result.[16]

In the following year, Nycolas Baud of Peissy was summoned on suspicion that he was mismanaging his property and selling so much of it that officials feared he would have difficulty supporting his family. The hearing began with "admonitions made by Monsieur Calvin." Baud explained his property transactions briefly, and asked for mercy from God and the government. The Consistory decided that this was a matter for the government to investigate. They also administered a remonstrance to Baud that he treat his wife better, that he attend church services more faithfully, that he set a better example for his children, and that he stop selling family property.[17] The identity of the person who administered this remonstrance is not revealed. In these cases, Calvin's interventions obviously filled a very different function than his concluding remonstrances. They were designed to begin, not end discussion. They were designed to make the person summoned more aware of the nature of the charge brought against him or her, and of the seriousness with which the Consistory took the charge.

[16]*RConsistoire*, 1:26 (4 April 1542).
[17]*RConsistoire*, 1:175 (1 February 1543).

To flesh out our picture a bit further, it would be well to look at cases in which Calvin did not administer the remonstrance, in which someone else took over this responsibility. One such case ended the first divorce suit brought by Calvin's brother Antoine against his wife Anne Le Fert on charges of adultery. That case led to a formal investigation by the Small Council, and concluded that while Anne had behaved with great imprudence there was no proof of adultery. The Council then recommended that she be reconciled with her husband in a ceremony to be held before the Consistory. That ceremony included remonstrances to Anne for her scandalous behavior and "her hypocrisy." They were not administered by Calvin, however, who had been deeply involved in the case, and in fact had personally brought before the Consistory the initial charge of adultery against his sister-in-law. They were rather administered by William Farel, the grand old man of the Genevan Reformation, then supervising the Reformed Church in Neuchâtel, who happened to be visiting Geneva that week. The hearing ended with Anne Le Fert falling to her knees before her husband and asking him for mercy and forgiveness, then turning to her brother-in-law with the same request. The two brothers both received her apology with gentleness and pardoned her. The three were then dismissed in peace, with a parting admonition to live in good friendship ("en bonne dilection") with each other.[18] In the circumstances it would have been inappropriate for Calvin to have administered the remonstrance. In this case, incidentally, the remonstrance was not effective. Several years later, Anne was back before the Consistory, faced with a fresh charge of adultery brought by her husband and his brother. This time the charge stuck and she was divorced and banished from the city.

Another celebrated case in which Calvin did not administer the remonstrance was that of François Favre, an elderly patrician whose children and in-laws held prominent positions in the city government. Favre was accused of multiple fornication with several servant girls. Calvin did not attend the Consistory session of 3 February 1547, in which this case came to a climax. His colleague Abel Poupin was asked to administer the usual remonstrance. Favre, however, announced that he simply would not listen to the remonstrance. He would not have anything to do with any of the ministers in attendance. He would accept correction only from the presiding syndic, a layman. And he would not even repeat for the syndic the charge for which he had been summoned. He pointed out that it was available in writing and he saw no need to embarrass himself by repeating it orally. After these statements of defiance, the session fell into chaos, with several of the ministers shouting at Favre. One of them, almost certainly Poupin, said that if Favre would

---

[18]A. E. G., RConsistoire, vol. 4, fol. 66 v (18 October 1548).

not recognize the ministers he could no longer be regarded as a sheep of the flock of Jesus Christ but rather as a dog, and excommunicate from the church.[19] This insult, particularly the reference to a dog, infuriated Favre and his relatives. They filed formal complaints against Poupin with the Small Council.[20] When his daughter, the wife of Ami Perrin, was summoned to the Consistory on different charges a short while later, she shouted insults at the ministers in general and at Poupin in particular for mistreating her father.[21] The whole mess led to formal trials of Favre and his daughter.[22] It ended several months later in yet another Consistory hearing. Favre now confessed his misbehavior and begged forgiveness. The presiding syndic, on behalf of the entire Consistory, formally requested Calvin to administer the remonstrances, point by point. Calvin began by observing that ministers are called by Our Lord. A part of their job is to administer his word, presumably by participating in Consistory hearings and issuing remonstrances. He then said that God is merciful to all who repent of their faults. He reminded Favre that he had provoked quite a scandal at his last appearance. Favre accepted everything Calvin said. His only explanation for his misbehavior was that he had been very upset because of the way in which his son had been treated by the Consistory in an earlier case. He said that if Calvin had always displayed the gentleness he had displayed that day, things would never have gotten out of hand. He then shook hands with each of the ministers and his case was dismissed.[23]

This is one of a number of cases that involve the powerful patrician Favre family. Clearly, this family gave Calvin a lot of trouble. They resented the growing influence in their city of Calvin and his colleagues, a group of hired pastors, almost all of whom were imported from France. The Favres did not object to the pastors' theology, but they felt that the newcomers were trying to root out old Genevan customs and impose French culture on the community. In this particular case, however, it is clear that it was not anything Calvin himself said that provoked the initial uproar; rather it was an attempted remonstrance from Calvin's colleague Abel Poupin. When it finally came time for Calvin to administer the remonstrance, the Favres had all simmered down and the problem was resolved. It

---

[19]Cf. *RConsistoire*, 3:14 (3 February 1547) with the somewhat fuller account, from a loose leaf in RConsistoire, published in *CO* 21.395–96. Only the latter includes the dog insult.

[20]*CO* 21.399–400, from A. E. G., RC, vol. 42, fol. 63v (21 March 1547).

[21]*RConsistoire*, 3:99–100 (23 June 1547)

[22]See Henri Fazy, "Procès et démêlés à propos de la compétence disciplinaire du Consistoire (1546–1547)," in *Mémoires de l'Institut National Genevois*, vol. 16 (Geneva, 1886), for a full account of this affair, with texts of the trial records and other related documents.

[23]*RConsistoire*, 3:1477 (6 October 1547). Cf. Robert M. Kingdon, "Anticlericalism in the Registers of the Geneva Consistory, 1542–1564," in Peter A. Dykema and Heiko A. Oberman, eds., *Anticlericalism in Late Medieval and Early Modern Europe* (Leiden: Brill, 1993), 618–22, for more on the Favre cases.

did, to be sure, flare up again, but not between François Favre and the Consistory. It was François' son-in-law, Ami Perrin, who became the new center of controversy.

It could be argued on the basis of these stories that Calvin was far more skillful in administering remonstrances than his colleagues. His remonstrances, on this showing, even if often harsh, were more likely to be effective in inducing repentance. That may very well be an important reason that he was asked often enough to administer the remonstrances that at the end of his life one of his colleagues could say that he administered them all.

III. Ceremonies of Reconciliation

Not only was Calvin frequently asked to administer the remonstrances with which most cases ended; he was also asked to superintend at least some of the ceremonies of reconciliation that sometimes followed a remonstrance. Reconciliation was often a part of the Consistory hearing itself. This was true of two of the cases already considered. The clear if implicit intent of the hearing involving Marquet, the hatmaker, and his wife had been to resolve a domestic quarrel and reconcile a husband and wife. The explicit intent of the hearing involving Antoine Calvin and his wife, following the first charge of adultery brought against her, had been to mend a marriage and bring a husband and wife back together.

The process of reconciliation, however, could be even more formal, and could become a separate ceremony following a hearing. We find examples of these ceremonies in the first years in which the Consistory was operating. The Consistory was particularly concerned to reconcile people before one of the quarterly communion services. It was generally agreed that people involved in a violent quarrel, with "hate in their hearts" toward others—whether family members, business partners, or neighbors—should not take communion. In fact, a fair amount of the Consistory's business in the sessions immediately preceding communion services could be devoted to reconciliations. For that matter, a certain amount of the Consistory's business after communion services could be devoted to exploring cases of people who had not received communion because they were involved in unresolved quarrels, in the hope that a process toward reconciliation could be started that would make it possible for them to receive communion the next time around. A ceremony of reconciliation took place a day or two after the related Consistory hearing, in one of the city's parish churches. It was presided over by two members of the Consistory, one layman and one minister. Calvin was often the minister assigned to these ceremonies.

Again, let me provide examples: On 28 August 1543, as plans were being made for the next communion service, the noble Bartholomie (widow of Claude

Richardet and at the time wife of the noble Jean Achard) was summoned before the Consistory, charged with "papist superstition." She flatly denied the charge, saying that she had never taught papistry to anyone, that she did not remember even talking about papistry with anyone. The Consistory asked her if she could think of anyone who might have wanted to get her into trouble by circulating such a story. She replied that the only person with whom she had had a recent argument was a man named Hippolite, who had misappropriated some of her money. She said she pardoned him for the love of God, did not want to damage him in any way, and would leave vengeance to God.[24]

Three days later the noble Bartholomie and Hippolite Revit, along with his brothers, came to the parish church of the Madeleine for a reconciliation ceremony. Antoine Chicand, that year's syndic responsible for presiding over the Consistory, and John Calvin presided together over this ceremony. Bartholomie and Revit were asked to explain their problem. Revit complained that Bartholomie had insulted him roundly, calling him a traitor, wicked, and other things. Bartholomie replied that she had never called him a traitor, but confessed that she had indeed called him wicked for losing a sum of money that her former husband, now dead, had given to yet another man of prominence. Revit apparently had been a servant or business agent of this other man. She did not seem sure of the facts, however, and was not inclined to press the charge. It would seem that the alleged misappropriation had taken place some time earlier. The two were asked to "pardon each other in order to receive the holy communion of Our Lord, and to live in peace and charity with each other." They both readily agreed and promised not to speak about the matter again. Revit asked for a written copy of the agreement. Apparently he wanted to be sure that she would not revive the charge later. The noble Bartholomie said she was now prepared to accept Revit as an "homme de bien," a man of property and good social standing, and would no longer insult him.

At this same ceremony, Chicand and Calvin also arranged the reconciliation of two sisters, Claudaz and Jana Dentant, both now married. Claudaz had criticized Jana too sharply about the price she had paid for some grain and for some other things. They were reconciled. Following admonitions and remonstrances, they agreed to abandon all harsh words and reproaches.[25]

Shortly before the next communion service, late in October 1543, the Consistory arranged yet another ceremony of reconciliation, once more in the parish church of the Madeleine, after the daily religious services, and once more presided

---

[24]*RConsistoire,* 1:250 (28 August 1543). For more on Bartholomie Achard, see Jacques-Augustin Galiffe, et al., *Notices généalogiques sur les familles genevoises,* 7 vols. (Geneva, 1829–1895), 1:530.

[25] RConsistoire, 1:255 (31 August 1543).

over by Chicand and Calvin. The members of the Consistory were apparently so pleased with the success of the earlier reconciliation ceremony that they thought it worth another try. This time the people who were to be reconciled were of even greater social prominence. They included Pierre Tissot, then treasurer of the republic, who had held and was to hold in the future a number of the most important positions in the city government. They also included Tissot's mother, Françoyse, his wife Loyse Favre (a daughter of the François Favre who was in later years to become notorious in ways already observed), and his brother Jean. This case had come to the attention of the Consistory the day before this reconciliation ceremony, when Tissot's mother, Françoyse, had been summoned for reasons that are not specified. She thought she had been summoned for investigation of her religious beliefs and began by assuring the Consistory members that she went to religious services every morning. She then added that her prominent son did not. She also said that her son had not even talked to her for months, and that she did not get along at all well with her son's wife. She apparently felt they mistreated their own children and ignored her.[26]

This time the reconciliation ceremony was not effective, for the simple reason that Françoyse was the only member of the Tissot family who showed up at the Madeleine that day. Chicand and Calvin immediately asked that Pierre Tissot, his wife Loyse, and his brother Jean, all be summoned officially before regular Consistory sessions to explain themselves.[27] Pierre Tissot and his wife dutifully appeared at the next Consistory session, where the case was discussed at some length. Jean appeared at a later session. In the earlier session, Françoyse repeated and elaborated her complaints that her illustrious son was mistreating and ignoring her, alleging that he had not supported her properly, had supplied her with bad wine, had ignored her when she was sick, and so on. Pierre and Loyse politely but firmly refuted the charges, and promised that they would continue doing all that they could to help her. It appeared that Françoyse had become not only querulous but also forgetful, with no longer any very clear idea of what was going on around her. The Consistory finally worked out the desired reconciliation at this session.[28] But the role of Calvin in that final agreement is not specified.

I trust that these selected examples will give you some idea of what Calvin did within the Consistory, in the administration of remonstrances and in the arrangement of reconciliations. They reveal him to be a pastor continually concerned with bringing people back into good relationships both with their own relatives and neighbors and with the wider Christian community. It is my hope that fur-

---

[26] *RConsistoire*, 1:264 (25 October 1543).
[27] *RConsistoire*, 1:266 (26 October 1543).
[28] *RConsistoire*, 1:266–67 (1 November 1543).

ther work with these Consistory registers will make it possible to fill out in even greater detail our understanding of this important but neglected side of Calvin's career.

Albrecht Dürer, *Mercenary Love*. The horse may refer to Jeremiah 5:8, "They were as horses in the morning: every one neighed after his neighbor's wife."

Docere/Movere: Les catégories rhétoriques et leurs sources humanistes dans la doctrine calvinienne de la foi

Olivier Millet

I. L'Approche rhétorique de la pensée religieuse de Calvin

Je ne pense pas qu'il soit aujourd'hui nécessaire de justifier une approche rhétorique de l'oeuvre de Calvin, mais en guise de préliminaire à cet exposé, une explication est nécessaire au sujet de ce que l'on est en droit d'attendre d'une telle approche pour le sujet particulier que nous intéressera ici—il s'agit en effet d'une doctrine théologique sur un point précis et crucial de la pensée religieuse du réformateur. Il va de soi que l'oeuvre de Calvin relève d'une étude rhétorique si l'on s'intéresse chez lui à l'exercice cultivé de la parole (*oratio*), qu'elle soit écrite ou prêchée, en langue latine ou en langue vulgaire. La rhétorique, comme tradition héritée de l'antiquité, cultivée sans interruption au Moyen Age et revivifiée à la Renaissance, est en effet la doctrine à visée pratique dont relève entièrement cet exercice de la parole dans *la mesure où* il se veut efficace, c'est-à-dire persuasif.

Les traités de Calvin (*Institutio* comprise), ses lettres, ses sermons, assument plus ou moins cette fonction éloquente, et supposent, pour être aujourd'hui perçus et interprétés correctement, une prise en compte de cette dimension. Cela est d'autant plus vrai que le courant rhétorique auquel appartient Calvin, celui ce que j'ai appelé ailleurs[1] la nouvelle rhétorique germanique, largement représentée à Paris dans les années d'études du Réformateur (cf. la lignée Agricola, Mélanchthon, puis Ramus), se caractérise par l'union intime de la dialectique avec la rhétorique: elle est à la fois une méthode heuristique de réflexion et une méthode efficace d'exposition et d'enseignement. Cette dimension rhétorique concerne donc les genres littéraires pratiqués par Calvin, mais aussi les méthodes et les procédures du raisonnement, la portée exacte et le statut des énoncés, les procédés de la disposition et enfin les moyens de l'élocution du discours.

---

[1]Je me permets de renvoyer à *Calvin et la dynamique de la parole, étude de rhétorique réformée*, Paris, Champion, 1992. Voir aussi Quirinus Breen, "John Calvin and the Rhetorical Tradition," in *Christianity and History: Studies in the History of Ideas*,éd. N. P. Ross (Grand Rapids, 1968), 107–29; E. David Willis, "Persuasion in Calvin's Theology," in *Calvin and Christian Ethics: Papers and Responses Presented at the 5. Colloquium on Calvin*, éd. P. de Klerk (Grand Rapids: Calvin Studies Society, 1987), 83–94, 95–99; William J. Bouwsma, *Calvinism as "Rhetorica theologica": Protocol of the 54. Colloquy, 28 sept. 1986* (Berkeley: Center for Hermeneutical Studies in Hellenistic and Modern Culture, 1987).

Si nous nous tournons vers le commentateur biblique, l'exégèse des textes bibliques repose chez lui, comme chez ses collègues Bucer et Mélanchthon (et bien d'autres exégètes contemporains), sur une très large utilisation de notions héritées de la tradition rhétorique et précisées encore notamment par Erasme dans l'application que l'on peut et doit en faire au langage biblique. La rhétorique est donc partout présente, non seulement dans la manière d'écrire du Réformateur, mais aussi dans sa manière d'argumenter et jusque dans les règles herméneutiques qui commandent l'interprétation des textes bibliques.

La question reste cependant posée d'un présence prégnante de la culture rhétorique dans ce qui relève de la théologie à proprement parler de notre auteur. Dans quelle mesure des catégories rhétoriques informent-elles sa pensée religieuse telle qu'elle est formulée dans ses traités doctrinaux? Il convient ici d'être prudent, si l'on veut éviter d'expliquer de façon réductioniste cette pensée en recourant à un modèle qui ne se situe évidemment pas sur le même plan. On se gardera peut-être d'employer une expression trop facile ou trop vague comme "théologie rhétorique," déjà appliquée à propos d'autres auteurs de la renaissance comme Erasme, à moins de préciser le contexte historique humaniste exact qui confère un sens pertinent à cette expression. Deux précautions, et deux hypothèses sont nécessaires *a priori*, qui peuvent rendre d'autant plus rentable le recours au modèle rhétorique qu'elles en limiteront immédiatement la portée.

D'abord, la rhétorique a pu servir de modèle intellectuel à Calvin pour penser la matière de la doctrine théologique dans la mesure, et seulement dans la mesure, où la tradition rhétorique propose des catégories susceptibles d'éclairer la révélation divine en tant que processus de communication verbale efficace entre Dieu comme locuteur divin et l'homme (singulièrement l'homme croyant) comme auditeur de la parole divine. D'autre part, de la rhétorique à la doctrine chrétienne de la révélation, il ne peut y avoir, pour toute sorte de raisons, de transposition directe: l'exercice cultivé et efficace de la parole interhumaine et la révélation divine offerte à l'homme sont à certains égards deux réalités incommensurables. C'est pourquoi le recours au modèle rhétorique de la communication résulte chez Calvin d'une transposition indirecte et complexe des catégories en question, transposition qui s'appuie elle-même sur des médiations culturelles, où l'on rencontre notamment saint Augustin et l'humanisme philologique de la Renaissance. L'intérêt de l'approche rhétorique, ainsi limitée, que je propose ici, comme j'ai déjà fait partiellement dans mon livre sur Calvin et la rhétorique résidera donc en ceci: cette approche permet de mettre en valeur la philosophie religieuse, soit un ensemble cohérent d'idées et de valeurs, à l'intérieur de laquelle les doctrines théologiques de Calvin prennent place et reçoivent tout leur sens. Un parallèle suffira pour me faire entendre. De même que Calvin explicite la doctrine

chrétienne dans le cadre d'une philosophie religieuse (héritée de l'antiquité, refor-
mulée par l'humanisme chrétien et adaptée par Calvin à ses propres objectifs) où
les notions de *religio,* de *pietas,* d'*aequitas* etc. jouent un rôle majeur,[2] de même sa
doctrine de la révélation s'appuie, sans s'y réduire, sur des notions provenant de
l'humanisme rhétorique mais qui sont en retour remodelées en fonction de la
signification nouvelle qu'elles revêtent dans le nouveau contexte de la théologie
réformatrice.

Et maintenant, venons-en au fait. Il s'agit de la doctrine calvinienne de la foi
(*fides*), et du couple des catégories rhétoriques du *docere* (instruire) et du *movere*
(émouvoir), dans la mesure où ce couple est utilisé par Calvin pour expliquer la
nature de la foi chrétienne. Afin de ne pas répéter ce que j'ai écrit dans mon livre,
j'examinerai ici des aspects de ce problème que je n'y ai pas abordés. Nous analy-
serons d'abord la tradition humaniste dans laquelle Calvin s'insère ici, de Lorenzo
Valla à Martin Bucer, au sujet de la *fides* comme *persuasio,* à la lumière du couple
docere/movere. Cet examen, qui ne portera pas sur les textes de Calvin lui-même,
sera en fait déjà un commentaire de *l'Institutio* de celui-ci (édition de 1559[3]:
notamment livre 3, chapitres 1 et 2). Puis nous soulignerons, autour de trois
grands textes de Calvin sur cette topique, certains accents du même complexe
d'idées chez lui, et la manière dont il interprète personnellement la même théma-
tique. Enfin, j'aborderai en conclusion certaines conséquences que l'interprète
moderne peut tirer des faits ainsi mis en évidence.

II. De Valla, Budé, Bucer (et Mélanchthon) à Calvin

1. *Lorenzo Valla: Persuasio et fides*

Tout remonte à L. Valla,[4] plus précisément au chapitre 30 du Livre 5 de ses
Elegantiae.[5] Rappelons ici que l'objectif de l'ouvrage de cet humaniste philologue
italien (1407–1457) est de définir une des trois qualités (*virtutes*) de *l'elocutio,*
l'*elegantia*: à la fois la pureté et la clarté, notamment la correction (*latinitas*) et la
netteté (*explicatio*), ce qui inclut le sens usuel et le sens propre des termes. Au plu-
riel, le terme *elegantia* reçoit une acception esthétique (élégance) qui s'ajoute aux
dimensions précédentes. L'usage des grands écrivains classiques (notamment

---

[2]Voir à ce sujet l'ouvrage majeur de Josef Bohatec, *Budé und Calvin: Studien zur Gedankenwelt des französischen Humanismus* (Graz: Böhlaus, 1950); Charles Partee, *Calvin and Classical Philosophy* (Leiden: Brill, 1977).

[3]Dans les *Opera Selecta,* vol. 4, éd. Peter Barth et Wilhelm Niesel (Munich, Kaiser, 1931, 1968).

[4]Cf. Marijn de Kroon, *Martin Bucer und Johannes Calvin, Reformatorische Perspektiven, Einleitung und Texte* (Göttingen, Vandenhoek & Ruprecht, 1992), 145, qui n'a pas répéré cette source chez Valla.

[5]Dans les *Opera omnia,* avec une préface d'Eugenio Garin, vol. 1, *Scripta in éditione Basiliensi anno 1540 collecta* (Torino: Bottega d'Erasmo, 1962), 172.

Cicéron et Quintilien) doit prévaloir, dans l'emploi des termes et des locutions, contre celui du latin scolastique; nouveauté profonde qui est la source essentielle de l'humanisme philologique de la Renaissance. Le contexte du chapitre dans lequel Valla traite du terme *fides* est celui des verbes munis du suffixe latin *per-*: il distingue *suadere* de *persuadere*. Le second terme désigne l'action dans son résultat (*est in effectu*), alors que le premier ne désigne que l'effort en vue du résultat (*est in actu*). Celui qui produit la *persuasio* est appelé en bon latin *autor*, d'où découle la notion d'*autoritas*. Quant à la *persuasio* elle-même, c'est une "opinion et un avis arrêté, dont nous sommes persuadés." C'est ici qu'intervient le terme *fides*:

> Cette persuasion (c'est du moins mon avis) semble signifier ce que les chrétiens appellent *fides*. Et si nous considérons l'origine grecque, je ne sais pas si nous ne devrions pas dire, de façon plus appropriée que *fides*, *persuasio*, d'autant que les faits sont pour nous. *Fides* en effet se dit en latin au sens propre de la *probatio* (argument probant), comme 'je produis la persuasion (*fidem facio*) au moyen de documents, d'arguments, de témoins'. Or la religion chrétienne ne s'appuie pas sur la *probatio*, mais sur la *persuasio*, qui est supérieure à la *probatio*. Car souvent les arguments probants (*probationes*) ne suffisent pas à nous convaincre: ainsi, un mauvais serviteur, un mauvais fils, une mauvaise fille, une mauvaise épouse, ne donne pas son assentiment (*non acquiescit*) à l'avis pourtant le meilleur, qui ne peut être réfuté. Celui qui est persuadé, donne son complet assentiment, et ne réclame pas d'argument supplémentaire. En effet, il n'estime pas seulement avoir été convaincu (*sibi probatum*), mais reconnaît avoir été poussé (*commotum*) à accomplir [les ordres donnés]. Mais puisque la *fides* est prise aussi dans l'acception, pour ainsi dire, de la facilité à croire [*credulitas*],... il est normal que notre religion ait reçu le nom de *fides*, comme chez les Grecs de *pistis*.

Dans ce texte, Valla n'insiste pas davantage sur la différence entre la simple *probatio*, qui relève du *docere* et des preuves d'ordre rationnel, et la *persuasio*, qui relève du *movere* (cf. *commotum*: "poussé," mais au moyen d'une émotion) et donc des affects. Cela va de soi dans le contexte de la culture rhétorique, auquel toutes ces notions sont empruntées. Le caractère supérieur et achevé (à vrai dire surnaturel, caractère ici passé sous silence) de la *fides* chrétienne est indiqué par le terme *persuasio*, qui devrait la désigner proprement. Mais du fait la *fides* en général, comme la *fides* chrétienne en particulier, comportent la facilité à croire (*credulitas*:[6] sens non péjoratif ici), Valla n'insiste pas pour que le terme de *persuasio* remplace celui de *fides* dans le langage chrétien correct. Retenons aussi le fait qu'il est impossible de produire la *fides* auprès de personnes moralement peu prêtes à obéir: auprès d'elles, la *persuasio*, c'est-à-dire le recours aux sentiments (au pathos) et aux moyens extraordinaires sera nécessaire.

2. *Erasme et Dolet*

Ce texte n'est pas passé inaperçu bien qu'Erasme, grand lecteur de Valla, ne semble pas en faire cas explicitement dans ses propres travaux exégétiques.[7] Mais l'emploi, sinon l'assimilation de *persuasio* pour *fides*, fait l'objet d'un débat assez vif entre les humanistes dans les années 1520–1530. L'Erasme du *Ciceronianus* (1528)[8] reproche aux cicéroniens trop épris de purisme d'employer l'un pour l'autre et d'effacer ainsi les caractéristiques du langage et de la tradition chrétiens; inversement, un cicéronien comme E. Dolet récuse à l'occasion, dans ses *Commentarii linguae latinae* de 1536,[9] l'assimilation des deux notions. Calvin est au courant de ces débats, je l'ai montré ailleurs.[10] A partir de Valla, deux voies étaient devenues possibles. Soit on pouvait remplacer, en bon latin, *fides* au sens chrétien par *persuasio*, par souci de purisme classicisant et sans en tirer de conséquence doctrinale ou spirituelle; c'est le choix des humanistes cicéronisants. D'autre part, on pouvait conserver le terme traditionnel, mais en rappelant que la *fides* chrétienne est une *persuasio*, et en tirer toutes les conséquences.

C'est la voie choisie par les auteurs que je vais maintenant mentionner, disons celle de certains humanistes évangéliques. Martin Bucer, au moment où il s'appuie à ce sujet sur Valla dans ses *Enarrationes* sur les Evangiles, profite de cette référence précise pour rendre un hommage exceptionnel à l'humaniste italien, ainsi qu'à Guillaume Budé, l'humaniste français qui s'était fait l'écho de Valla sur ce point. Une chaîne d'autorités s'est ainsi formée, qui comprend (outre les références négatives sur la question, mais au courant du problème, d'Erasme et de Dolet), avec Budé et Bucer, deux références importantes pour Calvin. Analysons-en les étapes.

---

[6]Sur les positions catholiques face à la doctrine réformatrice de la *fides*, voir par exemple Th. de Vio Cajetanus, *De fide et operibus*. Nous avons consulté l'édition (Lyon: J. Fellon, 1536), qui dénonce dans la *fides* réformatrice une simple *credulitas*, p. 4: "credulitatem qua homo credit se justificari per Christum...."

[7]Sur la *fides* comme *fiducia* (mais non comme *persuasio*) chez Erasme, voir Jacques Chomarat, *Grammaire et rhétorique chez Erasme* (Paris, les Belles Lettres, 1981), 1:341, 566.

[8]*Il Ciceroniano o dello stile migliore*, testo latino critico, éd Angiolo Gambaro, Brescia, La Scuola editrice, 1965, ligne 3929, où le reproche suivant est fait au cicéronien Longueil: *nunquam usurpans fidei vocabulum, sed in ejus locum substituens persuasionem.*

[9]*Commentarii linguae latinae* (Lyon: Gryphius, 1536), 1:23: "Fides hic nec persuasionem christianam significat."

[10]Millet, *Calvin et la dynamique*, 52 sq.

3. Budé

Budé revient à plusieurs reprises sur le fait que la *fides* chrétienne doit être appelée proprement *persuasio*. Dans ses *Annotationes* sur les *Pandecte* (1508, nombreuses rééditions) ouvrage que Calvin a lu de près au cours des ses études, il revient sur la différence entre *suadere* et *persuadere*, pour adopter la position de Valla, qu'il cite et approuve au sujet de la *fides* comme *persuasio*. Le contexte[11] où cette mise au point apparaît n'est pas indifférent. On y trouve, après la mention de Valla, une longue et enthousiaste charte de l'humanisme comme discipline, souveraine et encyclopédique, de la parole cultivée et suprêmement efficace, une exaltation de Pithô, déesse de la persuasion, une longue évocation de l'Hercule gallique, figure mythologique qui incarne les pouvoirs de l'éloquence agissant par la douceur de la persuasion, un plaidoyer aussi pour la lecture des Pères de l'Eglise contre les théologiens scolastiques actuels, et une conclusion sur la puissance psychologique du verbe:

> [Pithô] est appelée aussi *flexanima*, pour ainsi dire "emouvant l'esprit" (*animum flectens*), chez les Grecs *psychogogos*, pour ainsi dire conductrice et charmeuse de l'âme.

Ailleurs, dans ses *Commentarii linguae graecae* (1529), Budé rappelle le parallèle entre *fides* au sens chrétien et le terme grec *pistis*, mais pour corriger, en meilleur helléniste de son temps qu'il est lui-même, Valla sur ce point:

> *Fides* (dans son acception chrétienne) en effet, ne désigne pas seulement, comme l'a dit Laurent lui-même, la facilité de croire, mais la confiance en un fait avéré et parfaitement établi (*rei compertae explorataeque fiduciam*), par imitation du terme grec.... C'est pourquoi *fides* ne signifie pas moins que *persuasio*."[12]

Par une voie différente, et même opposée à Valla, Budé en arrive ici à la même conclusion: la *fides* chrétienne est une *persuasio*. Dans ce texte cependant, le complexe d'idées rhétoriques *docere/movere* a été effacé: la *persuasio* budéene porte ici sur une évidence plutôt qu'elle ne repose sur les ressources affectives de la persuasion. Les deux textes budéens que j'ai cités se complètent donc dans deux directions différentes: psychagogie ou action sur les profondeurs de la personne, et évidence totale. Bucer, et surtout Calvin, retiendront la leçon. Budé tira en tout cas les conséquences de sa définition en employant lui-même, par exemple dans

---

[11]Nous nous référons à l'édition suivante: *Annotationes Guglielmi Budaei ... in quatuor et viginti Pandectarum libros ... auctae et recognitae* (Paris: J. Badius Ascensius, 1530); le passage se trouve en c ii(v)–c iii(r).

[12]*Commentarii linguae graecae*, cité d'après les *Opera omnia* (1557; reprinted Farnborough: Gregg International Publishers, 1969), 4:152–53.

son *De contemptu rerum fortuitarum*, le terme *persuasio* pour *fides* au sens religieux. Une édition de 1526 de ce traité,[13] accompagnée d'un commentaire explicatif, explique d'ailleurs à ce sujet, sous la plume du commentateur: *persuasio = rerum divinarum fides*. Cet emploi est constant chez le maître français de l'humanisme chrétien.

4. Bucer

Bucer forme, avant Calvin, le dernier maillon de la chaîne. Aux arguments de Valla et de Budé qu'il cite, il ajoute, nouveau progrès dans la chaîne, des références hébraïques: *émunah* = *pistis* = *fides* = *persuasio*. Conscient de son originalité dans le camp des théologiens évangéliques, il s'en explique longuement dans ses *Enarrationes* (in Matthew 8).[14] L'appellation de *persuasio* pour la foi chrétienne est à la fois conforme au langage biblique, hébreu et grec, et plus adaptée doctrinalement pour désigner l'objet et l'attitude du *credere*. La foi est en effet une "certitude et une constance ferme que Dieu procure dans ses promesses"; ce sens objectif est complété par un sens subjectif: "On ne peut être plus pleinement certain et assuré dans son avis que lorsqu'on en est pleinement persuadé."

Ce sens subjectif s'accomplit, pour la *fides* chrétienne, grâce à l'Esprit de Dieu, qui persuade les "élus" au sujet des paroles de Dieu. Bucer précise cette dimension subjective, qui repose sur l'efficacité de l'Esprit, et non de la parole humaine: "l'Esprit [*Spiritus*] persuade plus efficacement que l'homme d'autant qu'il a lui-même plus de pouvoir que l'homme sur les esprits [*mente persuasus*]. Le jugement conceptuel (*animi judicium*), les affects aussi et les forces de l'homme suivent."

Les termes latins (surtout *animus*) sont ici délicats à rendre en français. Mais il est clair que la *persuasio* de la *mens* est supérieure à la simple *fides* parce qu'elle emporte, avec l'*animum*, qui comporte encore un aspect intellectuel (*sententia*) les sentiments, ou affects, et les "forces" humaines, soit la totalité des facultés ou des instances anthropologiques qui définissent l'homme. La définition de la foi chrétienne que Bucer donne alors est à peu près la même que donnera Calvin dans son *Institutio*.

Bucer est plus explicite encore dans son commentaire sur l'Epître aux Romains. Le chapitre IX[15] de sa Préface est consacré à la *fides* et au *credere*. Bucer y reprend la distinction de Mélanchthon (*Loci Communes*) entre la simple *notitia*,

---

[13]Paris, *Prelum Ascensianum*, 1526, p. 54 (il s'agit d'une note explicative des éditeurs), et renvoi à titre d'exemple au texte de Budé, fol. LV, où *persuasio* désigne effectivement la foi chrétienne.

[14]*In sacra quatuor Evangelia enarrationes ...* (Bâle: J. Herwagen, 1536), 218D–221A

[15]Nous nous référons par commodité à l'édition tardive *Metaphrasis et enarratio in Epist. D. Pauli Apostoli ad Romanos* (Bâle: P. Perna, 1562), Praefata, chap. 9, p. 15sq., qui cite Melanchthon (voir *infra*).

connaissance qui n'engage pas le sujet sinon momentanément, et *l'assensus,* qui résulte de la *persuasio* exercée par l'Esprit divin. L'*assensus* concerne non seulement l'intelligence (*intellectum*) mais aussi la volonté. En effet, "Là où manque une raison [*ratio*] qui fasse que notre esprit reconnaisse la véracité de ce qui est dit, et là où la seule autorité de celui qui parle fait que l'on croie, il est nécessaire que la volonté soit favorable à l'égard de celui qui parle, et soit tenue par l'amour et l'admiration pour sa personne."

Le couple *do*cere (ici *notitia*) / *movere* (ici, *assensus* de la volonté) gouverne ici implicitement cette analyse, présentée dans les termes généraux et sur le modèle d'un processus de communication verbale interhumain. Pour que l'autorité (cf. Valla et Budé sur l'*autor* comme *persuasor*) s'impose, il faut que nous concevions une opinion remarquable au sujet de la personne qui parle. Ainsi, la *persuasio* dépend non pas de l'*intellectus*, mais d'un préjugé favorable d'ordre personnel, mais fondé objectivement, qui permettra ensuite au *movere* de s'exercer pleinement; Bucer précise ce dernier point dans le cas de la communication/révélation divine, sur le coeur (*corda*) de l'homme.

5. *Premier Bilan*

Nous pouvons maintenant récapituler, et établir un premier bilan, afin de ne pas nous répéter ensuite à propos de Calvin, qui présente, en termes un peu différents, les mêmes analyses. La tradition rhétorique connaît en fait trois types de moyens de conviction/ persuasion, distingués depuis Aristote, puis Cicéron, puis saint Augustin[16]: *docere/conciliare/movere.* Le premier est celui des *probationes,* faits et arguments qui s'adressent à la part rationnelle de l'homme pour produire la *fides,* sans prétendre cependant à l'évidence absolue des axiomes et des raisonnements philosophico-scientifiques. Nous sommes sur le plan du *docere.* Le second plan relève en rhétorique de l'*ethos,* destiné à produire le *conciliare:* il s'agit de tout ce qui dans la personne de l'orateur et dans son discours produit une impression assez favorable pour faire pencher la conviction dans le sens de l'approbation; la *dignitas* de l'orateur est ici essentielle; nous avons vu que Bucer intègre cet élément à ses analyses. Calvin la transposera en *majestas* divine, qui s'impose d'elle-même aux fidèles. Ce second aspect joue un rôle tout particulier dans la tradition rhétorique latine, celle où l'orateur doit être d'abord un *vir bonus* et s'imposer par son autorité. Enfin, le *movere* doit intervenir pour achever l'oeuvre de persuasion, sur le plan irrationnel des affects. Dans la tradition latine, notamment cicéronienne, la véritable éloquence repose sur l'articulation judicieuse des trois dimensions, et des moyens rhétoriques (arguments et figures) qui leur sont

---

[16]Voir sur l'utilisation par Calvin de ce schéma, et sur ses sources, notre livre; Millet, *Calvin et la dynamique,* 214 sq.

respectivement propres. Définir, comme le fait Valla, puis Budé, la foi chrétienne comme *persuasio*, c'était distinguer nettement la foi comme croyance ou simple conviction, de la foi comme persuasion, produite par la mise en oeuvre des trois instances que je viens de rappeler.

A la suite de Mélanchthon, Bucer articule la distinction entre la simple *fides* et la vraie *persuasio* selon le couple *notitia/persuasio* (*assensus* chez Mélanchthon). A l'arrière-plan de cette distinction, l'opposition du simple *docere* et du *conciliare*. Cette opposition recouvre celle, anthropologique, de l'*intellectus* et de la *voluntas*. Les catégories rhétoriques sont ainsi utilisées, mais transformées dans leur signification lorsque nos auteurs y recourent pour préciser leur doctrine théologique. Du *docere* (la simple *notitia* mélanchthonienne) relève, dans le régime de la révélation chrétienne, tout ce qui appartient au discours en tant qu'il est exprimé dans un langage humain, et qu'il fait l'objet d'une prédication orale et "externe," comme dit Calvin, ainsi que les arguments qui relèvent en rhétorique de la *probatio*. Bucer précise, toujours dans le même contexte de son commentaire de Romains, qu'il s'agit des *probationes* ou type d'arguments rhétoriques suivantes: *opinio mentis humanae*, miracles, *probabilis sermo, experimenta.*

Sur le second plan, celui de l'*ethos* et de la *conciliatio*, plan de l'autorité sociale, morale et personnelle de celui qui parle, l'assentiment porte ici sur l'autorité de Dieu; le fidèle adhère à la personne de celui qui se révèle en tant qu'il est Dieu. Bucer insiste sur le fondement suivant de l'autorité divine: son amour pour nous, là où Calvin a tendance à valoriser l'autorité divine en tant que telle à partir de sa majesté (*majestas*), sans considération particulière de cette qualité aimante. Néanmoins, chez Calvin comme chez Bucer, la *fides/persuasio* a pour contenu concret moins une autorité nue conçue comme puissance que les promesses de salut de l'Evangile offertes par un Dieu en qui la confiance peut être totale.

Enfin, sur le plan du *movere*, celui qui provoque la *persuasio* totale, bien que jamais achevé (Calvin insistera sur ce point), nous trouvons les affects du coeur, que l'Esprit divin pénètre, bouleverse et transforme.

L'anthropologie réformatrice rejoint ainsi l'anthropologie rhétorique, elle-même d'origine philosophique. En effet, déjà la *rhétorique* d'Aristote repose essentiellement sur la distinction *docere/movere*, celle de la raison accessible aux arguments des *probationes* et celle des *affectus*. Dans l'anthropologie réformatrice,[17] vigoureusement réductrice comme on le sait, les facultés de l'âme se réduisent à deux instances, l'intelligence et la volonté. Or la volonté dépend

---

[17]Voir à ce sujet pour son contexte rhétorico-philosophique les travaux de Klaus Dockhorn, "Luthers Glaubensbegriff und die Rhetorik: Zu Gerhard Elelings Buch *Einführung in theologische Sprachlehre,*" *Linguistica Biblica* (Bonn) 21/22 (1973): 19–39; "*Rhetorica movet*: protestantischer Humanismus und karolingische Renaissance," *Rhetorik: Beiträge zu ihrer Geschichte in Deutschland vom 16 –20 Jahrhundert,* éd. Helmut Schanze (Frankfort/M., Athenäum, 1974).

entièrement, on le sait également (cf. Luther et Mélanchthon), des *affectus*, et l'homme n'est pas le maître de son coeur, ce coeur étant radicalement perverti (cf. le "mauvais fils" de Valla, auprès de qui le *docere* ne suffit pas! Mais Valla ne pensait bien sûr pas à la future doctrine réformatrice). Dieu doit prendre possession des affects pour réorienter le coeur humain. Or, dans l'anthropologie rhétorique héritée d'Aristote et élaborée notamment par Cicéron et Quintilien, la *persuasio* est envisagée comme une psychagogie, qui "fléchit" (*flectere*), ébranle entièrement la sensibilité et l'imagination (*afficere, commovere*) de manière à emporter de façon décisive l'assentiment. C'est sans doute ce parallèle entre anthropologie rhétorique et anthropologie réformatrice qui explique l'importance des catégories sous-jacentes, *docere/movere*, dans l'analyse réformatrice des conditions de la *fides* comme *persuasio*.

Erasme ayant rejeté l'anthropologie réformatrice lors de sa querelle avec Luther sur le libre-arbitre, on comprend aussi qu'il n'ait pas cru bon d'insister sur cette identification des deux notions, *fides* et *persuasio*. Cette identification le gênait déjà, pour d'autres raisons, de la part des cicéroniens, mais elle pouvait comporter, dans le contexte doctrinal de la réforme, des conséquences opposées à sa conception du libre-arbitre. Erasme ne s'y est pas trompé.

III. Accents de ce complexe d'idées chez Calvin

Je commenterai brièvement les trois passages principaux où le couple *docere/movere* est en jeu chez Calvin à propos de la foi chrétienne. Tous ces passages datent au plus tôt de 1539, et signalent ainsi clairement l'influence de Bucer.

1. *Institutio de 1559, 3.1–2*

La première se trouve dans l'*Institutio* de 1559, livre 3, chapitre 1 et chapitre 2, qui définissent la foi chrétienne. Calvin y oppose au §4 la parole de Dieu perçue extérieurement, qui ne peut produire qu'une "opinion" ou "cuyder," et l'effet intérieur produit par cette parole sous l'effet du saint Esprit. Ce que la première "enseigne" (*docuerat*), le second le "suggère" (*suggerere*), c'est-à-dire le produit en l'insinuant:

> §4: … quia sine profectu clamarent doctores nisi Christus ipse interior magister suo Spiritu ad se traheret qui dati sunt a patre.

Je reviendrai sur l'expression de *magister interior*: notons pour l'instant que le *movere* apparaît à travers l'expression biblique et johannique de "tirer," *trahere*. Mais c'est au chapitre 2, §7, que la foi est définie comme *persuasio*, dans des termes qui rappellent Bucer, et au § 14 que l'opposition *docere/movere* est explicitée: les fidèles sont *divinae veritatis persuasione* confirmati magis quam rationali demonstratione *edocti.* Notons en passant que la notion de *confirmatio,* constante chez Calvin à ce sujet, appartient aussi au langage rhétorique: la *confirmatio* est la partie du discours qui vient établir au moyen d'une argumentation ce qui a déjà été énoncé. Liée sous la plume de Calvin à la *persuasio* qui dépasse le simple *docere,* le terme de *confirmatio* prend un sens nettement psychologico-rhétorique, notamment dans ses commentaires bibliques.[18] Par ailleurs, les deux directions que j'ai signalées à propos de Budé apparaissent ici: la foi est à la fois une persuasion qui éclaire la *mens* et transforme les affects du "coeur," mais aussi une certitude qui porte sur une évidence (*plena et fixa, qualis de rebus compertis et probatis esse solet, certitudo*).

2. *Institutio de 1559, 1.7.4*

Un autre passage de l'*Institutio* sur le fameux témoignage intérieur du Saint Esprit (1559: 1.7.4), qui date de 1539, est particulièrement impressionnant par la présence des catégories rhétoriques; je le citerai dans la version française de 1541 en donnant en latin les termes essentiels:

> Car jaçoit qu'en sa propre majesté elle ait assez de quoy estre reverée (*majestate reverentiam conciliat*), néantmoins elle commence lors à nous vraiment toucher (*afficit*), quand elle est scellée en noz coeurs par le Sainct-Esprit. Estans donc illuminez par la vertu d'iceluy ... nous ne cherchons point ou arguments ou verisimilitudes auxquelles notre jugement repose.... C'est donc une telle persuasion (*persuasio*), laquelle ne requiert point de raisons (*rationes*), toutesfois une telle cognoissance (*notitia*), laquelle est appuyée sur une très bonne raison (*ratio).* C'est à sçavoir d'autant que notre esprit ha plus certain et plus asseuré repos qu'en aucunes raisons."[19]

3. *Institutio de 1559, 4.14.10)*

Docere (notitia) conciliare (a majestate Dei), movere (afficit): la certitude de la foi qui accueille la parole de Dieu comme telle est une persuasion parfaite, bien que d'un autre type que la persuasion humaine et supérieure à elle. L'évidence absolue (cf. Budé) repose, à travers les trois instances traditionnelles, sur un processus surnaturel conçu d'après le modèle, transcendé, de la conviction/persuasion rhétorique. En ce qui concerne la seconde fonction, celle du *conciliare,* Calvin est plus explicite ailleurs (*Institutio* de 1559, 4.14) sur l'origine rhétorique du schéma *docere/conciliare/movere* qu'il adopte, et très clair sur le rôle de l'illumina-

---

[18]Voir notre livre, *Calvin et la dynamique,* 304 sq.
[19]Calvin, *Institutio,* ed. Ja. Pannier (1559; Paris: Les Belles Lettres), 1:67.

tion intérieure comme équivalent de la *conciliatio* rhétorique. Dans ce passage, il développe en effet, à propos des sacrements comme forme visible de la parole, une similitude entre Dieu et les fidèles d'une part, l'orateur et ses auditeurs d'autre part, dans les termes suivants. Je cite par commodité le texte (qui date de 1539), toujours dans la version française de 1541; si l'on se reporte au texte latin (1539), on pourra constater que la phraséologie rhétorique est encore plus riche (le français laisse tomber tout l'aspect technique de cette phraséologie), et plus précise:

> Si on veut persuader [*persuadere*] quelqu'un de faire une chose, on meditera toutes les raisons, par lesquelles il soit attiré à cette sentence, et quasi soit contreinct d'obtemperer [= le *docere*]. Mais encore il n'y a rien de faict, si le personnage auquel on a affaire [= l'auditeur] n'est d'un jugement vif et aigu; s'il n'est pareillement docile, et enclin obéyr à bonne doctrine [= la *docilitas*]; si finalement, il n'a conçu une telle opinion [*praejudicium*] de la loyauté et prudence de celuy qui donne conseil [= problème de l'*autoritas*, et fonction du *conciliare*]. Quand la preudhommie est suspecte, on ne proffite de rien, voire envers ceux qui sont aisez à mener. L'opération de Dieu est pareille en eux [il s'agit ici des sacrements]. Car afin que la parolle ne batte point en vain les aureilles [= risque du simple *docere*] il déclare que c'est Dieu qui parle là [=*conciliatio*, et *autoritas* divine rétablie], et amollit la dureté de nostre cueur [=*movere*], pour nous apprester à l'obéissance.[20]

4. *La foi chrétienne (Institutio de 1559, 3.2.15 sq.)*

Si nous revenons à l'*Institutio*, livre 3, §8, la dimension psychologique est cependant prévalente sur la dimension intellectuelle: *assensionem cordis esse magis quam cerebri, et affectus magis quam intelligentiae*. La "plérophorie" paulinienne désigne pour Calvin, contre Erasme,[21] cette foi, qui inclut un fort moment sensible et affectif, notamment au titre de la douceur, *suavitas*, ou d'une expérience aussi subjectivement sensible que le suggère le terme, fréquent chez notre auteur, de *gustatio* (§15). Les §§33–36 enfin définissent clairement les différents plans de la *persuasio*: parole extérieure, nue et inefficace d'une part, et d'autre part illumination de la *mens* par l'Esprit saint ainsi que "confirmation du coeur." Ici réapparaît une notion essentielle à tous ces développements, celle de l'Esprit saint comme "docteur intérieur" (*doctor interior*), ou encore du Christ toujours comme *magister interior*. C'est là la grande différence avec les textes de Bucer que j'ai men-

---

[20]Calvin, *Institutio*, ed. Ja. Pannier (1559; Paris: Les Belles Lettres), 3:207-8.

[21]Cf. la polémique contre Erasme dans le Commentaire de l'Evangile selon saint Luc (2:1): Calvin reproche à l'humaniste d'avoir traduit *plérophoria* par "plenitude"; il s'agit pour Calvin d'une "certitude et persuasion."

tionnés ou cités plus haut. Bucer est soucieux de *comparer* le processus de la foi avec celui de la communication verbale interhumaine efficace et persuasive; Calvin, lui, utilise ces mêmes données, qui proviennent de Valla et Budé (*fides/persuasio*), et en partie de Mélanchthon (*notitia/assensus*), avec l'opposition du *docere/ movere*, mais, généralement sans expliciter les références rhétoriques qu'il emploie, il les subordonne à la notion augustinienne[22] de l'Esprit de Christ comme maître intérieur qui confère à la vérité une puissance psychagogique et transformatrice du coeur. L'opposition *docere/movere* prend tout son sens dans une opposition intérieur/extérieur elle-même interprétée dans un sens nettement augustinien. Cette référence augustinienne du "maître intérieur" n'a pas été repérée, autant que je sache, par les éditions critiques de l'*Institutio* ni par les études portant sur Calvin et saint Augustin; elle est cependant la clef de voûte de la doctrine calvinienne de la foi comme *persuasio*.

5. *Commentaire du psaume 143:10*

Nous en avons un autre indice dans le second passage topique sur la question. Il s'agit du Commentaire des psaumes, à propos du psaume 143:10 ("Enseigne-moi pour que je fasse ta volonté, car tu es mon Dieu; que ton esprit bon me conduire sur la terre de droiture"), commentaire que je traduis en français:

> Mais il faut noter avec soin la façon de parler: parce qu'il ne désire pas seulement être instruit (*non tantum doceri*) de ce qu'est la volonté de Dieu, mais aussi être instruit et formé (*formari*) à son obéissance, afin de la réaliser. En effet le premier mode de l'instruction (*docendi munus*) serait trop peu efficace, parce que quand Dieu montre ce qui est droit, nous ne suivons pas immédiatement son appel, jusqu'à ce qu'il ait tiré à lui nos affects (*affectus nostros traxerit*). C'est pourquoi il est indispensable que Dieu soit notre maître et notre docteur non seulement par la lettre qui est morte, mais aussi par une inspiration divine. Bien plus, il exerce à nostre égard une triple fonction de maître (*tribus magistri officiis*), du fait qu'il nous instruit (*docet*) par sa parole, qu'ensuite il nous illumine l'intelligence par son Esprit (*mentes illuminat*), que troisièmement il grave dans nos coeurs l'instruction afin que nous obéissions avec un véritable et sérieux assentiment (*consensu*).... [David] souhaite l'Esprit de Dieu comme guide non seulement dans la mesure où celui-ci illumine les intelligences, mais où, fléchissant le coeur, il nous conduit

---

[22] Saint Augustin, *De magistro*, 14:46; *De trinitate*, 14:15,21; sur le "maître intérieur chez Calvin, voir aussi son commentaire de Romains 1:16 et 7:5; sur l'interprétation calvinienne de ces passages augustiniens, voir notre livre, *Calvin et la dynamique*, t. 32, col. 403.

pour ainsi dire par la main à l'assentiment (*efficaciter cordem flectens in consensum*).[23]

J'ai longuement commenté dans mon livre ce passage. On y reconnaît une transposition de la doctrine rhétorique de la persuasion avec ses trois "offices" de l'orateur (*docere/conciliare/movere*). Transposition, et non application, parce que le *conciliare* est ici représenté par l'illumination par l'Esprit, dont le rôle est d'établir, ou plutôt de rétablir l'autorité de Dieu et de sa parole auprès du fidèle; d'autre part le couple du *docere/movere* est ici essentiel, au point que tend à s'effacer la triade rhétorique complète. Transposition enfin, et surtout, parce qu'il ne s'agit pas de Dieu comme "orator," mais comme "doctor," ou maître intérieur. L'origine augustinienne de ce schéma oratoire, transposé à l'efficacité de la parole divine, est indiquée par le fait que saint Augustin cite et commente, dans son *De doctrina christiana*, le même verset du même psaume et rappelle à cette occasion la triade rhétorique, bien que dans une autre version classique de celle-ci, typiquement cicéronienne, celle où "charmer," "plaire" (*delectare*) remplace le *conciliare*:

> Celui donc qui, dans son discours, s'efforce de persuader le bien, doit, sans dédaigner aucun de ces trois objectifs: instruire, charmer, et toucher, parler après avoir prié.[24]

Saint Augustin utilise cette référence rhétorique pour dire, à propos du même verset psalmique, que c'est Dieu, et non l'homme, qui est l'agent de l'efficacité persuasive propre à la parole divine. De même Calvin. Dieu est un *doctor interior* suprêmement efficace; pour représenter cette idée, Calvin après Augustin emprunte le modèle rhétorique de la communication persuasive. Dieu est ainsi conçu comme un *doctor eloquens* parce qu'il sait toucher tout en communiquant son message. Mais le réformateur, lui, insiste, ce que ne fait pas Augustin, sur *l'opposition* entre la lettre de la parole de Dieu, et son efficacité intérieure sous l'effet de l'Esprit. Cette opposition est illustrée dans de nombreux autres textes calviniens, sûrement connus de vous, dont le troisième que je mentionnerai, brièvement, pour finir d'illustrer le sujet.

6. *Commentaire de 2 Corinthiens, 3:6*

Le troisième texte topique de Calvin sur la question se trouve dans son Commentaire de 2 Cor. 3:6.[25] Calvin y développe à partir de saint Paul le thème de l'opposition de la lettre et de l'esprit. Il identifie en partie cette opposition avec

---

[23] CO, 32, col. 403.
[24] Augustin, *De doctrina christiana*, 4.16.33–4.17.34.
[25] CO, 50:39–40.

celle de l'Ancien Testament et de l'Evangile, tout en y mettant certaines nuances. La lettre est la "prédication externe," qui n'est "perçue que par les oreilles" et qui n'atteint pas le coeur" (*quae cor non attingit*), l'esprit la "doctrine vive, qui opère efficacement dans les âmes par la grâce de l'Esprit: elle n'est pas seulement prononcée par la bouche, mais pénètre jusque dans les âmes avec un sentiment vif" (cf. Jérémie 31). L'origine, ou le modèle rhétorique de cette opposition, est indiquée par l'opposition sous-jacente *docere/movere*, mais aussi par la mention suivante: la lettre est identifée avec la "loquacité des Thrasons qui déclament sans l'énergie de l'esprit." On reconnaît là un topos rhétorique bien connu, celui des mauvais orateurs, qui parlent de manière "froide" (*frigide*), incapables de produire et l'impression favorable et l'émotion susceptibles de conduire à une véritable persuasion. Le terme énergie (*energia*), qui traduit le grec *vis*, est revêtu ici de sa double signification: théologique (cf. saint Paul: *dunamis*) et rhétorique.[26]

Dans ce dernier sens, la référence à la déclamation, exercice purement scolaire sans enjeu réel, exercice qui risque d'être confondu avec la véritable éloquence, sert à traduire dans un langage humaniste l'opposition paulinienne entre l'éloquence simplement humaine et la force de la prédication évangélique. Mais, de manière significative, c'est à la rhétorique elle-même que Calvin emprunte ses références pour interpréter cette idée paulinienne: la prédication verbale et extérieure est à la vraie prédication évangélique ce que la déclamation est à la vraie éloquence humaine, un discours sans force, où le *movere* n'intervient pas, ou, çe qui revient au même, un discours où il intervient de manière inadaptée ou inefficace. Enfin ce passage est intéressant parce que Calvin y critique, comme le font les autres réformateurs, la conception de l'opposition de la lettre et de l'esprit telle que l'avait fixée la tradition patristique et médiévale. La lettre opposé à l'esprit, explique ici l'exégète, ce n'est pas le sens littéral-historique de l'Ecriture opposé à son sens spirituel. La tradition distinguait en effet, on le sait, des plans de signification différents de la parole divine. Comme le redisait après d'autres Nicolas de Lyre:

> *Littera gesta docet, quid credas allegoria*
> [*oralis quid agas, quo tendas anagogia*][27]

et ces sens étaient offerts à une exploration exégétique. Calvin lui, comme les autres réformateurs, distingue dans une même parole offerte à la foi un seul sens,

---

[26]En rhétorique, l'*energèia* est volontiers confondue avec l'*enargèia*, figure par laquelle l'expression du discours revêt une force qui rend présentes les choses.

[27]Cité par Nicolas de Lyre, *Postille sur Galates*, 4:3, ce distique se trouve aussi dans une page de son célèbre Prologue à la Glose ordinaire; voir Henri de Lubac, *Exégèse médiévale, Les Quatre sens de l'Ecriture*, Paris, 1959), t. 1.

qui se donne sous une forme extérieure, humainement perceptible, et se réalise dans le coeur du croyant sous l'effet de l'Esprit. L'opposition anthropologique de l'*intellectus* et de la *voluntas* (gouvernée, elle, par les *affectus*), et celle, rhétorique, du *docere* et du *movere*, convergent ici pour indiquer à la prédication évangélique son objectif ultime: produire la *fides* comme *persuasio*. Calvin aurait donc pu réécrire ce distique traditionnel, sous la forme suivante que je soumets à votre critique:

Littera quid credas docet, persuadet spiritus

ou encore,

Littera docet, movet spiritus.

7. *Deux points importants de la pensée religieuse de Calvin*

En guise de conclusion, je voudrais ici insister sur deux points. Nous avons rencontré, je crois, les références principales qui permettent en général de comprendre sur des points importants la pensée religieuse de Calvin. D'abord, avec Valla et Budé, l'humanisme philologique et rhétorique; il identifie la foi chrétienne avec la persuasion oratoire, à la lumière du couple *docere/movere*. Ensuite, la médiation théologique de M. Bucer (secondairement de Mélanchthon), qui développe ce thème et le met au service de la doctrine réformatrice. La résistance d'Erasme sur ce point me semble significative de sa prudence philologique, mais aussi idéologique. Enfin, la référence augustinienne, la plus importante peut-être, parce qu'elle offre à Calvin un cadre où les notions rhétoriques sont assumées dans une réflexion plus large sur le rôle de l'esprit du Christ comme *doctor interior*, et de Dieu comme *doctor eloquens*, et une réflexion plus précise dans ses références rhétoriques. C'est ainsi que Calvin utilise de manière parfois plus explicite que Bucer un schéma complet, *docere/conciliare/movere*, pour rendre compte du processus de communication et d'appropriation par l'homme de la parole divine, processus dans lequel la vérité se révèle subjectivement grâce au "maître intérieur," à la fois lumière éclairant l'intelligence et grâce transformatrice des affects.

Deuxièmement, il reste à évaluer la portée de cette topique. Il y a des aspects doctrinaux, herméneutiques et exégétiques, sur lesquels je ne peux pas m'étendre ici. Mais il n'est par exemple pas indifférent pour l'exégèse d'interpréter l'Ecriture en vertu des valeurs attachées à la voix comme parole vive et plénière, véritablement persuasive. Au-delà de ces aspects, ce qui me semble en jeu, c'est le statut, dans la culture chrétienne du XVIᵉ siècle, de la parole de Dieu, à la fois Bible, livre écrit et imprimé, et message proposé à une prédication orale salvatrice. En décrivant le processus de la foi née de la prédication comme un processus de persuasion plénière où le *docere* doit être impérativement relayé par le *movere*, et en recourant pour cela à des notions ou à des schémas servant à décrire la véritable éloquence, celle qui persuade vraiment, Calvin ne fait pas que manifester sa culture humaniste. Il invite, après Budé et Bucer, à retrouver dans la *Verbum Dei* une vérité qui est aussi une puissance. Ce motif biblique, et singulièrement paulinien, est cependant exprimé dans un langage qui fait constamment allusion à la culture rhétorico-humaniste, celle qui exalte la puissance humanisante de la parole cultivée, parole plénière parce qu'elle s'adresse à la totalité de l'homme comme intelligence, comme être social, comme être sensible, affectif et d'imagination. A cet égard, les références rhétoriques que j'ai signalées dans le cas de Calvin (cf. à propos de Luther et Mélanchthon les travaux de Dockhorn), prennent un sens tout particulier dans le cadre de la réforme protestante. Au moment où celle-ci écarte le magistère de la foi exercé par l'Eglise, pour ne retenir que l'autorité de l'Ecriture, il importait aussi de rappeler que la voix de Dieu n'est pas séquestrée par l'écrit. Cette voix est à la fois objet d'un enseignement, et présence. Entre une foi fondée en lecture, et offerte à une pure intériorisation méditative, voire mystique, et la conception traditionnelle du rite religieux comme geste sacral objectif, le chemin était étroit. La foi définie comme persuasion restaure la prédication chrétienne, parole prononcée comme instrument du salut, elle invite aussi implicitement les prédicateurs chrétiens à assumer dans toutes ses dimensions les ressources du langage humain. Mais d'autre part, l'insistance sur un *movere* purement intérieur, distinct du simple *docere*, et qui ne dépend pas de l'homme, mais que le prédicateur a la mission de désigner comme objectif de son message, oriente la réflexion dans un double sens. Cette insistance met en garde la prédication chrétienne contre la tentation de chercher dans ses propres ressources (qui seraient alors celles d'une sophistique sacrée), des moyens de conversion des auditeurs, moyens qui n'appartiennent qu'à Dieu. Elle invite aussi les auditeurs à un processus d'appropriation subjective et de spiritualisation pourvu d'une formidable valeur émotive. En recourant comme il l'a fait à des références rhétoriques pour appréhender la foi comme *fides*, Calvin, parmi d'autres, a ainsi indiqué que la foi doit être transmise et partagée collectivement selon les normes les plus élevées de la tradition occidentale en matière d'élaboration de la parole humaine, et qu'elle doit être reçue et vécue individuellement dans une expérience qui excède les moyens de cette parole.

COMMENTAIRES
DE M. IEAN CALUIN,
SUR LES CINQ LIURES DE MOYSE.
GENESE EST MIS À PART,
LES AUTRES QUATRE LIURES SONT DISPOSEZ
EN FORME D'HARMONIE :

AVEC CINQ INDICES, DONT LES DEVX CONTENANS LES PAS
SAGES ALLEGUEZ ET EXPOSEZ PAR L'AUTHEUR SONT
ADIOUSTEZ DE NOUUEAU EN CESTE TRADUCTION.

A GENEVE.

Imprime par Francois Eſtiene.

M. D. LXIIII.

Calvin as an Interpreter of Genesis

David C. Steinmetz

I. The Task: Explanation of Genesis 32:24–32

Between 1536 and 1545 Martin Luther lectured on the book of Genesis, finishing his last lecture on November 17, 1545. His lectures were collected from notes by some of his students and published in four volumes. The first volume appeared in 1544, while Luther was still lecturing on Genesis; the last three appeared after Luther's death in 1546. The final volume was published in 1552 and was devoted to the story of Joseph, the last of the patriarchs.[1]

Two years later, in 1554, Calvin published his own commentary on the book of Genesis and dedicated it in a foreword letter, dated 31 July, to the three sons of Johann Friedrich, the elector of Saxony, who had died in March.[2] Calvin had intended the dedication to be an ecumenical gesture toward the Lutherans and was therefore chagrined when the princes rejected the dedication on the recommendation of their theological advisors. The letter to Calvin from the Saxon chancellor, Francis Burckhardt, indicates that the Lutheran theologians were convinced that Calvin taught an entirely unsatisfactory doctrine of the eucharist, a charge that Calvin tried to answer in his long controversy with Joachim Westphal and Tilemann Hesshusen (1554–1561).[3] Furthermore, they complained that Calvin had made insulting remarks about Luther in his commentary on Genesis, an accusation that Calvin flatly denied. Calvin admitted he was critical of some of Luther's exegesis but not in a spirit that denigrated Luther's contribution. Perhaps the Lutherans took offense at Calvin's dismissal of Luther's exegesis of Genesis 11:27 as "frivolous" or of 13:14 as "lacking solidity."

In his reply to Chancellor Burckhardt, Calvin regretted the rejection of his dedication by the Lutherans, though he noted wryly there was very little he could do about the unwanted dedication since the books in which it appeared had already been printed and placed in circulation.[4] While he confessed that he accepted as serenely as he could the decision of the princes, he repudiated the grounds on which they had made it. It seemed to Calvin that the Lutheran theolo-

---

[1]The four volumes correspond to the Weimar edition according to the following pattern: vol. 1 (1544) = WA 42.1–428; vol. 2 (1550) = WA 42.429–43.364; vol. 3 (1552) = WA 43.365–44.231; and vol. 4 (1554) = WA 44.232–825.
[2]Wulfert de Greef, *The Writings of John Calvin: An Introductory Guide*, trans. by Lyle D. Bierma (Grand Rapids: Baker Book House, 1994), 104–5. Cf. CO 15:196–201.
[3]CO 15:260–61.   [4]CO 15:453–55.

gians in Saxony brooked no deviation from Luther's exegesis, thereby demonstrating what Calvin could only regard as a supine veneration for Luther's words. If Luther were beyond criticism, there would be no need for any future commentaries on Genesis. "This was the point to be examined," wrote Calvin, "whether I had eagerly sought after different meanings, whether I had wantonly attacked, or spitefully carped at, or insultingly inveighed against him. In truth, most accomplished sir, if your leisure permitted you to read over the whole book, you would find in it nothing of the kind."[5]

In a letter to Melanchthon written in early March 1555, Calvin complained bitterly that Melanchthon was not doing enough to restrain the Lutheran theologians who were looking for a suitable pretext to crush him (and, by extension, Calvin as well).[6] It would not be easy "to bridle such wild beasts," he admitted, but we must "accomplish what God requires of us, even when we are in the greatest despair respecting the results." In a letter to a colleague at Erfurt, Calvin contrasted the Gnesio-Lutherans in Saxony with Luther. Although "they do not possess a single one of Luther's virtues, by their lusty bawling they give themselves out for his genuine disciples." Furthermore "they cannot assent to anything that comes from this quarter" (and Calvin may have had the rejection of his commentary on Genesis in mind), "because we do not chime in with all the opinions of the Saxons." They are violent, obstinate, incapacious, frenzied, implacable, contumacious, ignorant, barbarous, and arrogant. They go out of their way to "raise disturbances without a motive." While they ape Luther, they do not imitate his virtues. In short, cried Calvin, "would that Luther were alive today!"[7]

In this essay I want to accept Calvin's challenge to Chancellor Burckhardt to examine his exegesis of Genesis in the light of Luther's interpretation of the same text. I am not interested in demonstrating that Calvin was critical of Luther (he freely admitted to the Saxon theologians that he was) or in measuring the degree of Luther's influence on Calvin's interpretation of Genesis (though that influence is measurable and can to a certain degree be tracked). What I have in mind is a somewhat more modest goal; namely, to compare their exegesis of Genesis in order to identify more accurately their similarities and differences as Biblical commentators. The point of this exercise is not merely to clarify the nature of their relationship (though that is, in itself, a worthy goal) but also to set in sharper relief than would otherwise be possible the image of Calvin as an interpreter of Genesis.

In order to provide a larger context for this reassessment of Luther and Calvin, I want to sketch in briefly a picture of the interpretation of Genesis on the eve of the Reformation. Although this could be done in a variety of ways, I have

---

[5]*CO* 15:454.   [6]*CO* 15:488–89.   [7]*CO* 15:501–2.

chosen to do it by examining the Genesis commentary of the great fifteenth-century Biblical commentator, Denis the Carthusian (1402/3–1471). Denis's commentary on the literal and spiritual senses of the Pentateuch was available to Calvin's contemporaries in printed editions such as the attractive folio volume published by Peter Quentel in Cologne in 1534, the same year in which Calvin wrote his first theological treatise, *Psychopannychia*.[8]

Obviously it is not possible within the limits of one essay (or even a dozen) to examine the interpretations of the whole book of Genesis by Denis, Luther, and Calvin. What I propose to do is examine in detail the exegesis of what Luther called one "of the most obscure passages of the whole Old Testament," namely the story of the wrestling match beside the brook Jabbok between Jacob, who was returning to the Promised Land to meet his alienated brother, Esau, and a mysterious man who appeared to attack Jacob by night without provocation and who dislocated Jacob's hip shortly before dawn.[9] The story is found in Gen. 32:24–32.

> Jacob was left alone; and a man wrestled with him until daybreak. When the man saw that he did not prevail against Jacob, he struck him on the hip, and Jacob's hip was put out of joint as he wrestled with him. Then he said, "Let me go, for the day is breaking." But Jacob said, "I will not let you go, unless you bless me." So he said to him, "What is your name?" And he said, "Jacob." Then the man said, "You shall no longer be called Jacob, but Israel, for you have striven with God and with humans, and have prevailed." Then Jacob asked him, "Please tell me your name." But he said, "Why is it that you ask my name?" And there he blessed him. So Jacob called the place Peniel, saying, "For I have seen God face to face, and yet my life is preserved." The sun rose upon him as he passed Penuel, limping because of his hip. Therefore to this day the Israelites do not eat the thigh muscle, that is on the hip socket, because he struck Jacob on the hip socket at the thigh muscle. (NRSV)

---

[8]Denis the Carthusian, *Enarrationes piae ac eruditae in quinque Mosaicae legis libros* (Cologne: Peter Quentel, 1534). Citations are taken from the critical edition, *Doctoris Ecstatici D. Dionysii Cartusiani Opera Omnia*, vol. 1 (Monstrolii, 1896). Although there is no evidence that Calvin consulted Denis in his interpretation of Genesis 32, Denis was one of the few medieval authors collected by the library of the Academy in Geneva. See in this connection Alexandre Ganoczy, *La bibliothèque de l'Académie de Calvin* (Geneva: Droz, 1969).

[9]*WA* 44.93.

II. Denis the Carthusian

1. *The Wrestling Match: Physical or Spiritual?*

The first question that troubled Denis was whether the wrestling match was physical or spiritual.[10] Did Jacob actually wrestle with a mysterious stranger beside the Jabbok or did he receive a private vision, unwitnessed by anyone else and in the nature of the case unverifiable? Supporters of the hypothesis that Jacob received a vision have to explain how Jacob could have been lamed by it. Supporters of the hypothesis that the match was wholly physical have to account for the fact that wrestling seems at times to be used metaphorically as a synonym for prayer. Although Denis did not take a strong position on the issue, physical or spiritual, he appears to agree with Hugh of St. Cher that Jacob's wrestling match was both, though in what proportion it was impossible for him to say.[11]

2. *The Mysterious Stranger*

On the other hand, Denis was in no doubt whatever who the mysterious stranger was.[12] Jacob's opponent was a good angel appearing in the form of a man. Denis was eager to refute what he reported as a Jewish legend, namely that the angel with whom Jacob wrestled was Esau's guardian angel.[13] According to this reading of the text, Esau's guardian angel had met Jacob at the Jabbok to impede his progress into Palestine and to wrest from him, if possible, the primogeniture and blessing Esau had lost to Jacob. When the angel could not overcome Jacob, he wept and pled, both for himself and for Esau. The difficulty with this story, of course, was that an angel would have known the mind of God in this matter and not have gone against it. God had judged Esau unworthy to receive the primogeniture and the blessing and had given them to Jacob. What had transpired had taken place by the will and direction of God. No angel would have attempted to undermine the plan of God. Besides, Denis added, angels do not cry; it is incompatible with their perfection.[14]

An alternative theory identified the stranger as Jacob's guardian angel rather than Esau's.[15] According to this account the angel had accompanied Jacob from Mesopotamia to Palestine and wanted to leave him at the Jabbok. But because Jacob feared his brother too much and did not trust God enough, he refused to let the angel go and kept him in place through prayer. The so-called wrestling match

---

[10] Denis, *Enarrationes*, 357.

[11] Hugh of St. Cher, "Liber Geneseos," *Opus Admirabile, Tomus Unus* (Venice: Nicolaus Pezzana, 1731), 45v.

[12] Denis, *Enarrationes*, 356.

[13] Denis, *Enarrationes*, 359.

[14] Denis, *Enarrationes*, 359.

[15] Denis, *Enarrationes*, 356–57.

occurred because Jacob's mind had withdrawn from God through diffidence. When the angel lamed Jacob, he did so as a punishment for his lack of faith.

3. The Match

Other interpreters found no grounds in the story for assuming that Jacob was being punished by God for his faults. The story could be read in a far more hopeful vein. God wanted to give Jacob greater spiritual gifts and greater gifts presuppose a greater struggle.[16] At any event, the point of the struggle was comfort. Through it "the angel saved [Jacob] from unadulterated human fear and comforted him in the Lord." Denis was even willing to claim that the angel "confirmed him in the hope of eternal salvation."[17] The question not unnaturally arose in the minds of the readers of the Jacob story why the angel was unable to defeat Jacob. As a heavenly being the angel was surely more powerful than any mortal, even a patriarch who bore a divine blessing. Denis answered the question by appealing to the theological distinction between *potentia absoluta* or absolute power and *potentia ordinata* or ordained power.[18] Considered absolutely, the angel could have crushed Jacob at any time. But it would have been unfitting for the angel to unleash overwhelming force against Jacob. It was never a question of "cannot" but only of "will not." What was at stake in the angel's defeat was not sheer energy (*potentia absoluta*) but divine purpose (*potentia ordinata*). In the end Jacob kept the angel in place by humility, devotion, love, and prayer, and not by his skill as a wrestler.[19]

Equally puzzling is why the angel asked to be released at daybreak.[20] Angels are creatures of light and ought not to be alarmed at the rising of the sun. Devils may scatter at dawn but surely not angels. Denis offered several traditional exegetical suggestions to explain the baffling urgency of the angel's request.

Perhaps the angel was late for choir, since it was time to appear in the heavenly court and sing the praises of God.[21] Perhaps the angel thought it was time for Jacob to be on his way to the meeting with Esau he dreaded so much.[22] Or perhaps the angel thought no one should see him except Jacob, although, as Denis noted, this explanation was not very convincing.[23] Angels can only be seen by mortals when they want to be. An army of angels could be camped on the banks of the Jabbok without drawing attention to itself.

[16] Denis, *Enarrationes*, 357.
[18] Denis, *Enarrationes*, 357.
[20] Denis, *Enarrationes*, 357.
[22] Denis, *Enarrationes*, 357.

[17] Denis, *Enarrationes*, 358–59.
[19] Denis, *Enarrationes*, 358.
[21] Denis, *Enarrationes*, 357.
[23] Denis, *Enarrationes*, 357.

4. The Blessing

The angel then asked Jacob his name. Of course, the angel knew Jacob's name already; it would be unthinkable that he did not. The wrestling match was no random encounter. The angel asked Jacob his name (much as a priest asks the name of a child at baptism) so he could do more fittingly what he intended.[24] What he intended was to change Jacob's name to Israel. Denis engaged in some discussion of the philological history of the two Hebrew names and, like Jerome, accepted the interpretation of the names offered by Moses. Jacob was no longer the supplanter but, like the angel, a prince with God. The point of the change of name was to signify that if Jacob had not been conquered by the angel, he would not be conquered by Esau.[25]

Jacob in his turn asked the name of the angel, but the angel refused to tell him. Denis could find no fault in Jacob for asking, since Jacob only wanted to increase his knowledge of divine things and invoke and honor the angel by his own name.[26] Why the angel denied Jacob's request is less clear. Perhaps the knowledge Jacob sought from the angel was too high for a mortal to grasp without the gravest difficulty. Or perhaps the question was unanswerable because most angels have no fixed names but derive their names from the tasks they are assigned (Michael and Gabriel are obvious exceptions).[27] Instead of disclosing his name, the angel blessed Jacob. The form of the blessing was not recorded in the Biblical text. Because of this silence concerning the words of the blessing some interpreters have concluded that the blessing was in fact the change of name.[28]

5. God Seen Face to Face

After his encounter with the angel Jacob made the astonishing claim that he had seen God face to face (*clare et facialiter*) and lived.[29] Denis was inclined to discount this claim. Jacob was no Moses. Unlike Moses, Jacob did not see God in the incomprehensible and invisible nature of his deity. Jacob's experience was not a theophany in that sense of the term. What Jacob saw clearly with his exterior eyes was an angel in human form who appeared and spoke to him in the person of God.[30] In that sense and that sense only was it appropriate for Jacob to claim that he had seen God and lived.

However, if one sets aside the literal sense of the text, one could agree with Augustine and Isidore that the angel with whom Jacob wrestled was Christ.[31] After all, Denis believed that Scripture contained both a spiritual and a literal

---

[24]Denis, *Enarrationes*, 358.
[26]Denis, *Enarrationes*, 358.
[28]Denis, *Enarrationes*, 358.
[30]Denis, *Enarrationes*, 358.

[25]Denis, *Enarrationes*, 358.
[27]Denis, *Enarrationes*, 358.
[29]Denis, *Enarrationes*, 358.
[31]Denis, *Enarrationes*, 360.

sense, even though he devoted his primary attention to the literal. On the spiritual level Denis compared Jacob to contemplatives who wrestle with God in prayer and who will not let God go until God blesses them.[32] Such a wrestling match is never with a mere angel, but always with Christ.

III. MARTIN LUTHER

1. *Jacob's Antagonist*
What Denis accepted as the spiritual sense of the text, Luther advocated as its literal-historical meaning. Jacob's antagonist was not an angel (certainly not Esau's guardian angel!), not a devil, and not flesh and blood. Jacob's antagonist was God (or as Luther would also say, Christ) appearing in hostile form.[33] Although God was not in reality hostile to Jacob—quite the contrary, he was and remained a loving Father—he nevertheless showed a dark and threatening face to Jacob in order to test his faith.[34]

2. *The Boldness of Faith*
To provide a New Testament frame of reference for Jacob's ordeal, Luther appealed to the story of the encounter between Jesus and the Syrophoenician woman. According to Matthew's account (15:21–28) an unnamed woman asked Jesus to heal her daughter. Jesus refused on the ground that she was not an Israelite and even compared her to a dog. "It is not fair," said Jesus, "to take the children's bread and throw it to the dogs." "Yes, Lord," replied the woman, "yet even the dogs eat the crumbs that fall from their master's table." Jesus was so impressed with her answer and her faith that he granted her request and healed her daughter.

In his *Fastenpostille* published in 1525 Luther included a sermon on this pericope.[35] The Syrophoenician woman provided for Luther an outstanding example of the boldness faith must exercise in the presence of a seemingly hostile God. She accepted without a murmur the judgment of Jesus that compared her to a dog. Rather than defend herself from such a comparison, she demanded from Jesus a dog's rightful share. "Where could Jesus turn?" Luther asked triumphantly. He was trapped by his own words. What the woman discovered by boldly confronting Christ was that his "no" was not "no" at all, but what Luther called "a deeply hidden yes." "Therefore," concluded Luther, "sweep your heart clean of such feelings and trust firmly in God's Word and grasp from above or from underneath the 'No' the deeply hidden 'Yes' and hold on to it as this woman did and keep a firm belief in God's justice. Then you have won and caught him with his own words."[36]

[32]Denis, *Enarrationes*, 360.
[33]*WA* 44.99; cf. 96–97 on Esau's guardian angel.
[34]*WA* 44.105.   [35]*WA* 17(2).200–4.   [36]*WA* 17(2).203.

In his lectures on Genesis Luther returned to this text and its themes.[37] Faith should not draw back when it feels the wrath of God or endures his inexplicable hostility. Like the Syrophoenician woman, Jacob did not falter or turn aside when faced with God's opposition in his lonely vigil beside the Jabbok. But against God's relentless opposition Jacob pressed forward and conquered God's wrath by God's promise. Although God appeared unfriendly, he was in reality a loving Father. Undeterred by the unexpected opposition of God, Jacob grasped the deeply hidden "yes" underneath God's "no." "I will not let you go," he cried, "unless you bless me!"

3. The Wrestling Match

Luther's reconstruction of the wrestling match turned what Genesis described as a quiet struggle by night into a noisy and inelegant brawl.[38] Only three brief conversations are recorded in Genesis, all of which occurred at the end of the match. Luther found such silence unnatural. In his view the opponents "struggled" in the darkness "with arms and words alike as two wrestlers usually do." The stranger in a terrifying voice bombarded Jacob with a string of disquieting thoughts as they wrestled: "You must die, Jacob, for you are not the man to whom God gave the promise. God does not want to keep even the promise that has been given. You must perish, Jacob; you are in for it!" To which Jacob responded "No, that is not God's will, I shall not perish! I may be pushed, assailed, and thrown down, yet I shall not die."[39] In the deep darkness of that night, declared Luther, "'yes' and 'no' there assailed each other very sharply and violently."[40]

When the traditional questions were asked about Jacob's conflict with God, Luther gave a somewhat narrower range of answers than Denis had given: (1) Why was the stranger unable to defeat Jacob? Of course, the stranger could have defeated Jacob at any time, but did not want to use more strength against Jacob than a man could use.[41] In addition, God helped Jacob in his struggle against the stranger through the power of the Holy Spirit.[42] (2) Why did the stranger demand to be released at daybreak? The stranger wanted Jacob to let him go because he needed to return to his own proper tasks.[43] (3) What was the name of the man who wrestled with Jacob? Luther believed that Jacob was completely in the dark about the stranger's identity until the very end of the conflict, when the stranger told him that he had triumphed over God and humans.[44] Only at that point did Jacob know he had wrestled with God in human form. That is why Jacob claimed

---

[37] WA 44.103–4.   [38] WA 44.100–101.   [39] WA 44.100–101.
[40] WA 44.100.   [41] WA 44.101–2.   [42] WA 44.100–1.
[43] WA 44.103–4.   [44] WA 44.106–8.

to have seen God face to face; he saw him both hidden and disclosed in Christ. (4) What was the content of the blessing Christ gave to Jacob? Moses did not reveal the text of the blessing but Luther suggested it must have been the same as the blessing given to Abraham and Isaac.[45]

4. The Renaming of Jacob

The renaming of Jacob offered Luther an opportunity to underscore what he regarded as the main point of the story. Jacob's name was changed from Jacob to Israel, i.e., from supplanter of Esau to conqueror of God.[46] Jacob had conquered God with God's own promises; he had grasped God's "deeply hidden yes." The notion that Jacob had conquered God as the Syrophoenician woman had trapped Jesus with his own words was and remains absurd to philosophy. Nevertheless, theology is willing to claim that God is conquered by faith, though it does not claim that God is thereby made submissive to human will.[47] God can be conquered; God cannot be tamed.

Against God's opposition but by God's will, Jacob triumphed over God by holding fast to the promises God seemed to have abandoned. He bravely and stubbornly opposed God's apparent hostility and refused to accept God's "no." For Luther bold opposition is what faith is all about; it is tested and triumphs in the dialectic of God's "yes" and "no." "Let us compose a proverb from this history," Luther concluded, "when you think our Lord God has rejected a person, you should think that our Lord God has him in his arms and is pressing him to his heart."[48]

5. Historical and Allegorical Interpretation

Throughout his exposition Luther maintained a clear distinction between historical and allegorical interpretations of the Jacob narrative. Although he complained about the misuse of allegory by some theologians, he did not reject a limited use of allegorical approaches to the Bible. At the end of his exposition of the literal meaning of Jacob's ordeal he appended a fairly detailed allegorical interpretation. The principle that Luther invoked for his use of allegory was not new with him but a theological commonplace since the time of Augustine; namely, that only the literal sense can be used as a foundation for doctrine. Allegory has a lesser role and can be used for the illustration of meanings firmly grounded in the literal sense.[49]

---

[45] WA 44.107–8.   [46] WA 44.105.   [47] WA 44.105.
[48] WA 44.111.   [49] WA 44.93, 108–9, 114–15.

Luther claimed that on the allegorical level Jacob could be viewed as the whole body of the faithful in every age. From this perspective Jacob provided the Church with a picture of all the saints who are tempted and tested by God.[50] In the history of Jacob, Christians can see their own history as well. Luther ended his allegorical exposition with an extended discussion of the meaning of eating or not eating the sinews of the thigh, over which we shall draw a merciful curtain.[51]

IV. JEAN CALVIN

1. Jacob as an Exemplary Model

Whereas Denis was interested in overcoming Jacob's all too human fear of Esau and Luther in resolving Jacob's crisis of faith, Calvin was interested in Jacob as an exemplary model. What Luther regarded as the allegorical sense of the text (namely, Jacob as an example of a tested believer) was collapsed by Calvin into the literal sense. Or to state that more precisely, the text as Calvin read it had two purposes: (1) to warn Jacob of the conflicts that still awaited him and to assure him that he would triumph over them, and (2) to represent all the servants of God as they are tested by God in this world and to remind them that what was once exhibited in visible form in Jacob is daily fulfilled in individual members of the Church.[52] As in Jacob, so also in us.

2. The Vision

Unlike Denis and Luther, who thought the conflict was both physical and spiritual, Calvin insisted that Jacob's wrestling match was a vision.[53] Calvin did not deny that Jacob's struggle was a real event with real physical consequences and commentators like Denis were, of course, correct to point out that Jacob's lameness was no figment of his imagination. But the wrestling match was not an external event that anyone else could have seen; it was a divine self-disclosure to Jacob alone. By the same token, Jacob's vision was not private; it was given to Jacob in order to benefit the Church.[54] That is why Jacob built a monument and named it Peniel; namely, to celebrate his vision and remind the Church of its continuing relevance for the life of the whole people of God in every age.

3. Jacob's Adversary: God's Testing His Faith

Calvin agreed with Luther that Jacob's enemy was not an angel, not a devil, and not flesh and blood. Jacob's adversary was God appearing in the form of a man.[55] Like Luther, Calvin conceded that this notion appeared absurd, but

---

[50] WA 44.114–15.   [51] WA 44.115–16.   [52] CO 23.442.
[53] CO 23.442.   [54] CO 23.446.   [55] CO 23.442.

assured his readers that reason and experience taught it to be true.[56] Jacob's enemy was God.

However, Calvin drew back from Luther's position, when he refused to identity the stranger who attacked Jacob with Christ. Instead he drew an analogy between the stranger and the Holy Spirit. Just as the Holy Spirit is sometimes called a dove, so Jacob's antagonist was called a man, even though the dove is really the Holy Spirit and the man was really God appearing in human form.[57] Obviously, such an analogy (the dove is to the Holy Spirit as the man is to God) precludes any notion of hypostatic union. For what seem to be reasons grounded in his understanding of the unfolding history of salvation, Calvin was reluctant to call Jacob's vision a revelation of Christ, although he did concede in the *Institutes* that Jacob's vision was a disclosure of the Logos in human form.[58]

Yet this disagreement between Luther and Calvin ought not to obscure the degree of agreement between them. God in human form (if not yet Christ) was Jacob's enemy. Even though God's intentions toward Jacob were loving and kind, he showed Jacob a harsh and unfriendly face in order to test his faith. The harshness, however, is more apparent than real. Indeed, God opposed Jacob with much less force than he used to assist him in his resistance.[59] Jacob did not flee from the hostile face of God but trusted in God's providential care and so triumphed over God's opposition. By so doing Jacob left an example, not only for Christians who are tested by God's open hostility in the way Jacob was but also for Christians subjected to any kind of conflict in which God exercises the faithful.[60]

Calvin raised the interesting question why Jacob had not been tested earlier. His answer was that raw recruits are often spared from conflicts in which veterans engage. Once Jacob had been seasoned by suffering, he was led out to real war.[61] The timing was not accidental but guided by God's providential hand.

Calvin also offered a new reason (or at least a reason not mentioned by Denis or Luther) for God's withdrawal from the struggle. God wanted to withdraw so that Jacob could rejoice in the grace afforded him.[62] In this connection Calvin was particularly impressed by what he called Jacob's "invincible perseverance."[63] Jacob provided for Calvin a model of how one ought to contend with God; namely, by never growing weary until God leaves the conflict of his own accord.

---

[56] *CO* 23.442. [57] *CO* 23.443. [58] *CO* 23.445–46. Cf. *Institutes* 1.13.10.
[59] *CO* 23.442–43. [60] *CO* 23.443. [61] *CO* 23.443.
[62] *CO* 23.444. [63] *CO* 23.444.

4. The Indelible Mark

Calvin did not explain how Jacob could be wounded by a vision but he did explain why. God wanted to leave an indelible mark on Jacob so that he would not dismiss his vision as an idle dream.[64] Jacob rose from his vision with a permanent, but apparently painless, limp.[65] Furthermore, Jacob's wound continues to remind Christians that they emerge conquerors from their temptations only by being wounded in the conflict. The limp serves as permanent sign that Jacob triumphed in God's strength and not in his own; and as in Jacob, so also in us.

5. The Blessing

Calvin agreed with Luther that Jacob did not know who his assailant was until daybreak. The key indicator that Jacob knew what had transpired was when he asked the stranger to bless him. Since in Calvin's view blessing is the act of a superior to an inferior, Jacob's request signaled his realization that the mysterious man was in fact God.[66] God then changed Jacob's name to Israel to indicate that his victory over God implied that he ought not to fear any lesser enemy.

Like Denis, Calvin tended to discount Jacob's claim to have seen God face to face. His vision of God appearing in human form was a lesser revelation than the self-disclosure of God to Moses or the apostles.[67] Jacob was not yet living in the time of the fuller self-revelation of God. Far better than Jacob's imperfect vision of God is the sight of Christ, the living image of God, in the mirror of the gospel.[68]

6. Similarities and Differences

When we place the three expositions of Genesis 32 by Denis, Luther, and Calvin side by side, we can see clearly several important similarities and differences. For example, Calvin is the only one of the three interpreters to opt for the story of Jacob's conflict with a mysterious stranger as a vision. Denis and Luther seem to accept it as both an internal and external event, partly vision, partly physical trial. Similarly Calvin is the only one not to refer to Jewish exegesis of the text. Both Denis and Luther mention especially the Jewish suggestion that the stranger was Esau's guardian angel, even though they emphatically reject it as a silly fable. Calvin does not allude to it at all.

7. Literal and/or Spiritual Sense of the Text

More importantly, Calvin is the only one of the three not to use the distinction between the literal (or historical) and the spiritual (or allegorical) senses of the text. Luther praises the historical sense over the allegorical and may even at

---

[64] *CO* 23.444. [65] *CO* 23.447. [66] *CO* 23.444–45.
[67] *CO* 23.445–46. [68] *CO* 23.447.

times create in some of his hearers the false expectation that he will reject the allegorical sense entirely. However, he has nothing of the sort in mind, preferring merely to restrict it. Allegory may properly be employed by theologians and preachers for the decoration and illustration of doctrine.

Because Denis accepts with a tranquil conscience the traditional notion that the Bible contains a spiritual sense as well as a literal, his literal exposition is remarkably free from spiritual applications. He focuses on the narrative and its meaning and postpones a discussion of its spiritual application until he has finished his discussion of its literal sense. His separation of letter and spirit and postponement of a discussion of the spirit gives his literal exposition a curiously modern feel, at least in comparison with Luther and Calvin.

Luther finds spiritual meanings on both levels of the text. On the level of letter Luther uses the Jacob narrative to show how faith conquers God by opposing God with God's own promises. Jacob's opponent is not an angel but Christ, a view that Denis had reserved for the spiritual sense. On the other hand he labels as allegorical the notion that Jacob provides an image of all the saints who are tempted and tested by God.

Calvin rejects, or, perhaps I should say more accurately, makes no reference to or use of, two levels in the Biblical text. He does not believe it is appropriate to identify Jacob's opponent with Christ on either an allegorical or a literal level. Jacob's opponent is not Christ (contra Luther) and not an angel acting in the person of God (contra Denis) but God appearing in human form. Luther is also wrong to appeal to allegory in order to make the point that Jacob is the model of believers who are tested by God. Jacob as model clearly belongs to the literal sense.

While Calvin rejects two levels of the Biblical story, he nevertheless affirms a twofold sense of the letter. The story as letter focuses both on Jacob, who provides an exemplary model of perseverance through severe testing by God, and on all believers who are similarly tested in this life. The exposition moves back and forth between Jacob and the Church, between narrative and application, until it creates a layered effect in Calvin's exegesis. If we label the Jacob narrative "a" and the application to the Church as "b," Calvin's exposition of the story scans as follows: ababababab, etc. What this scanning does not convey is the relative length of the two parts. Generally speaking, the application to the Church is longer than the interpretation of the narrative.

8. The Hostile and Fatherly Face of God

The most important similarity between Luther and Calvin may be the point at which both differ with expositors like Denis. It may also, perhaps, be their most important difference. Calvin agrees with Luther that Jacob's enemy is God, who shows a hostile face to Jacob (and by extension to all believers). Both agree that there is a difference between the appearance to us, which is hostile, and the reality that lies behind it. The underlying reality is that God is a loving father who means such testing to be for our own good. Luther even speaks of a playful God who tests us.

Yet there is a very different development of this common theme by the two authors. For Luther the wrestling match is a boisterous and raucous brawl, in which the opponents shout at each other and strain for an advantage. Luther even suggests what the two wrestlers might have bellowed at each other. Although the outcome is not in doubt *sub specie aeternitatis*, it is not altogether clear to Jacob in the heat of battle that the hostile God will not win and that his "no" will not be his final word. Jacob must counter God's sharp "no" (which is, after all, not the "no" of any creature, but the "no" of God the Creator) with an equally sharp "yes." He must exercise the boldness and cunning of faith in order to trap Christ with his own words. He must grasp the "deeply hidden yes" underneath the terrifying and implacable "no." When Jacob is finally proclaimed a conqueror of God and given a new name, he is lying exhausted on the banks of the Jabbok, weakly hanging on to the stranger who has wounded him.

For Calvin the atmosphere of the conflict is more serenely Augustinian. Gone are the noise and sweat of battle. The conflict is viewed from the perspective of God's providential care and not from the perspective of Jacob's terror. God is against us and for us; he fights against us with his left hand and for us with his right. While God opposes Jacob, he wills him to be conqueror and so opposes him less with his left hand than he supports him with his right. Unlike Luther, Calvin does not add dialogue not found in the Biblical text or portray the conflict as the clash of a sharp and implacable "no" with an equally sharp and implacable "yes." Instead of a harsh dialectic of "yes" and "no," Calvin offers a gentler dialectic of "left" and "right," a left hand that never offers more resistance than the right hand can overcome. What Calvin commends in Jacob is his perseverance and not his boldness. Victory is certain for those who trust in the goodness of God's providence and persevere through their trials.

I do not want to overemphasize these differences or suggest that they are more important than they really are. In spite of differences of style and, to some degree, of substance, Luther and Calvin are allies in their interpretation of the Jacob narrative. They are never, as the Saxon court theologians unfairly alleged, irreconcilable rivals. For them the story is finally about a God who opposes Jacob and a faith that triumphs over God's opposition. It is about God's "yes" and God's "no," God's left hand and God's right. It is about terror and courage, about promises and perseverance, and about the conquest of God.

Calvin and the Fathers in *Bondage and Liberation of the Will*

Anthony N. S. Lane[1]

HOW DID CALVIN USE THE FATHERS in his *Bondage and Liberatin of the Will?*[2] How did he work at his desk? How did he handle the fathers? This work contains more patristic citations than any of Calvin's other works apart from the *Institutio* and contains more such citations than any three similar works.[3] This is not surprising since a major thrust of Calvin's controversy with Pighius was the dispute about the teaching of the fathers, especially Augustine. It is not just the number of citations that reflects this emphasis, but the length of the quotations as well. In book 3, for example, about a third of the text is composed of patristic quotation.

How did this work come to be written? In his 1539 *Institutio* Calvin twice claimed that apart from Augustine, the early fathers are so confused, vacillating, and contradictory on the subject of free choice that almost nothing can be determined with certainty from their writings.[4] This claim so incensed the Dutch Roman Catholic theologian Albertus Pighius that he devoted much of the ten books of his *De libero arbitrio* to refuting it.[5] Calvin made haste to reply. Pighius'

---

[1]I am grateful to David F. Wright for his help both in the preparation of this paper and on many other occasions.

[2]This title is used for John Calvin, *[Defensio sanae et orthodoxae doctrinae de servitute et liberatione humani arbitrii adversus calumnias Alberti Pighii Campensis] The Bondage and Liberation of the Will: A Defence of the Orthodox Doctrine of Human Choice against Pighius*, ed. Anthony N. S. Lane, tr. G. I. Davies (Grand Rapids: Baker Books, 1996). I am also editing this work for the Ioannis Calvini Opera Omnia series, ed. Brian G. Armstrong et al. (Geneva: Droz, 1992–).

For details of the controversy, see Pierre Pidoux, "Albert Pighius de Kampen, Adversaire de Calvin, 1490–1542" (Ph.D. dissertation, Lausanne University, 1932); L. F. Schulze, *Calvin's Reply to Pighius* (Potchefstroom: Pro Rege, 1971); G. Melles, *Albertus Pighius en zijn Strijd met Calvijn over het Liberum Arbitrium* (Kampen: Kok, 1973).

Neither Calvin nor Pighius mentions the exchange between Luther and Erasmus on this issue and there is no internal evidence to suggest that either of them had the earlier debate in mind. Pighius attacks Luther's *Assertio omnium articulorum* but does not mention his *De servo arbitrio*.

[3]For these figures, see the tables in R. J. Mooi, *Het Kerk- en Dogmahistorisch Element in de Werken van Johannes Calvijn* (Wageningen: H Veenman, 1965), 365–97. While his figures may be not be not entirely accurate, they suffice for comparative purposes like this. On Mooi's figures, the 1559 *Institutio* has 866 citations; the *Bondage and Liberation of the Will*, 310; the *Defensio orthodoxae fidei de sacra Trinitate*, 108; the three replies to Westphal, 194; the reply to Heshusius, 99; the commentaries on 1 and 2 Corinthians, 98; the *De aeterna dei praedestinatione*, 98; the *Articuli a facultate sacrae theologiae Parisiensi terminati*, 81. For a different comparison, the 1539 *Institutio* has 301, the 1543 edition has 418 new citations.

[4]*OS* 3:245, 251 (*Inst.* 2:2:4, 9).

[5]Albertius Pighius, *De libero hominis arbitrio et divina gratia* (Köln: Melchior von Neuß, 1542). Pighius returns to Calvin's claim on fols.10b, 28a, 32b, 35b, 36b, and in many other places.

work was published in August 1542. Calvin was concerned that his reply might be ready in time for the 1543 Frankfurt Book Fair (1 to 20 March), which meant that he had, according to his own testimony, barely two months in which to write it.[6] The work was published by February;[7] so which two months did Calvin have in mind? Since he was already engaged in the work on 15 December, it could not have been the two months immediately prior to the book fair. More likely, he was thinking of December and January, the two months in which it would have to be written to be ready for Frankfurt. If we allow for an element of rhetorical exaggeration in the two-month claim, we can safely conclude that the work was written during November, December, and January.

It is possible that during some of this time Calvin was released from preaching, except for one Sunday sermon. Such a dispensation was granted to Calvin by the city council on 11 September 1542.[8] This was not because his normal load was too heavy,[9] but was to free him for the task (together with Claude Roset) of recodifying the Genevan laws and constitution.[10] However, it seems that the draft that Calvin and Roset had been asked to prepare was completed by 2 October, so Calvin presumably resumed weekday preaching from that date.[11] It is unlikely,

---

[6] Calvin stated early in the work that he had to be brief because of the pressure of time, with barely two months before the book fair; CO 6:236. Aimé-Louis Herminjard, _Correspondance des Réformateurs dans les pays de langue française_ (Geneva: H Georg / Paris: M Levy, 1866–1897), 8:341, n. 1, gives the dates of the fair. In a letter of 15 December 1542 Calvin states that he is replying to Pighius and wishes the work to appear at the next book fair; see ibid, 8:221; CO 11:474.

[7] On 31 January Simon Sulzer wrote from Bern thanking Calvin for what is generally understood to be a copy of the work, perhaps unbound; Herminjard, _Correspondance_, 8:256, n.1; CO 11:501, n.1. On 16 February Calvin wrote to Melanchthon announcing its recent publication; Herminjard, _Correspondance_,. 8:286–87; CO 11:515.

[8] _Annales_ for 11 September 1542, taken from the _Registres du Conseil_ (CO 21:302). I am grateful to William G. Naphy for drawing my attention to the fact that Calvin had a sabbatical around this time.

[9] Contra Thomas H. L Parker, _Calvin's Preaching_ (Edinburgh: T & T Clark, 1992), 60.

[10] Williston Walker, _John Calvin_, rev. ed. (New York: Schoken, 1969), 275–76. On the constitution, see Robert M. Kingdon, "Calvin et la Constitution Genevoise" in _Actualité de la Réforme_ 12 (Geneva: Labor et Fides, 1987), 209–19; idem, "Calvinus Legislator: The 1543 'Constitution' of the City-State of Geneva" in Wilhelm H. Neuser, ed., _Calvinus Servus Christi_ (Budapest: Ráday-Kollegium, 1988), 225–32.

[11] Robert M. Kingdon, "Calvin and the Government of Geneva" in W. H. Neuser, ed., _Calvinus Ecclesiae Genevensis Custos_ (Frankfurt: Peter Lang, 1984), 60, gives 2 October as the terminus for Calvin's release from preaching. In a private letter of 12 September 1995, Kingdon explains that the latter date is based upon the submission of the draft by Calvin and Roset, as recorded by Amadae Roget, _Histoire du Peuple de Genève depuis la Réforme jusqu'à l'Escalade_ (Geneva: Jullien, 1870–1883), 2:63, presumably drawing upon the _Registres du Conseil_. Kingdon also states that the Consistory registers show that Calvin attended all of the meetings of the Consistory for this period (7, 14, 21 September). This suggests that Calvin was released only from weekday preaching and not from other duties. He was certainly not released from other duties while responding to Pighius, as can be seen from the complaints noted at n.14, below. On 17 November 1542 the city council granted Calvin "ung bossot de vin vieulx de celluy de lhospital" in recognition of the pains that he was taking on behalf of the city (CO 10.1:125, drawing on the _Registres du Conseil_). This reinforces the conclusion that Calvin's labors over the constitution were completed before he embarked upon his reply to Pighius in November.

therefore, that Calvin worked on his reply to Pighius during the period that his preaching load was lightened. It does seem, however, that he probably had no other writing commitments while responding to Pighius.[12]

I. WORKS USED BY CALVIN

Which patristic works does Calvin use? He names or cites twenty-five of Augustine's works, three of pseudo-Augustine, and thirty-three from nineteen other authors[13]—quite an impressive array of patristic learning, one might think. But it would be rash to assume that Calvin at that stage handled all or even most of these works. First, the response to Pighius was written in a couple of months. Indeed Calvin complains not only about the brevity of the time available, but also about the weight of other responsibilities with which he continued to be burdened, in contrast to the leisure available to his Roman Catholic antagonists like Pighius,[14] so we can expect to find evidence of haste and must expect our author to take shortcuts. Second, Calvin was short of cash and books during his stay at Strassburg.[15] It is likely that he built up his library during his time at Geneva, but by the time he began to answer Pighius he had been back in Geneva for little over a year. It is unlikely, therefore, that he had a large library at his disposal.

In examining Calvin's citations we will adopt a hermeneutic of suspicion, assuming that he did not have a particular work to hand unless there is clear evidence to the contrary. We will consider alternative sources available to Calvin. First, some of the passages that he cites are simply taken from Pighius. If, in responding to a quotation in Pighius, Calvin gives no indication of knowing more of the work than is found in Pighius, we may safely assume either that he did not have the original to hand or that he did not bother to turn to it. Secondly, some passages are simply drawn from the 1539 *Institutio*, which Pighius was attacking. If Calvin betrays no more knowledge of the work than is already found in the 1539 *Institutio*, we may again safely assume either that he did not have the original to hand or that he did not bother to turn to it. Thirdly, some works are cited in a very

---

[12]This is determined by an examination of Calvin's other works from around this time. Rodolphe Peter and Jean-François Gilmont, *Bibliotheca Calviniana*, vol.1 (Geneva: Droz, 1991), 104–43) suggests that those works published in 1542 would have been completed, that the 1543 *Institutio* was probably already with the printer, and that he was unlikely to have begun any of the other works published in 1543.

[13]See the table of works at the end of this paper. Note there the different categories of works included. Works which are possible or even likely, but not certain, sources (such as Bernard's *Sermones in Cantica* in CO 6:334f.) have not been included. To include such works could extend the list indefinitely and make it highly subjective and unreliable.

[14]CO 6:229–232, 236.

[15]See nn. 51–52 below. For precise details of Pighius' extensive library, see Maria Elizabeth Kronenberg, "Albertus Pighius, Proost van S. Jan te Utrecht, zijn Geschriften en zijn Bibliotheek, " *Het Boek* 28 (1944–46), 125–58. Pighius also had money problems; ibid., 119–21.

imprecise manner. One is left with the impression that Calvin has in the past read the work, but does not at present have it open before him—either because he does not have it or because of haste. Finally, and much harder to assess, is the possibility that some of the quotations are derived from an intermediary source, such as an anthology. In order to establish this, one needs more substantial evidence than just the fact that Calvin's quotation is also found in another work.[16]

1. *Augustine*

Applying this hermeneutic of suspicion, how wide a selection of works does Calvin have to hand? He cites twenty-five Augustinian works.[17] Twelve of these he quotes at such length that one must conclude that he had them before him. Ten of these, it will come as no surprise, are anti-Pelagian works. The others are the *Retractationes* and the *Epistolae*, to four of which (all anti-Pelagian) he must have turned.[18] But how did he use these works? Did he constantly turn to them for quotations? Detailed study of the quotations yields the following conclusions: Occasionally he clearly had the volume open before him. This can be seen where there is a sustained volume of quotation from one work,[19] or where he refers to the position of the text in the volume.[20] On other occasions the quotations are briefer and looser; here it is likely that Calvin read Augustine for material in response to a particular point and then quoted from memory as he wrote.

For six of the works, there is no evidence that Calvin used them. For two, Calvin discusses Pighius' quotations without any indication that he went back to the original. For an additional three works Calvin discusses Pighius' quotations, drawing on material from the *Retractationes*, but giving no indication that he has

---

[16]Ford Lewis Battles, "The Sources of Calvin's Seneca Commentary," in Gervase E. Duffield, ed., *John Calvin* (Appleford, Abingdon: Sutton Courtenay, 1966), 38–66, shows the use of intermediary sources by Calvin at that stage. Luchesius Smits, *Saint Augustin dans l'oeuvre de Jean Calvin*, 2 vols. (Assen: van Gorcum, 1956, 1958), 1:206–11, notes Calvin's use of Lombard and Gratian in his early years, but detects none in the *Bondage and Liberation of the Will*. Annette Zillenbiller, *Die Einheit der Katholischen Kirche: Calvins Cyprianrezeption in seinen ekklesiologischen Schriften* (Mainz: von Zabern, 1993), 75–81, gives evidence for Calvin's use of Gratian as a source in the "Prefatory Address" to the *Institutio*, which is later recycled in the *De scandalis*. Anthony N. S. Lane, "Calvin's Sources of St. Bernard," *Archiv für Reformationsgeschichte* 67 (1976): 253–83, finds little evidence for Calvin's use of anthologies in his Bernard citations. My own examination of Lombard and Gratian has yielded no evidence that Calvin was dependent upon either of them in this work.

[17]See the table of works at the end of this paper. For the Augustinian and pseudo-Augustinian material I am indebted to the work of Smits, *Saint Augustin dans l'oeuvre*, vol.2, in tracing sources. My own study, based on one work of Calvin's only, has been more thorough and my conclusions differ from his in many points of detail and a number of substantial points. Some of the claims made below will therefore contradict the claims made in his tables. The basis for my claims appears more fully in Calvin, *Bondage and Liberation*, ed. Lane, tr. Davies.

[18]*Epistolae* 46–47, 105, 107, in his edition; pp. 194, 214–15, 217 in today's editions.

[19]E.g. from *De praedestinatione sanctorum* in *CO* 6:320–323.

[20]See nn. 71, 74 below.

gone back to the original. Why should he have neglected to go to the originals? One explanation would be that he did not have them to hand. This is possible with two of the works, but the other three are found in the same volume of the Erasmus editions as the *Retractationes*.[21] There is a simpler explanation. These are works of early Augustine, and Calvin's concern in discussing them is simply damage limitation. His aim is no more than to cast doubt on Pighius' appeal to them, his own attack coming from the later writings of the mature Augustine. He has neither the need nor the time to study these early writings. To unravel the complexities of Augustine's *De libero arbitrio* would have taken even Calvin more time than he could then afford. Finally from the *Confessiones* Calvin once quotes Augustine's famous prayer[22] ("Give what you command ..."), but this had already been quoted in the 1539 *Institutio*[23] and was also available via Augustine's anti-Pelagian works.[24]

This leaves seven other works which Calvin might have used. These are discussed in alphabetical order. From the *De civitate dei* there is a brief and rather loose quotation.[25] This is probably quoted from memory and almost certainly from earlier reading.[26] Calvin would not have scoured such a long work merely to give a single inaccurate three-line quotation.[27] The *Enarrationes in Psalmos* is four times named, [28] but always with less than four lines of quotation and generally not very accurately. This also looks like quotation from memory of earlier reading. Another possibility for these brief quotations is that Calvin kept a book of quotations, as did some other reformers.[29] Annette Zillenbiller argues that he must have done so because he is dependent upon Martin Bucer's *florilegium*, which was handwritten, in his 1543 *Institutio*.[30] But the latter work was largely completed by January 1542, [31] and the most likely explanation is that Calvin made use of Bucer's *florilegium* while he was still at Strassburg. So the verdict so far must be that there is no evidence that Calvin compiled his own book of quotations. But

---

[21] *De libero arbitrio, De quantitate animae,* and *De vera religione* are in the first volume, together with the *Retractationes*. The other two, *De duabus animabus* and *De actis cum Felice manichaeo,* are in vol. 6, together with *De haeresibus,* a work which we maintain that Calvin used. The assumption that Calvin used an Erasmus edition is justified below.

[22] Quoted in *CO* 6:348.   [23] *OS* 3:305 (*Inst.* 2:5:7).

[24] *De dono perseverantiae,* 20:53.   [25] In *CO* 6:304.

[26] For Calvin's earlier use of this work, see Smits, *Saint Augustin dans l'oeuvre,* 2:159–63.

[27] Here and throughout, the number of lines is counted in the original 1543 edition, where lines are slightly longer than those in *CO*.

[28] In *CO* 6:337, 342, 353, 386.

[29] Bucer's handwritten collection is in the library of Corpus Christi College, Cambridge, and has been edited by Peter Fraenkel, *Martin Buceri Opera Latini,* vol.3 (Leiden: Brill, 1988). Comparison of this with Calvin's works does not encourage the idea that Calvin was influenced by it and it was not, of course, available to him when he wrote his *Bondage and Liberation of the Will.*

[30] Zillenbiller, *Die Einheit der Katholischen Kirche,* 82–100.

[31] *OS* 3:xix-xx.

absence of evidence is not evidence of absence and Zillenbiller has reminded us that this is a question which must continue to be posed and investigated.

From the *Enchiridion* Calvin thrice cites a passage earlier quoted in the 1539 *Institutio*.[32] He also adds a new, lengthy, and accurate quotation from another passage, which he quotes a second time, more briefly.[33] This seems to be clear evidence that he turned to the work. The passage concerns the interpretation of Rom. 9:16, which was in dispute, and Calvin may have been drawn to it via the scripture index of the Augustine *Opera*, where it is found.

Augustine's *In evangelium Iohannis tractatus* is named five times by Calvin. Three times Calvin is simply repeating a quotation from the 1539 *Institutio*, and a fourth time he does so and adds extra material quoted by Pighius.[34] The fifth time the work is simply named as one of the sources for Augustine's statement that God crowns his gifts in us.[35] We can assume that Calvin knew this from his earlier reading of the sermons or via an intermediate source[36] rather than that he searched through them there and then to check whether this quotation might appear.[37]

One double citation of the *Contra Faustum Manichaeum* is simply drawn from Pighius.[38] But there is also a brief quotation, which appears nowhere else in Calvin's writings.[39] Since Calvin first began to quote this work in his 1543 *Institutio*,[40] which was largely completed by the time he took up his pen in response to Pighius, this two-line quotation is probably drawn from the memory of earlier reading.

Calvin repeatedly cites Augustine's *De haeresibus* as a source of knowledge about early heresies.[41] The only reason that one might question whether Calvin has the volume in front of him is his mistakes, attributing to the Montanists and Priscillianists ideas of which other heretics are accused. This clearly suggests that Calvin is working from memory. But since this book is not directly cited prior to our present work,[42] it is likely that the memory is of reading done specifically to

---

[32]In *CO* 6:293, 295, 336; cf. *OS* 3:250 (*Inst.* 2:2:8).   [33]In *CO* 6:343–44, 392.
[34]In *CO* 6:265, 314–15, 380. Cf. *OS* 3:249–50, 254, 305 (*Inst.* 2:2:8, 11, 2:5:7).
[35]In *CO* 6:337.
[36]It is cited in Peter Lombard, *Sententiae* 2:27:6 (*PL* 192:718–19). Calvin also cited this work repeatedly in the 1539 and 1543 *Institutio* (see Smits, *Saint Augustin dans l'oeuvre*, 2:189–97), so probably knew of the passage from that reading.
[37] The index volumes to the Erasmus editions list other sources for the saying, but none from the sermons on John.
[38]In *CO* 6:300.   [39]In *CO* 6:358. Cf. Smits, *Saint Augustin dans l'oeuvre*, 2:197.
[40]Cf. Smits, *Saint Augustin dans l'oeuvre*, 2:197–199.
[41]In *CO* 6:260, 262–64.
[42]Cf. Smits, *Saint Augustin dans l'oeuvre*, 2:206–7. Smits sees some parallels with the 1539 *Institutio*, but this work is not named and no knowledge of it is there required. Calvin mentions the work in the 1534 preface to his *Psychopannychia* (*CO* 5:170–71), but gives the *Decretum Gratiani* as an intermediate source. Gratian is not the source for Calvin's extensive citations here.

answer Pighius. Thus the inaccuracies would reflect the pressure of time rather than the inaccessibility of the original.

Finally, Calvin twice briefly cites the *Contra Julianum*, expanding even briefer references from the 1539 *Institutio*.[43] It is hard to be sure whether he has returned to the work or whether he is relying upon the memory of his earlier reading.

Where does this leave us? It appears that Calvin turned to the works of Augustine for fourteen or fifteen works, making use of at least five of the ten volumes of the Erasmus edition. Despite this, his reading was confined to the anti-Pelagian writings and the *Retractationes*, apart from brief forays into the *De haeresibus*, necessitated by Pighius' attack on that ground, and the *Enchiridion*. Given the subject matter and the time constraint, this restrictiveness is hardly surprising.

What of pseudo-Augustine? Calvin cites only three works, each in response to Pighius' use of them. Two of them he quotes at length and clearly had before him. These are found in the volumes of the Erasmus edition that he used for genuine works. The third he knew only through Pighius.[44]

2. The Augustine Edition Used by Calvin

Which edition of Augustine did Calvin use? This question is addressed by Luchesius Smits.[45] He notes that the choice is between the edition of Johann Amerbach at the beginning of the century and that of Erasmus, first published in 1528/29 and subsequently revised.[46] Before considering the evidence he notes three a priori reasons why Calvin should have used one of the Erasmus editions. His early humanist education, his humanist commentary on Seneca's *De clementia*, and his ongoing humanist inclinations would all have disposed him towards them. Secondly, his other writings contain evidence of his acquaintance with the latest works of humanist scholarship. Finally, Calvin's links with Basel would have predisposed him to the Erasmus edition, first published there. This last argument is perhaps less persuasive, not just because Amerbach's edition had also been published at Basel but also because factors like quality and, even more important, availability would presumably be much more important than place of publication.

Smits then proceeds to the evidence for the Erasmus editions. First, in discussing works of dubious authenticity Calvin showed independence of judgment, but in fact always reached the same conclusion as Erasmus, for ill and for good.[47]

---

[43]In *CO* 6:294, 354. Cf. *OS* 3:249, 275 (*Inst.* 2:2:8, 2:3:4).
[44]See n. 66, below.   [45]Smits, *Saint Augustin dans l'oeuvre*, 1:196–205.
[46]On these editions, cf. Joseph de Ghellinck, *Patristique et Moyen Age*, vol.3 (Brussels: Edition Universelle, 1948), 371–92; cf. Smits, *Saint Augustin dans l'oeuvre*, 1.197–201.
[47]For the details, see Smits, *Saint Augustin dans l'oeuvre*, 1.183–96.

Secondly, Calvin uses for Augustine's sermons on the Psalms the title coined by Erasmus: *Enarrationes.* Again, where there are textual variants Calvin always follows Erasmus' reading against that of Amerbach.

These arguments may be accepted as sound, though with qualifications. The a priori arguments show why Calvin might have preferred to use an Erasmus edition; they do not prove that he was actually able to do so. There is often a gulf between the editions that we would like to use and those that are actually available to us. The appeal to variant readings is legitimate, but must be used with caution. Those who have examined Calvin's quotations in detail know that he often quotes very loosely, so we must be cautious about using differences in wording as evidence. Smits claims that Calvin always follows Erasmus over Amerbach and then proceeds to give four examples. He says that he could continue the list, but gives no indication of how many such examples he has found,[48] which makes it hard to assess the strength of this argument.

There is another, more fundamental, weakness in Smits' case. Implicit is the assumption that Calvin used the same edition of Augustine throughout his literary career. But this is a presumption. We might reasonably suppose that while in one place Calvin used just the one edition, though if that edition was not his own personal copy there is no guarantee that he might always have had access to the same one. But until such time as Calvin possessed his own copy of Augustine's works, we must suppose that he used a different set in each place. Even if he did possess a copy at one time, he might have parted with it at some stage, especially at the time of his moves to and from Geneva.

There is solid evidence to support these reservations. In a study some years ago I showed that Calvin almost certainly used different editions of the works of Bernard during his time at Strassburg and during his later time at Geneva.[49] This shows the danger of assuming that Calvin used the same edition throughout. Where Augustine is concerned, Calvin himself is explicit. He had to respond to Pighius' charge that in the 1539 *Institutio* he failed to name all of the fathers who oppose him on a particular point.[50] Calvin justifies himself in part on the grounds that he had no books to hand at that time, save one volume of Augustine, which had been loaned to him. He proceeds to state that he had then been destitute of books.[51] While it suited Calvin's purpose to exaggerate his destitution, the basic

---

[48]Smits, *Saint Augustin dans l'oeuvre,* 1.204–5.
[49]Lane, "Calvin's Sources of St. Bernard," 253–283.
[50]*De libero arbitrio,* fol. 63a; the 1539 *Institutio, OS* 3:299:1–8 (*Inst.* 2:5:2).
[51]*CO* 6:336.

picture fits what is known of his poverty at Strassburg.[52] It is quite possible, therefore, that by the end of his stay at Strassburg[53] Calvin was using a copy of Augustine different both from the one(s) he had used before his stay in the city and from the one(s) that he used on his return to Geneva. Our goal here is not to discover one edition which Calvin used always, but simply to establish which edition of Augustine Calvin used for *The Bondage and Liberation of the Will*.[54]

Smits seeks not just to show that Calvin used an Erasmus edition but also to establish which of these editions he used. By the time Calvin responded to Pighius there were four available.[55] The first edition was begun by Johann Froben at Basel and completed by his sons in 1528 and 1529.[56] Three years later, in 1531 and 1532, Claude Chevallon at Paris printed a further edition, with some corrections by Jacobus Haemer, together with some newly discovered sermons.[57] In 1541, also at Paris, Yolande Bonhomme and Charlotte Guillard printed another edition.[58] Finally, Hieronymus Froben and Nikolaus Episcopius produced another edition at Basel, with corrections by Martin Lipsius, between 1541 and 1543.[59]

How might one discover which of the Erasmus editions Calvin used? Smits relies entirely upon one passage, which conveniently for us occurs in the work that we are considering. We will explore a number of possible indicators, also seeking positive proof that Calvin was not using the Amerbach edition. We will examine first the inconclusive evidence, then the evidence which excludes the Amerbach edition, and finally the evidence that might indicate which Erasmus edition Calvin did use.[60]

---

[52]See Lane, "Calvin's Sources of St. Bernard," 255; Jacques Pannier, "Calvin à Strasbourg," *Revue d'histoire et de philosophie religieuses* 4 (1924): 509–10. Emile Doumergue, *Jean Calvin: Les hommes et les choses de son temps*, vol. 2 (Lausanne: Bridel, 1902), 455–57, argues that while Calvin certainly sold the books that he inherited from Pierre Olivétan and also sold copies of his own works, there is no explicit reference to Calvin's selling any of his own library while at Strasbourg. But absence of evidence is not evidence of absence and it is quite possible that Calvin also sold some of his own books.

[53] This leaves open the possibility that he brought a copy of Augustine to Strasbourg and had to sell it there; see the previous note.

[54]One might hope that Calvin's copy of Augustine would have ended up in the Genevan library, as probably did his copy of Bernard (Lane, "Calvin's Sources of St. Bernard;," 265, 278), but the library contains Peter Martyr's copy; see Alexandre Ganoczy, *La Bibliothèque de l'Académie de Calvin* (Geneva: Droz, 1969), 183. In 1569, the library sold some of the books that had belonged to Calvin and Peter Martyr (ibid., 18–19). It may well have sold Calvin's copy because it was older (a conclusion reached below for the edition used in this work) or because it was not a complete set (a possibility that is also considered below).

[55]See n.46, above.

[56]*Index Aureliensis: Catalogus librorum sedecimo saeculo impressorum* (Baden-Baden: Koerner, 1965—), 110:175; (hereafter *IA*).

[57]*IA*, 110.201.   [58]*IA*, 110.258.   [59]*IA*, 110.256.

[60]For the Amerbach 1528/29 and 1541 editions, the copies in the Cambridge University Library were examined; for the 1541/43 edition, the copy in the British Library; for the 1531/32 edition, the copies in both libraries.

First, Calvin quotes (loosely) a number of passages from *De haeresibus*. Two
of these are not found in the earliest manuscripts,[61] but are found in both the
Amerbach and Erasmus editions. Second, there is a small but vital textual variant
in a quotation from *De correptione et gratia*. Calvin has "inseparabiliter" where
there is an alternative reading "insuperabiliter."[62] Since Calvin's reading weakens
the desired force of the quotation, it is unlikely that he would have introduced the
variant himself. Unfortunately though, his reading is found in both the Amerbach
and Erasmus editions. Third, Calvin queries the authorship of *Sermon 236*, denying that the style is Augustine's and conceding no more than the possibility that
this might be an early work of Augustine.[63] His doubts were well founded since
this is in fact Pelagius' *Confession of Faith to Pope Innocent*.[64] The Erasmus editions do not indicate that this particular sermon is spurious, but there are general
warnings both at the beginning of the *Sermons* volume and at the beginning of the
Sermones de Tempore, which indicate that not all of the sermons are genuine. But
none of this helps us discover which edition Calvin was using. The work is quoted
by Pighius who, unusually, gives no indication of his source.[65] Calvin is totally
dependent upon Pighius' quotation and clearly has no idea about the identity of
this work, other than that it is alleged to be by Augustine.[66]

One instance marginally favors the Erasmus editions. Calvin denies the
authenticity of the *Hypognosticon*, citing "the established opinion of the
learned."[67] The Amerbach edition states that the work is not found in the *Retractationes*, but adds that it is still useful. The Erasmus editions clearly state that it is
not by Augustine, and give the reasons why.

Two other instances strongly favor the Erasmus editions. First, Calvin discusses the pseudo-Augustinian *De dogmatibus ecclesiasticis*, and gives reasons why
it is not authentic. The Erasmus editions, unlike Amerbach's, make clear its inau-
thenticity, but, as Smits notes,[68] Calvin's reasons are independent of Erasmus' and
more developed. Calvin also notes that the author refers to Pope Innocent as
"magister" and speaks of the African synods of Milevis and Carthage. But the document itself refers to the author not as Innocent but as "magister in epistola ad

---

[61]*CO* 6:260, 262, quoting from *De haeresibus* 1 and 11 (*PL* 42:26, n.1; 42:28, n.3). In the former
passage, Calvin used "Selene" where Augustine used "Helen" (*PL* 42:25, n.1). The Amerbach and Erasmus editions read "Selene." Intriguingly, the French translation of Calvin has "Heléné."

[62]*CO* 6:324, citing *De correptione et gratia* 12:38 (*PL* 44:940, n.1).

[63]*CO* 6:319.   [64]*PL* 39:2181, n.b.

[65]Perhaps he did not know it. Peter Lombard, *Sententiae* 2:28:8 has a similar quotation, missing
the last line, attributed to Jerome "in Explanatione fidei Catholicae ad Damasum"(*PL* 192:718–19).
Pighius may have derived it from some such source.

[66]*CO* 6: 319, following Pighius, *De libero arbitrio*, fol. 58a ("ex quadam ad populum concione,
quae Augustino adscribitur").

[67]*CO* 6:306.   [68]Smits, *Saint Augustin dans l'oeuvre*, 1:187–88.

Milevitanum concilium."[69] How did Calvin know that the "magister" was Innocent? Erasmus' *censura*, found in all of the Erasmus editions, states that chapter 25 is Pope Innocent's letter to the council. Here, then, is further evidence that Calvin was working with an Erasmus edition. Finally, there is in another work a textual variant between the Amerbach and Erasmus editions where Calvin follows the latter.[70]

Most significantly, there are two passages that might indicate *which* Erasmus edition Calvin used. The first is used by Smits as the sole item of evidence to settle the issue. Calvin cites a passage from *De correptione et gratia* and then introduces another extract with the words "five lines earlier he had said."[71] As Smits notes, in all the Erasmus editions save the first, the text is divided into two columns and so it is in the latter only that one needs to return only five lines to reach the second extract.

This simple test appears to settle the case. But the simplicity is only apparent. How does one arrive at the total of five lines? Does one measure from the beginning or the end of the first passage and does one measure back to the beginning or the end of the second passage? It is yet more complicated. The first passage is a loose quotation in which only two words are adjacent in both quotation and original. The second passage is a paraphrase in which only two words come from the original. So from where to where does one count the gap? According to where the measurements are taken, the 1528/29 Erasmus edition yields results of four or five lines, the later editions' results varying between six and ten lines (at least seven lines for the 1541 edition). If this were the only piece of evidence, it would favor the first edition—but only marginally.

Apart from the question of what to measure, one must ask whether "five lines earlier" is intended as a precise mathematical measure or just another way of saying "a few lines above." On two other occasions Calvin makes similar statements where we know precisely which volume he had before him: Pighius' *De libero arbitrio*. Once he claims that Pighius contradicts himself ten lines later.[72] He then, after a brief summary of what follows, paraphrases a short passage which begins exactly ten lines after the end of the first. Another time Calvin claims that Pighius contradicts what he had said twenty lines previously.[73] Having summa-

---

[69] *De dogmatibus ecclesiasticis* 25 (*PL* 58:986).

[70] Amerbach has "quicquid"; Erasmus and Calvin have "quisquis" in *De correptione et gratia*, 7:12, quoted in *CO* 6:342. Cf. *PL* 44:923, n.3. This is one of Smits' textual variants; see Smits, *Saint Augustin dans l'oeuvre*, 1:205.

[71] *CO* 6:293º94., citing *De correptione et gratia*, 13:42. Cf. Smits, *Saint Augustin dans l'oeuvre*, 1:205.

[72] *CO* 6:301, Pighius, *De libero arbitrio*, fol. 47b.

[73] *CO* 6:367–68, Pighius, *De libero arbitrio* fol. 80a–b.

rized a passage of nine lines long, he proceeds to summarize an earlier passage which is eight lines long. The gap between the two is twenty lines. So to move from the beginning of the passage first summarized to the end of the second requires a move of twenty-one lines, while to move from the end of the passage first summarized to the beginning of the second (the more obvious measurement to make) requires a move of thirty-six lines.

There are two ways of interpreting this evidence. If we think that Calvin was seeking to give precise measurements, this would mean that when measuring distances *backwards* he did so by measuring the *gap* between the two passages. If the Augustine passage is measured this way, the 1528/29 Erasmus edition has a gap of just three lines, the 1531/32 and 1541/43 editions have gaps of exactly five lines, while the 1541 edition has a gap of six lines. By this way of measuring, the first Erasmus edition turns out to be the least likely. Alternatively, it may be that Calvin was not concerned to measure distances precisely. The fact that he speaks in terms of five, ten, and twenty lines would support this contention, though the evidence allows all three statements to be taken literally. If he was being precise throughout, the evidence excludes the 1528/29 edition; if not, the evidence from the Augustine passage does not significantly favor the 1528/29 edition over the other editions, in which case we must look elsewhere.

There is a second passage, not noted by Smits: Calvin is arguing with Pighius about the interpretation of Augustine's *De libero arbitrio*. He responds to a quotation made by Pighius by inviting him to "turn the page" to another passage, which he proceeds to quote.[74] Since these two passages are twenty-two columns apart in Migne, there is no way that one could move from one to the other just by turning the page in an Erasmus edition or any other edition. But Calvin has inadvertently alerted us that he was using not the *De libero arbitrio* itself, but the extracts from it found in the *Retractationes*. What happens when we turn from one passage to the other in the Erasmus editions? In the 1541/43 Basel edition the two passages are found on the same page. In the 1528/29 Erasmus edition they are found on facing pages. In the other two editions they are on opposite sides of the same leaf, so that one literally has to turn the page over to move from the one to the other. This strongly favors these two editions.

Where does this leave us? The 1541/43 edition seems to be excluded. This also follows from its date. Some of the volumes were not published until 1543, which

---

[74]*CO* 6:296, with quotations from *De libero arbitrio* 3:3:7 and 3:18:51. It might be argued that "turn the page" means "turn a handful of pages" from one passage to the other in the *De libero arbitrio*, but since the whole point is the closeness of the two passages, this is unlikely. It is also excluded by the fact that Calvin's next words are "Then he adds," followed by a quotation not from *De libero arbitrio* but from the *Retractationes*.

is too late since it appears that Calvin completed his work by February of that year. What of the 1528/29 Erasmus edition? One might argue that "turn the page" is as likely to be metaphorical as "five lines earlier." But there is a difference. In the one case the issue is *how many* lines one has to move up the page; in the other case the issue is *whether* one needs to turn the page.

My judgment is that Calvin used not the 1528/29 Erasmus edition but one of the two Paris editions. If Calvin (as he says) did not have a copy while at Strassburg and if he bought one in Geneva (rather than borrowed one), the 1541 edition appeared at just the right time. On the other hand, if we take the "five lines earlier" as a precise measurement of the gap between the two passages, the 1531/32 edition is indicated.[75]

3. Other Fathers.

What of the thirty-three works by other authors?[76] Here would appear evidence of a wide range of patristic learning. But those who read the treatise will be struck by the paucity of reference to other fathers compared to the wealth of material on Augustine. This paucity cannot be explained solely by the fact that the others do not support Calvin to the same extent as does Augustine.

Nineteen of the thirty-three works are easily eliminated. With five Calvin is simply discussing his citation in the 1539 *Institutio*, and provides no evidence of any further knowledge of the work. With an additional eight Calvin contents himself simply with discussing the quotation given by Pighius, and provides no evidence of any further knowledge of the work. Another four are drawn from Augustine's works.[77] One is taken from both the 1539 *Institutio* and Pighius, and another one from Augustine as well as these two.

This leaves fourteen works. Some of these can also be eliminated. Calvin cites Eusebius' mention of the letters of Clement of Rome, without implying that he himself had seen the letters.[78] He appeals to Bernard without mentioning any source.[79] His citations are based upon the *De gratia et libero arbitrio*, which Calvin cited in the 1539 *Institutio*. Here he appears to be drawing upon memory of earlier

---

[75]Another possibility, which should not be discounted, is that Calvin possessed the first volume of one edition (with the *Retractationes*) and the seventh volume of another edition (with *De correptione et gratia*). We cannot simply assume that Calvin had a complete set of the *opera omnia*. He claims that while preparing the 1539 *Institutio* he had only one volume of Augustine to hand (*CO* 6:336). But if one edition (like the 1531/32 or 1541 editions) fits all of the evidence it is most likely that he did have a complete set, or at least that all of the volumes that he used were from the same edition.

[76] See the table at the end of this article.

[77]The entire discussion of Cyprian (*CO* 6:282–83) and most of the discussion of Ambrose (*CO* 6:287) is based upon Augustine's quotation of and interpretation of these authors.

[78]In *CO* 6:262.

[79]In *CO* 6:291, 333, 334–35, 378.

reading.[80] There is a brief and loose quotation from Theodoret's *Historia eccle-siae*.[81] Both the text of the quotation and Calvin's general usage indicate that he was reliant upon Cassiodore's *Historia tripartita*. He had made good use of this work prior to 1543[82] and the present brief reference was probably drawn from memory of that study.

Three other works can be considered together. Calvin evidences some knowledge of the contents of the pseudo-Clementine *Recognitiones*.[83] Since he had never before referred to this work the most likely scenario is that he now turned to it in order to combat Pighius' claims. We shall shortly return to the question of which edition he might have used. In opposition to Clementine authorship he cites both Eusebius' *Historia ecclesiae* and Rufinus' *De adulteratione librorum Origenis*, found as the epilogue to his Latin translation of Pamphilus' *Apologia pro Origene*.[84] There was nothing new in opposing the authenticity of the *Recognitions*. This had been done by Johannes Trithemius, drawing on a comment made by Gratian.[85] But where did Calvin find the two witnesses for the opposition? They are found together in *later* compilations of evidence,[86] but a search of literature available to Calvin has failed to find them. There is no good reason to question that Calvin read them for himself; by this time he was certainly familiar with Eusebius and may here have been quoting him from memory.[87] The reference to an obscure work of Rufinus is more suspicious, but there is a simple explanation: it is found in at least some of the contemporary editions of Origen's works.[88] Calvin's use of Origen prior to 1543 was not excessive, but wide enough to suggest that Calvin had read his works.[89] It is not unlikely that he may at the same time

---

[80]This is also confirmed by the evidence that Calvin did not bring to Geneva the edition of Bernard that he used at Strassburg and did not acquire another copy until the 1550s (Lane, "Calvin's Sources of St. Bernard"). It is possible that the citation in CO 6:334–35 is based upon the *Sermones in Cantica*, which Calvin quoted extensively in the 1543 *Institutio*, largely completed by this time.

[81]In *CO* 6:276.

[82]Cf. Mooi, *Het Kert- en Dogmahistorisch Element*, 292–96. Theodoret and Cassiodore have been counted as two separate works.

[83]In *CO* 6:261.   [84]In *CO* 6:261–62.

[85]J. Trithemius, *Catalogus Scriptorum Ecclesiasticorum* (Köln: P. Quentel, 1531), fol. 2a, citing *Decretum Gratiani*, pars 1, dist.15, c.3, §29 (*PL* 187:76). It is also declared to be apocryphal by J. Driedo, *De ecclesiasticis scripturis et dogmatibus*, bk. 4, ch. 5, pt.5 (Louvain: R. Rescius, 1533), 602.

[86]E.g., *PG* 1:1159–62, taken from a work of Andreas Gallandi of the 1760s.

[87]Cf. Mooi, *Het Kert- en Dogmahistorisch Element*, 289–92; Irena Backus, "Calvin's Judgment of Eusebius of Caesarea: An Analysis," *Sixteenth Century Journal* 22 (1991): 419–37. The Greek text of Eusebius was not published until 1544, so Calvin was dependent upon the Latin translation by Rufinus, printed in 1473 and many times thereafter; *Die Griechischen Christlichen Schriftsteller der ersten drei Jahrhunderte* 9/3(Leipzig: Hinrichs'sche Buchhandlung, 1903), xliii, cclvi.

[88]It is found, together with Pamphilus' *Apologia pro Origene* in the *Opera omnia* of Origen (Paris: Parvus, Badius and Resch, 1522). Pighius quotes Origen via Pamphilus' *Apologia*; see *De libero arbitrio*, fols.22a–24a.

[89]Cf. Mooi, *Het Kert- en Dogmahistorisch Element*, 209–212.

have read Rufinus' *De adulteratione librorum Origenis*. Since there was no particular reason why someone interested in pseudo-Clement should think to look at Rufinus, the chances are that the brief reference here is from memory of that earlier reading.

This leaves seven works. How many of these did Calvin use in preparing his response to Pighius? One author that he undoubtedly used was Basil. Pighius quoted from two works by Basil.[90] Calvin responds to Pighius' quotations, adds some more material from one of the works, and quotes from two more works.[91] We can be more precise about what happened because there are different translations of Basil. Pighius was using the Latin translation by Raphael Maffei Volateranus, which appeared in five editions of Basil's *Opera* between 1515 and 1531.[92] Calvin, by contrast, in the passages that he cites, uses the translation by Janus Cornarius in the edition of the *Opera omnia* published in 1540 by Froben at Basel.[93] This fits the hypothesis propounded above. Calvin built up his patristic library on his return to Geneva. How better to start than to purchase the fresh translation of Basil recently published by Froben at Basel?

Apart from Basil we are on uncertain ground. There are four remaining works which Calvin might have used. Pighius quotes from Ambrose's *De Iacob et vita beata*.[94] Calvin discusses Pighius' quotations and then adds two short (three-line) quotations of his own. As he had twice cited this general passage in the 1539 *Institutio*, [95] he was already familiar with it. Whether he was now quoting from memory or turned again to the text is not clear, though there is a clue that suggests he did have the work at hand. He notes that he is quoting "ex eadem pagina, ex qua sumpsit Pighius quod adducit."[96] If this statement is accurate, it suggests that he had the volume open before him; if inaccurate, it suggests that he relied on memory. There were six editions of Ambrose between 1506 and 1539 and in two of these, both published by the Chevallons in Paris, Pighius' and Calvin's quotations are found on the opposite sides of the same leaf.[97] Calvin's claim would thus

---

[90]Pighius, *De libero arbitrio*, fol. 33a–b.   [91]In *CO* 6:284–286.

[92]*IA*, 114:428, 440, 448–49, 486. Cf. I. Backus, *Lectures Humanistes de Basile de Césarée* (Paris: Institut d'Études Augustiniennes, 1990), 15–27.

[93]*IA*, 114:485. On this edition, see Backus, *Lectures Humanistes* , 43–48, 232–38. Knowledge of which editions were used is quite important because they vary considerably (ibid., 9, 27, 48). The 1572 catalogue of the Genevan library contains Peter Martyr's copies of the 1532 Greek and the 1552 Latin editions of Basil; Ganoczy, *Bibliothèque de l'Académie*, 168, 181.

[94]Pighius, *De libero arbitrio*, fol. 34b-35a.

[95]*OS* 3:333, 506 (*Inst*. 2:7:7, 2:16:18).

[96]*CO* 6:287. The 1572 catalogue of the Genevan library contains Peter Martyr's copy of the 1555 edition of Ambrose; Ganoczy, *Bibliothèque de l'Académie*, .182).

[97]The editions are *IA*, 104.633, 644, 648, 651, 662, 663. *IA*, alleges another edition (104.647), citing the Nürnberg Stadtbibliothek as its only source. There are a number of suspicious features about this entry and a letter from the Stadtbibliothek has confirmed that the copy referred to (Theol.172.2° & 173.2°) is not a 1526 Basel edition but is in fact the 1516 Basel edition (*IA*, 104.644). In both of the Chevallon Paris editions (1529 & 1539, nos. 651 and 663) the quotations are found on fols. 289a and b.

be literally true if we allow "pagina" here to mean leaf instead of page. That this translation is possible is shown by the French translation of the earlier passage where Augustine is cited, which renders "cur non vertit paginam?" as "Que ne tourne-il le fueillet …?"[98]

Calvin cites Jerome repeatedly.[99] All save one of these citations are drawn from either the 1539 *Institutio*, Pighius, or Augustine. The one exception is a brief statement about Jerome's *Epistola* 133.[100] Calvin already knew this letter since he had cited it in the 1539 *Institutio*,[101] so was probably here referring to it from memory. That he did not have Jerome to hand is confirmed by the way he handles Pighius' material.[102] He parries it without saying much at all about Jerome, which might indicate that he is unable to consult Jerome.

Tertullian's *De praescriptione haereticorum* is also cited. Calvin displays a definite knowledge of the work, but never quotes more than a single sentence[103] and makes mistakes.[104] This all suggests that he cited from memory without consulting the text.[105]

Finally, Calvin repeatedly cites Irenaeus.[106] Mostly he makes general statements about the *Adversus Haereses*, but he also twice quotes from the work.[107] The first quotation is loose enough for Remko Mooi to suggest that Calvin quoted from memory having shortly before read the text,[108] but the second is longer (eleven lines) and more accurate. It appears, therefore, that Calvin had the text of Irenaeus to hand and this likelihood is reinforced by the existence in the 1572 Genevan library catalogue of the 1528 Basel edition of Irenaeus, bound together with the 1526 Basel edition of the pseudo-Clementine *Recognitions*.[109] Irenaeus is named, but not quoted in the 1543 *Institutio* (largely completed in Strassburg) yet is quoted in the present work and also twice in 1544.[110] This might indicate that

[98]*CO* 6:296. Cf. n.74, above. The French is found on p.325 of the *Recueil des opuscules* (Geneva: B. Pinereul, 1566).

[99]In *CO* 6:267, 286, 291, 299, 336   [100]In *CO* 6:267.   [101]*OS* 3:299 (*Inst.* 2:5:2).

[102]In *CO* 6:286. In his later works of 1543–44 (excluding the 1543 *Institutio*) Calvin shows more knowledge of Jerome (cf. *CO* 6:446, 516; 7:18, 22, 28, 38, 104; 9:827). The 1572 catalogue of the Genevan library contains Peter Martyr's copy of the 1553 edition of Jerome (Ganoczy, *Bibliothèque de l'Académie*, 179).

[103]Which he twice does in *CO* 6:275.

[104]He gives a faulty chapter reference (*CO* 6:260); he incorrectly claims that Tertullian lists all of the bishops of Rome to his time (*CO* 6:261) and that he commented on the small number of bishops in succession to the apostles up to his time (*CO* 6:278).

[105]The 1572 catalogue of the Genevan library contains Peter Martyr's copy of the 1550 edition of Tertullian (Ganoczy, *Bibliothèque de l'Académie*, 177).

[106]In *CO* 6:260–61, 274–75, 278, 281–82, 288, 290, 339.

[107]In *CO* 6:275, 282.

[108]Mooi, *Het Kerk- en Dogmahistorisch Element*, 196 n.3.

[109]Ganoczy, *Bibliothèque de l'Académie*, 168. The pseudo-Clementine edition is *IA*, 140.921. The library also had Peter Martyr's copy of the 1548 edition of Irenaeus (ibid., 180).

[110]In *CO* 7:15, 125.

Calvin acquired a copy of his works after returning to Geneva. It is possible—to put it no stronger—that he used the copies of Irenaeus and pseudo-Clement that found their way into the Genevan library.

What works of non-Augustinian fathers did Calvin consult in preparing his response to Pighius? He definitely used the 1540 Froben edition of Basil's works. He probably used an edition of Irenaeus, perhaps the one that was bound with the Clementine *Recognitions*. It is probable that he turned briefly to Ambrose. Otherwise there is no indication that Calvin used any other patristic writings.

Finally, Calvin quotes from a number of councils: those of Carthage, Milevis, and Orange. The number and length of the quotations leave no doubt that he has the source before him. The Council of Orange, which he cites extensively, is found not in the editions of Jacobus Merlin but first in Peter Crabbe's two-volume *Concilia omnia*.[111] All the present citations from the councils can be found in the first volume of that work. Smits noted that almost all of Calvin's citations of the canons of Orange and the African councils appear in works published in 1543. Apart from repetitions of these citations, there are only three exceptions, from 1541, 1544, and 1547.[112] This would indicate that Calvin studied them soon after his return to Geneva, which reinforces the conclusion that he had a copy of Crabbe to hand, instead of relying on earlier reading, from Strassburg say.

*   *   *

What conclusion have we reached? Here is Calvin's second most important work as regards his use of the fathers. He cites twenty-eight works of Augustine or pseudo-Augustine, thirty-three from nineteen other authors and three councils—a grand total of sixty-four works. How many books did he have to hand for this task? For certain, he had five volumes of Augustine's *Opera omnia*, the 1540 Basel edition of Basil, and the first volume of Crabbe's councils. He probably used editions of Irenaeus and of pseudo-Clement as well as a Chevallon edition of the works of Ambrose. Otherwise there is no firm evidence for the use of any other patristic sources. Thus this work may have been written with the help of as few as seven patristic volumes, probably with another two or three. But it is important to be clear about what is and is not being claimed. There is no firm evidence that Calvin used more than ten patristic volumes. In other words, there is no need to

---

[111]Smits, *Saint Augustin dans l'oeuvre*, 1:232. This work was published by Peter Quentel at Köln in 1538. Cf. also *OS* 5:113, n.1. The medievals relied on compilations for their knowledge of the councils and these, including the most influential, the ninth-century pseudo-Isidorian *Decretals*, did not include Orange. Thus the canons of this council were unknown and unquoted from the tenth century to the publication of Crabbe (Henri Bouillard, *Conversion et Grâce chez S. Thomas d'Aquin* (Paris: Aubier, 1944) 98–102, 114–121).

[112]Smits, *Saint Augustin dans l'oeuvre*, 1:229–30.

postulate the use of more than ten volumes to account for the evidence that we have. But this is not to be confused with the statement that Calvin definitely used only ten volumes. Absence of evidence is not evidence of absence and it may be that Calvin consulted a further twenty volumes. But if he did consult further volumes, they had no discernible effect upon the final outcome.

Why is this? Two reasons were noted at the beginning. First is lack of availability. At some stages in his career Calvin may have had access to a wide range of books, as during his stay with Louis du Tillet or his time at Basel. At other times this would not have been true, and the early years at Geneva must have been among the most barren. Second is lack of time. *Bondage and Liberation of the Will* was written in haste and Calvin did not have time to check all his references or to follow up all the issues that interested him. There is also a third reason. On this topic Calvin turns to Augustine for support. Where the writings of the other fathers or the young Augustine are concerned, his main aim is to parry Pighius' attack. There was little to be gained by discussing them at length.

Confirmation of this is found with Chrysostom. Calvin contributes nothing beyond what was said in the 1539 *Institutio* with the exception of one reference to a passage quoted by Pighius. Yet it is likely that Calvin had a copy of Chrysostom to hand, even if he did not use it. His copy of the 1536 edition of Chrysostom's works, complete with his own underlinings and marginal notes, is at present in the Genevan library.[113] The passages marked by Calvin appear especially in the 1543 *Institutio*,[114] which would suggest that Calvin had been reading Chrysostom not long before the time that he wrote his response to Pighius. But if he already possessed the volumes by this stage, why did he not use them? Probably because there was no point, because no amount of interpretation would bring Chrysostom into line with Calvin on this issue. Already in the 1539 *Institutio* he had criticized Chrysostom's views, so there was no need to delay further with him.

4. Calvin's Reading

Having sought to ascertain which works Calvin *consulted* in writing his *The Bondage and Liberation of the Will,* we can now ask a different question. Which works was Calvin *reading* around this time? There is a simple method to test this. From the works used we can eliminate all of those which Pighius introduced into the debate and all of those derived from an intermediary source.[115] What remains

---

[113]Cf. Ganoczy, *Bibliothèque de l'Académie,* 182; Alexandre Ganoczy and Klaus Müller, *Calvins handschriftliche Annotationen zu Chrysostomus* (Wiesbaden: F Steiner, 1981).

[114]Ganoczy & Müller, *Calvins handschriftliche Annotationen,* 24–27, 162.

[115]Some citations are drawn from the 1539 *Institutio;* some are taken from Augustine; some come from another source, such as Eusebius or Cassiodore. For details, see the table of works at the end of this paper.

is a list of twelve works that Calvin introduced into the debate. The fact of his doing so *might* indicate that he was then reading these works or had done so recently.

Five of the works are by Augustine. Two of those are anti-Pelagian works which Calvin had already used for the 1539 *Institutio*.[116] He is likely to have turned to these in his intense use of the anti-Pelagian works while responding to Pighius. Another is the *De haeresibus*, which Calvin here cites directly for the first time.[117] Calvin's use of it probably reflects not prior reading but the need to challenge Pighius' equating of his views with those of the early heretics. The other two Augustinian works are the *De civitate dei* and the *Enarrationes in Psalmos*. From the former there is only one brief sentence of quotation, too little to suggest recent reading, but the three brief quotations from the latter, probably drawn from memory, could well indicate that Calvin had recently been reading it.[118]

Of the non-Augustinian works, four do not necessarily indicate Calvin's *current* reading. Calvin's citations of Eusebius and Rufinus over the question of the Clementine *Recognitions* probably come from memory of earlier reading of Eusebius and Origen.[119] The citation of Theodoret via Cassiodore probably reflects memory of earlier reading of the latter.[120] Calvin also cites Tertullian's *De praescriptione haereticorum*, the only time before 1550 that he does so. This might suggest that he might have been reading it at around this time, but there are indications to the contrary. The brevity of his quotations and the mistakes that he makes[121] suggest that his encounter with the work was less recent. It may well be that the book was brought into the debates at the colloquies of 1539 to 1541 at which Pighius, who had recently been quoting from it, [122] was present. Calvin's knowledge of it may well derive from that time.

Three works remain. As mentioned, Calvin's appeals to the African councils almost all appear in 1543. This would indicate that he was probably studying Crabbe's 1538 edition around this time, maybe having only recently acquired a copy.[123] Finally, Calvin quotes from two works of Basil which had not previously entered the debate.[124] These are drawn from the recently published Cornarius

---

[116]*De dono perseverantiae* and *De perfectione iustitiae hominis.*
[117]Cf. n. 42, above.
[118]It is suggested above that Calvin may have relied on memory for citations from *In evangelium Iohannis tractatus*, *Contra Faustum manichaeum*, and *Contra Julianum*. The brevity of citation of these works does not encourage the idea that Calvin had read them near the time he made the citations.
[119]Cf. nn.83–89, above.   [120]Cf. nn.81–82, above.   [121]Cf. nn.103–5, above.
[122]Pighius does not cite this work in his *De libero arbitrio*, but he did cite it on the present topic in his 1538 *Hierarchiae ecclesiasticae assertio;* see Pontien Polman, *L'Élément historique dans la controverse religieuse du XVIe siècle* (Gembloux: J Duculot, 1932), 288; P. Fraenkel, *Testimonia Patrum* (Geneva: Droz, 1961), 279.
[123]Cf. nn.111–12, above.   [124]Cf. nn. 91, 93, above.

translation. Why did he quote these two works? The choice of one is not surprising since it was entitled *De libero arbitrio*. A perfunctory glance at the Basil volume
could have led Calvin to this work. But the other work is less obvious. Calvin
quotes from Basil's *Homiliae in Psalmos*. Why this work? The quotation is not
especially relevant and contributes little to the argument. The natural interpretation is that Calvin was at this time reading Basil and so introduced a quotation
from a passage that he remembered.[125] This conclusion is strengthened by the fact
that prior to his response to Pighius and including the 1543 *Institutio* (which was
largely complete by this time) Calvin's citations of Basil are rare and extremely
brief.[126] It is likely that Calvin was beginning his first serious reading of Basil.

What conclusion have we reached? There is clear evidence that Calvin at this
time was studying two books, the Crabbe edition of the councils and the Cornarius translation of Basil. He makes good use of these in his response to Pighius,
introducing works which had not previously been used either in his 1539 *Institutio* or in Pighius' attack on it. Apart from these two books, there is little evidence
of Calvin's reading, other than the study of Augustine's anti-Pelagian works and
his *De haeresibus* needed to answer Pighius. There is evidence of earlier reading of
the *Enarrationes in Psalmos*, but no clear indication that this reading was recent.
The same applies to Tertullian's *De praescriptione haereticorum*, the use of which
does not indicate recent reading.

II. Calvin's Use of the Fathers

In the second part of the paper we consider the manner in which Calvin uses the
fathers in *The Bondage and Liberation of the Will*. Calvin and Pighius differed fundamentally concerning the relation between Scripture and tradition. Calvin maintained that he was defending God's truth against Pighius' attacks.[127] But where is
this truth to be found? For Calvin, God's truth is the "sure truth of Scripture," the
light of truth shining in the word of God.[128] The rule of faith is to be sought in the
Word of God, in Scripture, in the oracles of God, not in tradition.[129] The teaching
of the fathers has value, but is always open to correction in the light of Scripture.[130] Pighius, however, regarded the consensus of the tradition of the Catholic

---

[125]This is paralleled by the way in which Calvin acquired the 1552 Basel edition of Bernard's
works and two years later began to introduce new Bernardine material (Lane, "Calvin's Sources of St.
Bernard," 278).
[126]In *CO* 1:442, 508, 646, 891; 5:181, 394; 9:834.
[127]*CO* 6:235–37. For this paragraph especially, a computer word search was used to examine
Calvin's use of *consensus, definitio, evangelium, oraculum, scriptura, verbum,* and *veritas.*
[128]*CO* 6:271, 273–84, 277, 327–29, 347-48, 391.
[129]*CO* 6:267–271.
[130]*CO* 6:276–278. Cf A. N. S. Lane, "Calvin's Use of the Fathers and the Medievals," *Calvin Theological Journal* 16 (1981): 167–74.

Church as normative. Scripture without the definitions of the church is obscure and is a nose of wax which can be turned this way and that by heretics. A norm for correct belief is required and is found in the tradition of the church, which is the pillar and bulwark of the truth. Indeed, he goes so far as to say that any Scripture that goes against tradition is to be disregarded.[131] There is a certain irony in this. Pighius maintains that Scripture is obscure, but that the fathers nonetheless managed to interpret it correctly. Calvin, on the other hand, maintains that Scripture is clear, but that most of the fathers had nonetheless failed to grasp its meaning, at least on this issue.

Calvin responds to Pighius' charges by accusing him of exalting human tradition above God's Word; his approach involves twisting Scripture to make it conform with human decisions, and thus subordinating it to them. It is true that heretics distort Scripture, as did Satan when tempting Christ. But the latter in his response relied on Scripture alone. Calvin also defended his stance from other passages of Scripture.[132] The underlying issue is the nature of the true church. For Pighius this is the institutional Catholic Church, which cannot err and whose teaching is the true Christian faith. For Calvin the true church is that which adheres to the Word of God.[133] Here is the fundamental divide of the Reformation.

This issue of the relation between Scripture and tradition was also fought out in the arena of the early fathers. Pighius claimed their support for his approach.[134] Calvin denies this. Irenaeus, he claims, regarded Scripture as normative.[135] Tertullian's own practice does not match what he says in his *De praescriptione* and, furthermore, he himself falls into error.[136] Origen's essentials of the faith include opinions now regarded as heretical.[137] Calvin also goes on the attack by citing Constantine's words to the Council of Nicea and by appealing to Augustine.[138] He does, however, concede that there is value in the agreement of the churches concerning matters of faith, as long as Scripture remains the norm. Where the agreement of the churches is added, it is an exceptional witness to seal the certainty of our faith.[139] Thus, just as the Spirit bears witness to Scripture, yet the church and

[131]Pighius, *De libero arbitrio*, fols.18b–19a, 20a–21b, 58b, 84a-b. Pighius repeatedly referred to the Bible as a nose of wax; P. Polman, *L'Elément historique*, 286–87.).
[132]*CO* 6:267–74, 277, 288, 326, 373–74. Calvin uses the phrase "sola scriptura" with approval (6:268) and chides Pighius for rejecting the principle of "nuda scriptura'"(6:269). But of course neither of these was yet a slogan in the way that "sola scriptura" was to become; see A. N. S. Lane, "Sola Scriptura? Making Sense of a Post-Reformation Slogan" in Philip E. Satterthwaite and David F. Wright, eds., *A Pathway into the Holy Scripture* (Grand Rapids: Eerdmans, 1994), esp. 298.
[133]Pighius, *De libero arbitrio*, fol. 58b; *CO* 6:326–27.
[134]Pighius, *De libero arbitrio* fols.21b–22a.
[135]*CO* 6:274–75.   [136]*CO* 6:275–78   [137]*CO* 6:277–78, 291.
[138]*CO* 6:276.   [139]*CO* 6:276–77. Cf. *CO* 6:288.

rational proofs are secondary helps, so also the agreement of the churches can be a secondary confirmation of Christian doctrine.[140]

The dispute over the fathers falls into two distinct halves: Augustine and the other fathers. This distinction had already been made by Calvin in the 1539 *Institutio*, where he twice claimed that apart from Augustine, the early fathers are so confused, vacillating, and contradictory on the subject of free choice that almost nothing can with certainty be ascertained from their writings.[141] Pighius devoted much of his second book to refuting this claim. In return, he claimed the clear and universal consent of the orthodox fathers for his own belief in free choice.[142] Calvin responded in a variety of ways.

First, he clarified what it is that he had claimed. He had been completely frank in the 1539 *Institutio* about the fact that the fathers exalted human powers excessively, through the pressure of Greek philosophy and for fear of encouraging laziness. He also stood by his claim that their teachings were obscure and inconsistent, in particular about the limits of human power.[143] But by this he had meant that they differed from one another, not that they were internally inconsistent, though he also maintained that these fathers were confused inasmuch as they failed to take fully into account the effects of the Fall.[144]

Second, he engages in a protracted discussion of the teaching of the fathers: Origen, pseudo-Clement, Tertullian, Irenaeus, Cyprian, Hilary, Basil, Jerome, Ambrose, and Chrysostom.[145] There is a standard reply that he uses. Where Pighius cites a passage which suggests that free choice is unimpaired, Calvin presents him with a dilemma. Either the father was referring to *unfallen* human nature (in opposition to Gnosticism, say), in which case the passage is irrelevant, or he had failed to distinguish between human nature as created and fallen, in which case he was heretical by the standards of later Catholic orthodoxy.[146]

Calvin concludes his discussion of these fathers with a number of observations. First, in opposition to Pighius' claim, he maintains that the only consensus of the church is that which is in accord with the Word of God.[147] Such a dogmatic dismissal of historical evidence would, of course, render superfluous all the preceding discussion of the fathers, so Calvin does not stop there. He proceeds to question what is meant by the consensus of the church. Merely to produce badly selected quotations here and there from six or eight patristic writings does not

---

[140]For further reasons why Calvin needed to dispute the teaching of the fathers rather than appeal to Scripture alone; cf. Lane, "Calvin's Use of the Fathers and the Medievals," 165–67.

[141]Cf. n. 4, above.   [142]Pighius, *De libero arbitrio* fols. 21a-b., 58b.

[143]*CO* 6:284, *OS* 3:244 (*Inst.* 2:2.4).   [144]*CO* 6:291–92.

[145]*CO* 6:280–291. Bernard is mentioned in the conclusion (291), but not previously.

[146]*CO* 6:280–285, 290, Origen, Tertullian, Irenaeus, Hilary, and Basil.

[147]*CO* 6:288.1

suffice. The common agreement of the church is not found in the private opinions of a few writers.[148]

These vague statements are made more specific in one instance. Calvin juxtaposes a series of statements from Hilary, quoted by Pighius, and canons from the Council of Orange that condemn those views. He then challenges Pighius' claim that Hilary represents the official tradition of the church.[149] The Council of Orange so effectively undermined Pighius' claim that Calvin twice returns to it.[150] It also encouraged him to claim against Pighius that there is no such thing as a lasting consensus of teaching in the church on this matter.[151] Finally, Calvin quotes Augustine's observation that those who wrote before the rise of the Pelagian controversy are not the best guides because they were not forced to address the points at issue.[152]

Calvin concludes his second book by briefly surveying the disputed fathers.[153] The Clementine *Recognitions* are counterfeit. Irenaeus and Tertullian wrote about human nature as originally created. Ambrose and Basil, he claims, offer little support to Pighius. Origen is an unreliable witness.[154] This leaves Pighius with Hilary (who is refuted by the Council of Orange), Jerome (who was more careful after the rise of Pelagius), and Chrysostom (whom Calvin would not defend). Finally, Calvin claims that Bernard, mentioned elsewhere by Pighius, is predominantly on his side.

In addition to appealing to the consent of the fathers, Pighius seeks to identify the Reformers' teaching with that of the early heretics.[155] Calvin denies the charge, contrasting his own teaching with that of the heretics as set out by Augustine.[156] He also regularly accuses Pighius of Pelagianism, [157] as well as once, more imaginatively, calling him a Manichee![158]

Calvin, in the 1539 *Institutio*, claimed the support of Augustine, a claim which Pighius denies. He accuses Calvin of quoting Augustine out of context and without understanding him, of quoting mutilated passages contrary to Augustine's meaning.[159] Calvin was stung by this charge and took care that his third

---

[148] *CO* 6:277, 288. [149] *CO* 6:288–89. [150] *CO* 6:305, 363–64.
[151] *CO* 6:289–90. [152] *CO* 6:290. [153] *CO* 6:290–91.
[154] Calvin, *CO* 6:291, accuses Origen of heresy, drawing on the judgment of Jerome, but was unaware that Origen had been condemned by an ecumenical council, an argument that he could not have failed to use had he been aware of it. He also refers to 'those crazy ideas of Tertullian and Origen which we all equally reject' (*CO* 6:278), but shows no awareness that Tertullian's status as a Catholic church father might be questioned.
[155] Pighius, *De libero arbitrio* fols.16b-17b, 19a, 72b–73a.
[156] *CO* 6:260–264, 308–9, 350–51.
[157] *CO* 6:304, 336, 338–39, 360, 363–65, 372, 384, 397.
[158] *CO* 6:361.
[159] Pighius, *De libero arbitrio*, fols.37a-b, 64a.

book would not face such an accusation.[160] He quotes lengthy passages with reference to their context. He concludes the book with extended quotations from some of Augustine's last works, and ends by stressing that these are not mutilated, maimed statements.[161] Calvin also responds by accusing Pighius of twisting Augustine and, in one place, of inserting his own phrase into a quotation.[162]

But the dispute over Augustine hung on more than accusations of dishonest exegesis. Both men recognized the importance of discerning the changes in Augustine's position. Pighius divided his writings into three groups: those before the Pelagian controversy, those written during the heat of the controversy, and those written on the subject without polemical heat.[163] Calvin was happy to accept this division, though with one qualification.[164] Pighius tried to minimize the effect of the anti-Pelagian works by suggesting that Augustine's teaching there was sometimes excessively one-sided because of his polemic. He wanted, therefore, to place more reliance upon the works from the third stage. This was an unwise move in that Augustine's last writings are more consistently "Augustinian" than some of the earlier anti-Pelagian writings. It is interesting that neither writer acknowledges the fact, noted by Augustine himself, that the fundamental shift in his thought took place not with the beginning of the Pelagian controversy but nearly twenty years earlier, in the mid-390s.[165]

Pighius quotes at length from Augustine's anti-Manichean works.[166] Calvin responds, mainly by interpreting these in the light of Augustine's *Retractationes*.[167] The author of the *Retractationes* and Calvin both had the same aim: to bring these writings as far as possible into harmony with Augustine's mature views. For each of them, this is essentially an exercise in damage limitation. Many statements about free will are referred to human nature as originally created, on the grounds that this was the issue against the Manichees. Augustine himself excused the paucity of reference to original sin and the corruption of fallen human nature on the grounds that he was then debating the Manichees, who did not accept the Old Testament.[168] As a last resort, Calvin concedes that the young, anti-Manichean Augustine still had much to learn about grace, a deficiency that the Pelagian controversy would help to resolve.[169]

---

[160]He responds to these charges in *CO* 6:292–294, 337, the specific passages mentioned by Pighius.
    [161]*CO* 6:320–326.   [162]*CO* 6:299, 307, 314–15.
    [163]Pighius, *De libero arbitrio*, fols. 37b–38a.
    [164]*CO* 6:294, 297.
    [165]*De praedestinatione sanctorum* 4:8. Cf. Eugene TeSelle, *Augustine the Theologian* (London: Burns & Oates, 1970), 156–65, 176–82.
    [166]Pighius, *De libero arbitrio* fols.38b–47a.
    [167]*CO* 6:294–301.   [168]*CO* 6:297.   [169]*CO* 6:297, 301.

Pighius then moves to the anti-Pelagian works.[170] Calvin is very happy to fight on this ground, though he rejected Pighius' attempt to weaken the force of these writings.[171] Here it is Pighius who is on the defensive, accusing Augustine of a sophistry unworthy of him.[172] Calvin responds with a thorough examination of the works cited by Pighius, as well as other Augustinian works. He argues that where Augustine speaks of fallen humanity as free, he means by this not that good and evil are equally in our power, but rather that our choices are voluntary. This is true despite our being subject to a necessity to sin. Finally, Pighius turns to the third group of writings. Calvin finds much material for his cause here and suggests that the whole controversy should be settled on the basis of Augustine's last works.[173]

Much of the battle revolved around language. Augustine, when his views changed, continued to affirm both free will and free choice, but redefined them. This enabled him to claim considerable continuity both with earlier writers and with his own early writings, as in the *Retractationes.* Calvin, like Luther, adopted a different strategy. Already in the 1539 *Institutio* he affirmed that he believed in the freedom of the will as it is understood by Augustine, but did not wish to retain the term.[174] Calvin repeats this in his response to Pighius, defining precisely the senses in which the will is and is not free.[175] But Pighius treats passages where Augustine affirms free choice as refutations of Calvin and the latter has to devote much energy to refuting this. There might have been less heat and more light had Calvin been willing to follow Augustine's approach and to affirm free choice, while defining it carefully.

III. Conclusions

What conclusions can we draw? Here is Calvin's second most important work as regards his use of the fathers. He makes use of at least seven, probably nearer ten, patristic volumes. He also draws on his extensive earlier reading of the fathers and at least some current reading. Drawing on these resources, and making the most of the material presented by his opponent, he puts together an impressive case—the more impressive when one remembers the shortness of time at his disposal. He displays a thorough mastery of the anti-Pelagian Augustine. With the other fathers he shows himself a skilled debater who could argue a good case with minimal resources at his disposal.

[170]Pighius, *De libero arbitrio* fols.47a–53a.
[171]CO 6:301–312.   [172]Pighius, *De libero arbitrio* fol. 47b; CO 6:301–2.
[173]CO 6:312–26.
[174]OS 3:249–251 (*Inst.* 2:2:7–8). Cf. A. N. S. Lane, "Did Calvin Believe in Freewill?" *Vox Evangelica* 12 (1981): 72–90.
[175]CO 6:279–80, 292–93, 311–13.

Table of Works Used in Calvin's Bondage and Liberation of the Will

WORK OR COUNCIL	USED	SOURCE	NAMED BY CALVIN	NOT NAMED BUT CITED BY CALVIN	NAMED BY PIGHIUS & REFERRED TO BY CALVIN	QUOTED BY PIGHIUS (W/O NAMING THEN & REFERRED TO BY CALVIN)	NAMED BY CALVIN IN 1539 INST. & REFERRED TO IN BONDAGE	UNNAMED BUT CLEAR INTERMEDIATE SOURCES OF CALVIN'S QUOTATION
Augustine								
De civitate dei	Probably not	Memory	X					
Confessiones	No	1539 Institutio		X				
De correptione et gratia	Yes	Augustine (Erasmus, ed.), vol. 7	X					
De dono perseverantiae	Yes	Augustine (Erasmus, ed.), vol. 7	X					
De duabus animabus	No	Pighius, De libero arbitrio, Augustine, Retractationes	X					
Enarrationes in Psalmos	Probably not	Memory	X					
Enchiridion	Yes	Augustine (Erasmus, ed.), vol. 3	X					
Epistolae	Yes	Augustine (Erasmus, ed.), vol. 2	X					
In evangelium Iohannis tractatus	Probably not	1539 Institutio, Pighius, De libero arbitrio, Memory	X					
Contra Faustum manichaeum	Probably not	Pighius, De lib. arb. + Memory	X					
De actis cum Felice manichaeo	No	Pighius, De libero arbitrio	X					
De gratia Christi et de peccato originali	Yes	Augustine (Erasmus, ed.), vol. 7	X					
De gratia et libero arbitrio	Yes	Augustine (Erasmus, ed.), vol. 7	X					
De haeresibus	Yes	Augustine (Erasmus, ed.), vol. 6	X					

WORK OR COUNCIL	USED	SOURCE	NAMED BY CALVIN	NOT NAMED BUT CITED BY CALVIN	NAMED BY PIGHIUS & REFERRED TO BY CALVIN	QUOTED BY PIGHIUS (w/o NAMING THEN & REFERRED TO BY CALVIN	NAMED BY CALVIN IN 1539 INST. & REFERRED TO IN BONDAGE	UNNAMED BUT CLEAR INTERMEDIATE SOURCES OF CALVIN'S QUOTATION
Contra Julianum	Cannot say	Augustine (Erasmus, ed.), vol. 7 or Memory	X					
De libero arbitrio	No	Pighius, De libero arbitrio, Augustine, Retractationes	X					
De natura et gratia	Yes	Augustine (Erasmus, ed.), vol. 7	X					
De peccatorum meritis et remissione	Yes	Augustine (Erasmus, ed.), vol. 7	X					
Contra duas epistolas pelagianorum	Yes	Augustine (Erasmus, ed.), vol. 7	X					
De perfectione iustitiae hominis	Yes	Augustine (Erasmus, ed.), vol. 7	X					
De praedestinatione sanctorum	Yes	Augustine (Erasmus, ed.), vol. 7	X					
De quantitatae animae	No	Pighius, De libero arbitrio	X					
Retractiones	Yes	Augustine (Erasmus, ed.), vol. 1	X					
De spiritu et littera	Yes	Augustine (Erasmus, ed.), vol. 3	X					
De vera religione	No	Pighius, De libero arbitrio, Augustine, Retractationes	X					
PSEUDO-AUGUSTINE								
De dogmatibus ecclesiasticis	Yes	Augustine (Erasmus, ed.), vol. 3	X					
Hypognosticon	Yes	Augustine (Erasmus, ed.), vol. 7	X					
Sermo 236	No	Pighius, De libero arbitrio					X	
AMBROSE								
Expositio evangelii secundum Lucam	No	Augustine	X					
De fuga saeculi	No	Augustine	X					

WORK OR COUNCIL	USED	SOURCE	NAMED BY CALVIN	NOT NAMED BUT CITED BY CALVIN	NAMED BY PIGHIUS & REFERRED TO BY CALVIN	QUOTED BY PIGHIUS (w/o NAMING THEN & REFERRED TO BY CALVIN	NAMED BY CALVIN IN 1539 INST. & REFERRED TO IN BONDAGE	UNNAMED BUT CLEAR INTERMEDIATE SOURCES OF CALVIN'S QUOTATION
De Jacob et vita beata	Probably	Paris: Chevallon, 1529 or 1539, edition of Ambrose		x	x			
BASIL								
Homiliae	Yes	Froben edition		x	x			
Homiliae in Psalmos	Yes	Froben edition		x				
Constitutiones asceticae	No	Pighius, *De lib. arb.*			x			
PSEUDO-BASIL								
De libero arbitrio	Yes	Froben edition		x				
BERNARD								
De gratia et libero arbitrio	No	1539 *Institutio* + Memory		x				
CASSIODORE								
Historia tripartita	Probably not	Memory						x
CHRYSOSTOM								
Homiliae in Genesim	No	1539 *Institutio*, Pighius, *De libero arbitrio*			x			
Homiliae in Matthaeum	No	1539 *Institutio*		x				
Homilia de ferendis reprehensionibus	No	1539 *Institutio*		x				
PSEUDO-CHRYSOSTOM								
Homilia in dominica I adventus domini	No	1539 *Institutio*					x	
CLEMENT								
Epistolae	No	Eusebius	x					
PSEUDO-CLEMENT								
Recognitiones	Probably	Edition	x					
CYPRIAN								
De dominica oratione	No	Augustine		x				
Testimonia	No	Augustine		x				

WORK OR COUNCIL	USED	SOURCE	NAMED BY CALVIN	NOT NAMED BUT CITED BY CALVIN	NAMED BY PIGHIUS & REFERRED TO BY CALVIN	QUOTED BY PIGHIUS (w/o NAMING THEN & REFERRED TO BY CALVIN)	NAMED BY CALVIN IN 1539 INST. & REFERRED TO IN BONDAGE	UNNAMED BUT CLEAR INTERMEDIATE SOURCES OF CALVIN'S QUOTATION
CYRIL								
Commentarius in Joannis evangelium	No	Pighius, *De libero arbitrio*				X		
EUSEBIUS								
Historia ecclesiae	Probably not	Memory	X					
HILARY								
Tractatus super Psalmos	No	Pighius, *De libero arbitrio*			X			
IRENAEUS								
Adversus Haereses	Probably	Edition		X				
JEROME								
Adversus Jovinianum	No	Augustine; 1539 *Institutio*, Pighius, *De libero arbitrio*				X		
Dialogi contra Pelagianos	No	1539 *Institutio*						X
Epistolae	No	1539 *Institutio*, Pighius, *De libero arbitrio* + memory	X					
Questiones hebraicae in Genesim	No	Pighius, *De libero arbitrio*			X			
ORIGEN								
De principiis	No	Pighius, *De libero arbitrio*			X			
PAMPHILUS								
Apologia pro Origene	No	Pighius, *De libero arbitrio*			X			
PETER LOMBARD								
Sententiae	No	1539 *Institutio*						X
PROSPER								
De vocatione gentium	No	Pighius, *De libero arbitrio*			X			
RUFINUS								
De adulteratione librorum Origenis	Probably not	Memory	X					

WORK OR COUNCIL	USED	SOURCE	NAMED BY CALVIN	NOT NAMED BUT CITED BY CALVIN	NAMED BY PIGHIUS & REFERRED TO BY CALVIN	QUOTED BY PIGHIUS (W/O NAMING THEN & REFERRED TO BY CALVIN	NAMED BY CALVIN IN 1539 INST. & REFERRED TO IN BONDAGE	UNNAMED BUT CLEAR INTERMEDIATE SOURCES OF CALVIN'S QUOTATION
TERTULLIAN								
Adversus Marcionem	No	Pighius, *De libero arbitrio*	x					
De praescriptione hereticorum	Probably not	Memory	x					
THEODORET								
Historia ecclesiae	No	Cassiodore		x				
COUNCILS								
Carthage (416)	Yes	Crabbe, *Concilia Omnia*	x					
Milevis (416)	Yes	Crabbe, *Concilia Omnia*	x					
Carthage (418)	Yes	Crabbe, *Concilia Omnia*	x					
Africanum	Yes	Crabbe, *Concilia Omnia*	x					
Orange (529)	Yes	Crabbe, *Concilia Omnia*	x					

Calvin's Polemic: Foundational Convictions in the Service of God's Truth

Charles Partee

A STUDY OF JOHN CALVIN'S POLEMICAL THEOLOGY begins with the recognition that among the categories of the western intellectual tradition which Calvin accepts with considerable passion and without serious question is the distinction between truth and falsity. According to Calvin, the confidence in Christ's victory over opposition "should greatly encourage us never to break in our defense of truth, but to be sure of success. It will often happen that the enemy continue their wild assaults to the very last; but at length God has their frenzy turn back upon their own heads and despite all, truth comes out victorious."[1] Truth is assumed to be the correspondence between human thought and divine reality, and Calvin's claim to expound this truth is so constant that it is easy to overlook. For example, Calvin asserts that "the theologian's task is ... to strengthen consciences by teaching things true, sure, and profitable."[2] Thus he declares, "I most religiously endeavored to deliver divine truth purely and sincerely."[3] Moreover Calvin cries out against Joachim Westphal, the Lutheran pastor who wrote against Calvin concerning the Lord's supper, "I appeal to thee, O Christ, the Son of God, supreme Judge of the world, whose authority is dreaded by devils themselves, that thou wouldst make it manifest now and on that day whether my mind has ever entertained the mad thought of tainting thy doctrine by any falsehood."[4]

The declared intention of Calvin's theology, then, is the presentation of the truth of God, and the defense of God's truth is the purpose of his polemic. Clearly the latter depends on the former in that Calvin's polemical writings are motivated by his conviction that dangerous falsehoods which claim to be truth must be exposed as lies. Calvin's narrower polemical targets cannot be isolated from his broader theological aims because they are interrelated aspects of the same real-

---

[1]Com. Mk. 12.34 (*CO* 45.616).

[2]*Inst.* 1. 14.4 (*OS* 3.157.11–13). The citations in English of the *Institutes* are from *Calvin: Institutes of the Christian Religion,* trans. Ford Lewis Battles, ed. John T. McNeill, Library of Christian Classics, vols. 20, 21 (Philadelphia: Westminster Press, 1960).

[3]Joachim Westphal, *Second Defense of the Sacraments,* 2:278 (*CO* 9:71) (hereafter cited Westphal, treatise no.: page no.). The three treatises against Westphal are cited from volume 2 of *Selected Works of John Calvin,* ed. and trans. Henry Beveridge (1849; reprinted Grand Rapids: Baker, 1983).

[4]Westphal, 3:475 (*CO* 9:237). Earlier, when responding to Westphal, Calvin claims "for myself this praise, that there is scarcely an individual who can take more pleasure than I do in a candid confession of the truth"; see Westphal 1:222 (*CO* 9:16).

ity—the service of God's truth. Since Calvin's polemical opposition is based on his dogmatical affirmations, obviously, the most basic, as well as most sweeping theological question, is Calvin's understanding of the truth of God and the crucial polemical question is the application of this truth to specific errors.

This essay addresses Calvin's concept of truth in part 1, the content of truth in part II, and the application of truth in part 3. It argues that since Calvin's view of truth is not precisely defined, his polemical stances are necessarily difficult to predict. The explanation suggested for this situation is that Calvin's most fundamental theological doctrines are based on unquestioned convictions and heartfelt certainties rather than on articulated, principled positions for which arguments are advanced.[5] Among these foundational convictions—or fundamental doctrines—are (1) the precedence of Word above Church, (2) of Faith before Love, and (3) (what might be called) the continuing flesh of Christ.

I. THE CONCEPT OF TRUTH

Calvin assumes that truth is an absolute category.[6] Additionally, he seldom questions and never fundamentally addresses his own ability to distinguish between truth and its opposite. Thus, while Calvin discusses the content of truth at great length, he devotes scant attention to the category of truth and how it is known. Calvin takes for granted that God's truth certainly exists, can be truly known, and must be both presented and defended by those with gifts to do so. This twofold

---

[5]Cf. *Inst.* 1.5.9 (*OS* 3:53.10–14). The recent discussion of Calvin as rhetorician rather than dialectician permits interpreters to understand his theology more as persuasion than demonstration. However, the need remains to identify Calvin's foundational convictions as well as his fundamental doctrines—and their relationships. According to Thomas F. Torrance, *The Hermeneutics of John Calvin* (Edinburgh: Scottish Academic Press, 1988), 63, if the appeal to God's Word is disregarded then "the appeal must be beyond all ecclesiastical or Biblical citation to the truth of God (*Veritas Dei*) itself for that is the ultimate authority upon which all must cast themselves and upon which everyone must rely. Ultimately it is by reference to that Truth [capital in original] directly that judgment must be passed upon the truth or error of theological interpretation or statement." A stronger statement on the centrality of "Truth" for Calvin would be difficult to imagine. However, instead of pursuing the *content of truth*, Torrance turns to "*questions of method* in interpretation or in determining the truth of doctrine" (emphasis added, see ibid., 64–65).

[6]This assumption is no longer widely shared. For example, Allan Bloom, *The Closing of the American Mind* (New York: Simon & Schuster, 1987), 1, observes, "There is one thing a professor can be absolutely certain of: almost every student entering the university believes, or says he believes, that truth is relative." Peter Berger, *A Rumor of Angels* (Garden City, N.Y.: Doubleday, 1969), 144, writes, "There is also a fact in the realm of human consciousness, namely the relativization of beliefs and values, which … is endemic to the modern situation." Yet William J. Bouwsma, "Renaissance and Reformation: An Essay in Their Affinities and Connections," *Luther and the Dawn of the Modern Era*, ed. Heiko Obermann (Leiden: E. J. Brill, 1974), 131, uses "the relativity of truth" to characterize the Renaissance view as opposed to scholasticism. The contemporary discussion of "truth" involves questions such as "the impossibility of literal predication in theology" and "the possibility of irreducible metaphor in talk about God." See William P. Alston, *Divine Nature and Human Language: Essays in Philosophical Theology* (Ithaca: Cornell University Press, 1989), chaps. 1, 2.

understanding of the pastor's task is expressed in his *Reply to Sadoleto*: "For then only do pastors edify the church, when, besides leading docile souls to Christ, placidly, as with the hand, they are also armed to repel the machinations of those who strive to impede the work of God."[7] Obviously, it is Calvin's purpose to expound the truth of God in his theological writings and to defend against falsehood in his polemical writings.

According to Calvin, a preconceived conviction of God's truth is the foundation of faith which he defines as the knowledge of God's will toward us perceived in his Word.[8] In the same exposition Calvin defines faith in more trinitarian terms as a certain knowledge of divine benevolence founded upon the truth in Christ, revealed to our minds and sealed upon our hearts through the Holy Spirit.[9] In other places Calvin declares that the Lord Christ is truth,[10] that truth flows from God,[11] that the Spirit of God is the sole fountain of truth,[12] that Scripture is unassailable truth,[13] that truth is not sustained by external props but serves as its own support,[14] and that the church is the faithful keeper of God's truth.[15] This truth Calvin intends to present and defend although he does not analyze or synthesize his assertions about its nature.

Nevertheless, in spite of his intention, strong objections were raised to some of Calvin's teachings, and he was obliged to deal with the fact that common agreement on theological truth could not always be achieved. Recognizing that disagreements often lead to disunity, Calvin expresses his abiding concern that "among Christians there ought to be so great a dislike of schism, as that they may always avoid it so far as it lies in their power."[16] Ideally, then, Christians should agree completely, but since that is impossible, Calvin allows for error in matters which do not affect what he calls the sum of religion. Thus he writes: "First and foremost, we should agree on all points. But since all men are somewhat beclouded with ignorance, either we must leave no church remaining or we must condone delusion in those matters which can go unknown without harm to the sum of religion (*summa religionis*) and without loss of salvation."[17] Unfortunately, Calvin does not identify exactly the doctrines which constitute the sum of religion nor those delusions which must be gently condoned rather than vigorously denounced. In short, Calvin offers no precise conceptual guidance for iden-

---

[7]To Sadoleto, 29 (*OS* 1:460). The letters (1) from Sadoleto and (2) to Sadoleto are cited from vol. 1 of the *Selected Works of John Calvin*.
[8]*Inst*. 3.2.6 (*OS* 4:15.12–13): *Huius autem fundamentum est, praesumpta de veritate Dei persuasio.*
[9]*Inst*. 3.2.7 (*OS* 4:16.31–35).   [10]*Inst*. 2.8.31 (*OS* 3:373.17–18).   [11]*Inst*. 1.2.1 (*OS* 3:34,35).
[12]*Inst*. 2.2.15 (*OS* 3.258.14–18).   [13]*Inst*. 1.7.5 (*OS* 3:70.32).   [14]*Inst*. 1.8.1 (*OS* 3:72.27–29).
[15]*Inst*. 4.1.10 (*OS* 5:15.3–4).   [16]Letter of 24 Oct. 1538 (*CO* 10: 275).
[17]*Inst*. 4.1.12 (*OS* 5:16:21–25).

tifying the truth in such a way that disagreements about its nature could be adjudicated.

One possible response to disagreement about true doctrine would be an abiding mutual humility, a virtue which Calvin regards very highly but tends to recommend of our relation to God more than our attitude toward each other.[18] Calvin acknowledges that "God has never so blessed his servants that they each possessed full and perfect knowledge of every part of their subject. It is clear that his purpose in so limiting our knowledge was first that we should be kept humble, and also that we should continue to have dealings with our fellows."[19] Again he asserts, "I do not dream of a perspicacity of faith which never errs in discriminating between truth and falsehood. On the contrary, I admit that pious and truly religious minds do not always attain to all the mysteries of God, but are sometimes blind in the clearest matters—the Lord, doubtless, so providing, in order to accustom them to modesty and submission."[20]

In addition to humility, according to Calvin, strong disagreements about the truth call for something like patience with each other. Calvin suggests a truly pious person will sometimes rather suspend judgment than separate by dissent on slight grounds from one who otherwise knows Christ and his Word[21] Calvin admits that if he personally did not choose to bear many attacks he would spend all his time writing to correct them. "Now, I confess that we should patiently endure many false accusations, and keep silent when we are maligned, and it is known all over the world that we practice this doctrine. For otherwise we should always have the pen in hand, considering how many of the maligners do not cease to disparage us."[22] Thus, on some occasions, in humility and patience Calvin acknowledges disagreements about the truth of God, expresses his willingness to accept instruction, discusses the degrees of his convictions, and offers his best judgment concerning the debatable issue. However, these are attitudes adopted on certain occasions and not a settled strategy for dealing with disagreements about the truth. At some times Calvin recognizes the need for humility and patience. At other times strong polemic is required. The theoretical distinction between these times is impossible to determine without an adequate definition of Calvin's view of truth and its relation to the sum of religion.

Another possible way for Calvin to understand conflicts about the truth is the application of the notion of things indifferent or *adiaphora* to some of them.[23]

---

[18]*Inst.* 2.2.11 (*OS* 3:253.29–30).   [19]Dedication of Romans (*CO* 10:405).
[20]To Sadoleto, 53–54 (*OS* 1: 478). [21]To Sadoleto, 54 (*OS* 1:478–79).
[22]Letter of 20 Feb. 1555 (*CO* 15:436).
[23]See T. W. Street, *John Calvin on Adiaphora: An Exposition* (doctoral dissertation, Union Seminary in New York, 1954). Also, E. F. Meylan, "The Stoic Doctrine of Indifferent Things …," *Romantic Review* 8 (1937): 135–45.

Presumably there could be doctrinal formulations which, being only partially true, are finally inadequate but not exactly—and therefore not dangerously—false. Since Calvin applies the notion of *adiaphora* to ethical and ceremonial matters,[24] the idea of things indifferent is available to modify the sharp dichotomy between true and false. That is, Calvin could regard some ideas as indifferent not merely in *use* but in *reality* (metaphysical adiaphora). Additionally, there might be ideas which humans must consider as indifferent because no one is able to determine their truth or falsity (epistemological adiaphora). Calvin does not consider these options and, although he mentions it at least once when predictably he objects to including the doctrines of Trinity, predestination, and free grace as *choses indifférentes*,[25] he does not utilize the idea of doctrinal adiaphora at all. In his heart Calvin seems to believe that no doctrine which he considers as certain and important could ever be regarded as anything less than true.

The possibility of a category of doctrinal adiaphora between those of true and false is not the same issue as fundamental versus nonessential doctrines. Nevertheless, Calvin charges Philip Melanchthon with extending "the distinction of nonessentials (*res medias et indifferentes*) too far. Several of those things which you consider indifferent are obviously repugnant to the word of God." He continues the admonition in the confidence that Paul, like Calvin himself, contends for the truth of God, and tells Melanchthon, "I would prefer to die with you a hundred times rather than to see you surviving the doctrines you surrendered."[26] Although on such issues as predestination and free will Calvin seems to have exercised a certain charity and forbearance, and in spite of the fact that Calvin has the highest regard for Melanchthon's scholarship[27] and cherishes his friendship, Calvin's perception of truth here denies Melanchthon the right to decide on things indifferent.

Most philosophers and theologians in the western intellectual tradition apply the abstract noun "truth" to intellectual constructions as the highest accolade. For Calvin the recognition and consequences of learned disagreements about theological truth do not modify and are not incorporated into a theory of truth which could be evaluated or utilized. For example, in discussing the will of God, Calvin admits "we do not grasp how God wills to take place what he forbids to be done." In explanation Calvin reminds us first of our mental incapacity and then that the light in which God dwells is unapproachable before concluding "in a wonderful and ineffable manner nothing is done without God's will, not even that which is

---

[24]For the former see *Inst.* 3.19.7–8 (*OS* 4.286:27–28). For the latter see *Inst.* 4.10.22. (*OS* 5.184. 30) and *Inst.*4.17 43. (*OS* 5:408.20).

[25]Letter of 20 Feb. 1555 (*CO* 15:441)

[26]Letter of 18 June 1550 (*CO* 13:594, 595).   [27]Westphal 3, 354 (*CO* 9:147–48).

against his will." According to Calvin, the proposal that two contrary wills exist in God is a cavil "not hurled against me but against the Holy Spirit."[28] It is not clear to what conceptualization of truth Calvin is appealing when he claims to represent the Holy Spirit in teaching the singularity of the will of God. In other words, the specific concept of truth which Calvin employs, and by which error is identified, while both passionately assumed and asserted, is never precisely defined. If, therefore, Calvin does not develop a concept of truth which provides adequate guidance in theological disputes, we would seem to be entirely dependent on his exposition of the content of truth to which we turn in part 2.

II. THE CONTENT OF TRUTH

Calvin devotes an immense effort to expounding the content of God's truth. Indeed all his work contributes to that end. However, the judgment of degrees of truth and error requires the application of some kind of manageable standard of evaluation. That is to say, the identification of truth and error would seem—if not based on a clear concept of truth external to the exposition—to depend on the clear content of truth internal to the exposition. Doubtless, Calvin intends the *Institutes of the Christian Religion* as a compendium of the truth of God, but it would be extremely helpful to possess Calvin's own summary of essential elements since using the whole *Institutes* as a standard is extremely unwieldy—if it is not impossible.

In this context Calvin, unlike Luther,[29] does not advance one doctrine as first in a hierarchy of essential truths nor develop a single doctrine in such a way that the adequacy of other doctrines could be measured by fidelity to it. In the past students of Calvin responded to this situation by asserting the sovereignty or glory or honor of God as Calvin's central dogma and expounding his theology in terms of it. More recently Alfred Göhler spoke for many in concluding, "There is no central doctrine in the theology of Calvin; rather all his doctrines are central doctrines in the sense that from their own standpoint they aim to understand independently what is central."[30] Having declared there is no central doctrine in Calvin, Göhler unfortunately does not explain the intriguing reference to "what is central."

---

[28]*Inst.* 1.18.2 (*OS* 3:224: 3–7).
[29]Luther declares justification to be the "master and prince, the lord, the ruler, and judge over all kinds of doctrines"; see WA 39.1. 205. According to Einar Billig, *Our Calling*, trans. Conrad Bergendoff (Rock Island, Ill.: Augustana Book Concern, 1950), 7, "Whoever knows Luther, even but partially, knows that his various thoughts do not lie alongside each other, like pearls on a string, held together only by common authority or perchance by a line of logical argument, but they all, as tightly as the petals of a rosebud, adhere to a common center, and radiate out like the rays of the sun from *one* glowing core, namely the gospel of the forgiveness of sins."
[30]Alfred Göhler, *Calvins Lehre von der Heiligung* (Munich: Chr. Kaiser Verlag, 1934), 81. See also Alister McGrath, *A Life of John Calvin* (Cambridge, Mass: Basil Blackwell, 1990), 147–48.

Göhler is also representative of much Calvin scholarship in awarding the subject of his own study a special importance, affirming "the central place of sanctification in the perception and interest of Calvin."[31] This trait leads Wilhelm Niesel to conclude, "There is hardly an aspect of theology which someone or other has not considered as quite specially typical for Calvin's doctrine." Niesel himself suggests the Christological formula of Chalcedon as Calvin's basic paradigm.[32] Nevertheless the insuperable difficulty with all attempts to find Calvin's starting point remains that without strong textual support provided by Calvin himself, every suggestion about the central dogma—however helpful—will remain an evaluation rather than an exposition of Calvin's theology.

If, then, Calvin does not exposit the truth from the point of view of a clearly defined central dogma, one might expect the existence of a declared or undeclared set of doctrines which could be called "fundamental" and by reference to which the truth could be judged. That is, in the absence of a central dogma, a cluster of essential doctrines would serve the same purpose. In dealing with Calvin's thought scholars have often studied specific doctrines or groups of doctrines, asserted their historical and theological significance, and then traced their relationships within Calvin's total theology. In contrast other scholars have surveyed Calvin's entire theology from various perspectives and have come to differing conclusions. While the former works presumably suggest aspects, the latter should contain all of "the essence of Calvin's theology" but the reader is ordinarily left alone to extract the essentials.

Occasionally, however, a Calvin scholar offers to abstract "the main emphases and chief peculiarities of Calvin's theology." They are, according to Williston Walker: (1) The sovereignty and glory of God (2) Who is known to faith as revealed in the Word by the Holy Spirit. (3) All men in their fallen state are totally depraved, but (4) The work of Christ effects the salvation of some (5) Who being justified seek to live the Christian life (6) In the Church.[33]

Such synoptic summaries of Calvin's theology may be useful for certain purposes, but they do not purport to represent Calvin's own understanding of foundational doctrines and must be evaluated as conclusions traceable to the mind of the scholar who produces them. In short, the attempt to expound the fundamental doctrines of Calvin's theology suffers the same problem as the search for a central dogma. As Calvin himself never adequately identifies a central dogma,

---

[31]Göhler, *Calvins Lehre*, 105.

[32]Wilhelm Niesel, *The Theology of Calvin*, trans. Harold Knight (Philadelphia: Westminster, 1956), 247.

[33]Williston Walker, *John Calvin: The Organiser of Reformed Protestantism* (1906; reprinted New York: Schocken Books, 1969), 424, 409–28.

likewise he does not designate an adequate set of essential doctrines. Nevertheless, there is one sharp difference. While Calvin does not recognize or articulate the need for a central dogma, he does declare the importance of a central set of dogmas!

Strangely, the three references to the necessity of essential doctrines contained in the *Institutes* are quite casual and extremely brief. The first mention occurs in a discussion of purgatory and presents for reflection only the phrase itself: "the principal and necessary doctrines of the faith."[34] The second citation is not more specific in content and uses terms both singular (doctrine) and plural (articles). However, a vivid conclusion indicates the seriousness of the issue in Calvin's mind. In discussing the false and true church, Calvin says that fellowship should be maintained with those whose errors "do not harm the chief doctrine of religion," or "the articles of religion on which all believers ought to agree." Then Calvin adds, that when "the sum of necessary doctrine is overturned ... the death of the church follows—just as a man's life is ended when his throat is pierced or his heart mortally wounded."[35] In spite of the dramatic and violent images of the cut throat and heart attacked, the first two references are too vague to be helpful. They mention the necessity of essential doctrines but do not develop the subject. With only these two references one might conclude that Calvin means by the sum of necessary doctrine something like a generalized form of the Apostles' Creed. The references to various doctrines as fundamental which are scattered through his writings might then be understood as no more than a way of calling attention to the importance of the doctrine being expounded.[36]

However, the third reference is fuller. In discussing the marks of the true church Calvin says that any society which has a pure ministry of the Word and a pure celebration of the sacraments may be safely embraced as church. However, he immediately qualifies this comment by insisting that faults which damage the purity of word and sacrament ought not to estrange us from communion with

---

[34]*Inst.* 3.5.9 (*OS* 4:143.1–2).   [35]*Inst.* 4.2.1 (*OS* 5:31.1–3).

[36]In Com. Eph. 2.20 (*CO* 51, 175) Calvin says, "Christ is the only foundation since he alone supports the whole church." Also Com. 1 Pet. 2.6 (*CO* 55: 235). Com. Acts 8:5 (*CO* 48:177): "[T]he whole substance of the Gospel is comprehended in Christ." Faith, justification, sanctification, election — this is the *principium* of our Christianity according to Com. 2 Pet. 1:9 (*CO* 55, 448). At Com. 2 Tim. 2:18 (*CO* 54, 161) resurrection is called "*le principal article de nostre foy.*" In a personal letter of 16 Sept. 1994 Ulrich Mauser raises this important point: "Is it possible that Calvin felt carried along by the general agreement of a truly Catholic—not Roman— consensus and for that reason saw no need to establish some hierarchy of essential, less essential, and subordinate doctrines down to adiaphora?" Calvin certainly believes he is presenting the holy, catholic, and apostolic doctrine in its truth, and it may well be that at the deepest levels of his thinking he did not make distinctions between true and essentially true doctrines. Still a complex totality like theology is made up of parts and both construction and interpretation requires discrimination—even if unacknowledged—between what is foundational and what is not.

those in a defective church. The reason for continuing fellowship is that "*not all the articles of true doctrine are of the same sort.*" Some doctrines are *more necessary* to know than others. In contrast to these necessary doctrines some disputed doctrines, such as the place of the soul after death, are *nonessential* matters and do not break the unity of faith. In addition to recognizing the category of "nonessential doctrines," Calvin also apparently means that not all true doctrine is essential doctrine. In other words some true doctrines are more fundamental than other true doctrines!

Then Calvin offers examples of what he means by "the proper principles of religion." They are: "[1] God is one; [2] Christ is God and the Son of God; [3] our salvation rests in God's mercy; [4] and the like."[37] It is worth noting that this short statement ending with the remarkably vague imprecision of "and the like" is quite astonishing when compared with the confident ferocity of later debates about "the essentials of reformed theology" among Calvin's descendants. In citing these three doctrines as proper principles of religion Calvin does not explain the criteria by which they were selected nor how they are related to each other or to the wider body of true but nonessential doctrines. Moreover, Calvin does not specify the additional doctrines which should be added as fundamental, having indicated by the phrase "and the like" that there are other doctrines associated with these in his mind.

The reality and necessity of essential doctrines is also expressed in the Commentary on 1 Corinthians where Calvin writes, "We must pay attention to the order of doing things, so that a start may be made with general doctrine, and the

---

[37]*Inst.* 4.1.12–13 (*OS* 5:16: 6–11 ff.). I. John Hesselink, "Calvinus Oecumenicus: Calvin's Vision of the Unity and Catholicity of the Church," *Reformed Review* 44, no. 2 (Winter, 1990), 110, cites this passage and observes, "The inevitable question is, What kinds of doctrines does Calvin have in mind with the phrase, 'and the like'?" Hesselink suggests there is no answer beyond Westphal 2:251 (*CO* 9:50) "which contains a similar but considerably fuller list of what [Calvin] calls 'leading articles' of the Christian faith." The passage reads: "In regard to the one God and his true and legitimate worship, the corruption of human nature, free salvation, the mode of obtaining justification, the office and power of Christ, repentance and its exercises, faith which, relying on the promises of the gospel, gives us assurance of salvation, prayer to God, and other leading articles, the same doctrine is preached by both. We call on one God the Father, trusting to the same Mediator; the same Spirit of adoption is the earnest of our future inheritance. Christ has reconciled us all by the same sacrifice. In that righteousness which he has purchased for us, our minds are at peace, and we glory in the same head. It is strange if Christ, whom we preach as our peace, and who, removing the ground of disagreement, appeased to us our Father in heaven, does not also cause us mutually to cultivate brotherly peace on earth." Hesselink concludes that "[Calvin] was clearly trying to establish a basis for agreement which would include the essential doctrines of the historic faith without excluding anyone unnecessarily" (110–11). On the contrary, it seems to me that Calvin is not expounding, or expanding, his fundamental doctrines as a basis for agreement, but only indicating that many of the same doctrines are already preached by both Swiss and Germans. In this context the phrase "and other leading articles" is just as vague as "and the like."

more essential of the chief points, or the foundation."[38] Again, "A wise teacher has the responsibility of accommodating himself to the power of comprehension of those whom he undertakes to teach, so as to begin with basic elements when instructing the weak and ignorant, and not to move any higher than they can follow. But these rudiments will contain whatever is necessary for knowledge, no less than the fuller instruction given to the stronger."[39]

In this commentary Calvin seems to develop the *Institutes'* list.[40] He says that in spite of all their defects, the Corinthians "held on to the fundamental doctrine (*doctrina fundamentalis*)—[1] the One God was worshiped by them and [2] was invoked in the name of Christ—[3] they rested their confidence of salvation in Christ, and [4] they had a ministry that was not wholly corrupt."[41] The fourth phrase is new and might replace "and the like" in the previous formulation. If so, perhaps Calvin believes that the *Institutes* (as "fuller instruction given to the stronger") explains these heads of doctrine. Thus the proper interpretation of "God is one" is found in book 1. That Christ is God and the Son of God is expounded in book 2. That our salvation rests in God's mercy is developed in book 3, and true ministry is the subject of book 4. In any case, so far as I know, Calvin gives no more extended explanation of the essentials of theology although Calvin's own

---

[38]Com. 1 Cor. 3:12 (*CO* 49,355). The distinction between fundamental and nonessential doctrines was part of the debate between Sebastian Castellio and Calvin. Indeed Roland H. Bainton, "Sebastian Castellio, Champion of Religious Liberty," *Castellioniana* (Leiden: E. J. Brill, 1951), 56, claims, "Fundamentalism originated in the sixteenth century in the interest of liberty," and Castellio was its champion. According to Ferdinand Buisson, *Sébastien Castellion, sa vie et son oeuvre* (Paris: Librairie Hachette, 1892), 2:290, Castellio's view of freedom of conscience as the fundamental and characteristic condition of Christianity fostered a minimum of obligatory belief and a rejection of dogmatic uniformity. Emile Doumergue, *Jean Calvin: Les hommes et les choses de son temps* (Neuilly-sur-Seine: Édition de "La Cause," 1926), 6:430–42, believes that Castellio's view of tolerance is finally based on intellectual skepticism rather than theological commitment. In any case Calvin (and Beza) denied Castellio's application of adiaphora to doctrines such as Trinity, justification, predestination, baptism, and eucharist. It is probably fair to say that modern convictions of the diversity of Scripture, cultural relativism, the rights of individual consciences, and so on—whether called skeptical or enlightened — lead to the inapplicability of the concept of heresy and therefore the loss of a passionate concern for right doctrine. Castellio's preference for right living over right doctrine means that his idea of fundamental doctrines is a maximum reduction rather than a minimum basis for faithful expansion. Hans Martin Stückleberger, "Calvin und Castellio," *Zwingliana*, 7:91–128, addresses interestingly the question why Calvin continues to be studied so industriously if Castellio is the more modern man. See also Etienne Giran, *Sébastien Castellion et la Réforme Calviniste* (Geneva: Slatkin Reprints, 1914, 1970); Stefan Zweig, *The Right To Heresy: Castellio against Calvin*, trans. Eden and Cedar Paul (New York: Viking, 1936) is an interesting diatribe. Calvin's opposition to Castellio, Servetus, and others demonstrates that doctrine cannot avoid involvement with social, ecclesiastical, political, and historical realities and complexities, but this paper is focused on Calvin's own theological definitions.

[39]Com. 1 Cor. 3.2 (*CO* 49:347).

[40]If the *Commentary* offers a more careful discussion than the *Institutes*, McGrath, *Life of Calvin*, 147, might need to modify the following conclusion: "In dealing with any given topic in the 1559 edition, the reader can rest assured that he or she will encounter everything Calvin regarded as essential to grasping his position on that topic."

[41]Com. 1 Cor. 1:2 (*CO* 49:307).

understanding of fundamental doctrines must powerfully inform his work and most especially his polemical writings.

That Calvin does not discuss the essential doctrines of his theology in precise detail is presumably explained by his conviction that the proper principles of religion "should be clear and unquestioned by all." Therefore, Calvin seems to think it is sufficient only to *indicate* some of the essential doctrines but not necessary to *identify* them more exactly. Calvin also does not examine in detail the possible ramifications of this "clear and unquestioned" criterion. For example, it is possible that some necessary doctrines could become clear only as they are questioned and alternatives rejected. It is likewise possible that upon further examination some previously unquestioned doctrines might turn out not to be clear but quite confused. Moreover, there could be beliefs so clear and so unquestioned that they are taken completely for granted and never discussed at all. It is not likely that Calvin means "clear and unquestioned" in this absolute sense, or in any philosophical sense, but only that at the point where his head and heart intersect[42] some doctrines are so regarded and cherished that Calvin thinks they are (or ought to be) simply matters of affirmation rather than argumentation.

Apparently, within the content of God's truth which Calvin presents in the *Institutes* he thinks the essential doctrines are self-evident, but obviously they are neither clear to, nor unquestioned by, others. Furthermore, it is puzzling that Calvin considers the examples of fundamental doctrines which he offers are themselves clear and unquestioned. The summary he proposes is so broad and can be filled with such widely contrasting contents that it is virtually useless for purposes of theological discrimination. In fact Calvin's own lengthy "clarifications" of these very doctrines plead eloquently for the cause of their truth in the context of various possible misunderstandings of them. Perhaps Calvin believes that *intrinsic* clarity does not obviate the need for *expositional* clarity (or some such distinction), but he does not indicate when he is clarifying an unclear doctrine on the one hand and when (or why!) he is devoting a copious exposition to an essentially clear doctrine on the other hand. For example, eternal election would seem to be one of Calvin's fundamental doctrines—or at least based on a fundamental doctrine—but it is "clarified" at considerable length.

---

[42]In evaluating Calvin's "Nestorian tendency" Kilian McDonnell, *John Calvin, the Church, and the Eucharist* (Princeton, N.J.: Princeton University Press, 1967), 219, alludes to, without developing, "[Calvin's] manner of looking at things, a frame of mind, an underlying attitude, a theological disposition which characterizes his movements within the boundaries of Christological orthodoxy." Cf. W. T. Stace, "The Problem of Unreasoned Beliefs," *Mind* 54, nos. 213:27–49 and 214:122–147 (Jan. and April 1945), explores this subject and suggests there exist nonrational mental processes which are ways of discovering truth.

This problem indicates that the first part of Calvin's "clear and unquestioned" criteria is unusable and must be disregarded. The operative criterion of fundamentally true doctrines is taken to be that they are (by Calvin) and ought to be (by others) unquestioned and therefore are used by Calvin with little or no analysis. That is to say, Calvin's essential doctrines are those which he regards as self-evident and they can be identified by their central location in Calvin's writings and their taken-for-granted nature by the absence not of exposition but of argumentative support. In short, the distinction between an importantly true and a fundamentally true doctrine is that the latter is rather assumed than analyzed.[43]

Undoubtedly, Calvin believes that all the essentially true doctrines are presented in the *Institutes* (also in the general catechisms) but they are difficult to distinguish from the merely true doctrines. Therefore perhaps a more promising approach to the issue of fundamental truth in Calvin's theology can be made through his polemical efforts. Of course the subjects of his polemical writings are not selected by Calvin but by his opponents because Calvin has no need to defend the essential truth of what has not been attacked. However, Calvin's response to false views may be presumed to indicate not only the general importance of those doctrines he elects to defend, but also the specific importance of the doctrines he asserts foundationally in their defense. Part 3, therefore, is an attempt to identify several examples of fundamentally true, because centrally placed and essentially unquestioned, doctrines as they appear in selected polemical works.

III. The Application of Truth

The purpose of Calvin's polemical writings is the application of truth to erroneous views. Calvin acknowledges that his teachings are assailed from two sides—that of the Papists and that of the Anabaptists.[44] Although Calvin's first theological writing, the *Psychopannychia* (1534), oppugns the Anabaptists, the majority of his polemical efforts are directed against the Catholics and cover a broad front of doctrinal opposition. In contrast, Calvin's polemic toward other Protestants, like Joachim Westphal, forms a third and special set with a much narrower focus.

In his polemic against the Catholics Calvin claims, as one would expect, to represent "the perfect truth."[45] Thus he tells Cardinal Sadoleto that separation was

---

[43]William Placher, *Unapologetic Theology* (Louisville: Westminster/John Knox Press, 1989), offers the following: "'We cannot begin with complete doubt,' C. S. Peirce wrote back in 1868: 'We must begin with all the prejudices which we actually have when we enter upon the study of philosophy. These prejudices are not to be dispelled by a maxim, for they are things which it does not occur to us *can* be questioned.... Let us not pretend to doubt in philosophy what we do not doubt in our hearts,'" see Charles Sanders Peirce, *Collected Papers*, vol. 5 (Cambridge, MA: Harvard University Press, 1934), 265. The present concern is what is unquestioned for Calvin.

[44]To Sadoleto, 36 (*OS* 1:465).

[45]To Sadoleto, p. 61 (*OS* 1:484), p. 56; (*OS* 1:480), p. 59; (*OS* 1:482), p. 64; and (*OS* 1:486), p. 68 (*OS* 1:489).

necessary because in Roman theology, "the light of divine truth had been extinguished, the Word of God buried, the virtue of Christ left in profound oblivion and the pastoral office subverted."[46] Calvin even charges that the sole purpose of the Roman Church "is to defend their own cause in any way they can without regard for the truth."[47] In his "Prefatory Address to King Francis" (which Calvin describes as almost "a full-scale apology")[48] the design is not to present but only to summarize the truth of God in order that Francis might accept the divine truth which is presented in "our doctrine."

1. Word and Church

Among the fundamental convictions of Calvin's theology which are applied foundationally in opposition to Roman theology is the precedence of Word over Church. In the "Address to Francis," Calvin charges that "our doctrine" is the object of unbounded rage on the part of the ungodly.[49] In defense Calvin insists "all controversies should be decided by [God's] Word,"[50] which demonstrates that our doctrine is sound and must stand because it is the truth of Christ revealed in Scripture and properly interpreted according to the analogy of faith.[51] Calvin maintains the scriptural warrant for "our doctrine" is clear for all to see who are willing to admit the truth that God's word takes precedence over men's traditions. In contrast, Calvin argues, Roman doctrine is not sound because it is based on human customs and appeals away from Scripture to the analogy of being. Calvin charges that Catholics improperly and unbiblically exalt the church rather than God and Christ. That is, instead of proclaiming the glory of God, they promote the primacy of the Apostolic See and the authority of the church.[52]

In the same way Calvin describes Sadoleto's intent as recovering "the Genevese to the power of the Roman pontiff, or to what you call the faith and obedience of the church."[53] For this purpose Sadoleto appeals to the glorious heritage of the church of the apostles, saints, and martyrs which "has regenerated us to God in Christ, has nourished and confirmed us, instructed us what to think, what to believe, wherein to place our hope, and also taught us by what way we must tend towards heaven."[54] Calvin counters this doctrine of the church on the basis of the prior truth claim of the Word asserting, "Our opponents locate the authority of the church outside God's Word; but we insist that it be attached to the Word."[55] It is "a firm principle: No other word is to be held as the Word of God,

---

[46]To Sadoleto, 49 (*OS* 1:475).
[47]*Inst.* 4.2.2 (*OS* 5:32, 11–12).
[48]Prefatory Address to King Francis, 31 (*OS* 3:29–30).
[49]To Francis, 9 (*OS* 3:9).
[50]To Sadoleto, 60 (*OS* 1:83).
[51]To Francis, 12 (*OS* 3:12).
[52]To Francis, 14 (*OS* 3:14).
[53]To Sadoleto, 29 (*OS* 1:490).
[54]From Sadoleto, 10–1 (*OS* 1:447).
[55]*Inst.* 4.8.13 (*OS* 5:146, 29–31).

and given place as such in the church, than what is contained first in the Law and the Prophets, then in the writing of the apostles; and the only authorized way of teaching in the church is by the prescription and standard of his Word."[56] It is wrong, Calvin says, to ask anyone to trust the church since one who is "deprived of the Word of God is given up unarmed to the devil for destruction."[57] Calvin understands his task as that of a standard bearer who calls deserters to re-form around God's own banner—the Word. This Word allows Protestants to speak nobly of the church as it properly exists without the Roman pontiff. Calvin charges that apart from the Word Sadoleto's faction has produced strange doctrines, numberless superstitions, and worship of images.[58]

The centrality of the Word in Calvin's theology is unquestionable, but he advances the terms for a crucial question he never asks. *Institutes* 1.7 is devoted to a demonstration that the credibility of Scripture does not depend on the judgment of the church and interprets Augustine in agreement with this view. That Scripture is from God, Calvin insists, we affirm with utter certainty. "We seek no proofs, no marks of genuineness upon which our judgment may lean; but we subject our judgment and wit to it as to a thing far beyond any guesswork." In this view of Scripture Calvin claims to be "fully conscious that we hold the unassailable truth" which is "a conviction that requires no reasons."[59] Dealing with the Lord's Supper Calvin writes, "Surely what we teach perfectly agrees in all respects with Scripture. It contains nothing either absurd or obscure or ambiguous."[60] The same point is made against Westphal who appeals to Scripture—but falsely. According to Calvin, Westphal "boldly masks all his fictions with the Word of God ... just as if he were some comic Jupiter carrying a Minerva in his skull."[61] Obviously Calvin believes that all his own teachings are derived from, and therefore conform to, Scripture and need no other justification.[62]

---

[56]*Inst.* 4.8.8 (*OS* 5:139, 29–32—140:1).   [57]To Sadoleto, 53 (*OS* 1:478).
[58]To Sadoleto, 59 (*CO* 1:482); 67 (*CO* 1:488).[59]*Inst.* 1.7.5 (*OS* 3:70:31–32—71:8–9).
[60]*Inst.* 4.17.19 (*OS* 5:366, 4–6).   [61]Westphal 2:328 (*CO* 9, 108).
[62]In an important essay, John H. Leith, "Calvin's Theological Method and the Ambiguity in His Theology," *Reformation Studies: Essays in Honor of Roland H. Bainton*, ed. Franklin H. Littell (Richmond, Va: John Knox Press, 1962),110, correctly observes: "Calvin was ready to sacrifice logical consistency in order to do justice to the complexity of Christian revelation and experience." Likewise, while Calvin "avows the greatest loyalty to Scripture, he actually goes beyond Scripture as a result of an almost irresistible tendency to extrapolate rationally the scriptural data" (p. 110). Again (p. 113): "On the basis of the presupposition that the Bible supplies infallible material for theology and that reason is competent to manipulate and theologize about these materials, Calvin was convinced that he possessed the truth." It is true that Calvin sacrificed rationality to revelation as he himself asserts. It is also true that—in our judgment—Calvin goes beyond scriptural data in offering rational conclusions, a process which he never admits. However, it is essential to notice that Calvin moves directly from the Bible to the truth without analyzing the competency of reason "to manipulate and theologize about" Biblical material. In the dispute with Tileman Heshusius, Calvin mentions three kinds of reason: (1) natural reason (2) fallen reason, and (3) conformed (to Scripture) reason (*CO* 9:474). See also Charles Partee, "Calvin, Calvinism and Rationality," *Rationality in the Calvinian Tradition*, ed. Hendrik Hart, Johan Van der Hoeven, and Nicholas Wolterstorff (Lanham, Md.: University Press, 1983), 1–15.

Since Calvin regards Scripture alone as the unquestionable source of truth, he cannot accept the church and its traditions as either a prior or additional source. Nevertheless, in discussing the doctrine of the Trinity, Calvin asserts it is wicked to confine our thoughts and words within the limits of Scripture because this "condemns all interpretation not patched together out of the fabric of Scripture." Calvin insists that our thoughts and words should be conformed to Scripture, but not confined to Scripture because nothing "prevents us from explaining in clearer words those matters in Scripture which perplex and hinder our understanding, yet which conscientiously and faithfully serve the truth of Scripture itself, and are made use of sparingly and modestly and on due occasion."[63] Calvin does not consider the possibility that the doctrine of the Trinity could be the reverent result of the historical reflection of the community of faith guided by the Holy Spirit. Instead the doctrine of the Trinity is regarded as an explanation of Scripture in clearer words. Indeed Calvin's conviction of the Word as clear and unquestioned is so strong that it does not even occur to him to explain how words (and therefore doctrines) that conform our thoughts to Scripture are to be distinguished from those that distort them. Additionally, we are not instructed on how to recognize the "due occasion" when nonscriptural words may be used properly although "sparingly and modestly."

2. Faith and Love

In Sadoleto's letter to the senate and people of Geneva, Calvin sees a substantial attack not only on the truth of God, but a personal attack on his ministry in its service. In defending both, Calvin predictably asserts the doctrine of the Word's precedence over the Church—which Rome predictably denies. Not so often noticed is Calvin's equally fundamental insistence that Faith precedes Love.[64] Sadoleto's chief appeal is to the Genevans' hope for salvation, a subject which Calvin estimates to occupy about a third of his letter.[65] Sadoleto argues that salvation is achieved within the church by faith issuing in works. In his exposition Sadoleto employs the term "faith alone" but he includes within its meaning the human desire and intention to perform works pleasing to God. In Sadoleto's view non-Catholics mean by "faith alone" only a mere credibility and a confidence in God which excludes these works of love.[66] Therefore "faith alone" in the Protestant sense is not sufficient for salvation. Sadoleto writes, "We hold that in this very faith love is essentially comprehended as the chief and primary cause of our salvation."[67]

---

[63]*Inst.* 1.13.3 (*OS* 3:112, 11–14).   [64] Cf. *Inst.* 3.2.41 (*OS* 3:52, 7–10).
[65]To Sadoleto, 33 (*OS* 1:463).   [66]From Sadoleto, 9 (*OS* 1:446).
[67]From Sadoleto, 10 (*OS* 1:447).

Calvin agrees with Sadoleto that eternal blessedness is an important topic, but insists it is bad theology to confine a man's thoughts so much to himself and not to set before him, as the prime motive of his existence, zeal to illustrate the glory of God. The point is that God's mercy is not restricted to those who attempt to prove themselves worthy of it by good works.[68] In fact, true piety leads not to self-interest but to the sanctifying of God's name. In this way Calvin frames the main issue. He agrees with Sadoleto that nothing endangers salvation so much as false worship and this agreement sets the foundation for Calvin's defense. Since the central question is which side turns divine truth into a lie by false opinions, Calvin exclaims to Sadoleto, "I was amazed when I read your assertion, that love is the first and chief cause of our salvation." According to Calvin, the truth is the reverse. Love is not the cause of election because Scripture teaches that salvation depends on free adoption by the merciful God. We do not first love God but are chosen by God through the atonement effected in Jesus Christ.[69]

Calvin understands the view of love held by Sadoleto to include human merit (which it does) and concludes that it abrogates free grace (which Catholics deny). The distinction between faith and love in Calvin's mind also appears in the *Institutes* where Calvin teaches that the essence of righteousness is found more in honoring God with piety than in living among men with innocence. Of course piety toward God is exercised "in good works toward our neighbor." Still Calvin insists, "It is certain that the Law and the Prophets give first place to faith and whatever pertains to the lawful worship of God, relegating love to a subordinate position."[70]

The same point is made in his commentary on 1 Cor. 13:13. "Love is said to be greater here, not in every respect, but because it will last forever, and now has a primary role in keeping the church in being." Nevertheless, according to Calvin, the Papists are wrong to infer that love is of more value in justification than faith. Faith properly understood in its fullness is not only the mother of hope but love itself is produced by faith.[71] This view of faith is consonant with Calvin's understanding of justification as the Catholic view of love is consonant with their doctrine of justification. Both views may be appealed to Scripture but neither is self-evident.

In his understanding of Word preceding Church and Faith preceding Love, Calvin believes he is expounding obvious truth which Rome denies. These relations are discussed at different lengths but the issues in neither case can be resolved by appeal to Scripture, or to logic, or to tradition because they are ultimately based on personal convictions and intellectual preferences which become social and theological loyalties or vice versa. In other words, these are examples of

---

[68]To Sadoleto, 33 (*OS* 1:463), and 61 (*OS* 1:484).   [69]To Sadoleto, 44 (*OS* 1:471).
[70]*Inst.* 2.8.53 (*OS* 3:392.20–23).   [71]Com. 1 Cor. 13.13 (*CO* 49:515–16).

doctrinal positions Calvin regards as unquestionable truth requiring no further analysis or support.

3. *God and Man*

Calvin's polemic with Protestants is narrower in scope than against Catholics because he recognizes a "holy union" among the many churches which "preach the same doctrine."[72] However, in spite of these agreements the Protestant divisions over Eucharistic theology remained, and Calvin devoted considerable attention to the negotiations that resulted in the *Consensus Tigurinus* of 1549. This small document demonstrates Calvin's conviction that the presentation and defense of God's truth does not exclude concessions to, and accommodations with, those who maintain differing emphases. According to Calvin, the Zurich Agreement set forth sacramental doctrine in terms that were few, simple, clear, and gentle including a request for discussion and, if necessary, amendment.[73] Calvin hoped that this irenic presentation of Eucharistic doctrine would provide "an essential first step toward a wider pan-Protestant accord,"[74] and was pleased the agreement was either civilly embraced or silently approved. However the consensus between Geneva and Zurich aroused the ire of Joachim Westphal who began in 1552 a continuing attack on the Reformed doctrine of the Lord's Supper to which Calvin responded from his redoubts with angry rhetoric in the *Defense of the Sound and Orthodox Doctrine of the Sacraments* (1555), his *Second Defense of the Holy and Right Faith in the Matter of the Sacraments* (1556) and finally, the *Last Warning from John Calvin to Joachim Westphal* (1557).

Before Westphal's attack Calvin had concerned himself with the presentation of Eucharistic truth and dealt gently with conflicting interpretations. Thus Calvin claims that until Westphal "kindled the torch of discord," "I had never touched him or one of his faction, but had rather humbly begged, that if anything in our doctrine did not please, it might not be deemed too troublesome to correct it by placid admonition."[75] Under the force of Westphal's attack Calvin concludes that the time for discussion has passed and against Westphal a hard wedge must be used for a bad knot.[76] "All we asked was, that he would not deal roughly with a newly cured sore," [77]but Westphal opened wounds and Calvin was thoroughly roused to defend "the clear and indubitable truth,"[78] the "truth of Christ" which

---

[72]Westphal 2:251 (*CO* 9:50).   [73]Westphal 2:246 (*CO* 9:45).
[74]Timothy George, "John Calvin and the Agreement of Zurich (1549)," *John Calvin and the Church: A Prism of Reform*, ed. Timothy George (Louisville: Westminster/John Knox Press, 1990), 45.
[75]Westphal 3:348 (*CO* 9:143).   [76] Westphal 2:248 (*CO* 9:47); 3:347 (*CO* 9:141).
[77]Westphal 2:314 (*CO* 9:97).   [78]Westphal 2:268 (*CO* 9:64).

forbade silence.[79] According to Calvin, "[T]he hope of peace has been destroyed by their unreasonable rage."[80]

Obviously a sufficient exposition of Calvin's polemic with Westphal would involve, among other things, a lengthy discussion and comparison of Christology and its relation to Eucharistic theology especially on such topics as the *communicatio idiomatum* and the relation of ubiquity to the so-called *extra Calvinisticum*.[81] Most scholars agree that the ostensible disagreements between Westphal and Calvin are ultimately traceable to differing views on the doctrine of the two natures. Of course, both sides accept Chalcedonian orthodoxy and deny Nestorianism and Eutychianism. Commenting on these historical developments Calvin insists it is not permissible to commingle the two natures in Christ or to pull them apart.[82] Nevertheless, the traditional interpretation suggests that Calvin's emphasis on the integrity of the two natures appears to Lutherans to jeopardize the personal union while the Lutheran view of the unity of person appears to Calvin to deny the reality of Christ's humanity.[83] This essay takes the position that viewing Calvin's polemic against Westphal as a conflict between Calvin's (and Reformed theology's) so-called tendency toward Nestorianism versus Westphal's (and Lutheran theology's) so-called tendency toward Eutychianism, however useful as a generalization, is too crude to represent Calvin's own understanding of the issue. Calvin charges Westphal with Eutychianism,[84] but he does not regard himself as Nestorian—even in tendency. The point is Calvin defends his view of the two natures, not as historical choice or doctrinal preference, but as foundational truth.

Calvin believes his view carries the authority of Paul and Luke, thus those who disagree find "their quarrel is not with me but with the Spirit of God."[85] Calvin asserts, "[Westphal] and his band remain fixed in error, being prevented by mere obstinacy from yielding obedience to the truth."[86] The truth at issue is Calvin's fundamental and unquestioned conviction concerning the continuing and integral humanity of the risen Christ (including the flesh) which Calvin

---

[79] Westphal 2:246 (*CO* 9:45); 2:314 (*CO* 9:97).   [80]Westphal 2:324 (*CO* 9:105).

[81]See *Inst.* 2.13.4 (*OS* 3:458, 5–13) for the so-called *extra Calvinisticum*. On the communication of attributes: *Inst.* 2.12.1 (*OS* 3:437, 18–23); 2.14.1f. (*OS* 3:458f.); 4.17.29,30 (*OS* 5:384–9).

[82]*Inst.* 2.14.4 (*OS* 3:463, 1–2); 4.17.30 (*OS* 5:388, 16–17)

[83]Karl Barth, *Church Dogmatics*, 1, 2, 171, suggests that no resolution is possible between the opposing Lutheran and Reformed views of the communication of the divine and human attributes. We cannot say that one is right and the other wrong. The truth about the reality of Jesus Christ, according to Barth, does not allow a single conceptualization (either Lutheran or Calvinist) so that if there is to be an evangelical theology at all these *two* understandings must remain.

[84]*Inst.* 4.17.30 (*OS* 5:388, 24). In the dedication of the Com. Jere. (*CO* 20:72,75) to Frederick (who had been charged with Calvinism) Calvin asserts that only Eutyches taught that the ubiquity of God could belong to the flesh of Christ. Concerning his own understanding of the flesh Calvin affirms, "I am taught by the Holy Spirit."

[85]*Inst.* 4.17.20 (*OS* 5:369, 25–28). [86]Westphal 2:305 (*CO* 9:90).

declares in writing, "I deem it unlawful to think or speak of any other body than that which was offered on the cross."[87] According to Calvin there is an irreducible duality between Christ's divinity and humanity. Thus, "We wish Christ to remain complete and entire in regard to both natures."[88] Again, "We hold that Christ, as he is God and man, consists of two natures united but not mingled."[89] Of course in his divinity Christ is ubiquitous, but, Calvin will not allow that Christ's human nature could be understood according to the Lutheran notion because he believes such a view really means that Christ's human nature has disappeared instead of being elevated. "For we affirm his divinity so joined and united with his humanity that each retains its distinctive nature unimpaired, and yet these two natures constitute one Christ."[90]

According to Calvin the understanding of the two natures is fundamental to our salvation because Christ—being God—saves us by what he did *in his human nature.*[91] Therefore we must be brought into union with his human nature. Calvin acknowledges "that the sacred union which we have with Christ is incomprehensible to carnal sense. His joining us with him so as not only to instill his life into us, but to make us one with himself, we grant to be a mystery too sublime for our comprehension, except in so far as his words reveal it."[92] Nevertheless, Calvin insists that "ingrafted into the body of Christ by the secret agency of the Spirit, we have life in common with him."[93] Indeed while it may be possible to suggest the union with Christ as the central mystery of Calvin's theology,[94] on any evaluation

---

[87]Westphal 2:282 (*CO* 9:73–74). In Com. 1 Tim. 3.16 (*CO*:52:290) Calvin, commenting on "God manifested in the flesh," writes "In this single phrase the true and orthodox faith is powerfully armed against Arius, Marcion, Nestorius, and Eutyches. There is great emphasis laid on the contrast between the two terms, God and the flesh. [Y]et in Christ we see God's infinite glory joined to our polluted flesh so that the two become one." François Wendel, *Calvin: The Origins and Development of His Religious Thought*, trans. Philip Mairet (New York: Harper, 1963), 219, suggests that the *distinction* between the two natures "is a very important aspect of Calvin's theological thought and perhaps what is most original in it."

[88]Westphal 1:241 (*CO* 9:33).

[89]*Inst.* 2.14.4 (*OS* 3:463, 14–15); a special kind of duality also applies to Christ's humanity. In his commentary on Galatians 3.13 (*CO* 50:210) Calvin says, "[T]here are two things to be considered, not only in the person of Christ, but even in his human nature. The one is that he was the unspotted Lamb of God, full of blessing and grace. The other is that he took our place and thus became a sinner and subject to the curse, not in himself indeed, but in us; yet in such a way that it was necessary for him to act in our name."

[90]*Inst.* 2.12.1 (*OS* 3:437, 2–4) says the two natures are not the result of absolute necessity but of the heavenly decree. In the battle of images the Lutherans claimed that Calvin's view of Christ's humanity and deity was like putting two boards together. The Lutheran model was the glowing iron. Fire has the property of shining and burning but when fire unites with iron it manifests these properties in, with, and through the glowing iron. Calvin uses the image of our two eyes. We have two distinct eyes, but almost always they bring to us a unified vision (*CO* 53:326).

[91]*Inst.* 3.11.9 (*OS* 4:190, 23–24).   [92]Westphal 1:239 (*CO* 9:31).   [93]Westphal 1:238 (*CO* 9:30–31).

[94]See Charles Partee, "Calvin's Central Dogma Again," *Sixteenth Century Journal* 18/2 (Summer, 1987), 191–99. *Inst.* 3.11.10 (*OS* 4:191, 28–31). David Willis-Watkins "The Unio Mystica

the doctrine is centrally important and Calvin's understanding of the flesh of Christ is a crucial element in it. Calvin writes, "This union alone ensures that, as far as we are concerned, he has not unprofitably come with the name of Savior. The same purpose is served by that sacred wedlock through which we are made flesh of his flesh and bone of his bone, and thus one with him."[95] Calvin insists, "God's natural Son fashioned for himself a body from our body, flesh from our flesh, bones from our bones, that he might be one with us,"[96] The union of Christ's flesh with our flesh, his bone with our bone is maintained because Calvin believes that union with the body of Christ involves more than vivification by the Holy Spirit or faith in the merit of Christ. The real body of Christ is received as bread and the real blood of Christ as drink. Thus, true communion means a real nourishment by the real flesh of Christ. "The flesh of Christ is like a rich and inexhaustible fountain that pours into us the life springing forth from the Godhead into itself."[97] In this union Calvin understands any hint of transfusion or commingling of divine and human substance to be both absurd and blasphemous since it would deify us or dehumanize Christ.[98] Nevertheless, something like a communication/communion of Christ's human attributes with our humanity occurs as he "instills his life into us."[99]

In any case, Calvin regards it as "a settled point" that Jesus Christ has only a true and natural body,[100] and it is obvious to Calvin that true and natural bodies

---

and the Assurance of Faith According to Calvin," *Calvin: Erbe und Auftrag: Festschrift für Wilhelm Heinrich Neuser*, ed. Willem van't Spijker (Kampen: Kok, 1991), 77–84. On union and Eucharist see Ronald W. Wallace, *Calvin's Doctrine of the Word and Sacrament* (Edinburgh: Oliver and Boyd, 1953), esp. chapters 12, 13, 16.

[95]*Inst.* 3.1.3 (*OS* 4:5, 7–10).

[96]*Inst.* 2.12.2 (*OS* 3:438, 28–29—439:1). E. David Willis, *Calvin's Catholic Christology: The Function of the So-called extra Calvinisticum in Calvin's Theology* (Leiden: E. J. Brill, 1966), pp. 91–100 and 109–120 treats, but does not concentrate on, Calvin's view of *flesh* in the doctrine of the humanity of Christ.

[97]*Inst.* 4.17.9 (*OS* 5:50: 38—351:1–2). To explain our relation to Christ precisely as "union without confusion" is difficult for Calvin. He rejects *transfusion of substance* but insists upon *infusion of life.* See 1.238 (*CO* 9:31); 1.:240 (*CO* 9:33); 2:248 (*CO* 9:47); 2:277 (*CO* 9:70); 2:283 (*CO* 9:74); 3:447 (*CO* 9:216).

[98]At *Inst.* 4.17.11 (*OS* 5:354.24–25) Calvin says we are partakers of Christ's substance. In discussing the mode of participation in the Eucharist Calvin rejects the Papists' view of substance but speaks favorably of our union in one life and substance with Christ (Com. 1 Cor.11:24 [*CO* 49:487]. On substance see McDonnell, *John Calvin*, 232–33.

[99]Perhaps this is what Joseph McLelland, "Lutheran-Reformed Debate on the Eucharist and Christology," *Marburg Revisited*, ed. Paul C. Empie and James I. McCord (Minneapolis: Augsburg, 1966), 46–47, means by "Calvin relates all his theology [to] the believer's participation in the *new humanity* of the living Christ" and "[T]he Reformed understood the lordship of Christ as a communication of properties of the *new humanity* by the Spirit." Italics added.

[100]Westphal 1:207 (*CO* 9:10:31).

are located in a place[101] which for the risen and ascended Christ is at the right hand of God.[102] Calvin insists that the whole Christ is present everywhere but *in his flesh* Christ is contained in heaven until he appears in judgment.[103] This local, heavenly presence Calvin understands to preserve not only Christ's heavenly glory but the continuing reality and integrity of Christ's human nature which protects our human nature in union with him and thus our salvation.[104] In applying his Christological doctrine to the Eucharist Calvin intends to avoid both superstition and absurdity each of which transfers praise to the sacrament which is properly due to God alone.[105] Therefore, Calvin affirms the local, heavenly presence by insisting that Christ while present to faith is not present in, with, or under the elements. Christ is absent from us in the body which is in heaven, but Christ dwells in us by his Spirit.[106]

Calvin regards his doctrine of the Lord's Supper as real, true, and spiritual in contrast with Westphal's carnal view which understands the substance of Christ's flesh to be on earth.[107] For Westphal to declare of bread, "an ephemeral and corruptible element, that it is Christ [is] an intolerable blasphemy."[108] In support of his understanding of the truth Calvin appeals to the analogy of faith, plain reason, common sense, and piety which deny that Christ can be pulled "down from his throne, that he may lie enclosed in a little bit of bread."[109] Calvin believes that "to hold that the bread is the body is nothing else than to confound heaven and earth together."[110] Contrary to this carnal understanding of the Eucharist, "We assert that in the sacred supper we are truly made partakers of Christ, so that by the sacred agency of the Spirit, he instills life into our souls from his flesh."[111] Calvin understands that flesh is not in itself immortal and cannot of itself give life. Life resides intrinsically in Christ's divinity, but Calvin sees flesh as a channel to pour out life to us. Therefore, he concludes, "Although righteousness flows from God alone, we shall not have the full manifestation of it anywhere else than in Christ's

---

[101]*Inst.* 4.17.26 (*OS* 5:378.16–8) Calvin insists that he does not derive this view of body from Aristotle and, in Westphal 2:327 (*CO* 9:107) says he did not learn about bodies in the school of Archimedes but of Scripture. Calvin cannot believe that bodies exist if locality is taken away. Therefore while Christ is everywhere present as God, in respect of his human nature he is not everywhere diffused (Westphal 3:382 [*CO* 9:168]).

[102]*Inst.* 4.17.18. (*OS* 5:364:29–32), where sitting at the right hand of the Father means that Christ's reign is not "bounded by location in space nor circumscribed by any limits."

[103]*Inst.* 4.17.30 (*OS* 5:389.18–20).

[104]Westphal 3:391 (*CO* 9:174): "[T]he hope of future resurrection is overthrown, if a model of it is not exhibited in the flesh of Christ."

[105]Westphal 1:227 (*CO* 9:20–21). Idolatry is defined as worshiping the gifts in place of the Giver himself (*Inst.* 4.17.36 [*OS* 5:400.15–16]).

[106]Westphal 2:272 (*CO* 9:66).   [107]Westphal 1:240 (*CO* 9:32).   [108]*Inst.* 4.17.20 (*OS* 5:369, 4–6).

[109]Westphal 1:241 (*CO* 9:34).   [110]Westphal 3:438 (*CO* 9:209–10).

[111] Westphal 2: 276 (*CO* 9:69).

flesh" which remains in heaven.[112] Calvin asks of Westphal the scornful question, "Would he have the flesh of Christ eaten like the beeves of his country?"[113] Calvin insists that the efficacy of the sacrament does not depend on human beings but neither does it result from the external use of the elements. "For we deem it no less absurd to place Christ under the bread or couple him with the bread, than to transubstantiate the bread into his body."[114] Thus Calvin rejects Roman Eucharistic doctrine but also thinks the Lutheran notion that the body of Christ is immense or ubiquitous is a "monstrous phantom" which denies the resurrection, ascension, session, and return as taught in Scripture. Calvin also calls the Lutheran view of *manducatio oralis* a "monstrous sacrilege"[115] since it teaches that Christ can be received apart from faith. According to Calvin the sense of piety clearly dictates that Christ "infuses life into us from his flesh, in no other way than by descending into us by his power (*virtus*), while, in respect of his body, he still continues in heaven."[116] That "the living virtue of Christ's flesh penetrates from heaven to earth, and is in a wondrous manner infused into our souls," Calvin insists is not a doctrine learned from, or defended by, common sense, or natural reason, or philosophical speculation.[117]

This exposition of the real and continuing humanity of Christ which requires the doctrine of local, heavenly presence raises the question of communion with the flesh of Christ which is absent from earth. Calvin affirms that the mode of communion is miraculous and supernatural,[118] but insists that the true mystery is located in the power of the Holy Spirit connecting believers with the heavenly body of Christ rather than a physical claim to Christ's Eucharistic presence. Calvin describes this process with the language of both ascent and descent. That is, in faith by the power of the Holy Spirit we ascend to heaven to communicate with the flesh of Christ and, while his body remains in heaven, Christ descends to us on earth by the power of his Holy Spirit.[119] In both cases, Christ's descent and our ascent, the event is real but not physical and each is achieved by the power of the Holy Spirit. Presumably, Calvin could have conceived the power of the Holy Spirit and thus the mystery of the Eucharist as extending the true, real, and spiritual body (flesh) of Christ to earth for communion which might have mollified West-

---

[112]Com. John. 6.51 (*CO* 47:152). Com. Acts 7.56 (*CO* 48:168) where Calvin says Stephen sees Christ "reigning in that flesh in which he had suffered humiliation." Cf. *Inst.* 4.17.9 (*OS* 5:350, 22–26).
[113]Westphal 1:207 (*CO* 9:9).
[114]Westphal 1:219 (*CO* 7:742–43): "I confess that under the Papacy men were miserably infatuated in innumerable ways, but the most fearful and monstrous fascination was that of stupidly adoring the bread in place of God" (2:309 *CO* 9:93). Westphal 3:374 (*CO* 9:162): Calvin asserts that Westphal comes too close to the 'gross gulping' doctrine of the Papists which is abhorrent to our sense of piety."
[115]Westphal 2:260 (*CO* 9:58).   [116]Westphal 1:240 (*CO* 9:33). [117] Westphal 2:310 (*CO* 9:94).
[118]Westphal 3:399 (*CO* 9:181).   [119]*Inst.* 4.17.24 (*OS* 5:375, 33–34).

phal and might have obviated the difficulties of understanding how the believer who has an earthly, local presence can by faith commune with a heavenly, local presence. However, Calvin's mind did not work in this direction and his "realistic" (i.e. heavenly, local) conception of the flesh of Christ (which continues through the ascension, session, and return) does not invoke this possibility.

*   *   *

The theology of John Calvin is based on a conviction of truth so basic that it is never precisely defined. As we have seen, Calvin does not provide a clear analysis of either the category or content of fundamentally true doctrines. One result of this lack of definition is the difficulty of knowing at what point acceptable variations become polemical disagreements. Doubtless every leading article of the faith is to be found in the *Institutes of the Christian Religion*, at least implicitly, but the distinction between a true doctrine and a fundamentally true doctrine as well as the direction of possibly necessary, polemical expansions of the latter is extremely difficult, if not impossible, to draw. The explanation seems to be that Calvin takes for granted the existence of essential doctrines as clear and unquestioned and therefore applies them without recognizing a need to identify or analyze them further.

The present essay approaches the issue of Calvin's fundamentally true doctrines/convictions with the assumption that some of them can be identified in Calvin's polemical writings which are directed against fundamentally false doctrines/convictions. Thus, Calvin's belief in (1) the precedence of Word over Church, (2) of Faith over Love, and (3) the continuing humanity (flesh) of the risen Christ are claimed to be fundamental because at the deepest level they are presented on the ground of Calvin's conviction of their truth. That is, being asserted, they are clarified at various lengths but unargued in the sense that alternatives to them are not seriously considered as possibly legitimate options. In short, as the truth they are unquestioned by Calvin.

If by this—or some other method—a comprehensive list of Calvin's essential doctrines could be obtained, the immense task of understanding their relationship would still remain. Of the three fundamental doctrines suggested and considered here the continuing humanity of the risen Christ seems to be central to Calvin's Christology and the understanding of *Institutes*, book 2. Faith's precedence over Love is basic to Calvin's soteriology and his explanation of God's free grace in *Institutes*, book 3. The precedence of the Word seems to be prolegomenon to all theology. However, in addition to Scripture, reasonableness and historical tradition also appear to serve some very important but undefined role in determining the truth for Calvin. At least Calvin instructs Westphal to demonstrate his case by "furnishing himself with (1) the oracles of Scripture, (2) strong argument, and (3) the consent of the Church" before he comes forward as a defender of truth.[120]

In evaluating Calvin's view of truth, its presentation and defense, perhaps one may hazard this broader conclusion. While Calvin's exegetical writings start with a specific text, his dogmatical writings begin with the entire doctrinal tradition.[121] That is to say, Calvin's theology is not deduced from a single doctrine or set of doctrines although one might argue that it is developed from a single insight or from an undesignated set of fundamental convictions. In this context a reader might suggest the Lordship of Christ as Calvin's central conviction and our union with Christ as his central doctrine.[122] However that may be, in working within the generally established doctrinal boundaries Calvin seeks to straighten the lines wherever his conviction of God's truth requires, shaping and clarifying traditional

---

[120]Westphal 2:255 (*CO* 9:53).

[121]In a thought-provoking essay Brian G. Armstrong, "The Nature and Structure of Calvin's Thought according to the *Institutes*: Another Look" in *John Calvin's Institutes, His Opus Magnum: Proceedings of the Second South African Congress for Calvin Research* (Potchefstroom: Potchefstroom University, 1986), 55–81, asserts, "Try as we may, we are simply unable to come to any consensus when we wish to reduce [Calvin's] theological positions to one, or even several, central doctrinal position," insisting "there will always be two poles, two aspects, two dialectical and conflicting elements in each theological topic which he discusses" (56), and concluding "that Calvin's theology is not formal, that it is not formulated according to the traditional heads of doctrine, and that it is not devoted to intellectual ends at all" (58).

It is not clear to me in what sense devotion to intellectual ends is taken to abrogate the spiritual purpose of Calvin's theology since a "pious mind" is still a mind. In fact Calvin begins his *Second Defense against Westphal* by insisting, "I have always candidly and sincerely made profession according to the genuine convictions of my mind"; see Westphal 2:252 (*CO* 9:51). Additionally, I understand the *Institutes* to be formulated exactly according to the way Calvin chose to deal with the "traditional heads of doctrine." Further Armstrong suggests that "the whole general tenor and structure of Calvin's theology is built around a hypothetical or conditional base" (64–65). My own conviction is that Calvin's conviction of *truth* is more basic to his mind and heart than the obvious dialectic between ideal and real, universal and hypothetical, necessary and contingent, rhetoric and philosophy, divine initiative and human response.

To the extent that these are differing interpretations and in consideration of past disputes over Calvin interpretation (held with varying degrees of civility), for example, Barth versus Brunner on natural theology, Parker versus Dowey on knowledge, etc., one wonders whether some form of the ancient philosophical debate over the ultimacy of the One or the Many is being argued by the students of Calvin in the absence of their teacher.

In any case, Armstrong is quite right to observe that scholars have come to no consensus about Calvin's purported central dogma or his supposed set of central dogmas and to call for a reexamination of the structure and nature of Calvin's thought. My proposal, addressed to that situation, takes seriously Calvin's acknowledgment of the existence of fundamental doctrines and suggests they can be identified by the method of examining texts for doctrines whose truth Calvin assumes without question.

[122] In his Commentary on 1 Cor. 3.11 (*CO* 49:354), Calvin writes, "[T]he fundamental doctrine, which it is forbidden to overthrow, is that we might learn Christ. For Christ is the one and only foundation of the church." Cf. *Inst.* 4.2.1 (*OS* 5:31, 11–12). On 1 Pet. 1.20 (*CO* 55:226–27): "Hence all thinking about God without Christ is a vast abyss which immediately swallows up all our thoughts."

theological topics in the direction of as much coherence and scriptural fidelity as a single mind can encompass. Perhaps where Calvin does not articulate a dialectic of relationship between doctrines, they are essentially freestanding. In this endeavor Calvin assumes the existence of fundamental doctrines but does not expound them because this procedure does not represent the way he actually thought. Calvin intended a sum of piety not an exposition of foundational theology. Moreover, Calvin may have instinctively recognized the difficulties involved with a hard and nonnegotiable concept of essences.[123] Certainly the phrase "and the like" concluding a list of fundamental doctrines seems to point in the direction of a rather softer and discussable view of which doctrines must be included.

In any case, Calvin's overriding purpose is not logical consistency (as has sometimes been supposed) but fidelity to God's truth, as he understands it, which means that his theology is not a result of conclusions from fundamental logical principles and is misread as a closely (or loosely) reasoned deductive system. Indeed, Calvin asserts: "Our argument is not derived from philosophy but from the heavenly oracles of God."[124] Again: "Human reason did not dictate to us that the Son of God, to reconcile us to the Father by the sacrifice of his death, assumed our flesh."[125] He continues, "I would rather perish a hundred times than put one little word of Christ into the balance, and counter-weigh it by the whole body of philosophy."[126] Taken as a whole, Calvin presents a theological witness not a philosophical argument. He tells Westphal that it has been his greatest care "to deliver distinctly what I daily profess and teach in the church, and what God is my best witness and judge that I sincerely believe."[127]

Therefore, Calvin's theology is more correctly understood as a systematic confession of (and testimony to) the Christian faith utilizing traditional heads of doctrine and integrating various insights from various sources[128] into a structure which includes both examined (i.e.,clarified) and unexamined (i.e., unquestioned) doctrines. The result is a way of approaching God's reality with head and heart which claims to be the truth. Obviously this claim to truth was produced in a specific time, place, and culture. Calvin's sixteenth-century, western-European convictions of mind and habits of heart are often difficult to isolate just because so many twentieth-century people have learned to share them. Nevertheless, the

---

[123]Cf. Ludwig Wittgenstein, *Philosophical Investigations*, trans. G. E. M. Anscombe (New York: Macmillan, 1953), 1, 66–67 on essences and family resemblances.
[124]Westphal 3:380 (*CO* 9:167).   [125].Westphal 3:442 (*CO* 9:212–13).
[126]Westphal 2:289 (*CO* 9:79).   [127]Westphal 2:279 (*CO* 9:71).
[128]Undoubtedly Calvin thought Scripture was the single source of all his theological insights. However, on topics such as soul and body the western intellectual tradition—in this case especially Plato—seems to qualify as a source.

attempt to identify Calvin's own fundamental doctrines (to the extent they exist)—if that is possible or even if it is not possible—is useful both to sixteenth- and to twentieth-century theological reflection.

"I Came Not to Send Peace, but a Sword"

Francis Higman

Matt. 10:34: "Think not that I am come to send peace on earth; I came not to send peace, but a sword." In his commentary on the synoptic Gospels, Calvin glosses: "Since a good part of the world is not only contrary [to the Gospel] but bitterly fights against it, we cannot serve Christ without conflict and without attracting the hate of many. So Christ warns his disciples to prepare themselves for battle: since it is necessary to fight to give witness to the truth."

Contemporary readers of Calvin often had their attention drawn to the point; many of the early editions of his works were printed by Jean Girard of Geneva, who had adopted as his printer's mark a sword, usually accompanied by this motto. The reminder is entirely justified. At no stage in his life was Calvin an academic theologian, concerned only with the definition and exposition of the truth of the Gospel. The battle was omnipresent, real, urgent, and merciless—a battle on behalf of God, against Satan, against the Antichrist, against their minions.

William J. Bouwsma lays considerable emphasis on Calvin's commitment, on his need to convince, to persuade, to win the rhetorical battle of words. This leads him to some surprising formulations: "[Calvin] was often more concerned to sway a particular audience for particular purposes than to achieve the 'absolute balance' of a detached and systematic theology. Since he was more concerned to effect a change in behavior than to state abstract truths, his denunciations of human wickedness are sometimes particularly unbalanced." And later, Bouwsma goes further: "It should always be remembered, in assessing his intention, that he was a rhetorician, less concerned with the objective truth of his message than with its effect on his audience."[1]

Now it is clear that writing in a situation of conflict will influence the way in which the writing is formulated. But can we go along with the statement that Calvin is less concerned with the objective truth than with its effect? That is the question which underlies my attempt to survey Calvin's work as a polemist. I hope to present three aspects of the matter: (1) a summary of what Calvin wrote in terms of polemical treatises, (2) a brief section on how he perceived the possible audiences for whom he wrote, and (3) some notes on the techniques he used. To

---

[1] W. J. Bouwsma, *John Calvin: A Sixteenth-Century Portrait* (New York: Oxford University Press, 1988), 116, 141. See also Lynda S. Jones, "Fulfilled in Your Hearing": Rhetoric and Doctrine in John Calvin's *Institutes of the Christian Religion* (Ph.D. dissertation, Yale, 1991).

concentrate on the polemical treatises is of course to omit the fact that polemics are omnipresent—in the commentaries, in the sermons, in the *Institution*. But what is said about the polemical treatises will, I believe, be equally applicable to polemical contexts elsewhere.

I. Calvin's Polemical Treatises

Volumes 5 through 9 of Calvin's *Opera quae supersunt omnia* are devoted to the *Tractatus Theologici Minores*. In the new edition in preparation under the guidance of Wilhelm H. Neuser the group is differently defined: *Didactica et polemica*.[2]

I propose a distribution of the treatises, not as in the *Opera omnia* in one chronological sequence, but according to the particular battle fronts on which Calvin fought. The result (given in the appendix to this chapter) makes interesting reading. In a sense the sections I propose are somewhat arbitrary, since for example, some titles in the doctrinal section might have appeared in other categories like Rome or the radicals. But I think the outline holds: the "doctrinal" treatises concentrate on a single doctrine, whereas the first three sections are doctrinally more wide-ranging, but focused on an opponent. On the whole we have an overview of the major fronts on which Calvin gave battle in his treatises.

Calvin does not always wield a heavy, two-handed sword. There are occasions (not many, agreed, but some) where he indulges in what I would call "gentle polemics." His disagreement with Martin Bucer on the subject of compromise with Rome in matters of worship is a case in point.[3] The disagreement is a serious one; but the tone is reticent almost to the point of embarrassment:

> Several good people of holy life and sound doctrine think that not only [the believer] may but must do so [go to parish mass], and they have some reason, or at least excuse, to confirm their view. They say that in such an assembly there is a church, from which a Christian man may not cut himself off by his private authority. But one can reply that the "Church" can be understood in different ways. [There follows a tortuous passage where Calvin accepts that we recognize Roman baptism as valid, for example; so there is a sign of the Church. On the other hand, everything is so corrupt that it is hardly recognizable.] So I would not approve of those who entirely reject such an assembly or who excommunicate it by withdrawing from it. But to communicate fully with the leaders, who

---

[2]The question has been raised whether there is not a pleonasm there, whether there are any *didactica* which are not also *polemica*. I think there is at least the *Short Treatise on the Lord's Supper* to justify the inclusion of both terms.

[3]See Francis Higman, "Bucer et les nicodémites" in *Martin Bucer and Sixteenth-Century Europe*, ed. C. Krieger and M. Lienhard (Leiden: Brill, 1993), 645–68.

are ravening wolves and dissipators of the Church, or with its vicious members, in what is wholly wrong, I cannot see there is a case.

The other reason adduced by those who allow the believer to go to the papist parochial mass is that the mass derives from the Supper of our Lord, although it is greatly contaminated and corrupted. So, they do not deny that there are a lot of sacrileges and abominations committed there, which all good hearts must detest. But they excuse a private individual who, unable to receive the Lord's Supper purely administered, does not reject the traces which he can have, although there is much to criticize. Now I find this perplexing. For I consider that the papist mass is an entire abomination, which only has the name of the Supper in the same way as the Devil disguises himself as an angel of light. Since therefore the mystery of the Supper is there profaned and destroyed, I do not know how we can accept it instead of the Supper.[4]

He goes on for several pages in this vein. While there is nothing gentle in his view of the Roman mass, his treatment of his friend and colleague Bucer is remarkably restrained.

Another example of Calvin's gentle polemics is his tone in addressing texts to the Emperor Charles V (as emerges from our category 1.b). In particular, the *Actes de la journée de Reguesbourg* (1541) reflect the hope the reformers still had that the emperor, or at least the electors, princes, and cities of the empire, might accept the Reformation. Calvin published a French translation of the collection of documents which constitutes the Acts (Bucer and Melanchthon produced Latin and German versions). In his French, Calvin makes several revealing additions. He stresses, for instance, that the Protestants have done all they could for the sake of unity, but that doctrine, truth, is not negotiable (contrast human transactions); one cannot be a traitor to God. He continues:

Nonetheless one can see that [the Protestants] present their doctrine with the utmost moderation, and argue about nothing unless they are obliged to, although their intention is always that, once agreement is reached, the word of God shall be preached purely and clearly everywhere, as they have declared in their books. On this matter the faithful who fully understand, when they consider what has moved the Protestants not to oppose too directly on a lot of matters, should not be shocked. For, although they do not want to let anything get by which is counter to the truth, they do want to show that, far from causelessly stir-

[4]"Petit traité monstrant ...," *CO* 6:582–88.

ring up conflict and dissension because of their unlimited ambition, even when there is cause to dissent, they hold back and abstain, as long as the truth is maintained. In this way they have accepted several expressions to accommodate themselves to the uneducated and weak, or have fallen back on custom or previous practice. This should not shock the faithful and God-fearing, when it is clear that everything is being done in order to arrive at a good result.[5]

While hedging himself around with concessional clauses, Calvin moves closer to compromise here than one would have imagined. He is treating the emperor with kid gloves. But, when the papal legate Contarini intervenes to have the *Acta* submitted to Rome and judged by the future council, Calvin's tone changes abruptly. We have heard this all before, he says: for twenty-four years the pope has been promising a council. We all know that he has no intention of ever summoning it, or of reforming the Church either. Even if they did call a council, he continues:

Everyone knows what theology there is at Rome, especially in the pope's consistory and among the cardinals. Their first principle is that there is no God, the second point is that Christianity is lunacy, and the rest is what follows from that. So if today a council is summoned, the pope will preside and the bishops and prelates will be judges; will they come in the name of the Lord to seek his will, and to follow what he shows them by his Word with humility and obedience?[6]

The relative restraint of Calvin's writing when concerned with the imperial authorities disappears when Rome intervenes.

Once Calvin is launched in his polemics, the sword is out. As J.K.S. Reid put it many years ago: "So long as the differences were capable of being composed, Calvin shows an admirably irenical spirit. Once hope of concord was abandoned, he relapses with some suddenness into the prevailing acrimony of tone with which disputes were commonly conducted."[7]

More often than not, Calvin does not go out looking for a fight, it is brought to him. Most of these treatises are "replies" to, "responses" to, admonitions "against" (the Anabaptists, for example; someone had asked him to refute the Schleitheim articles). He responds to Cardinal Sadoleto, to the *Articles of the Faculty of Theology*, to the Paris book censures, to the *Articles of the Council of Trent*, to Cathelan, to Saconay— and, of course, to Joachim Westphal. The major exceptions to the principle of response are the series on compromisers (the Nicodemite

[5]*CO* 5:646–47.   [6]*CO* 5:654.
[7]Introduction to, *Calvin: Theological Treatises*, ed. J. K. S. Reid (London: SCM, 1954), 16.

treatises) and the *Treatise on Relics*. The Nicodemites are of course the last people to provoke a conflict; and the subject of the *Treatise on Relics*, Calvin's most popular work, is too juicy to let pass.

Many of these publications give not only Calvin's refutation, but the full text of the writing he is refuting: Sadoleto's letter to the Genevans, the articles of the Paris faculty, the *Admonitio Pauli III*, the *Acts* of Trent, the Regensburg *Acts*, the *Interim*. It is interesting to contrast this evenhandedness with the more usual technique of theological refutation in the period (for example by the Paris theologians), which consisted of quoting extracts, out of context, from the text being refuted—a method which renders the refutation much easier.

There is a marked change in the nature of Calvin's production about the year 1550. Prior to that date we find almost all of the titles aimed at individuals or groups, and the majority of the treatises written in French. After 1550 appear most of the "doctrinal" treatises; most of these titles are in Latin. It is as if, by 1550, Calvin's status as an international religious leader has been established, and he writes for an international audience on matters of universal truth (most clearly seen in his writings against the Polish antitrinitarians).

In the earlier period it is also noticeable that most of the controversial series begin with writings in Latin; here the reason is that the practice of debating in French was yet to be established, and Latin was the natural linguistic choice. These treatises, together with the *Institution* (first French edition in 1541), are what put French on the map of intellectual debate.

II. Calvin's Readership: Latin and French

The choice of language also implies a different public. In his Latin works Calvin clearly addresses himself to an audience of intellectual equals: he expects his reader to identify classical allusions, to draw deductions without his having to point them out, to be aware of irony. When he writes in French, he reduces or eliminates classical references, he makes each point explicit, and he uses irony only of the most heavy-handed sort.

This can be seen most clearly in those texts which Calvin himself translated from Latin into French. Let us take the *Acta synodi tridentinae* of 1547, translated into French (almost certainly by Calvin) in 1548. Calvin reproduces the text of the *Acta*, and follows each section with a refutation. In refuting the introduction, he stresses that the bishops assembled at Trent do not themselves produce theological statements, but are guided by a group of monks who "croak out some sort of buzzing in their quarrels, like Aristophanes' frogs."[8] In French, "these pen-push-

---

[8]"stridulum nescio quid ipsos rixando, tanquam ranas Aristophanis, coaxare" (*CO* 7: 383).

ing monks scribble on the paper"[9] to produce what then passes for a revelation from the Holy Spirit. A few lines further on, Calvin asks whether going to Trent has made ignorant bishops into expert theologians: in Latin, "must we think that, when they moved to another place, they are suddenly inspired with divine power, as if they were subject to the tripod of the Delphic priestess?"[10] This is weakened in French: "shall we think that by a change of air they are suddenly illuminated with divine inspiration?"[11] In any case, says Calvin, all the texts proposed at Trent are sent to Rome, where the pope and his counselors make whatever changes they see fit. He concludes: "We can, I believe, rightly reject what we know was composed by such doctors and corrected by such an Aristarchus."[12] In French: "We may be allowed to despise what has been scribbled by such doctors, and amended by such a corrector."[13] And finally, Calvin asserts: "These Neptunian Fathers are not so grand with their trident"[14] that they should not be punished by the Word of God. Again the French loses some of the effect: "Milords the prelates of Trent are not so precious that one may not touch them."[15]

The elimination of classical allusions generally leads to a weakening in the French. This is compensated by an increased energy in the vituperation in French, often accompanied by conversational, almost slang, elements absent from the Latin. Calvin's summary of how the Tridentine texts are vetted in Rome is an excellent example. The Latin is a model of succinct elegance:

> As soon as any decree is composed, the messengers fly to Rome, and implore peace and pardon at the feet of their idol. The most holy father hands over whatever has arrived to his private counsellors for study. They delete, add or change whatever seems right. The messengers return, a session is summoned. The secretary reads out what no one dares to criticize. The asses agree with their ears. Behold an oracle which religiously binds the whole world.[16]

---

[9] "ces moynes fallourdiers barbouillent le papier."

[10] "An eos, simul atque locum mutaverint, repentino afflari numine putabimus, ac si Phoebades Delphicam cortinam subiissent?"

[11] "Estimerons-nous donc que pour avoir changé d'air, ils soyent soudain illuminez d'inspiration celeste?"

[12] "Nobis vero impune, opinor, contemne relicebit, quod a talibus magistris compositum, a tali Aristarcho correctum esse agnoscimus"; *CO* 7:384–85.

[13] "Il nous sera bien licite de mespriser tout ce qui aura esté barbouillé par tels docteurs, et amendé par un tel correcteur."

[14] "Neptunios istos patres nec tam formidabiles esse cum suo Tridento…" (*CO* 7:385). The witticism appears several times in the correspondence between Calvin, Viret and Farel; see Rodolphe Peter and Jean-François Gilmont, *Bibliotheca Calviniana* (Geneva: Droz, 1991), 1: 238.

[15] "messieurs les prelats de Trente ne sont pas si precieux, qu'on ne les puisse toucher."

[16] "Simul atque compositum est decretum aliquod, Romam volitant cursores: veniam pacemque exposcunt a pedibus idoli sui. Privatis suis consultoribus examinandum tradit sanctissimus pater, quod est allatum. Demunt illi, addunt, et mutant quod videtur. Redeunt cursores, sessio indicitur.

The French is more lively:

> As soon as a decree is composed, the messengers run to Rome, to find out what it will please their idol to order. The holy father calls his privy council to examine the *bundle.* There they cut, or add, or change according to their view. The messengers return. A new session is held. The secretary announces what no one would dare to criticize. *Milords* the asses *bow* their ears to *make it seem* they agree. And there's an oracle to subject the whole world.[17]

In the *Articuli a facultate sacrae theologiae Parisiensi determinati … cum antidoto* of 1544, Calvin uses another technique. He quotes each of the twenty-six articles of faith as defined by the Paris theologians in 1543; but, before refuting them in serious vein (and in "pure" Classical Latin), he provides a burlesque "proof" of the article as if written by a "Sorbonnagre"—and in a scholastic Latin worthy of the Faculty (or of the *Epistolae obscurorum virorum*):

> Dico, quod contra negantem principia, non est arguendum. Item, nos habemus pro nobis unam aliam demonstrationem.[18]

This parodic element is more or less lost in the French:

> Je dis qu'il ne faut point disputer contre un homme, qui nie les principes. Aussi nous avons encore un autre bon argument pour nous.[19]

On the other hand, the French makes some points much more explicit than the Latin. Article I states that baptism is necessary for salvation:

Recitat notarius, quod improbare nemo audeat. Asini auribus annuunt. En oraculum, quod religione totum mundum obstringat"; *CO* 7:384.

[17]"Si tost qu'il y a un decret composé, les postes courent à Rome, pour savoir ce qu'il plaira à leur idole d'en ordonner. Le sainct Pere appelle son conseil estroit pour examiner le paquet. Là on retranche, ou on adjouste, ou bien on change selon l'advis qu'on a. Les postes retournent. Une Session nouvelle se tient. Le secretaire prononce ce que nul n'oseroit reprouver. Messieurs les asnes baissent les aureilles pour faire semblant d'y consentir. Voyla un oracle pour assujettir tout le monde."

[18]From article 4, on Works, *CO* 7:12.

[19]"I say that one must not dispute with a man who denies the principles. Also, we have another good argument for us."

Probatur sic: Quia alias baptisma per mulieres datum, nihil valeret, quod est expresse fundamentum in hac fide, quia baptismus sit de necessitate salutis: utcunque sit prohibitum in concilio Carthaginensi, quod mulieres baptizare non praesumant, sine aliqua exceptione.	Je le prouve. Car autrement le baptesme donné par les sages-femmes ne vaudroit rien. Lequel est expressement fondé en ceste foi, que le baptesme est necessaire à salut. *Et mesmes il appert combien ceste necessité est grande, vu que pour icelle on a permis aux femmes de baptiser,* comtre la defense expresse du Concile Carthage quatriesme, *où le contraire est resolu au centiesme decret.*

Calvin's "serious" refutations are also sometimes made more explicit in the French. On the question of auricular confession (article 3): "De confessione ad aurem sacerdotis de facienda, nulla usquam mentio Touchant: *susciller en l'oreille.* d'un prestre, il n'en fait nulle mention."

Examples could be multiplied to show that Calvin has in mind, for his Latin works, an educated reader who can follow the rapidity of his thought; in French, he is broadening his readership to include a less educated public, which needs more clear exposition—and, by the manipulation of polemical language, a firmer steering towards the "right" opinion.

III. Techniques

We now arrive at the question of stylistic techniques in Calvin's polemical works. These techniques are most visible in his writings in French (though, as we have just seen, there are techniques enough in his Latin as well). Ostensibly, Calvin's approach to writing is simple to the point of innocence:

> I have tried as far as I could to accommodate myself to the plainness of simple people, for whom I was mainly working. Thus the Anabaptists cannot quarrel … that I have tried to win them over by subtlety, or to crush them by the cleverness of human eloquence, since I have kept to as popular and simple a manner as one could wish.

> There is no better way to confute them than to set out and discuss each question distinctly, and raise one point after another in order; to weigh up and look closely at the words of Scripture in order to draw out the true and natural sense; to use simple and direct words not far removed

from everyday language.... For my part, I confess that as far as I am able I strive to set out in order what I am saying, in order to give clearer and easier understanding.[20]

This is a key text for understanding Calvin's literary aesthetic, at least in appearance. Accommodation to the needs of the simple audience (just as, on a higher level, God "accommodates" himself to human understanding);[21] the avoidance of rhetoric, the simplicity of vocabulary, the presentation in careful order of his arguments, the true sense of the Scripture: these are all that Calvin claims. He derives these principles from the simple language of Scripture, notably of the synoptic Gospels;[22] if they seem obvious to us, it is because Calvin succeeded in imposing them—they were by no means obvious to his contemporaries. The lucidity and trenchancy of Calvin's prose is what his contemporaries, both friends and enemies, most remarked (without being able to imitate those qualities); it is what set Calvin head and shoulders above his colleagues as a religious leader in the Reformation.[23]

But, as a statement of Calvin's literary practice, it is highly disingenuous. The apparent simplicity of his writing is underlaid by a systematic presentation of vocabulary, syntax, and imagery designed to guide and influence the reader, to orientate him towards the "right" attitude in the debate. Here is not the time or place to attempt a full exposition of Calvin's stylistic qualities;[24] but a schematic summary may be possible on the basis of the "sword" of our title.

Calvin's polemical weapon is definitely a two-edged sword. At every level, he practices oppositions between his own position and that of his adversaries, which underlie the contrast between truth and falsehood. He makes the point theoretically, and explicitly, in his preface to Viret's *Disputations chrestiennes* (1544):

One should note that Christianity can be discussed in two ways: firstly, in denouncing the mad superstitions which have grown up among Christians under the disguise of religion.... Secondly, in showing the pure and simple truth, as it is revealed to us in God's holy word. As regards this second sort, it is certain that, as soon as we open our mouths to speak of God, no jokes should come into our discourse; but, in all that we say, we

[20] *Contre les Anabaptistes, CO* 7:139–40.

[21] Ford Lewis Battles, "God Was Accommodating Himself to Human Capacity," *Interpretation, A Journal of Bible and Theology* 47 (1977):19–38; O. Millet, *Calvin et la dynamique de la parole: Étude de rhétorique réformée* (Paris: Champion, 1992), 247–256.

[22] See L. Wencelius, *L'Esthétique de Calvin* (Paris: Belles Lettres, 1937).

[23] See Francis Higman, "Calvin polémiste," *Études théologiques et religieuses* 69 (1994): 349–65.

[24] See Francis Higman, *The Style of John Calvin in His French Polemical Treatises* (Oxford: Oxford University Press, 1957).

must show the reverence we feel towards His majesty, and never speak a word other than in fear and humility. But when we take apart the superstitions and follies in which the world has been entangled until now, we cannot help, in talking of such ridiculous matters, but that we laugh out loud.[25]

This binary principle is systematically applied in his own writings. It is easily perceived in the way he introduces arguments for or against his doctrine. For example (to bring the *Institution* into the polemical context), he is refuting (3.23.7) the view of "the adversaries" that God did not will the Fall. (Introductions to the adversaries' arguments are italicized; citations of his own doctrines are in SMALL CAPS):

> *They say* that Adam was created with his free will.... *If such a frigid invention is accepted, where is the infinite power of God...? In any case, gnash their teeth as they will* [lit. "in spite of their teeth"], God's predestination IS SEEN in the whole descendance of Adam.... *Why should they waste their energies on wriggling?* // THE SCRIPTURE SAYS LOUD AND CLEAR that all mortal creatures are subject to death in the person of one man. SINCE THIS CANNOT be attributed to nature, IT MUST COME from God's admirable counsel. *It is too clumsy an inconsistency that these lawyers, who thrust themselves forward* to uphold the justice of God, are *brought up short by a straw, but hop over a great beam.*

The beginning of each sentence tells the reader how he is to evaluate what follows, either as an absurdity, or as plain fact.

More subtly, the orientation takes place at the level of choice of language. Thus, when he is presenting his own doctrine, his vocabulary is serious, much based on scriptural terms (including scriptural images like the Good Shepherd, the Way, the Fountain, the Bread of Life...); the syntax is balanced and harmonious, reflecting the true order of God's providential guidance. When he turns to the adversary, on the other hand, the vocabulary becomes popular to the point of vulgarity, the syntax is broken and disjointed, the images loaded with a heavy charge of distasteful associations (pigs, dogs, brigands, prostitutes, lavatory cleaners). Just one example to illustrate the way in which Calvin seeks confrontation:

> We must have such zeal for the honor of God that, when He is injured, we feel an anguish which burns our heart. We must have such love for our neighbors that, when we see them in danger of destruction, espe-

[25]*CO* 9:865.

cially as regards their soul, we should be moved with pity and compassion. // Satan, by these clowns, wants to make the world brutish, so that, whatever confusion we see, we couldn't care less; so that we should not be moved at all when we see the name of God blasphemed, his holy commandments violated, souls lost, wickedness triumph.[26]

The relentless orientation of the reader through linguistic techniques is one of the powerful elements in Calvin's persuasive success; and it is very far from the innocent claim that he does not "crush his adversaries with the tricks of human eloquence."

IV. Conclusions: Reflections on Calvin's Rhetoric

So far we have done little more than align a series of facts, many of them already well known to the reader. I should like, finally, to attempt to rise a little higher, and present a certain number of reflections in guise of conclusions.

1. The Limits of Calvin's Polemical Rhetoric

When Calvin is "accommodating" himself to the simplicity of his assumed readers, he is accepting a certain limitation on his scope.[27] His need to provide maximum forcefulness and clarity, reflected in his relentlessly binary structure, leads to a certain schematization of his presentation, and often to a simplification of his material.[28]

Besides this accommodation, a characteristic of Calvin's writing is his insistence on utility.[29] Whether he is discussing the attributes of God, or Christian wisdom, or the nature of man, he regularly refuses to delve too far into philosophical debate, and limits himself to "a knowledge of God which is not based on vain speculation, but which is useful and fruitful to us" (*Institution*, 1541, p. 56), or to "what is profitable and expedient." Again, Calvin is limiting himself in his potential scope.

Clear and simple his style may be; but it is not colorful (references to "black and white" are innumerable in Calvin; there are rarely mentions of colors). There are flights of poetic uplift in Calvin, but they are rare. The sword is a functional weapon.

---

[26] *Contre les libertins, CO* 7:197.
[27] Quite apart, of course, from his oft-stated awareness that all theological language is "accommodation" to human limitations of the divine, and therefore inaccessible, truth.
[28] An example is his definition of providence in *Contre les libertins*, chaps. 12–16. Compare the more detailed and more Scripture-based treatment, in particular of possible objections, in *Institution* 1.16.
[29] See the numerous references to *utilité* in the index of O. Millet, *Calvin et la dynamique*, 970.

2. *The "Objective Truth"?*

That Calvin was a rhetorician, as Bouwsma (and others) state, there can be no doubt. But do we go along with Bouwsma in asserting that Calvin was "less concerned with the objective truth of his message than with its effect on his audience"?

First, what, in the eyes of Calvin, is this "objective truth"? The answer is clearly the Word of God, as revealed in Holy Scripture. Scripture gives all the data (in principle) of Calvin's theology; by far the greatest part of his ministry was occupied in the exposition of Scripture, whether in sermons, commentaries, or lectures; the *Institution* itself is a "key" to the understanding of Scripture, or a "path" into it.

However much individual writers in the Scriptures have their individual styles, Scripture is nonetheless the work of one, divine author: Calvin constantly introduces biblical quotations with the words: "The Holy Spirit says by the mouth of Moses" or "by the mouth of David" or "by the mouth of St. Paul." And the Holy Spirit does not contradict himself. All Scripture is therefore consistent with itself, the Old Testament and the New Testament, St. James and St. Paul.

What of those places where, on the surface, Scripture does appear to be contradictory? In Calvin's mind, this must be due to the limitations of fallen human reason, not inherent in Scripture itself. The task of the theologian must be to winkle out the underlying coherence of the message[30]—and, having identified that coherence, to *communicate* it. Calvin conceives his job as *explanatory*, not as *exploratory*: he is not setting out to discover new truths—the truth is given; his job is to explain, to communicate, to convince of, the given truth. One may contrast Calvin's approach with the discursive, conversational, questioning, dialogic qualities of Montaigne's *Essays*. Montaigne is exploring, Calvin never: the truth is revealed.

3. *The Battle for Hearts and Minds, and the Holy Spirit*

The "objective truth" is central and obligatory in Calvin's thought, and I cannot go along with Bouwsma's "less interested...." But I can take a reformulation: the truth is objective, but the battle is not. The historical context of all Calvin's work is that of battle: battle to impose the "correct" understanding of the Word of God on limited, corrupt human beings, battle to oppose, fight down,

---

[30]The clearest example I know of comes not from a polemical work, but from the Commentary on James, chap. 2, presenting James' carefully constructed argument, culminating (v. 24) with the famous: "Ye see then how that by works a man is justified, and not only by faith." Calvin's lengthy gloss concludes that "justified" here means "justified before men," and that the "faith" referred to is a cold intellectual assent—which enables him to claim that there is no contradiction with Paul.

destroy the forces of evil, under whatever guise. This means that, not only by the cogency of the argument, but also by all his many techniques of orientating the reader and guiding his judgment, Calvin is backing up the "factual" argument by persuasive techniques.

It is thus not that the rhetoric ("effective speaking," to borrow a phrase from another context) replaces the "objective truth," but that the rhetoric gives that truth its communicative charge, enables it to touch its target and to have its effect of conviction. We rejoin Oliver Millet's categories of *movere* and *docere*: Calvin is doing both. The aim is the conviction of heart and mind.

Finally, it seems to me that the role of rhetoric, in terms of communicating persuasion on the level of human psychology (the heart), is in Calvin's thought and writing closely associated with the "inner conviction of the Holy Spirit" on the level of the soul. Calvin's rhetoric is the instrument that can open the way, in the heart of the reader, to the conviction, the conversion, which is the work of God alone.

[Appendix begins on next page.]

APPENDIX
Jean Calvin: Didactica/Polemica

4. Doctrines

4.1. Sacraments

4.2. Trinity

4.3. Predestination

CHÂTEAU OF AMBOISE.

Der Eigentumsbegriff Calvins angesichts der Einführung der neuen Geldwirtschaft

Hans-Helmut Eßer

I. Einleitung und Grundlegung

"Nostri non sumus sed Domini."[1] Mit diesem Leitsatz der Ethik Calvins ist die Eigentumsbeziehung zentral christologisch bestimmt und in der Konsequenz auch trinitarisch. Der Abschnitt 3.7.4 der *Institutio* trägt die Überschrift: "Summa vitae Christianae...."[2] Die christliche Gemeinde bekennt mit diesem Leitsatz doxologisch den lebendigen Gott als den einen Eigentümer; und das Eigentum des einzelnen Christen an Personen und Sachen, den je persönlichen Gaben Gottes in Schöpfung, Erlösung und Heiligung (Dankbarkeit), als in die Christusgemeinschaft der Gemeinde einbezogen.[3] Daß dieses Bekenntnis nicht gesetzlich, sondern evangelisch-freiheitlich zu verstehen ist, verdeutlicht seine klassische Interpretation in der von den Calvin-Schülern Ursinus und Olevian verfaßten *Frage 1 des Heidelberger Katechismus*,[4] welche gleichsam in einer vorweggesetzten Klammer rühmt, was "Christi eigen" sein in des Menschen Elend, Erlösung und in der Dankbarkeit, zu der der Christ gebracht wird, bedeutet: Trost als Gehaltensein, Befreiung von Sünde und Gewalt des Teufels, Bewahrtsein unter der Provi-

---

[1] *Inst.* 3.7.1 (*OS* 4.151.16 (mit Wiederholung Z. 18, 20, 21 der Negation; Z. 23–25 der Position, die 1559 durch "Dei sumus" ersetzt wird); als Auslegung von Röm.14,7–8.

[2] *Inst.* 3.7.1 (*OS* 4.151.1). Die Texthervorhebungen durch Kursivdruck stammen jeweils vom Verf. dieses Beitrags; die durchgehenden Unterstreichungen geben Sperrungen im zitierten Text oder formale Hervorhebungen des Verfassers wieder.

[3] Cf. dazu auch Gottfried Wilhelm Locher, "Calvin: Die Ehre Jesu Christi in Seiner Gemeinde und ihren Mitteln" in *Der Eigentumsbegriff als Problem evangelischer Theologie* (Zürich, 1962), 36–44, 53–55; bes. Anm. 99; ferner Ludi Schulze, *Calvin and "Social Ethics": His Views on Property, Interest and Usury* (Pretoria: Kital, 1985). Dieses Werk ist die subtilste Spezialuntersuchung zu unserem Thema. Der Verf. schließt den Abschnitt (2.1) seiner Studie: *John Calvin, His Views on Property*, mit dem Satz: "Domini sumus— we are the Lord's. From this wonder of his gracious gift sprang our responsibility toward one another"; dort, 48: Zum doxologischen Aspekt des Eigentumsbegriffs innerhalb der natürlichen (Schöpfungs–) Ordnung ist besonders zu erwähnen die Studie von Susan E. Schreiner, *The Theater of His Glory: Nature and the Natural Order in the Thought of John Calvin* (Durham, N.C.: Labyrinth Press, 1991), 4–5, 90, 95.

[4] Cf. Jubiläumsausgabe 1963: 400 Jahre nach der Erstausgabe 1563. Beachte auch im ersten Teil der Antwort zu Frage 1 die Formulierung: "der mit seinem teuren Blut für alle meine Sünden vollkömmlich *bezahlet*...." Eigentum u.a. auf Grund von Loskauf!

denz Gottes des Vaters zur Seligkeit; und durch den Heiligen Geist des ewigen
Lebens vergewissert und zu einem Christus dienenden Leben bereit gemacht.[5]
Das derart doxologisch-verantwortungsethisch begründete Verständnis des
Eigentums ermöglicht eine nicht einengende Auslegung biblischer Aussagen zur
Sache, die sich dynamisch den Herausforderungen der Reformationszeit stellt, die
Verlockungen verschwenderischen Luxuslebens ebenso meidet wie die des idealis-
tischen Güterkommunismus, aber das Dienstgefälle von reich zu arm in Liebe
wahrnimmt und nach der Goldenen Regel in aequitas ((Billigkeit/Rechtlichkeit)
ordnet, auch unter Überholen der traditionellen Lösungsangebote. Eine schwier-
ige Aufgabe in einer verarmten Stadt, in der Christengemeinde und Bürgerge-
meinde zu einer fragwürdigen, aber faktischen Identität gezwungen sind, die
politisch von Savoyen, Frankreich und vom Kaiser bedroht ist, Tausenden von
beruflich hochqualifizierten Glaubensflüchtlingen Fluchtstätte sowie beruflichen
Neubeginn bieten will und muß, und die sogar unter dem wirtschaftlichen Druck
ihrer eidgenössischen Verbündeten steht, der nur durch Kreditaufnahme der
Stadt und Anschluß an die aufbrechende Kapitalwirtschaft aufgefangen werden
kann.[6]

II. Der neue Eigentumsbegriff Calvins

1. Methodologische Zwischenüberlegung

Es ist hier aus Raum- und Zeitgründen nicht möglich, den weiten ontolo-
gischen Rahmen abzuschreiten, den Ludi Schulze in seiner Monographie präzise
absteckt.[7] Statt dessen folgen wir den Schwerpunktsetzungen Gottfried Wilhelm
Lochers,[8] die besonders das Calvin von seinen Mitreformatoren unterscheidende

---

[5]Die Auslegung des drei-fachen "Dei sumus" in *OS* 4:151: (1) "illi ergo vivamus ac moriamur"
(Z. 23); (2) "Cunctis ergo nostris actionibus praesideat sapientia eius et voluntas," (Z. 24–25); (3) "ad
illum igitur, tanquam solum legitimum finem, contendant omnes vitae nostrae partes [Rom. 14:6–8]"
(Z. 25–27). Diese Auslegung schließt mit dem Ausruf: "O quantum ille profecit qui se non suum esse
edoctus, dominum regimenque sui propriae ratione abrogavit, ut Deo asserat!" (Z. 27–29).
[6]Zur politischen und wirtschaftlichen Lage Genfs seit der Reformation und bis zum Ende des 16.
Jh. cf. die grundlegenden Untersuchungen: André Biéler, *La pensée économique et sociale de Calvin*
(Genf: Librairie de l'Université, 1961), und Alfred Bürgin, *Kapitalismus und Calvinismus. Versuch einer
wirtschaftsgeschichtlichen religionssoziologischen Untersuchung der Verhältnisse in Genf im 16. und
beginnenden 17. Jahrhundert* (Winterthur, 1960); ferner die Aufsätze: H. Lüthy, "Nochmals: Calvinismus und Kapitalismus: Über die Irrwege einer sozialhistorischen Diskussion," *Schweizerische Zeitschrift für Geschichte* 11 (1961): 129–56; Geiger, *Calvin, Calvinismus, Kapitalismus, in: Gottesreich und
Menschenreich* (Basel/Stuttgart: F. S. Ernst Staehelin, 1969), 230-86; Hans H. Eßer, "Calvins Sozialethik
und der Kapitalismus," *Hervormde Teologiese Studies* 48. Jg., 3. u. 4. (FS A.D. Pont, Pretoria 1992): 783–
800. In den angegebenen Titeln jeweils weitere Lit.
[7]Schulze, *Calvin and "Social Ethics,"* 15–47.
[8]Locher, *Eigentumsbegriff,* 36–44; 53–55.

Neue[9] in seinem Eigentumsverständnis markieren. Analoge Gesichtspunkte bei Ludi Schulze sollen dabei berücksichtigt werden.

2. *Eigentum ist unproblematisch, denn es ist eine Gabe Gottes*

Calvin empfindet im Unterschied zur kirchlichen Tradition,[10] aber auch zu Luther und Zwingli,[11] das Problem des Eigentums nicht mehr. "Der Besitz selbst wird nie verhandelt, er gilt überall als selbstverständliche Voraussetzung."[12] Überall, wo Calvin auf die Güte der Gaben Gottes eingeht, kritisiert er darum nicht die Gaben selbst, sondern er lobt ihre Vorzüge und weist ein in ihren angemessenen Gebrauch:

> Der Gebrauch der Gaben Gottes geht nicht vom rechten Wege ab, wenn er sich auf den Zweck ausrichtet, zu dem uns der Geber selbst diese Gaben erschaffen und bestimmt hat. Er hat sie nämlich zu unserem Besten erschaffen und nicht zu unserem Verderben.... Wenn wir nun also bedenken, zu welchem Zweck er die Nahrungsmittel erschaffen hat, so werden wir finden, daß er damit nicht bloß für unsere Notdurft sorgen wollte, sondern auch für unser Ergötzen und unsere Freude.[13]

Den gleichen Lobpreis der Güte Gottes gewinnt Calvin aus der Anmut der Kleidung, der Schönheit der Kräuter, Bäume, Früchte und Blumen, der Freude des Menschenherzens am Wein, der Schönheitswirkung des Öls (Ps. 104,15). Er schließt die lange Aufzählung u.a. der Schönheit der Farben, des Goldes, von Silber, Elfenbein und Marmor mit der Frage: "Hat er (Gott) nicht überhaupt viele Dinge über den notwendigen Gebrauch hinaus fruchtbar gemacht?"[14] Dieser Frage folgt eine barsche Abweisung "jener unmenschlichen Philosophie, die uns die Kreaturen nur zur Notdurft will brauchen lassen und uns damit einer erlaubten Frucht der göttlichen Wohltätigkeit beraubt."[15]

Erst nach dem Rühmen der Gaben Gottes und der Ermutigung zur Freude an ihrem freimütigen Gebrauch bringt Calvin drei Regeln zum Gott wohlgefälligen

---

[9]Locher, *Eigentumsbegriff*, 36; cf. dazu auch Geiger, *Calvin, Calvinismus, Kapitalismus,*, 248–53; Schulze, *Calvin and "Social Ethics"* 18–21.

[10]Cf. M. Hengel, *Eigentum und Reichtum in der frühen Kirche. Aspekte einer frühchristlichen Sozialgeschichte* (Stuttgart, 1973); Schulze, *Calvin and "Social Ethics"*18–21.

[11]Cf. Schulze, *Calvin and "Social Ethics,"* 21; Locher, *Eigentumsbegriff*, 536–37; Biéler, *La pensée*, 387 ff.

[12]Locher, *Eigentumsbegriff*; cf. Schulze, *Calvin and "Social Ethics,"* 18, 21.

[13]*Inst.* 3.10.2; das Kapitel trägt die Überschrift: Quomodo utendum praesenti vita, eisque adiumentis, s. *OS* 4.177.7–8, 4.178.11–14, 15–17. Die deutschen Texte der *Institutio* werden zitiert nach der 3. Aufl. der einbändigen Ausgabe der Übersetzung von Otto Weber (Neukirchen: Neükirchener Verlag, 1984).

[14]Zum ganzen Zusammenhang, cf. *OS* 4:178:15–32; hier, 32–34.

[15]*OS* 4:178:35–37.

Umgang mit den anvertrauten Gütern:[16] (1) Das paulinische Haben, als hätte
man nicht;[17] (2) Das geduldige Ertragen enger und karger Verhältnisse in Genüg-
samkeit;[18] (3) Die eschatologische Perspektive der *Rechenschaftgabe* über das aus
Gottes Freundlichkeit uns geschenkte Gut. Die Liebe gibt für diese Umgangsweise
das rechte Maß.[19]

Zum Schluß dieser Erwägungen bindet Calvin die angemessenen Verhaltens-
weisen *providentiell* ein: "in eine der *vocatio* entsprechende Wahrnehmung des
zugewiesenen *Berufs*. (Wobei zu beachten ist, daß im Lateinischen 'Beruf' und
'Berufung' *ein* und dasselbe Wort sind.)"[20]

Die providentielle Erleichterung des angemessenen Umgangs mit dem anvertrauten Eigentum erläutert Calvin an der Geschichte der Trennung Abrams von
Lot, Genesis 13:

> Es bestand Gefahr, daß Abram sich in seinem Glück zu sicher fühlte....
> Darum muß Abram diese bittere, aber heilsame Arznei trinken. Es ist
> gut, daß auch der Reichtum seine Beschwerde hat. Wir sollen den Gütern
> dieser Zeit nicht unbegrenzt nachhängen... Wer Überfluß hat, der hüte
> sich, daß ihn die Dornen nicht stechen. Wer bedrängt ist, der wisse, daß
> Gott ihm dies auferlegt.... Oft trifft Gott Vorsorge auf künftige Zeit. So
> wird Abram erzogen, daß Habsucht und Stolz für ihn keine versuchende
> Macht gewinnen.[21]

Schon zu Beginn der Auslegung des genannten Genesis-Kapitels hatte sich
Calvin gegen die mittelalterliche ethische Hierarchie gewehrt, an deren Spitze die
selbstgewählte Besitzlosigkeit steht. Er nimmt dabei einen Aspekt vorweg, den er

---

[16]*Inst.* 3.10.4–5; cf. *OS* 4:179:25–180:35.

[17]Cf. *OS* 4:179:25–28 (1 Kor. 7,29–31).

[18]Cf. *OS* 4:180:6–9.

[19]Cf. *OS* 4:180:22–28.

[20]*Inst.* 3.10.6; cf. *OS* 4:180:36–181:32; dort Z. 25–26: "dum quisque sciet Deus in his omnibus sibi
esse ducem."

[21]Kommentar zu Gen. 13:5 in *Johann Calvins Auslegung der Heiligen Schrift, Neue Reihe* (hereafter *AHSNR*), 1:143; cf. *CO* 23 (von 1554), Sp. 190: "Periculum erat ne sibi nimium placeret in sua for-
tuna.... Ergo opum dulcedinem quasi aceto temperat Deus: ne patitur servi sui Hanimum illa nimium
aliniri. Quum autem fallax opinio ad divitias plus *aequo* appetendas nos impellat, quia non sentimus
quantas incommoditates secum trahant, valeat huis historiae memoria ad cohibendum illum immodi-
cum amorem. Deinde quoties aliquid molestiae ex suis copiis sentiunt divites, hac medicina purgare
animos suos discant, ne praesentibus bonis ultra modum sint addicti.... (Die deutsche Übersetzung in
AHSNR ist hier gerafft.).... Denique, qui abundant, spinis se circumdatos esse, meminerint, et caveant
ne pungantur. Quibus res sunt arctae, et magis restrictae, sciant *divinitus* sibi prospici.... Deus saepe
... in futurum prospicit. Sic Abrae servi sui non correxit avaritiam vel superbiam, sed *anticipato reme-
dio* effecit ne quibus illecebris eius animum inficeret Satan." Cf. die englische Übersetzung bei Schulze,
Calvin and "Social Ethics," 17.

erst ein Jahr später in der Evangelienharmonie zu Luk 16:25[22] einbringen wird; dort heißt es:

> Man darf die Stelle "nicht so auffassen, als ob auf all die das ewige Verderben warte, die in dieser Welt gut und glücklich gelebt haben. Ja, Augustin bemerkt in kluger Weise, der arme Lazarus sei darum in den Schoß des *reichen*[23] Abraham getragen worden, damit wir erkennen, daß Reichtum niemandem die Pforte zum Himmelreich verschließt, sondern daß sie allen in gleicher Weise offensteht, denen, die sich in Maßen ihres Reichtums bedient, und denen, die ihn geduldig entbehrt haben."

In der Einleitung zu Gen. 13,1 kommentiert Calvin:

> Weiterhin zeigt uns Mose, daß aller Reichtum für Abram *kein Hindernis* war, unentwegt das Ziel zu verfolgen.... So mögen alle mit irdischem Gut Gesegneten auf die Berufung Gottes schauen. Dieses Vorbild Abrams nimmt uns alle Entschuldigung. Aber auch nach der anderen Seite hin haben wir etwas zu lernen. Manche meinen, sie müßten all ihr Gut wegwerfen, sonst könnten sie nicht Gott nachfolgen ... zahlreich sind die Schwärmer, welche den Reichen alle Hoffnung auf Seligkeit rauben möchten. Als ob Armut schon die Pforte des Himmels wäre. Sie kann manchmal den Menschen mehr Hindernis bereiten als Reichtum.

Und nun folgt die Vorwegnahme des Augustin-Zitates:

> Augustin hat ein feines Wort gesprochen: Der arme Lazarus sitzt in des reichen Abraham Schoß. So will Gott *dasselbe Erbteil* des ewigen Lebens Reichen und Armen geben. Hüten wir uns nur, daß nicht der Reichtum uns beschwere und hinderlich werde auf dem Weg zum Himmelreich.[24]

Daß alles, was Gott geschaffen hat, gut ist und nichts verwerflich, was mit Danksagung empfangen wird, betont Calvin ebenso im Kommentar zu 1. Tim.

---

[22]*AHSNR* 12:445 (Calvins Kommentar stammt aus den Jahr 1555); cf. Schulze, *Calvin and "Social Ethics"*; Tholuck, Ausg. 2 (1883), 51.

[23]In der Übersetzung gesperrt.

[24]*AHSNR* 1:142–43; cf. *CO* 23 (von 1554), Sp. 189 zu Gen 13:1–2: "Quare divitibus omnis excusatio tollitur, si in terra defixi, ad Dei vocationem non attendunt. Quanquam duo hic extrema cavenda sunt. Multi perfectionem angelicam constituunt in paupertate, ac si pietatem colere, et Deum sequi non liceret, nisi abiectis divitis.... Multi tamen phanatici, divites procul repellunt a spe salutis: ac si sola paupertas coelorum esset ianua: quae tamen pluribus impedimentis interdum homines involvit quam divitiae. Scite autem Augustinus qui divites pauperibus aggregari admonet a Deo *in eandem vitae hereditatem*: quia Lazarus pauper in sinum divitis Abrahae receptus fuerit. Rursus cavendum est ab altera vitio, ne scilicet remoram iniiciant divitiae, vel nos aggravent quominus expediti pergamus in regnum coelorum."

4:3–5. Die Beiseitenahme aller Güter Gottes für den besonderen Dienst (Heiligung) geschieht durch das Wort Gottes und Gebet. Calvin wehrt dabei in sinngemäßer Auslegung das Eheverbot und die Speiseverbote bestimmter gnostischer Sektierer konsequent ab:

> Wie groß ... ist die Anmaßung der Menschen, das zu verbieten, was Gott freundlich darreicht! ... ER, der sie (die Speisen) geschaffen hat, hat auch den Gebrauch freigegeben, den Menschen vergeblich zu verhindern suchen. Paulus fügt ... hinzu, daß wir seine (Gottes) Gaben *mit Danksagung* empfangen sollen, weil wir dem Herrn seine Freigebigkeit nicht vergelten können, es sei denn durch das Zeugnis der Dankbarkeit... Ohne Zweifel hat Gott eigentlich die ganze Welt und alles, was in der Welt ist, allein für seine Kinder bestimmt. Deshalb heißen sie auch Erben der Welt. Adam war unter der Bedingung, daß er Gott gehorsam blieb, zum Herrn über alles gesetzt worden. Also hat ihn und seine Nachkommen sein Ungehorsam gegen Gott des Rechtes auf das, was ihm übertragen worden war, beraubt. Da nun aber alle Dinge Christus untertan sind, werden wir durch seine Güte wieder in das alte Recht eingesetzt durch den Glauben.... In der Tat ist wahrer Glaube ... eine auf Gottes Wort gestützte klare Erkenntnis.... Nicht darum allein werden die Geschöpfe rein genannt, weil sie Gottes Werke sind, sondern weil Gottes Güte sie uns zum Gebrauch überwiesen hat.

Zu 5.5:

> Aber worin besteht die Heiligung all der Güter, die zur Erhaltung unseres gegenwärtigen Lebens gehören? Paulus bezeugt, sie bestehe im *Wort Gottes* und im *Gebet*.... Der gewöhnliche Menschenverstand redet uns freilich ein, daß die Vorräte der Welt von Natur zu unserem Gebrauch bestimmt seien. Aber da uns die Herrschaft über die Welt in Adam entzogen ist, so wird alles, was wir von den göttlichen Gaben berühren, durch unsern Schmutz verunreinigt; und es bleibt unrein, bis Gott in seiner Großmut uns zu Hilfe kommt, uns dem Leib seines Sohnes angliedert und uns von neuem zu Herren der Welt einsetzt, so daß wir alles, was er uns darreicht, erlaubterweise gleichsam als unser Vermögen genießen dürfen. Deshalb bringt Paulus mit Grund den rechtmäßigen Genuß mit dem Wort Gottes in Verbindung. Denn durch dieses allein erlangen wir wieder, was in Adam verloren war. Wir müssen Gott als unsern Vater anerkennen, wenn wir seine Erben sein wollen, und Chris-

tus als unser Haupt, wenn sein Eigentum auch unser Eigentum werden soll.[25]

Mit dieser Exegese Calvins ist eine Schlüsselstelle für sein Eigentumsverständnis erschlossen. In ontologischer Argumentation bindet der Reformator das rechte Eigentumsverständnis und das Verhältnis zum Eigentum ganz an den in der viva vox und im Gebet gründenden Glauben. Er nutzt dazu die klassische heilsgeschichtliche 3-status-Lehre des status integritatis, des status corruptionis und des status redemptionis. Bemerkenswert ist daran, daß er den Eigentumsbegriff positiv schon *praelapsarisch* ansetzt und zugleich dem außerhalb des status redemptionis Lebenden jegliches adäquate Verhältnis zum Eigentum abspricht. Damit ist eine deutliche Abweisung des "natürlich-theologischen" Zugangs zum rechten Eigentumsverständnis ausgesprochen. Susan E. Schreiner[26] weist zu Recht darauf hin, daß Calvin trotz zahlreicher Hinweise auf die "lex naturae" als Notordnung[27] seinem in der Offenbarung verankerten Grundansatz *nicht* widerspricht: "Calvin was not interested in natural law in and of itself.... Therefore, his appeals to nature and natural law were on the level of appropriation" [Anknüpfung], "not of doctrine." S. E. Schreiner stellt in ihrer Zusammenfassung zu "natural law and societal life" fest: "the abilities and activities of human beings are, in Calvin's thought, the objects of redemption and the instruments for the renewal of creation."[28]

---

[25]*AHSNR* 17:487–88; cf. *CO* 52 (von 1548!), Sp. 295–97 (Die Sperrungen in der Quelle sind übernommen.): "Quanta vero hominum arrogantia est, eripere quod Deus largitur? ... Creavit, inquam, cibos Deus *ad percipiendum*: hoc est ut illis fruamur. Hunc finem evertere nunquam poterit humana autoritas. Addit "(Paulus)...," *cum gratiarum actione*: quia nihil Deo pro sua liberalitate rependere possumus, quam gratitudinis testimonium.... Et sane, proprie loquendo, solis filiis suis Deus totum mundum et quidquid in mundo est destinavit. Qua ratione etiam vocantur mundi haeredes. Nam hac conditione constitutus initio fuerat Adam omnium dominus, ut sub Dei obedientia maneret. Proinde rebellio adversus Deum iure, quod illi collatum fuerat, ipsum una cum posteris spoliavit. Quoniam autem subjecta sunt Christo omnia, eius beneficio in integrum restituimur, idque per fidem.... Posteriore membro definit quos vocet fideles, nem qui notitiam habent sanae doctrinae. Neque enim fides, nisi ex verbo Dei ... non ideo tantum puras vocari creaturas quia Dei sint opera, sed quia eius beneficentia nobis sint datae." V.5: "Nunc videamus qualis sit omnium bonorum, quae ad sustinendam praesentem vitam pertinent, sanctificatio. Eam Paulus sermone Dei et oratione constare testatur... *Dictat quidem hoc communis sensus mundi copias naturaliter destinatas esse in usus nostros: sed quum in Adam nobis ademptum sit mundi dominium, quidquid attingimus donorum Dei, polluitur nostris sordibus: et nobis vicissim impurum est, donec liberaliter Deus succurrat et nos in corpus filii sui inserens, de integro constituat mundi dominos: ut omnibus quae suppeditat, tanquam nostris opibus licite fruamur. Quare merito Paulus iustam fruitionem verbo alligat, quo solo recuperamur quod in Adam erat perditum. Deum enim patrem agnosci oportet, ut simus eius haeredes: et Christum caput, ut quae eius sunt, nostra fiant."* Cf. zur Stelle auch Schulze, *Calvin and "Social Ethics,"* 17.

[26]Schreiner, *The Theater of His Glory,* 90, 94–95.

[27]ebd., S. 94.

[28]ebd., S. 95.

Zum Abschluß dieses Abschnitts nehme ich nach der Exegese Calvins zu Luk 16:25 (s.o. vor Anm. 23 u. 24) den Hinweis Gottfried Wilhelm Lochers auf, daß Calvin bei der Auslegung jener Texte, die vordergründig vor einem positiven Verständnis des Eigentums *warnen*, dennoch seiner Aufwertungs-Tendenz im Blick auf das Eigentum treu bleibt durch "auffällig schnelle Beschwichtigungen" der Warnung.[29] Als Beispiel: Mk. 10:21 par.; Luk 12:16–17 u. 20–21; Luk 12:33, mit solchen, die Radikalität der Forderung dämpfenden Aussagen. *Zur Aufforderung an den "reichen Jüngling"*:

> Wichtig ist aber, daß Christus nicht dazu auffordert, einfach alles zu verkaufen, sondern es den Armen zu geben, denn seinen Reichtum wegzuwerfen, wäre an sich noch keine Tugend.... Denn wenn, wie wir sicher sind, die Liebe das Band der Vollkommenheit ist, verdient bestimmt kein Lob, wer *sich und anderen den Nutzen des Geldes entzieht.* Darum wird von Christus nicht einfach der Verkauf gelobt, sondern die Großzügigkeit, den Armen zu helfen" ... Es "ist leicht zu erkennen, daß gar nicht allen ohne Unterschied geboten wird, alles zu verkaufen; ein Bauer z.B., der es gewohnt ist, von seiner Hände Arbeit zu leben und seine Kinder zu ernähren, würde sündigen, wenn er ohne zwingende Notwendigkeit seinen Grundbesitz verkaufen würde. Zu bewahren, was Gott in unsere Hand gegeben hat, wenn wir nur einfach und bescheiden uns und unsere Familie ernähren und einen Teil davon den Armen schenken, ist demnach eine größere Tugend als alles zu verstreuen.[30]

Calvin polemisiert dann gegen das Armutsverständnis der Mönche:

> Es ist nämlich ein vorzüglicher Tausch, wenn ihnen einerseits befohlen wird, den Armen zu verschenken, was sie gerechterweise besitzen, sie aber andererseits mit ihrem eigenen nicht zufrieden sind und fremdes Gut an sich reißen.[31]

Zu Luk 12:16–17 u. 20–21 (aus dem Gleichnis vom reichen Kornbauern):

> Dieses Gleichnis hält uns wie in einem Spiegel ein lebendiges Bild für Christi Behauptung vor, daß die Menschen nicht von ihrem Überfluß leben können. Doch wieviele sind es, die es sich wirklich zu Herzen nehmen? ... Darum haben es *alle* nötig, sich selbst wach zu machen, damit sie sich nicht auf Grund ihres Reichtums für glücklich halten... Dazu

---

[29]Locher, *Eigentumsbegriff,* 53, Anm. 86.
[30]*AHSNR* 13:135–36 cf. *CO* 45 z. St.; Biéler, *La pensée,* 322; Tholuck Ausg. 2, 164 ff.
[31]*AHSNR* 13:136; Biéler, *La pensée,* 322; Tholuck, Ausg. 2, 164 ff.

kommt ein drittes, das unausgesprochen bleibt ..., daß das beste Heilmittel für die Gläubigen ist, daß sie ihr tägliches Brot vom Herrn erbitten und allein in seiner Fürsorge ruhig werden, *ob sie nun reich sind oder arm*.... Doch verurteilt Christus nicht unbedingt das, was ein fleißiger Familienvater nach seiner Pflicht tut, wenn er die Ernte aufbewahrt. Er verurteilt an dem Reichen, daß er in seiner unersättlichen Gier wie ein bodenloser Schlund viele Scheunen verschluckt und sie verschlingt. Daraus folgt, *daß er keine Ahnung hat von der richtigen Anwendung einer reichen Ernte* ...—Der Ausdruck »*man wird fordern*« bedeutet in seiner Unbestimmtheit nichts anderes, als daß ein anderer das Recht über das Leben des Reichen hat ... Es war einfach Christi Absicht, zu zeigen, daß in jedem ... Augenblick den Menschen ihr Leben entrissen werden kann, das sie unter dem Schutz ihrer Güter so wohl behütet glauben. Aber darin überführt er den Reichen der Torheit, daß er nicht erkannte, daß sein Leben von ganz anderer Stelle abhänge...—Wir wollen also klarstellen, was das heißen soll, *reich zu sein in Gott*."... Es heißt, daß "das Ganze darauf hinausläuft, daß *reich* im Hinblick auf Gott einer ist, der nicht auf die irdischen Dinge sein Vertrauen setzt, sondern sich von seiner alleinigen Fürsorge abhängig macht. Es spielt *dabei keine Rolle, ob einer Überfluß oder Mangel hat,* wenn nur beide aufrichtig den Herrn um das tägliche Brot bitten. Denn der Gegensatz hierzu: *sich Schätze sammeln* heißt soviel wie die Segnung Gottes nicht beachten....".[32]

Zu Luk 12:33: "Verkauft, was ihr habt, und gebt Almosen!" bemerkt Calvin:

Wer dem Armen schenkt, der leiht dem Herrn (vgl. Spr. 19,17). Was er im übrigen über das Verkaufen von Besitz anordnet, *ist nicht so genau zu nehmen,* als ob es dem Christen nicht auch erlaubt wäre, etwas für sich

---

[32] *AHSNR* 12: 416–17; cf. *CO* 45:385–86: "Haec similitudo quasi in speculo vivam nobis effigiem proponit illius, quod homines sua abundantia non vivunt ... interim quotusquisque animum suum adiicit? ... Ergo necesse habent *omnes* se ipsos expergefacere, ne se divitiis beatos fingentes.... Addendum est tertium, quod non exprimitur ... optimum hoc esse remedium fidelibus, ut panem quotidianum a Domino petentes in sola eius providentia quiescant, *sive divites sint sive egeni*.... Neque tamen praecise hoc damnat, Christus, quod officium seduli patrisfamilias in reponendo provento faciat, sed quia velut profundus gorges famelica sua cupiditate absorbeat ac devoret multa horrea: unde sequitur, non tenere verum copiosi proventus usum....—Verbum 'repetet' quamquam pluralis est numeri, quia tamen indefinitum est, nihil aliud significat *quam alieni iuris esse,* quam dives in manu sua vitam ducebat ... Simplex autem Christi consilium fuit, docere singuli momentis vitam hominibus eripi, quam opum suarum praesidio probe munitam putant. Atque in hoc stultitiae coarguitur dives iste, quod vitam suam aliunde pendere non agnosceret. Definiamus ergo, quid hoc sibi velit, *divitem esse in Deo* ... huc redit summa, *divites* esse secundum Deum, qui rebus terrenis non confisi ab unica illius providentia dependent. *Nec refert, abundent ne an esuriant:* modo utrique panem quotidianum sincere petant a Domino. Nam eius oppositum *recondere sibi* tantundem valet ac, posthabita Dei benedictione...."

zurückzubehalten. Er wollte nur zeigen, daß wir nicht nur insoweit den
Armen schenken sollen, daß unser Überfluß auf sie überströmt, sondern
daß wir nicht einmal unser Kapital verschonen dürfen, wenn die *Ein-
künfte*, die zur Hand sind" (Zinsen?), "der Not der Armen noch nicht
abhelfen können. Als ob er gesagt hätte: Eure Freigebigkeit soll sich auch
bis zur Antastung der ererbten Gutes, bis zum Verkauf des Grundbesitzes
erstrecken."[33]

Im Anschluß an die letztzitierten Auslegungen Calvins läßt sich der ganze
Abschnitt 2.2 zusammenfassen: Eigentum als gute Gabe Gottes verdankt sich
Seinem Segen und darf deshalb unter dem Segen Gottes weitergegeben werden in
freier Verantwortung. Denn "Segen Gottes" bedeutet: Kraft Gottes hinein in den
Alltag der Gemeinde und durch die Gemeinde für die Welt.[34]

3. Die gemeindliche Einbindung des Eigentums und ihre Auswirkungen auf die Gesellschaft

"Calvin geht über seine Vorgänger hinaus, indem er ... auch in der Eigentumsfrage die christliche Gemeinde in ihrer wesentlichen Eigenart, Eigenständig-
keit und Unabhängigkeit, als verantwortliches Subjekt einführt. Das Problem ist
für ihn nicht in erster Linie ein individualethisches ..., auch nicht primär ein politisches ..., sondern ein ecclesiologisches, bei der Bedeutung der Kirche für die
Welt dann freilich ein allgemein soziologisches."[35]

Den Satz des Apostolikums:

"Ich glaube die Gemeinschaft der Heiligen" interpretiert Calvin in *Inst.*
4.1.3: "Er bedeutet doch soviel: ... die Heiligen werden nach *der* Ordnung zur Gemeinschaft mit *Christus* versammelt, daß sie all die Wohltaten, die ihnen Gott gewährt, *gegenseitig* einander mitteilen."[36]

Calvin schränkt sogleich ein:

Dadurch wird die Verschiedenheit der Gnadengaben nicht aufgehoben;
denn wir wissen ja, daß die Gaben des Heiligen Geistes vielartig ausge-
teilt wurden. Auch wird *dadurch die bürgerliche Ordnung nicht umge-*

---

[33] *AHSNR* 12, 217; cf. Tholuck, Ausg. 1, 173–74: "non ita precise urgendum est, quasi fas non sit
Christiano homini quicquam sibi reliquum facere: tantum docere voluit, non eatenus modo largien-
dum esse pauperibus, ut quod nobis superfluum est ad eos redundet, sed ne fundis quidem parcen-
dum esse, si pauperum necessitati non sufficiat reditus, qui ad manum est. Liberalitas vestra etiam
usque ad patrimonii diminutionem et agrorum alienationem se extendat."

[34] Cf. Locher, *Eigentumsbegriff*, 37 (Zitat aus *CO* 26.626, zu Deut. 8:17); cf. zum Ganzen ferner:
Schulze, *Calvin and "Social Ethics*," 16–18: "2.1.2 Breaking New Ground: Property is a Gift of God."

[35] Locher, *Eigentumsbegriff*, 37.

[36] Cf. *OS* 5:5:4–7.

stürzt, nach der *jeder einzelne für sich ein besonderes Vermögen* in Besitz haben darf; denn es ist ja zur Aufrechterhaltung des Friedens unter den Menschen erforderlich, daß *jeder unter ihnen sein eigenes, besonderes Eigentumsrecht an seinem Besitz* hat.[37]

Calvin zitiert dann sinngemäß für den Charakter dieser Gemeinschaft Apg 4,32: "Die Menge aber der Gläubigen war *ein Herz und eine Seele*", sowie Eph. 4:4: "*ein Leib und ein Geist*", "zu *einer* Hoffnung berufen,"[38] *nicht* jedoch Apg. 2:44–45 oder 4:32b—5:11! Der Schluß dieser Sektion argumentiert dann wieder idealtypisch *gesinnungsethisch:*

> wenn sie wahrhaft von der Überzeugung getragen sind, daß Gott für sie alle der gemeinsame Vater und Christus das gemeinsame Haupt ist, so kann es nicht anders zugehen, als daß auch sie, in brüderlicher Liebe miteinander verbunden, einander gegenseitig ihren Besitz mitteilen.[39]

Konkreter, jedoch nicht kasuistisch argumentiert Calvin in *Inst.* 3.7.5. In seiner Ermahnung zur innergemeindlichen Hilfsgemeinschaft nutzt er sogar die Begriffe des *Obligationenrechts*[40] (die lateinischen Begriffe sind jeweils in Klammern vermerkt), um die geldwirtschaftliche Umsetzbarkeit seiner Paränese vorzubereiten (schon 1539)[41]:

> deshalb mahnt sie [die Schrift] uns daran, daß uns alle Gnadengaben, die wir vom Herrn empfangen haben, mit der Bestimmung *anvertraut* sind [concreditum → Kredit], sie zum *gemeinen Nutzen* [commune bonum] der Kirche anzuwenden! Der *rechtmäßige Gebrauch* (legitimus usus) aller dieser Gnadengaben besteht also darin, daß wir sie freimütig und gerne mit anderen teilen! Es läßt sich keine zuverlässigere Regel denken, auch keine kräftigere Ermahnung, sie einzuhalten, als die, daß wir uns unterweisen lassen: alle die Gaben, die wir reichlich empfangen haben, sind Gottes uns *anvertrautes Eigentum* [deposita Depositum], das uns mit der *Bestimmung auf Treu und Glauben hingegeben ist* (lege fidei ... commissa Fideikommiß), daß wir es dem Nächsten zugut austeilen [dispensentur → Dispensation]!
> Die Schrift geht aber noch darüber hinaus und vergleicht jene Gaben mit den Fähigkeiten, die den Gliedern des menschlichen Körpers innewohnen. Kein Glied hat seine Fähigkeit für sich selber, wendet sie

---

[37]Cf. *OS* 5:5:7–11; cf. auch die Fassung von 1539: 5:5:29–33!
[38]Cf. *OS* 5:5:12–15.   [39]Cf. 5:5:15–18.
[40]S. den Hinweis bei Locher, *Eigentumsbegriff,* 54, Anm. 89 (dort auch der lateinische Text).
[41]Cf. *OS* 4:155:27–156:11.

auch nicht zu seinem eigenen [privatim] Nutzen an, sondern jedes über-
trägt sie auf die mit ihm verbundenen Glieder [*socia membra*] und hat
auch keinerlei Nutzen davon als den, der aus dem Wohlergehen [com-
moditas] des ganzen Leibes kommt.[42] So muß der Fromme alles, was er
vermag, für die Brüder vermögen—indem er für sich allein [privatim]
sein Gemerk auf nichts anderes lenkt als darauf, daß sein Herz auf die
gemeinsame Erbauung der Kirche gerichtet sei! Den Weg (methodus) zu
Freundlichkeit und Wohltun werden wir also finden, wenn wir beden-
ken: für alles, was uns Gott übertragen hat und mit dem wir dem Nächsten zu helfen vermögen, sind wir als Haushalter eingesetzt [nos esse
oeconomos], und wir sind verpflichtet, über die Verteilung solcher Gaben
einst Rechenschaft abzulegen (ratio reddenda → Rechenschaftsablage).
Die rechte Austeilung [Dispensation] wird aber einzig die sein, die sich
nach der Regel der Liebe richtet. So werden wir das eifrige Trachten nach
dem Wohlergehen des anderen nicht allein mit der Sorge um unseren
eigenen Nutzen stets verbinden—nein, wir werden diese Sorge jenem
eifrigen Trachten *unterordnen.*

Das harte Urteil G. W. Lochers über diese Ermahnung Calvins: "in diesem
Licht bleibt nun bei diesem Reformator, der das Eigentum als selbstverständliche
Ordnung hinnahm, zugleich von der berühmten 'freien Verfügung' und dem 'Ver-
fahren nach Belieben' nichts mehr übrig,"[43] scheint mir überzogen. Trotz des
Rück- und Vorgriffs Calvins auf Begriffe des Obligationenrechts, trotz des Ansat-
zes struktureller Regelung notwendiger Anteilgabe am Privateigentum bleibt die
Freiheit der Liebe (hier: *dilectio*) als Hauptregel gewahrt, und falsche Gesetzlich-
keit wird vermieden. Immerhin stellt Calvin der ganzen ausführlich zitierten
Ermahnung das—hier nicht zitierte—Hohelied der Liebe, 1 Kor. 13, voran.
Erwähnenswert noch, daß das innergemeindliche Blickfeld über die dienende
Brüderlichkeit hinaus erweitert wird auf die Begriffe "der andere" (alienus) und
"der Nächste" (proximus) und heilsgeschichtlich auf die *futurisch-eschatologische*
Rechenschaftgabe.

Calvin sieht offenbar die Aufgabe nicht darin, durch Abschaffung der
Armut den Unterschied zwischen Besitzenden und Darbenden zu besei-
tigen, *sondern ihren Gegensatz.* Das Wunder, das hier geschehen und
zeugnishaft auf das Reich Gottes hinweisen soll, setzt freilich starke
soziale Energien in Bewegung, es ist aber selbst *nicht ein soziales, sondern*

---

[42]Zum Organismusgedanken bei Calvin cf. Johann Bohatec, *Calvin und das Recht* (Graz, 1934);
ders., *Calvins Lehre von Staat und Kirche* (Breslau, 1937).
[43]Locher, *Eigentumsbegriff,* 37.

ein geistliches: das der Gemeinschaft zwischen Reich und Arm, die sonst in dieser Welt durch eine Kluft getrennt sind. Daß es an irdischen Gütern Arme gibt, wird aus der Schrift und aus Gottes Weltregierung hingenommen; aber neu ist ihre Wertung; eigentlich ist in der Gemeinde niemand "arm", denn reich sind wir, sofern wir dienen können und andere uns brauchen. Der Reiche aber hat den Armen ebenso nötig wie der Arme den Reichen.[44]

Das eindringlichste *Angebot*, solche *wechselseitige Bedürftigkeit* in der Gemeinde anzunehmen, gibt Calvin in einer berühmt gewordenen Predigt über Deut. 16,11[45] aus dem Jahre 1555; daraus einige Passagen:

"Dein Armer" sagt Gott. Als wollte er sagen: wenn ein Mensch arm ist, verachtet man ihn.… Ganz anders unser Herr: eben um solchen Dünkel und Hochmut niederzuschlagen, spricht er: Wer bist denn du, der du deinen Bruder so verachtest? Er ist *dein* Armer, dein Bedürftiger! Er wendet sich an unser eigenes Fleisch. So müssen wir hier die Worte wohl abwägen, deren sich hier der Heilige Geist bedient hat, damit kein Stolz uns hindert, Mitleid mit denen zu haben, die auf solche Weise mit uns verbunden sind. Merken wir uns: es sind unsere Armen, das heißt: die, die solchermaßen Mangel leiden—unser Herr ist's, der sie uns darbietet. Als wollte er sagen: Ich will eine solche Zerstreuung vornehmen [altfrz.:

---

[44]Locher, *Eigentumsbegriff*, 38.

[45]Cf. *CO* 27, Sp. 342 ff.; die Auswahl orientiert sich an der deutschen Übersetzung bei Locher, *Eigentumsbegriff*, 55, Anm. 91; cf. die englische Übersetzung analoger Abschnitte bei Schulze, *Calvin and "Social Ethics,"* 15–16: Weitere Auszüge aus Calvins Predigt über die Bestimmungen zum jüdischen Pfingst-(Wochen-)Fest, Deut. 16:9–12 (*CO* 27, Sp. 387–389): "Si donc Dieu a enrichi quelqu'un, il faut qu'il regarde de ne point supprimer la benediction de Dieu, de *ne la point tenir enclose*: car nous voyons qu'il y en a qui gourmandent, et ne leur chaut de la povreté des autres: il leur semble que nul ne doit avoir part en leurs biens, et qu'ils peuvent tout serrer. Au contraire il est ici declairé, selon qu'un chacun a receu abondance de la main de Dieu, qu'il se doit employer envers ses prochains: car voila a quelle fin Dieu pretend: et si nous n'y pensons, si faudra-il venir à conte: et nous sentirons en la fin que Dieu nous imputera à larcin" (kleiner Diebstahl / Mundraub), "quand nous aurons ainsi mangé ses biens sans avoir pitié de ceux qui en ont faute, pour les secourir." "Cependant si falloit-it qu'ils advisassent tousiours, qu'ils ne se pouvoyent acquitter, sinon *en distribuant de leurs biens à leurs prochains* qui estoyent en necessité. Voila donc ce que Moyse a ici entendu disant, … que ce n'estoit point assez que de bouche et de gestes ils recogneussent qu'ils estoyent tenus à Dieu de ce qu'il leur avoit envoyé de quoi se nourrir: mais qu'ils monstrassent aussi envers les hommes, qu'ils ne demandent sinon *à s'acquitter du bien qu'il leur a mis entre mains*, et qu'*ils en veulent estre fideles dispensateurs*." "Pensez (dit-il) que vous avez esté en la terre d'Egypte povres esclaves, et que vous eussiez bien voulu alors estre traittez humainement: quand on vous molestoit par trop, vous criyez à moi: maintenant cognoissez que ceux qui sont au milieu de vous, les povres indigens demandent aussi qu'on ait regard à eux: et moy ie les ay pour recommandez." "Comme aussi elle" (la sentence de Prophete Osee) "est alleguee par nostre Seigneur Jesus Christ, c'est assavoir que Dieu demande sacrifices d'aumosnes: comme s'il disoit, qu'il ne se contente pas qu'on ait usé de quelques ceremonies envers luy: mais qu'il veut que nous soyons humains pour aider à ceux qui ont faute de nostre aide, quand nous avons la faculté et le moyen de ce faire."

faire une telle discussion], daß Reich und Arm gemischt wird, daß sie
also einander begegnen, um miteinander Gemeinschaft zu gewinnen
[communiquer]; und daß der Arme empfängt und der Reiche gibt, und
daß ich vom einen wie vom andern geehrt sei, wenn der Reiche hat,
wovon er Gutes tun kann, und der Arme dafür dankt, daß er um meines
Namens willen zu essen hat, und daß beide mich preisen.... So sollen die
Reichen mit den Armen Gemeinschaft halten, nicht um ihnen gleich zu
werden, sondern um dem Mangel derer abzuhelfen, die ihnen Gott so
darbietet.

In seinem Kommentar zu Jak. 5:1–6[46] hält Calvin eine Gerichtspredigt gegen
jene Reichen, die sich auf das Angebot der wechselseitigen Bedürftigkeit in der
Gemeinde nicht einlassen. Er hält ihnen 3 Sünden vor: Habgier, Grausamkeit
gegen ihre Arbeitnehmer und "süßes," luxuriöses Leben. Aber er prangert auch
die allgemeine stumme Unterdrückung der Schwachen durch die Reichen an, der
die Gerechten nicht widerstehen. Wiederum liegt das Problem nicht im Reichtum
selbst, sondern im Verhalten des sündigen Menschen zu Gottes Gaben, deren
Güte der Mensch in ihr Gegenteil verkehren kann. Calvin legt auch hier Wert auf
die Feststellung, daß Jakobus nicht pauschal _alle_ Reichen verurteilt, sondern nur
jene, die "alles verschlingen, was sich ihnen in den Weg stellt."[47] Diese haben die
"Ordnung der Natur" zerstört, das "Gesetz ihrer Geschöpflichkeit" gebrochen und
damit Gott seine Ehre entzogen. Es ist nicht auszuschließen, daß Calvin in seinem
Jakobus-Kommentar jene altreichen Patrizier und auch jene neureichen Gewerbe-
treibenden und Kaufleute anspricht, die sich seinem wirtschaftlichen und sozialen
Reformprogramm, vor allem aber dessen geistlicher Begründung verweigern.[48]

4. Arbeit dient wie das Eigentum dem Aufbau der Gemeinde und dadurch der Weltgestaltung

Calvin übt im Blick auf die Beziehung von Glaubens- und Wirtschaftswirk-
lichkeit das "unvermischt und ungeteilt."[49] Jedwedes Feld menschlicher Aktivität
muß von den Christen der Königsherrschaft Jesu Christi unterstellt werden, aber

---

[46]Cf. CO 55, Sp. 422–25 (von 1556); ferner die ausführliche Interpretation bei Schulze, _Calvin and "Social Ethics,"_ 34; ferner ebd. zum Verhältnis "reich-arm", 39–48.
[47]CO 55, zu 5. 1 bzw. 2: "qui, tantum inexhausti gurgitis devorant omnia" bzw. "supprimunt quidquid undecunque possunt ad se trahere"; s.o. 9–11.
[48]S. schon die Ratsprotokolle (R.C.) vom 14.2.1542/14.1.1544/24.5.1547 (CO 21.291,328,404), cf. Biéler, _La pensée,_ 159 u. 107ff. sowie 145–66; 306–84. Zur biblischen Begrifflichkeit: "_arm_" cf. meinen Art. im _ThBLNT;_ dort auch den Art. "Besitz" v. Beyreuther/Eichler/Selter u. bes. den Abschnitt "Zur Verkündigung" von Lothar Coenen; Eßer, "Barmherzigkeit."
[49]Biéler, _La pensée,_ 512–13, unter Anspielung auf die Zwei-Naturenlehre des Chalcedonense; cf. Eßer, "Calvins Sozialethik und der Kapitalismus," 789.

zugleich werden Arbeit, wirtschaftliche Unternehmen und Geld dem ganzen menschlichen Wirkvermögen freigegeben.[50] Der Begriff "Arbeit" bekommt in Calvins Sprache eine eigentümliche Akzentuierung: "Arbeiten' ist ... das von der Gemeinde geforderte Durchhalten und Durchstehen im Glauben, das beharrliche Überwinden aller Anfechtungen und Widerstände."[51] Der dem unermüdlich wirkenden und tätigen Gott gehorsame Mensch kann kein untätiges, passives Geschöpf sein.[52] Auf die Einbindung des menschlichen Berufs in die Vorsehung Gottes wurde schon hingewiesen (s.o. 4).[53] Neu an der Weite des Arbeitsverständnisses Calvins ist neben der Würdigung der Arbeit von Bauern und Handwerkern seine positive Wertung und Förderung des *Kaufmannsstandes*. Bei aller Kritik an den Gefahren dieses Berufs wertet er den "Handelsgewinn als ein Geschenk der göttlichen Güte, als Lohn für den Fleiß des Handelsherrn und als wertvoll für das Gemeinwohl: 'Prosperitas, ut Dei donum est, non erit per se damnanda ...; non ... damnari per se debeat, quum republicae utilis et necessarius sit.'"[54] Anstelle einer Summierung aller Äußerungen Calvins über die Arbeit[55] sei seine Bestimmung der Arbeit als Durchstehen im Glauben einerseits und von daher geleitete verantwortliche Weltgestaltung andererseits, in dieser Doppelbeziehung und Zusammengehörigkeit, exemplarisch verdeutlicht an einem von ihm formulierten "*Gebet vor der Arbeit*," das dem Genfer Katechismus 1562 angefügt wurde[56]:

---

[50]Cf. Biéler, *La pensée;* Eßer, "Calvins Sozialethik und der Kapitalismus.:

[51]Geiger, *Calvin, Calvinismus, Kapitalismus,* 286, unter Berufung auf einen Brief Calvins an die Gemeinde in Aix vom 1. Mai 1561: "Si est ce que le temps que nous travaillions d'un coste, et souffrions de l'autre. Nous appelons travailler, nous porter virilement et passer par dessus tous obstacles, quand il est question de faire nostre devoir. Car plus tost cent fois mourir que de flechir"; *CO* 18:3379:436–37. Zum Verständnis des Begriffs der Arbeit ist auch auf Calvins Testament hinzuweisen; *CO* 20:4103:298 ff.; cf. dazu Geiger, *Calvin, Calvinismus, Kapitalismus,* 283–84, 286.

[52]Cf. *Inst.* 1.16–18.2.4.

[53]Biéler, *La pensée,* 413: "Calvin, se fondant sur les Ecritures, est l'un des rares théologiens qui ait mis en évidence avec tant de clarté *la participation du travail de l'homme à l'œuvre de Dieu. Il a ainsi conféré au labeur humain une dignité et une valeur spirituelles.*" Auch in dem Imago-Dei-Sein des Menschen ist die Verpflichtung zur Arbeit begründet: "Unde sequitur, homines ad aliquid agendum creatas esse, ne desides et ignavi iaceant"; *CO* 23, Sp. 44 zu Gen. 1,25. Zur Sache cf. auch Hans H. Eßer, "Zur Anthropologie Calvins. Menschenwürde: Imago Dei zwischen humanistischem und theologischem Ansatz," in *Wenn nicht jetzt, wann dann?* hrsg. v. H.-G. Geyer u.a. (Neukirchen: Kraus, 1983), 269–81.

[54]Cf. Locher, *Eigentumsbegriff,* 38–39, u. Anm. 93, 55, die aus Calvins Jes-Kommentar, *CO* 37, Sp. 167 u. *CO* 36, Sp. 394 zitiert.

[55]Cf. dazu Bürgin, *Kapitalismus und Calvinismus,* 204–5 u.ö.

[56]Übers. v. Verf. nach *CO* 6, Sp. 137: "Oraison pour dire avant que faire son œuvre.... D'avantage, Seigneur, qu'il te plaise nous assister par ton sainct Esprit, à fin que nous puissons fidelement exercer nostre estat et vocation sans aucune fraude ne tromperie, ainsi que nous regardions plustost de suyvre ton ordonnance, que de satisfaire à l'appetit de nous enrichir: que si neantmoins il te plait de faire prosperer nostre labeur, qu'aussi tu nous donnes le courage de subvenir à ceux qui sont en indigence, selon le pouvoir que tu nous en auras donné, nous retenant en toute humilité à fin que ne nous eslevions point par dessus ceux qui n'auront pas receu telle largesse de ta liberalité. Or si tu nous veux traitter en plus grande povreté ou indigence, que nostre chair ne desireroit, qu'il te plaise nous faire la grace d'adiuster foy à tes promesses..."

Vor allem, Herr, wollest Du uns beistehen durch Deinen Heiligen Geist, daß wir treu unsern Stand und Beruf ausüben, ohne Betrug und Täuschung, so daß wir eher darauf achten, Deinen Anordnungen zu folgen, als den Hunger nach Reichtum zu befriedigen. Wenn es Dir dennoch gefällt, unsere Arbeit gedeihen zu lassen, gib uns auch den Mut, denen zu helfen, die im Mangel leben, nach der Vollmacht, die Du uns dazu geben wirst. Halte uns in aller Demut, damit wir uns nicht über die erheben, die nicht solche Freigebigkeit von Dir erfahren haben. Und wenn Du uns größere Armut und Entbehrungen auferlegst, als unsere Schwachheit sie sich wünschen könnte, wollest Du uns die Gnade geben, unseren Glauben ganz auf Deine Verheißungen auszurichten.

5. *Das 8. Gebot als erschließender und abschließender Aspekt des Eigentumsbegriffs*[57]

Die eindringliche Auslegung Calvins in *Inst.* 2.8.45–46,[58] die sich, wie in der reformatorischen Auslegung seit Luther üblich, in die Deutung von *Ver*bot und *Ge*bot gliedert, nimmt in ihrer Mitte das zur Arbeit Gesagte auf (s.o. 4): "Denn wer nicht tut, was sein *Beruf* den andern gegenüber erfordert, der vergreift sich an fremdem Gut![59] ... Endlich soll jeder darauf achten, was er in seinem Beruf zu tun schuldig ist, und dann das Erforderliche auch erfüllen."[60]

Zum *Gesamtüberblick*: "Überraschend ist, wie" Calvin, "der auf die materielle und realistische Seite der Eigentumsfrage das ganze Gewicht letzter geistlicher Verantwortung legt, ... selbst diesen Begriff ausweitet, vertieft, meinetwegen 'spiritualisiert'":[61] "Der Zweck ist hier: Gott ist jede Ungerechtigkeit zuwider, und deshalb sollen wir jedem geben, was ihm gehört."[62]

Das stoische, umfassende "*Suum cuique*" wird als formale Definition des zur Offenbarung gehörenden Gebotes unbedenklich aufgenommen. Dementsprechend heißt es: "Stehlen kann man nun in der verschieden-

---

[57]Wir folgen für diese Überlegungen wiederum Locher, *Eigentumsbegriff,*, 40, und den Erwägungen von Schulze, *Calvin and "Social Ethics,"* 27–31.—Zur systematischen Einordnung des Gesetzesverständnisses Calvins in den Gesamtzusammenhang seiner Theologie cf. Hans H. Eßer, "Freude zum Gehorsam bei Johannes Calvin" in *Zukunft aus dem Wort*, hrsg. v. G. Metzger (Stuttgart: F.S.H. Claß, 1978), 45–55.

[58]*OS* 3:384:7–385,19 (im wesentlichen v. 1539).

[59]*OS* 3:385:1–3: "Alienum enim et retinet et praevertit qui non exequitur quod ex suae *vocationis* aliis debet" (Schlußsatz v. Sectio 45).

[60]Aus Sectio 46, Anfang des 2. Abs.: "Postremo respiciat unus quatenus *ex officio* aliis sit *obligatus*, ac quod *debet bona fide* persolvat"; *OS* 3:385:17–19. Auch hier wieder Schlüsselbegriffe des Obligationenrechtes (*s.o.* 149–50)!

[61]Locher, *Eigentumsbegriff,* 40.

[62]*OS* 3:384:7–8 (Anfang der Sectio 45): "Finis. Quoniam abominationi est Deo iniustitia, ut reddatur *unicuique* quod *suum* est."

sten Weise."[63] Von Gewalt, Betrug, Schmeichelei wie von siegreichen Prozessen und zahlreichen anderen Künsten ist die Rede.[64] Aber "*Gott urteilt*."[65] Und dann steht plötzlich der inhaltsschwere und doch so schlichte Begriff des *Menschenrechtes* da, des "ius cuisque,"[66] das man niemandem entziehen darf.... Ferner vergißt der leidenschaftliche Kämpfer für die Gottesehre bezeichnenderweise nicht, das zu unserm vor dem achten Gebot unantastbaren Eigentum auch die *Ehre* gehört, die wir Menschen einander schulden. "Bei alledem sollen unsere Gedanken sich immer auf den Gesetzgeber richten...."[67]

---

[63]Bei O. Weber, die deutschen Texte der *Institutio*, 245: "Es geht um sehr vielerlei Diebstahl"; OS 3: 384.14–15: "Plurima autem sunt furtorum genera."

[64]Locher, *s.o.* Anm. 61, *vergißt* in seiner ein wenig lässigen Aufzählung:
(1) den *Vorspruch*: "Was ein Mensch besitzt, das hat er nicht von irgendeinem Zufallsgeschick, sondern durch *Zuteilung Gottes*, des Herrn aller Dinge; wer sich also an seines Nächsten Vermögen vergreift, der übt Betrug gegen die *göttliche Ordnung*" (OS 3:384:10–14: "Sic enim cogitandum est, unicuique evenisse quod possidet, non fortuita sorte, sed ex *distributione* summi rerum omnium *Domini*: non posse igitur praeverti malis artibus facultates cuispiam quin fraus *divinae dispensationi* fiat.")
(2) die genauen juristischen Definitionen der einzelnen Diebstahlsformen (ich gebe hier nur die lat. Fassung wieder):
(a) "*violentia* = quum vi quacunque et praedatoria licentia aliena diripiuntur" (OS 3:384:15–16)
(b) "*in malitiosa* impostura: ubi fraudulenter intercipiuntur" (OS 3:384:16–17);
(c) "*in tectiori calliditate*: ubi per speciem iuris excutiuntur" (OS 3:384:17–18);
(d) "*in blanditiis*: ubi sub donationis praetextu emunguntur" (OS 3:384:18–19).
(3)die Gesamtdefinition: "alle falsche Kunst, mit der man des Nächsten Gut und Geld an sich bringt, sofern dabei die Lauterkeit der Liebe verlassen wird und dafür das Begehren sich einstellt, zu täuschen oder irgendwie Schaden zu tun," ist "für Diebstahl zu halten"; O. Weber, die deutschen Texte der *Institutio*, 246, (OS 3:384:20-23): "artes omnes, quibus *proximorum possessiones* et pecuniae ad nos derivantur, ubi a synceritate dilectionis, ad fallendi aut quovis modo nocendi cupiditatem obliquant, pro furtis noverimus esse habendas." Zum genauen Aufschlüsseln der Begriffe, juristisch und theologisch, cf. Schulze, *s.o.* Anm. 57!

[65]"Vor Gott gelten sie als das, was sie sind." (O. Weber, die deutschen Texte der *Institutio*, 246 = OS 3:384:24–25: "a Deo tamen non secus aestimantur"); oder: das alles ist "in Gottes Augen Diebstahl" (O. Weber, ebd.); OS3:385:1: "furti apud Deum tenetur."

[66]"Dergleichen Unrecht findet sich ... nicht nur ..., sondern *bezüglich aller Rechte, die der andere hat*" (O. Weber, ebd., = OS 3:384:31–32: "Neque haec iniuria ... modo ... locum habet, sed *in iure cuisque*"). Cf. L. Schulze, *Calvin and "Social Ethics,"* 27: "The expression 'human rights' comes in the same paragraph, where Calvin argues that this commandment does ... prohibit theft of *anything to which man has a right*. The rights of man open up a horizon, far wider than the usual political, economical or social rights to which we are used!"

[67]"Ad haec, referenda semper mens ad legislatorem" (OS 3:386:16).
Viermal kommt in der *Position* der Auslegung des 8. Gebots der Begriff der *Ehre* vor, die wir *Menschen einander* schulden:(1) nur ehrenhafter Gewinn ist zu erstreben (OS 3:385:5–6 (*Inst.* 2.8.46): "nullum nisi honestum ... lucrum facere." (2) Das Volk soll die ihm Vorstehenden in Ehren halten (OS 3:385:19–23: "populus omnes sibi praefectos in honore habeat." (3) Den Dienern der Kirche soll das Volk die Ehre geben, die der höchste Lehrer der Kirche ihnen zugeteilt hat (OS 3:385:29–31: "Populus ... eos pro nuntiis ...Dei suscipiat, eum iis honorem reddat quo summus Magister eos dignatus est"). (4) Die Jüngeren sollen das Alter ehren, da der Herr selbst es so will (OS 3:386:3–5: "Iuniores senilem aetatem revereantur, ut eam aetatem honorabilem esse voluit").

Die *Position* des 8. Gebots, der Ehrung Gottes in der Ehrung der Mitmenschen durch Trachten nach dem Nutzen und Vorteil des Nächsten, heißt am knappsten zusammengefaßt: "Daß ein jeder das Seine erhalte und darin *Gott* das erhalte, was wir ihm schuldig sind, das ist der scopus von Calvins Behandlung der Eigentumsfrage."[68] Damit ist auch die Ehrenhaftigkeit des Kreditgebens und nehmens vorbereitet coram deo, dem Eigentümer aller Eigentümer und allen Eigentums.

III. Die neue Geldwirtschaft und Calvins Argumentation zugunsten
der Zinsnahme für Produktions-Darlehen

1. *Die sich aufdrängende neue Geldwirtschaft im sozialen Kontext*[69]
In ihrer Sorge um das Wohlergehen der Stadt begünstigt die calvinische Reformation zwar die Finanzaktivitäten, aber es geht ihr in erster Linie um das Geschick der unteren Schichten der Bevölkerung, und sie streitet gegen jede Praxis, die dem ärmsten Teil der Bevölkerung schaden könnte. Sie ist unermüdlich darum bemüht, ein gerechtes Gleichgewicht zwischen wirtschaftlichem Aufschwung und sozialer Gerechtigkeit aufrechtzuerhalten.[70] Schon von ihren Anfängen an hat die Reformation in Genf seit 1535, auch auf Farels Initiative hin, das "soziale Netz" gespannt, zunächst durch die Errichtung und Unterhaltung eines Hospitals für die Kranken, Hilflosen und Waisen. Calvin baut dieses Netz, vor allem während der Teuerung der 50er Jahre, als Ratgeber der Stadtregierung durch folgende umzusetzende Vorschläge aus:[71]

(1) freie Krankenversorgung für die Armen, sowohl im Hospital wie in der Stadt;

(2) Preiskontrolle für die Hauptnahrungsmittel: Brot, Wein und Fleisch;

(3) Regulierung der Arbeitszeit;

(4) Gesuche für Gehaltserhöhung, speziell zugunsten der Lehrer;

(5) Schulpflicht für die Grundschule;

(6) Arbeitsbeschaffungsmaßnahmen der öffentlichen Hand und Umschulung der Arbeitslosen;

---

[68]Locher, *Eigentumsbegriff,* 40; Schulze, *Calvin and "Social Ethics,"* 30–31: "The positive meaning of this commandment is to 'aim faithfully to lend our counsel and aid to all so as to assist them in retaining their property' ... Further we must contribute to the relief of those in distress, 'assisting their want out of our abundance'. Finally each one must 'consider how far he is bound in duty to others and must pay what he owes' ... Thus the Law is an 'image of God's character' and an attestation of the correspondence, the correspondance that ought to exist between God and man."
[69]Cf. dazu u.a. Biéler, *La pensée,* 152 ff u.ö.; Geiger, *Calvin, Calvinismus, Kapitalismus,* 238–50; Locher, *Eigentumsbegriff,* 38–39; Schulze, *Calvin and "Social Ethics,"* 71–74.
[70]Cf. Biéler, *La pensée,* 170.
[71]Cf. Schulze, *Calvin and "Social Ethics,"* 72ff; Biéler, *La pensée,* 152ff.

(7) Hilfe auch für jene Glaubensflüchtlinge, welche die Stadt nur zum Zwischenaufenthalt aufsuchen;

(8) Einsetzung von Diakonen, die nach der Kirchenordnung von 1541 zur ständigen, gegliederten Gemeindeleitung gehören und von Gemeinde und Rat mit großen Vollmachten ausgestattet sind, zur Armen- und Krankenpflege;[72]

(9) Verbot des Bettelwesens, weil in Genf dafür kein Grund mehr besteht.—

Mit den genannten Sozialmaßnahmen wurde sowohl die soziale Katastrophe als auch der Aufstand eines Armutsproletariats verhindert, aber sie brachten allein noch keinen wirtschaftlichen Aufschwung in Gang. Die Stadt war nämlich durch die Befreiung vom Hause Savoyen und den Auszug der dem Herzoghause dienenden Stände schon zu Beginn der Reformation verarmt und außerdem durch handelspolitische Umstände (Entdeckung Amerikas!) in Isolation geraten, die sich in finanziellen Krisen auswirkte, denen nur ein mit 5% zu verzinsender Kredit der Stadt Basel in Höhe von 6.000 Talern vorübergehend abhelfen konnte. "Das Problem bestand somit in der Beschaffung fehlender Güter, nicht in der gerechten Verteilung vorhandener."[73]

Calvin hatte während seiner dreijährigen Straßburger Tätigkeit in den dortigen Wechselstuben die Transaktionen zwischen der Bank von Lyon und den süddeutschen Banken (Fugger u.a.) und damit die Bedeutung des aufkommenden Kapitalverkehrs aufmerksam beobachtet, aber ebenso die Schwierigkeiten der Integration von Glaubensflüchtlingen in eine Stadt mit hoher Asylantenquote erfahren. Auch aus der Erfahrung der potentiellen Macht des Kapitalverkehrs, der sich immer stärker durchsetzte und den Gütertausch sowie die Wechselschein-Praxis ablöste, zog Calvin für seine Einflußnahme auf die wirtschaftlichen Verhältnisse der Stadt Genf die Konsequenz, sich dem Druck der neuen Geldwirtschaft zu stellen. Das bedeutete die Verwerfung der seit Aristoteles gültigen Geldtheorie: "Geld erzeugt kein Geld."[74] Geld kann also als Startkapital für vermögenslose, strebsame Unternehmer zum fruchtbaren Arbeiten gebracht werden. Calvin förderte durch seine Anstöße und die Durchsetzung seines Konzepts die Integration einer großen Zahl hochqualifizierter Gewerbetreibender und Kaufleute, die als mittellose Flüchtlinge—vor allem nach dem Edikt von Châteaubriant 1551—in Genf ankamen, und er trug damit zur Begründung bzw. Erweiterung noch heute in Weltruf stehender spezieller Kleinindustrien bei: Uhrenherstellung, Goldschmiedekunst, differenzierte Textil-Produktion.[75] Der

---

[72]Cf. dazu die Untersuchung von Elsie Ann McKee, *Elders and the plural ministry*, Genf, 1988.
[73]Locher, *Eigentumsbegriff*, 38.
[74]Calvin hatte diese Theorie auslegungsgeschichtlich durch Ambrosius und Chrysostomus kennengelernt; cf. Geiger, *Calvin, Calvinismus, Kapitalismus*, 247.
[75]Cf. dazu Bürgin, *Kapitalismus und Calvinismus*, 102 ff.; 165–80; Biéler, *La pensée*, 148–70.

ökonomische, aber ethisch reglementierte Eigentumsbegriff (s.o. Teil 2 dieser
Arbeit) kam damit dem Kreditgeber wie dem Kreditempfänger zugute.

Es galt nun für den Theologen Calvin, mit theologischer Begründung das
immer noch gültige christliche Tabu, das über jeglichem Zinsnehmen lag, aber
stillschweigend und öffentlich in der Praxis des Wirtschaftslebens durch Spekula-
tion und Wucher (bis zu 20 Prozent) ständig durchbrochen wurde, wegzuräumen
und durch eine *vor Gott und den Menschen glaubwürdige Regelung zu ersetzen.*
Dies konnte nur durch ethische Einweisung, Exegese und Predigt geschehen.

2. *Calvins Unterscheidung zwischen zinslosen Konsumdarlehen und zins-
pflichtigen Produktionsdarlehen; Die neue Regelung des Zinsnehmens.*[76]

Unter den nicht zahlreichen, aber auch nicht nur vereinzelten Äußerungen
Calvins zur Frage des Zinses hat zu Recht immer wieder der unter die *Questiones
iuridicae* eingereihte Brief *Jehan Calvin à quelqun de ses amys* Aufmerksamkeit
gefunden; es handelt sich um ein gedrängtes Schriftstück von hohem theologischem Gehalt.[77] Dazu ist vor allem auch die Predigt über Deut. 23:18–20 vom 28.
Januar 1556 zu berücksichtigen.[78] Calvin bezeichnet die an ihn herangetragene
Frage als schwierig: Einerseits würde ein totales Zinsverbot eine Bindung der
Gewissen bedeuten, die selbst Gott nicht vornimmt, andererseits ermöglicht das
geringste Zugeständnis eine Zügellosigkeit, die Beschränkungen erfordert. Aus
den biblischen Schriften ist ein totales Zinsverbot nicht zu erheben. Die (für das
traditionelle kirchliche Zinsverbot klassische) Stelle Lk. 6,34: "Und wenn ihr
denen leiht, von denen ihr zurückzuerhalten hofft, was für einen Dank habt ihr?"
läßt sich für ein allgemeines Zinsverbot nicht in Anspruch nehmen, sondern weist
uns den Weg, ohne Rücksicht auf eigene materielle Sicherheit mehr den Armen als
den Reichen beizustehen. Auch die alttestamentlichen Stellen, die vom Zins reden,
erfordern eine neue Interpretation. Deut. 23,19 ("Du sollst von deinem Volksge-
nossen keinen Zins nehmen, weder Zins für Geld noch Zins für Speise, noch Zins
für irgend etwas, was man leihen kann") ist als "politisches Gesetz" (loy politique)
des jüdischen Volkes für uns nur hinsichtlich der in ihm enthaltenen "Billigkeit"

---

[76]Für diesen Abschnitt folge ich weitgehend der Zusammenstellung bei Geiger, *Calvin, Calvinismus, Kapitalismus,* 246 ff.; verwiesen sei außerdem auf die ausführliche Behandlung dieses Themas bei
Biéler, *La pensée,* 453–76, u. auf Schulze, *Calvin and "Social Ethics,"* 48–71.

[77]*CO* 10, Sp. 245–49, ebenfalls wiedergegeben in *OS* 2:391–96. Das Schreiben wurde veranlaßt
durch eine Claude de Sachin zugeschriebene Anfrage. Biéler, *La pensée,* 456, nennt den 7 November
1545 als Datum dieser Anfrage; die Datierung ist aber umstritten und darum weder in *CO* noch in *OS*
angeführt. Eine Drucklegung des Textes wurde erst 1575 durch Theodor von Beza veranlaßt.

[78]*CO* 28, Sp. 111–24; Biéler, *La pensée,* 453 ff., führt außerdem noch den Kommentar zu Ex.
22:25 auf, der auch Lev. 25:35–38, und noch einmal Deut. 23:19–20 berücksichtigt (*CO* 24 z. St.);
ferner den Komm. zu Ps. 15,5 (*CO* 31 z. St.) und die Vorlesungen über Ez. 1–20, die Calvin als letzte
vor seinem Tode hielt (*CO* 40 v. 1565), dort speziell zu Ez. 18,8 u.17!

(équité) und "Menschlichkeit" (raison d'humanité) verpflichtend. Ps. 55:12 ("Verderben wohnt in ihrer Mitte, Bedrückung und Trug weicht nicht von ihrem Markt") meint nicht eigentlich den Zins als solchen, sondern die mit dem Zinsnehmen so oft verbundene "tyrannische Grausamkeit" (cruaulte tyrannique) und "Täuschungskunst" (l'art de tromper). Hez. 22,12 schließlich ("Bestechung nimmt man in dir, um Blut zu vergießen; Zins und Zuschlag nimmst du und übervorteilst deinen Nächsten mit Gewalt, und meiner vergissest du, spricht Gott der Herr") spricht zwar spezieller vom Zinsnehmen, muß aber auf dem Hintergrunde der politisch-jüdischen Ordnung des allgemeinen Zinsverbotes verstanden werden. Hier nimmt Calvin einen wichtigen Einwand auf: Müßte die jüdische Regelung des Zinsverbotes nicht auch von uns übernommen werden, da doch auch wir eine "brüderliche Gemeinschaft" (coniunction fraternelle) bilden? Calvin verneint die Frage mit der Begründung, daß zwischen den damaligen und den gegenwärtigen "politischen Umständen" (coniunction politique) eine Differenz bestehe. "Der Zeitpunkt, zu dem Gott die Juden angeredet hatte, und viele andere Umstände machten es notwendig, daß sie untereinander rücksichtsvoll ohne Zinsen Handel trieben. Unsere heutige Lage ist damit überhaupt nicht vergleichbar."[79] Zins ist daher für uns unter dem Vorbehalt von "Billigkeit" (equite) und "Nächstenliebe" (charite) nicht einfach verboten.

Damit holt Calvin—seine am Anfang des Briefes betonte Zurückhaltung mehr und mehr vergessend—zu einer bewegten, fast leidenschaftlich werdenden Bekämpfung der auf Aristoteles zurückgehenden bekannten Anschauung aus, "daß Geld kein Geld erzeugt" (que largent *nengendre point* largent).[80] Sollte man das Geld anders betrachten und behandeln müssen als irgend etwas, das zu unserem Lebensunterhalt dient? Wenn Häuser, Felder und Waren Gewinne bringen, sollte es unerlaubt sein, auch vom Gelde einen Gewinn zu erwarten? Kauf und Hypothekarisierung eines Grundstückes sollten erlaubt, die bloße Gewährung eines verzinslichen Darlehens zum Kaufe des Grundstückes sollte unerlaubt sein? Hier muß Klarheit in der Sache geschaffen werden: "Die Sache und nicht die Worte, noch die Redeweise stehen hier zur Beurteilung an."[81]

Die Klarheit der Sache gewinnt Calvin durch eine Grundregelung und 8 Einzelregelungen: *Die Grundregelung:* Calvin trifft "die klare Unterscheidung zwischen dem Zins für produktiv angelegtes Kapital und dem fremde Not

---

[79]"la situation du lieu auquel Dieu avoyt colloque les Iuifz et beaucoup autres circonstances faisoient quilz traffiquoient entre eulx commodement sans usures. Nostre coniunction na point de similitude"; *OS* 2:393:33–36.

[80]Cf. o. Geiger, *Calvin, Calvinismus, Kapitalismus,* zu Anm. 75.

[81]"les choses et non pas les parolles ne les manieres de parler sont icy appellees in iugement" *OS* 2:395:4–6.

ausbeutenden parasitären Wucher." Er stellt "den ersten unter strenge Regelungen, den zweiten unter Verbot und Verfolgung."[82]

Calvin setzt folgende 8 Einzelregelungen des Zinsnehmens fest:[83]

(1) Geldleihen auf Zins sollte nicht zu einem eigentlichen Beruf gemacht werden (die Genfer Pastoren widersetzten sich zu Lebzeiten Calvins der Gründung einer Bank).

(2) Von Armen und wirtschaftlich Bedrängten darf kein Zins genommen werden.

(3) Zinstragende Kapitalinvestitionen dürfen nur insoweit vorgenommen werden, als sie die Hilfe an die Notleidenden nicht beeinträchtigen (s.o. III.1 dieser Arbeit!).

(4) Zinsverträge dürfen nur im Sinne der "natürlichen Billigkeit" (équite naturelle) und der Goldenen Regel Christi geschlossen werden (Mt. 7,12); *Zinsfuß zwischen 5 und 6,6 Prozent.*[84]

(5) Der Kapitalschuldner muß von dem ihm geliehenen Betrag den größeren Gewinn machen können als der Zinsempfänger.

(6) Maßstab für die Festsetzung des Zinsfußes darf nicht einfach Gewohnheitsrecht, sondern muß das Wort Gottes sein (s.o. 4).

(7) Zinsgeschäfte dürfen nicht nur unter privaten Gesichtspunkten getätigt werden, sondern es ist ihre Wirkung auf das allgemeine Wirtschaftsleben zu berücksichtigen.

(8) Bestehende gesetzliche Regelungen müssen stets nach dem Grundgesetz der "Billigkeit" angewendet werden (dürfen also nicht zur Rechtfertigung von Zinsgeschäften dienen, die sich aus anderen Überlegungen verbieten).

3. Abschließende Erwägungen zur Charakterisierung des sozialethischen Ansatzes Calvins und seiner entsprechenden Hermeneutik

Zur Gesamtcharakterisierung der "Sozialehtik" Calvins nennt Biéler vier Merkmale, die ihre Ausrichtung auch auf die neuen sozialen Dimensionen der

---

[82]H. Lüthy, Lüthy, "Nochmals: Calvinismus und Kapitalismus," 155 Lüthy ergänzt: "Jeder Wirtschaftshistoriker weiß, daß ... der Unterschied zwischen protestantischen und katholischen Ländern Europas nicht der war, daß in den ersten auf Zinsen und in den andern zinsfrei geliehen wurde, sondern daß in den ersten die Billigkeit des *anerkannten, öffentlich geregelten und präzis definierten Kapitalzinses* ein wesentlicher Faktor des wirtschaftlichen Aufschwungs war, während in den Ländern kanonischen Rechts der Wucherzins für Kapitaldarlehen eines der Haupthindernisse der wirtschaftlichen Entfaltung blieb."

[83]Sie sind im wesentlichen schon 1545 in seinem "Brief an einen Freund" (ibid., Anm. 77) eindeutig ausgesprochen (OS 2:395–96).

[84]Cf. die "Ordonnances sur la police des églises de la campagne" v. 3.2. (1547); CO 20:1: 56–57.

industriellen Welt ermöglichen, damit also die Situation im 16. Jh. und die Beziehung zum Frühkapitalismus transzendieren[85]:

(1) Sie ist fest in der Theologie verankert. Sie ist vollständig abhängig vom Mittelpunkt des evangelischen Glaubens, von der Person und dem Werk Christi. Es ist eine christozentrische theologische Ethik.[86]

(2) Sie stammt aus einer genauen Kenntnis der biblischen Offenbarung, die sie aber sehr dynamisch auslegt im Lichte der geschichtlichen Veränderungen der Gesellschaft.[87] Es ist eine biblische Ethik, die auf die Lebendigkeit der Geschichte ausgerichtet ist.

(3) Sie wird immer wieder aktuell und konkret durch eine klare Analyse der sich ständig entwickelnden Umstände. Sie enthält eine wissenschaftliche Methode für die Analyse sozialer und wirtschaftlicher Fakten.[88]

(4) Sie erreicht eine außergewöhnliche geschichtliche Wirksamkeit, weil sie ein Handeln verlangt, das den Umständen angepaßt und unermüdlich durch den Kontakt mit der Wirklichkeit erneuert wird. Es ist eine dialektische Methode des Handelns.[89]

---

[85]Cf. André Biéler, *Gottes Gebot und der Hunger der Welt: Calvin Prophet des industriellen Zeitalters. Grundlage und Methode der Sozialethik Calvins*, Polis 24 (Zürich,1966), 12; Eßer, "Calvins Sozialethik und der Kapitalismus," 794.

[86]Generell ist hier auf die Verankerung des 3. Gebrauchs des Gesetzes in der Christologie, *Inst.* 2.7.12–17, und auf die Heiligungslehre als Zuwendung der Wohltaten Christi im 3. Buch der *Institutio*, also in der Pneumatologie, zu verweisen.

[87]Calvin hätte vermutlich nicht vom "Lichte der geschichtlichen Veränderungen" gesprochen, sondern vom Subjekt der Tagesordnung, der *providentia dei*.

[88]Biéler, *Gottes Gebot*, 36. Biéler bringt als Beispiel die Erkenntnis Calvins, daß sich die Bezahlung von Zinsen auf die Gesamtlebenskosten einer Gesellschaft auswirkt, also trotz bestehender Privat-Darlehensverträge nicht Privatsache ist (s.o., Regel 7).

[89]Als Beispiel nennt Biéler, *Gottes Gebot*, 37–49, die "Prozeßethik" bei der Festlegung des Zinssatzes in den 50er Jahren des 16. Jh., an der die Kirchenglieder, der Rat und die einschlägigen Interessenten und Betroffenen beteiligt sind. Heute würden wir wohl von einer "konzertierten Aktion" aller an einem solchen "Prozeß" Beteiligten reden.

JOHN ŒCOLAMPADIUS.

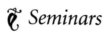 *Seminars*

Two Commentaries on The Epistle to the Romans: Calvin and Oecolampadius

Akira Demura

I. Preliminary Remarks

1. The Significance of Romans Commentaries in Church History

In church history, the appearance of a new commentary on the Epistle to the Romans has often marked a turning point in theological trend, as was the case with Luther's commentary in the sixteenth century or Karl Barth's in the twentieth. This was especially true in 1525 for the Basel Reformer Johannes Oecolampadius' *In Epistolam B. Pauli Apost. ad Rhomanos Adnotationes*[1] as well as in 1540 for Jean Calvin's *In Epistolam Pauli ad Rhomanos*.[2] The popularity enjoyed by Oecolampadius' *Adnotationes* is well attested by its second printing, which appeared the very next year.[3] There is no need to emphasize the importance of Calvin's Romans commentary, the first of the series of Biblical expositions that he worked on throughout his life. According to Richard C. Gamble's careful studies,[4] Calvin frequently used the same scriptural texts for a triple purpose: one for lessons in the *auditoire*, another on homiletic occasions in the pulpit for the sake of his congregation; and finally, for publication aimed at the learned world. Regrettably, Gamble's list covers only the publications after the year 1549; consequently, there can be found no reference to the Romans commentary from Gamble's perspective.

The chief objective of this seminar is a comparative study of Oecolampadius' and Calvin's commentaries on Romans in order to find out whether the Geneva Reformer was influenced by his Basel predecessor in his growth and formation as a Reformed theologian. It was in Basel where the French refugee found his much needed shelter in the summer of 1535 and where he added a few finishing touches to the manuscripts of his *Institutes*, which was to be published in the following

---

[1] Johannes Oecolampadius, *In Epistolam Pauli ad Rhomanos: Per Andr. Cratandrum MDXXVI* (hereafter *Adnotationes*). I am grateful to Prof. Wilhelm H. Neuser for the complete copy of this second edition.

[2] Thomas H. L. Parker, ed., *Iohannes Calvini in Epistolam Pauli ad Romanos* (Leiden: E. J. Brill, 1981) (hereafter: Parker, page nos., line nos.). English Translation: Ross Mckenzie, tr., *The Epistles of Paul the Apostle to the Romans and to the Thessalonians* (Grand Rapids: W. B. Eerdmans, 1980).

[3] Ernst Staehelin, ed., *Oekolampad-Bibliographie* (Nieuwkoop: B. De Graaf,1963), nos. 111:122.

[4] Richard C. Gamble, "Exposition and Method in Calvin," *Westminster Theological Journal* (1987): appendix I.II (esp. pp. 30–31).

spring. By this time Oecolampadius had been dead for nearly four years, but no doubt his writings had some influence on Calvin's Romans commentary, the first edition of which was eventually printed during his three-year sojourn in Strasbourg. We shall consider the major theological loci of justification, sanctification, and sacraments to discover a possible influence of Oecolampadius on Calvin or an identifiable parallelism between their commentaries.

2. *Some Problems*

Calvin dedicated his Romans commentary to Simon Grynaeus, a theologian with broad humanistic training and Oecolampadius' successor to the same chair of professor of theology at Basel University since 1532. In the well-known dedicatory preface, Calvin summarizes his fundamental standpoint in Biblical hermeneutic in a single phrase: "perspicua brevitas,"[5] which was his objective throughout his long career as a Bible exegete. Some theologians "not only study to be comprehensible, but also try to detain [their] readers too much with long and wordy commentaries," while Calvin himself stresses his love of abbreviation (*amor compendii*).[6]

In the preface Calvin refers to works by three of his predecessors that influenced his writing of Romans commentary: Philip Melanchthon, Heinrich Bullinger, and Martin Bucer.[7] According to Calvin's own characterization, Melanchthon seems to "discuss the points which were especially worth noting," with the result that he dwells "at length on these, deliberately passing over many matters" and "neglecting many points which require attention."[8] This is to say that Melanchthon was brief, but was not lucid enough. In contrast, Bullinger "expounded doctrines with an ease of expression, and for this he has been widely commended."[9] This testifies to the high respect Calvin had for Bullinger, as we shall later see in our discussion on sacraments.[10]

---

[5]Parker, p.1, line 8.   [6]Parker, p. 1, line 18.
[7]See Philip Melanchthon, *Dispositio Orationis, in epistola ad Romanos* (Hagenau: 1529). Rolf Schafer, ed., *Melanchthons Werke in Auswahl*, vol. 5. Römerbrief-Kommentar (Gütersloh: Mohn, 1965). Heinrich Bullinger, *In omnes Apostolicas Epistolis, Divi videlicet Pauli XIIII... Commentariis Heinrichi Bullingeri* (Zurich, 1537). Martin Bucer, *Metaphrasis et Enarratio in Epistolam ad Romanos...* (Strasbourg, 1532).
[8]Parker, p. 2. lines 45–49.   [9]Parker, p. 2, lines 50–52.
[10]Professor Fritz Büsser's numerous articles on the relation between Bullinger and Calvin, and especially on the significance of the former as a "model in Biblical exposition," were particularly helpful in this research. See especially Fritz Büsser, "Bullinger as Calvin's Model in Biblical Exposition: An Examination of Calvin's Preface to the Epistle to the Romans," *In Honor of John Calvin*, ed. E. J. Furcha, (Montreal: McGill University Press, 1987), 64–95 (in: *Calvin and Calvinism*, vol. 6. *Calvin and Hermeneutics*, 1992). And, in greater detail, "Calvin und Bullinger," in: *Calvinus Servus Christi: Die Referate des Congrès International des Recherches Calviniennes*, ed. Wilhelm H. Neuser (Budapest: Presseabteilung des Raday-Kollegium, 1988), 107–126.

In reference to his predecessors, Calvin says that Bucer tends to be "too verbose to be read quickly ... and too profound to be easily understood."[11] In other words, Bucer may have been lucid but not brief. All in all, Calvin's own aspiration was "praesertim quum ita omnia succincte perstringere instituerem, ut non magnam temporis iacturam facturi essent lectores."[12]

In this connection Calvin makes no reference to Oecolampadius in this preface. Does this omission necessarily exclude the possibility of Calvin's accessibility to, and knowledge of, Oecolampadius' Romans commentary? Thomas H. L. Parker also makes no reference to Oecolampadius in his modern critical edition. His references to Oecolampadius in his more comprehensive work, *Calvin's New Testament Commentaries*, are similarly scarce.[13] In it only two passages that mention Oecolampadius are quoted from Calvin. One is from the Daniel commentary, where Calvin is cited to have remarked: "Oecolampadius teaches correctly and wisely" in connection with an attack by a certain rabbi against the Christian interpretation of the Old Testament.[14] Another quotation is from Calvin's letter to Pierre Viret dated 19 May 1540.[15] Viret seems to have asked Calvin for advice on the commentaries of Isaiah. Calvin writes back: "Nemo ergo adhuc diligentius Oecolampadio in hoc opere versatus est, qui tamen etiam scopum non semper attingit."[16] Scant as these quotations are, they clearly point out that Calvin had some opportunities for carefully reading and consulting Oecolampadius' expository works; he profoundly appreciated them, even though, in some scattered cases, he says that he had some reservations. Exactly where Calvin found Oecolampadius not entirely satisfying is not quite certain. The reason may have been critico-historical or dogmatico-theological, or perhaps both. Without a doubt, Calvin had Oecolampadius' exegetical works beside him and consulted them with reasonable frequency. Parenthetically, in 1558, nearly thirty years after the death of Oecolampadius, a Genevan printer, Jean Crespin, published the corpus of Oecolampadius' commentaries on the Old Testament under the title of *Commentarii Omnes in libros Prophetarum*.[17] We must remember that a stringent censure system was in operation in Geneva under Calvin's strong leadership. The silence on the side of Calvin, therefore, is all the more unintelligible to us. We shall pursue this question in what follows.

---

[11]Parker, p. 2, lines 52 ff.   [12]Parker, p. 3. lines 89–90.
[13]Thomas H. L. Parker, *Calvin's New Testament Commentaries* (London: SCM Press, 1971).
[14]Parker, *Calvin's New Testament Commentaries*, 87.
[15]Parker, *Calvin's New Testament Commentaries*, 88.
[16]CO 11:217:36   [17]Staehelin, *Bibliographie*, no. 209:1–5.

3. Precedents of Parallel Studies

There are few comparative studies of commentaries on Romans. One of the more recent is Cristina Grenholm's doctoral dissertation, published as *Romans Interpreted: A Comparative Analysis of the Commentaries of Barth, Nygren, Cranfield and Wilckens on Paul's Epistle to the Romans.*[18] Although the commentaries analyzed are by contemporary authors, the similarity in methodological interest and treatment is meaningful, especially the sections in which she discusses the problem of ἐγώ in chapter 7. This classical problem received special attention by Paul Althaus in *Paulus und Luther über den Menschen: Ein Vergleich.*[19] His contradistinction between "Mensch ohne Christus," and "Christenmensch" may have stimulated Grenholm to contrast "Paul ante Christum" with "Paul post Christum." In section III of this essay, I compare Calvin's and Oecolampadius' interpretations of the problem of ἐγώ. In a broader perspective, Thomas F. Torrance's *Calvin's Doctrine of Man* points out the major themes of Calvin's anthropology, but it is not basically "comparative" in method and is somewhat remote from our present concern.[20]

II. The Doctrine of Justification

1. Romans 1:16, 17

a. *Oecolampadius.* Commenting on the phrase "uirtus enim dei est," Oecolampadius says: "Clausula haec bene obseruanda erit. Nam hic ingressum habemus in epistolam totam.... Igitur status rei tractandae est, Verbo dei credentes saluos fieri. Et haec potentia uerbi, ut ipsum uerbum sit potentia dei.... Et uide quam necessarius sit auditus uerbi dei. Nam satius soret omnes caeremonias tolli, quàm uerbum dei intermitti."[21] In these sentences Oecolampadius shows himself clearly to be a theologian of the Word of God. According to him, faith comes from hearing the Word (fides ex auditu[22]), and the Word itself has authority, power, and virtue. Commenting on verse 17, Oecolampadius continues: "Nam dum uerbo Christi credimus, Christo credimus."[23]

These statements remind us of a passage in Calvin's preface: "quando siquis eam intelligat, aditum sibi quendam patefactum habet ad totius Scripturae intelligentiam."[24] Whereas Calvin regards *The Epistle to the Romans* as the key to under-

---

[18]Cristina Grenholm, *Romans Interpreted: A Comparative Analysis of the Commentaries of Barth, Nygren, Cranfield and Wilckens on Paul's Epistle to the Romans* (Stockholm: Almqvist & Wiksell, 1990).
[19]Paul Althaus, *Paulus und Luther über den Menschen: Ein Vergleich,* Studien der Luther-Akademie, 14 vols. (1938; reprinted Gütersloh: C. Bertelsmann Verlag, 1951).
[20]Thomas F. Torrance, *Calvin's Doctrine of Man* (London: Lutterworth, 1947).
[21] *Adnotationes,* 10a.   [22] *Adnotationes,* 33b,   [23] *Adnotationes,* 10b.
[24]Parker, p. 2, lines 39–41.

standing the entire Bible, Oecolampadius' view is that the passage in Romans 1:16–17 is an "entrance" into this letter. In spite of this difference regarding the context, we may still hear resounding echoes between the two Reformers.

At this point, it will be helpful to make a brief digression for the purpose of considering the textual criticism of both Reformers. Oecolampadius and Calvin are quite free in determining the scriptural text, although the former does not usually give the entire text as he translates it into Latin. The formal title, *Adnotationes à Joanne Oecolampadio Basileae praelectae*, may suggest that the book was for the most part lecture notes taken and abbreviated by someone else. Accordingly, Oecolampadius does not have a great interest in discussing the problem of textual criticism as such. Nonetheless, he maintains complete independence not only from the Vulgate but also from Erasmus' *Novum Instrumentum* (1516), the completion and publication of which he had wholeheartedly committed himself to while he was still a young assistant to Erasmus. The following example is a good illustration: Oecolampadius translates "virtus" in accordance with the Vulgate, while Calvin uses "potentia," as Erasmus does in *Novum Instrumentum*, even if Erasmus himself uses "virtus" in his *Annotationes*. Since both words have practically the same connotation, these variances may be of small significance. Nevertheless, such liberty and independence were quite characteristic of Oecolampadius, as can be noticed throughout the whole book.

To verse 1:16, "Non enim pudet me Euangelii Christi," Calvin comments as follows: "Observa autem quantum verbi ministrio tribuat Paulus quum testatur Deum illic suam ad salvandam virtutem exerere, non enim de arcana aliqua revelatione, sed vocali praedicatione hic loquitur."[25] Calvin continues: "Verum quia non operatur in omnibus efficaciter, sed tantum ubi Spiritus interior magister cordibus illucet."[26] Such an expression as this, so characteristic of Calvin, focusing on the theme of the internal illumination by the Holy Spirit, is not explicit in Oecolampadius, even though he was firmly convinced of the divine inspiration of Scripture, as is testified, for example, by his expository lecture on 1 John 4:1, where he so clearly indicates: "Ante omnia enim Christianos persuasum esse oportet, scripturas sacras divinitus inspiritas."[27]

What do both annotators have to say on the central theme of "iustitia dei"? A statement by Oecolampadius, "Caue ne intelligas hic per iustitiam dei, iudicium dei, ... Iustus deus reuelatur per Euangelium.... Et est iustitia dei, quae gratis ius-

---

[25]Parker, p. 25, lines 80–83.
[26]Parker, p. 25, lines 85–87.
[27]Calvin, *Epistolam Ioannis Apostoli Catholicam primam* (Basel: Andreas Cratander, 1524). Equally, on 1 John 5:24, "necesse est ut corda audiat. Internum magistrum audiamus, spiritum sanctum.""

tificat impium, absque operum respectu,"[28] reminds us of Luther's doctrine of justification. In contrast, Calvin sounds more "forensic" in his understanding of justification. In regard to the same verse, Calvin remarks: "Iustitia Dei accipio, quae apud Dei tribunal approbetur.... Alii exponunt, Quae a Deo nobis donatur.... Plus in eo momenti est, quod iustitiam hanc non in gratuita modo peccatorum remissione sitam esse quidam putant: sed partim quoque in regenerationis gratia."[29] We should notice that, among those whom Calvin calls *alii* expositors, in fact, no less a figure than Augustine himself is included, as we see it in his exegesis on Romans 3:22.

On the latter half of verse 17 "Iustus autem in fide sua vivet," Oecolampadius annotates:

> Viuet in futuro dicit, ostendens quod iusti in hoc seculo contempti uiuant, et computentur cum mortuis, crucifixi scilicet huic mundo.... Unde et frequenter dominus dicit in Euangelio: Fides te saluum fecit. Proinde fides ad opera confert, sicut uita ad alimentum.[30]

Calvin is aware that Erasmus paraphrased this word into the participle ("Iustus autem ex fide victurus est"). He points out that it suggests "perpetuo constaturam,"[31] because,

> quia quantum progreditur fides nostra, quantumque in hac cognitione proficitur, simul augescit in nobis Dei iustitia, et quodammodo sancitur eius possessio ... quo magis augescit pietatis eruditio, velut propiore accessu clarius ac magis familiariter Dei gratiam perspicimus.... Paulus, sed quotidianum in singulis fidelibus progressum notat.[32]

Here we perceive the central theme of Calvin's doctrine of sanctification, i.e., "the daily progress of repentance," in an unambiguous way.

2. Romans 3:21–28

a. *Oecolampadius.* On verse 3:21, which is, so to speak, the climax of *The Epistle to the Romans* so far as the doctrine of justification is concerned, Oecolampadius tries to clarify and amplify what he has stated on 1:17 ("iustitia enim dei ... omni credenti, ex fide, in fidem").[33] He says: "Etiam hoc loco iustitia est, qua nos deus iustos reputat, quando scilicet in eius gratia sumus."[34] Once one admits that righteousness is what is granted to us by God's grace, it can in no case be attrib-

---

[28]*Adnotationes*, 11a.   [29]Parker, p. 26, lines 22–32.
[30]*Adnotationes*, 12b–13a.   [31]Parker, p. 27, line 51.
[32]Parker., pp. 26–27, lines 36–45. [33]*Adnotationes*, 12b.   [34]*Adnotationes*, 33a.

uted to us as if it were the reward for our merit. "Iustitia dei" is that righteousness by and through which God regards the sinners as if they were already righteous and sinless. Here we find a clear-cut statement on the imputation theory of justification in Oecolampadius. According to his exposition of verse 22, the cause or ground of this gratuitous gift consists in God's promise: "Causa haec est, quia inititur promissionibus. Iusti autem est praestare promissa."[35] Richard Muller's essay on the hermeneutic of promise and fulfillment is enlightening in this context, although he appears to depend heavily upon Henri Strohl's earlier works.[36]

On the phrase "absque lege," Oecolampadius notes: "Non quod omnino prohibeamur facere opera legis, sed liberum est illa facere, prout fides et charitas dictant. Dicit autem illa opera non reputari ad iustitiam."[37] This sentence is reminiscent of the fundamental ethical code in Calvin: "Non per opera, sed non sine operibus," as Calvin repeatedly expounds it in his *Institutes.*

Oecolampadius again takes up the same strain of the daily progress of the faithful already referred to in 1:16–17. On 3:23 ("omnes enim peccauerunt"), Oecolampadius observes: "Habes hic manifeste et sanctos peccasse. Et non dicit imperfecti fuerunt, neque ad malum propensi sunt: sed, Peccauerunt. Agnoscamus ergo nos peccatores....Semper enim sanctis adhaesit labecula quaedam."[38] Here is unmistakably echoed the cardinal refrain of Luther's theology of "simul iustus ac peccator," although Oecolampadius does not use the term in an explicit way. We are well aware that his conversion to the Evangelical position took place under the overwhelming impact of Luther.

What, then, does Oecolampadius have to say on the difficult question of "reward," a reward apparently promised even by the Evangelists, for good works, in seeming conflict with the teaching of justification by faith alone? Already by the time he was lecturing on *The Epistle to the Romans* in Basel, the controversy between Luther and Erasmus over the problem of "free will" was reaching its height. Although Oecolampadius remained strongly critical of the proponents of free will, he offered the following noteworthy sentences on this matter: "Haec enim iustitia est in praesenti tempore. Nam in futuro tempore post hanc uitam iustitia dei est, ut unicuique tribuat secundum opera sua."[39] We shall refrain from inferring that Calvin would ever support such an interpretation.

Finally, his remarks on verse 28 are worth notice. As the ground of his assertion, "fide iustificari hominem absque operibus legis, qualiacunque praecepta

[35]*Adnotationes,* 33b.
[36]Richard A. Muller, "The Hermeneutic of Promise and Fulfillment in Calvin's Exegesis of the Old Testament Prophecies of the Kingdom," in *The Bible in the 16th Century* (Durham, N.C.: Duke University Press, 1990), 68ff.
[37]*Adnotationes,* 33a.   [38]*Adnotationes,* 33b.   [39]*Adnotationes,* 34b.

sunt in lege,'[40] he takes up the utterances of one of the robbers who was crucified together with Jesus:

> Huius exemplum idoneum arbitror latronem cum Christo crucifixum: cuius cum non describitur aliud bonum opus, quam quod clamauit: Memento mei domine, dum ueneris in regnum tuum, et pro sola hac fide audiit: Hodie mecum eris in paradiso. Opponatur ergo latro ille alteri abundanti operibus apparebit hic latro iustificatus sine operibus legis.[41]

As is widely recognized, this was a favorite subject for Erasmus in his struggle to restore simple and undogmatic Christianity. Remote as the years may have been when Oecolampadius was an ardent admirer and follower of Erasmus, memories of the latter may have lingered on. This stream of perception was no other than the expression of the piety of *devotio moderna,* which was also traceable in Oecolampadius. More than a quarter of a century later, Sebastian Castellio, for example, would ground his claim for religious tolerance and the freedom of conscience exactly on the same passage. We wonder if Calvin could ever pronounce in a similar tone.

   b. *Calvin.* Next, let us give special attention to some notable passages from Calvin's comments on verse 3:21 ("Nunc autem sine Lege iustitia dei"). Calvin says: "Dubium est qua ratione Dei iustitiam appelet, quam per fidem obtinemus: ideone quia sola coram Deo consistit: an quod eam nobis Dominus sua misericordia largiatur. Quoniam utraque interpretatio bene quadrabit: neutra ex parte contendimus."[42] Here Calvin dares to oppose the authority of Augustine when he writes: "Neque vero me latet, Augustinum secus exponere: Iustitiam enim Dei esse putat regenerationis gratiam: et hanc gratuitam esse fatetur, quia Dominus immerentes Spiritu suo nos renovat."[43] The reason behind his negative attitude toward Augustine is that some recent Schoolmen took the liberty of founding their doctrine of justification and sanctification in this very statement by Augustine. Calvin tries to sever himself from their position when he says:

> Mihi etiam plus satis notum est, quosdam novos *speculatores* hoc dogma superciliose proferre.... Putant haec duo optime convenire, Fide iustificari hominem per Christi gratiam: et tamen Operibus iustificari, quae ex regeneratione spirituali proveniant: quia et gratuito nos Deus renovat, et eius donum fide percipimus.[44]

---

[40] *Adnotationes,* 35a.   [41] *Adnotationes,* 35a.   [42] Parker, p. 68, lines 45–49.
[43] Parker, p. 68, lines 57–59.   [44] Parker, p. 68, lines 1–63, 72–74.

There is no doubt that those "novi speculatores" referred to are the School-men belonging to the so-called *via moderna*, who vindicated a fine distinction between the "meritum de congruo" and "meritum de condigno." Calvin criticizes them in his comment on verse 27 ("Ubi ergo gloriatio?"), saying: "Gloriationem autem haud dubie exclusam dicit, quia nihil possumus nostrum producere quod Dei sit approbatione aut commendatione dignum. Quod si materia gloriandi est meritum, sive de congrue sive de condigno nomines, ... hic utrunque everti vides."[45] Calvin's conclusive remark on verse 21 is: "At Paulus longe aliud princi-pium sumit;"[46] on verse 27, similarly: "sed Paulus ne guttam quidem reliquam facit."[47]

In short, Calvin is convinced "non iustificari homines quia re ipsa tales sint, sed imputatione."[48] In order to fortify what he has said, he talks about the "iusti-tiae communicatio," by which "suas divitias Deus apud se minime tenet suppres-sas, sed in homines effundit."[49] There is no room here, unfortunately, to discuss further the issue of whether these concepts of the "communication" or "effusion" of righteousness has something to do with the Lutheran teaching of the "commu-nicatio idiomatum" in the process of justification.

3. Romans 5:1–11

Our final section on the doctrine of justification is concerned with the anno-tations on Romans 5:1–11, where the Apostle Paul's understanding of justification by faith alone and the fruits of sanctification seems to reach its climax.

On verse 1 ("pacem habemus apud deum"), Oecolampadius remarks: "Transit nunc ad opera et fructus fidei, immo beatitudines, quae ex fide proueniunt. Primus fides iustificat coram deo.... Secundo, peccatas reddit conscientias nos-tras. Tertio, constantes et perseuerantes fecit. Quarto concedit ut gloriemur et gaudeamus."[50] Like Erasmus, Oecolampadius translates the main verb into the present tense (*habemus*), and does not adopt the Vulgate version of the imperfect tense (*habebamus*). In the commentary itself, however, he says: "plus placet sim-plicitas veteris translationis, aditum habuimus."[51] This is in the perfect tense. Erasmus refers to this grammatical problem in his *Annotationes* and defends his preference for the present tense on the basis that later Greek tended to use the imperfect to express the present. Insignificant as such an argument may sound, it may be indicative of Oecolampadius' skill as a classical linguist.

"Juxta tempus" in verse 6 is interpreted to mean "praedestinato tempore." That is to say: "Noluit autem mox filium mittere post lapsum Adae, ut cog-

---

[45]Parker, p. 76, lines 9–13.   [46]Parker, p. 69, line 2.   [47]Parker, p. 76, lines 14–15.
[48]Parker, p. 74, lines 46–47.   [49]Parker, p. 75, lines 96–97.
[50]*Adnotationes*, 42a–b.   [51]*Adnotationes*, 43b.

nosceretur peccati gravitas: neque expectavit usque ad consummationem seculorum, ne nimia desperatione animos desponderemus."[52] Admitting the danger of a precipitous judgment, we might tentatively say that Oecolampadius was inclined more toward the so-called infralapsarianism than toward supralapsarianism. At any rate, he was not allowed to live long enough to develop his doctrine of predestination to full maturity, concerning which Calvin may later have had some complaint regardless of differences in the historical context.

What, then, does Calvin say on the same passage? While he uses the present tense for the first verse ("pacem habemus"), he changes it into the perfect tense in the next case ("accessum habuimus"). The matter itself may not be of great significance, except that he draws the attention of his readers to this word "accessus," on which he makes the following remarks: "Et accessus quidem nomine, initium salutis a Christo esse docens, praeparationes excludit, quibus stulti homines Dei misericordiam se antevertere putant."[53]

Such a critical attitude toward Augustine as the following should be understood in this context. On verse 5 ("dilectio Dei diffusa est in cordibus nostris") he goes so far as to say that Augustine was mistaken ("hallucinatur,"[54] or rather "under an illusion"!), because he had expounded "nos constanter adversa tolerare, et hac ratione in spem confirmari, quia Spiritu regenerati, Deum diligamus. Pia quidem sententia, sed nihil ad Pauli mentem. Dilectio enim hic non activa, sed passiva capitur."[55] Calvin was firmly determined not to attribute anything to man as the ground of faith, hope, love, and perseverance even though Augustine took care to explain it as the gift of the Holy Spirit to the regenerate.

On the other hand, Oecolampadius does not sound so thoroughgoing and unreserved. Probably it was an unavoidable limitation for a first generation Reformer. It may have been the ground of Calvin's slight discontent. It can fairly be said that Oecolampadius was prone to emphasize responsive human love toward God and charity among men, although he too was careful enough to say, in his commentary on 1 John, "quamvis autem charitas magna sit, non tamen iustificat.... [f]ide enim iustificamur, et filii dei efficimur: at charitate non tribuitur iustificatio."[56] Without doubt or reservation, we must say that Oecolampadius was also a theologian of the Reformation.

---

[52]*Adnotationes*, 44b. Cf. Erasmus, *Annotationes*, ed. Heinz Holeczek (Stuttgart: Bd. Frommann-Holzboog, 1986), 431.

[53]Parker, p. 102, lines 13 et al., p. 103, lines 33 et al.

[54]Parker, p. 106, line 47.

[55]Parker, p. 106, lines 47–50.   [56]*In Epistolam Ioannis*, 54a-b.

III. The Use of the Law: Romans 7:7–25

1. *Oecolampadius*

a. *The Use of the Law.* As to the size of the two commentaries, the one by Oecolampadius is scarcely two hundred octavo pages, whereas that by Calvin, in the critical edition by Thomas H. L. Parker, is well over three hundred pages. Because Oecolampadius does not normally give the full text, the total number of pages tends to be fewer. In view of this simple fact, it is remarkable that the annotation on chapter 7 is practically the same size as Calvin's, as if it exemplifies the importance Oecolampadius ascribed to the question of the Law and its role.

On verse 7 ("Quid igitur dicemus?"), Oecolampadius observes: "Ex his quae dicta sunt, emergit quaestio de sanctitate legis. Dixerat enim legem operari iram: et eos qui sub gratia, iam non esse sub lege. Praeterea compararat ueterem hominem et peccati fomitem legi."[57] Does not, however, this suggestion that the law is sinful imply blasphemy to Moses and his divine law? The answer is "absit," because

Quasi dicat: Non dixerim legem, quae per Mosen data, impiam, cum peccatum sit transgressio: sed uelim deplorare infirmitatem et debilitatem nostram hisce uerbis: Nam post peccatum primorum parentum ita uitiata est natura nostra, ut lex a deo data, quamuis uere sancta sit, non solum tamen non iuuet, sed et deteriores reddat.[58]

The Law, far from being sin or sinful, is, in itself, as Paul clearly affirms, holy and righteous. What is termed ἀδύνατον τοῦ νόμου (Romans 8:3) can only be explained by way of human sinfulness that has made the Law ineffective and inappropriate for the soteriological end. Basically, there could neither be a conflict nor a contradiction between Moses and Christ, Law and Gospel, although it must be clear that the Law is subordinate to the Gospel. In his commentary on Matthew, Oecolampadius states unequivocally: "Lex sancta erat, iusta et bona. Nostrae autem infirmitatis erat, quae bono pharco deterior fiebat.... Proinde Moses Christo contrarius non erit, sed ancillabitur."[59]

To return to the Romans commentary, we find an interesting remark on 7:14, where Oecolampadius says: "Obserua tamen, quod non idem est dicere, legem esse spiritus, et legem spiritualem esse."[60] Note that he makes a fine distinction between "spiritus" and "spiritualis." Commenting on Isaiah 24:5, he has a similar

---

[57] *Adnotationes,* 54b.   [58] *Adnotationes,* 54b.
[59] Johannes Oecolampadius, *Enarratio in Euangelium Mattaei* (1536), 3a.
[60] *Adnotationes,* 56b.

expression that reads: "Charitatis autem lex, lex est spiritus."[61] Nonetheless, the Law has become incapable of salvation. To be sure, Christ said that not even an iota of the Law would be abolished. We must hurry to add, however, "Omnino ostendit Christus legem fore necessariam, etsi ex lege non salvabimur. Non sequitur, lex necessaria est, ergo salvat,"[62] to quote from Oecolampadius' same commentary on Matthew.

The very reason of this impotence of the Law consists in the reality of sin and the fact that all sins are derived from the sin committed by Adam. Here, Oecolampadius expounds his theology of the contemporaneity of Adam and all his descendants. To quote from his commentary on Job: "In Adam enim omnes peccavimus, non imitatione sola qua sponte peccamus, sed et carnis eius participes facti, in qua habitare ceparat peccatum."[63] He goes so far as to say that this sin, namely, the disobedience or the rebellion of flesh, reaches us through hereditary transmission. On Romans 5:12, he comments: "quia habitauit in nobis peccatum, quod haereditatuimus."[64] In interpreting the essence of Original Sin in this way, Oecolampadius was a faithful follower of Augustine.

According to him, "debebat homo absque lege deo hilariter seruire omnibus suis affectionibus," while, in reality, sinners do not and cannot recognize their sins. "Uerum ut peccator erat, non cognoscebat malitiam suam, quod tanta pronitate ad peccandum ferretur."[65] It is almost as much as to say that sin is the ignorance of sin, as Luther put it in his Romans commentary.

What does Oeclampadius have to say on the use of the Law, especially, the so-called third use of the Law, reputedly so characteristic of the Reformed tradition? As did Luther and Calvin, Oecolampadius affirms that the first use or purpose of the Law consists in the recognition or disclosure of sin. He says on 7:7, "Hoc unum praestitit mihi lex, ut aperiret mihi oculos ad cognoscendum peccatum."[66] Since before the coming of the Law, man tried to measure the purity of life by the standard of external blamelessness, he was not able to come to the true knowledge of his sinfulness. When the Law was given, however, man was able for the first time to realize the profundity of his sinfulness. "Nunc post legem, quia illa uideo esse in me, et disciplicere deo, necesse est ut fatear me esse peccatorem."[67] Similarly, on 10:4, Oecolampadius says that the Law makes us despair of our own capabilities "desperantes de nostris uiribus"[68] so that one looks to grace from above. Thus, Oecolampadius is quite certain in his understanding of the accusatory or indicting function of the Law. However, on the civil or legislative use of the Law,

---

[61]Johannes Oecolampadius, *In Iesaiam Prophetam Hypomnematon* (1525), 150a (on Isa. 24:5).
[62]*Enarratio in Mattaei*, 65b.   [63]*In Librum Iob exegemata* (on 14:4), 80a.
[64]*Adnotationes*, 46a.   [65]*Adnotationes*, 54b.
[66]*Adnotationes*, 54b.   [67]*Adnotationes*, 55a.   [68]*Adnotationes*, 76a.

he was not as expressive as could well have been expected. And in the case of the third use of the Law, he was even less expressive. In regard to the legislative and third uses of the Law, he may, in fact, have been closer to Luther than to Calvin, although we know that Oecolampadius did exert himself to establish church discipline in the city of Basel.

b. *The Problem of ἐγώ.* As we hinted in our preliminary remarks, one of the touchstones of the Romans commentaries is in the interpretation of ἐγώ in the seventh chapter. Let us hear what Oecolampadius says concerning this problem:

> Ego ... iuxta primam generationem ab Adam, carnalis et crassus sum: non specto gloriam dei, fugio crucem, amo commoda propria: et non solum carnalis, et sicut minister addictus carni, sed sicut empticium mancipium, qui non possum suffigere imperium domini, et facio quicquid caro imperat. Lex spiritualem requirit, ego autem carnalis sum: lex uult liberum, ego autem captiuus sum.... [c]ognouimus autem per legem nos esse uenditos.[69]

Consequently, "ego miser" in 7:24, according to Oecolampadius, is no other than the Apostle Paul himself, who has already been under the reign of grace and now stands in it. On verse 15, he comments: "Non introducit apostolus alienam personam, sed suam propriam. Dicit autem: Quod ago, in carne scilicet, improbo per legem, et odi spiritu. Et agnoscit in se adhuc Apostolus etiam iustificatus peccatum, et peccandi cupiditatem."[70] Here is perceived, unmistakably enough, the well-known paradox, common among the Reformers, that only the saved can know and confess their sins. On verse 24, Oecolampadius remarks succinctly: "Deplorat seipsum, et haec est uera et perpetua causa deplorandi nos ipsos.... Non solum dicit se infirmum uel captiuum, sed plane miserum, et omnia auxilio alio-qui destitutum."[71]

It is in this conjunction that the shift from the first use of the Law to the third takes place, as we have just seen. On 7:16, Oecolampadius observes: "Hic apparet uitam iustorum esse perpetuam palaestram: impelluntur enim a spiritu sancto ad facienda bona, sed obstat caro, et deformat opus."[72] An assertion such as this by Oecolampadius, that human life is a perpetual progress and continuous self-discipline, is to be found in many other passages. To quote only a few, on 4:14 he says: "concupiscentia quandiu uiuimus, in nobis relinquit: quae tamen quamuis peccatum dicatur, non imputatur in peccatum."[73] Similarly, on 9:20: "Quandiu igitur uiuimus, inhabitamus crassa corpora, atque diuina perspicere non possumus: sed absoluti a corporibus, et facti spirituales, illa sciemus."[74]

---

[69] *Adnotationes*, 56b.
[70] *Adnotationes*, 56b–57a.
[71] *Adnotationes*, 57b–58a.
[72] *Adnotationes*, 57a
[73] *Adnotationes*, 41a.
[74] *Adnotationes*, 73a.

These examples correspond precisely with what we have noticed in his remarks on chapters 3 and 5.

2. Calvin

a. *The Use of the Law.* Since there have already been a large number of thoroughgoing studies on Calvin's view of the Law and its use, for example those by Edward Dowey and John Hesselink, the following discussion is restricted to Calvin's exposition of 7:7 as a typical example of his thought on this theme.

On the much debated word "concupiscentia" in 7:7, Calvin remarks:

Nam politicae quidem Leges consilia se, non eventus punire clamant: Philosophi etiam subtilius tam vitia quam virtutes locant in animo: sed Deus hoc praecepto ad concupiscentiam usque penetrat, quae voluntate occultior est.... Atqui Paulus se reatum suum deprehendisse ex hoc latente morbo dicit.[75]

On the clause "Ego autem vivebam sine Lege aliquando," he says: "istud Vivebam habet propriam connotationem: quia absentia Lege faciebat ut viveret, hoc est inflatus iustitiae suae fiducia vitam sibi arrogaret."[76] This word "inflatus" immediately reminds us of Oecolampadius' comment on the preceding verse which runs: "Occasione autem accepta peccatum," where it is said: "Nihil ne profuit tibi lex ad emendationem tui, postquam cognouisti te esse peccatorem? Dicti nihil se a lege emendatum, sed excitatum, et inflammatus ab ea ad peccatum."[77] Etymologically, Calvin's expression of "inflatus'" conveys practically the same range of nuance as Oecolampadius' "inflammatus," although, of course, it does not guarantee in any way that Calvin had been influenced by his senior Reformer of Basel. It is certain, however, that they both spoke from the same theological point of view.

b. *The Problem of ἐγώ.* On verse 8, Calvin explains why he uses the imperfect tense by saying: "In praeterio imperfecto, acsi Paulus de se loqueretur: quum facile sit videre, illum a propositione universali incipere, deinde rem explanare suo exemplo."[78] This is equivalent to saying that the ἐγώ in the seventh chapter is none other than the Apostle Paul himself. The natural question, then, would be just which stage of his life he had in his mind, as he wrote this letter to the

---

[75]Parker, p. 142, lines 7–13. Cf. *Encyclopedia of the Reformed Faith*, ed. Donald K. McKim (Edinburgh: St Andrew Press, 1992), 215–17.
[76]Parker, p. 143, lines 46–48.
[77]*Adnotationes*, 55a.
[78]Parker, p. 143, lines 38–43.

Romans. To put this question in the way it is expressed by Calvin in regard to verse 9: "Verum quaeritur, quod fuerit illud tempus quo per Legis ignorantiam, sive (ut ipse loquitur) absentiam, sibi confidenter vitam arrogaret."[79] The answer is to be sought in the annotation on verse 15, where Calvin unambiguously declares:

> Quo igitur tota haec disputatio fidelius ac certius intelligatur, notandum est, hoc certamen de quo loquitur Apostolus, non prius extare in homine, quam Spiritu Dei fuerit sanctificatus. Nam homo naturae suae relictus, totus sine repugnantia in cupiditates fertur.... Pii contra, in quibus coepta est Dei regeneratio, sic divisi sunt.[80]

Further on, Calvin continues to say:

> Haec est lucta Christiana de qua Paulus ad Galatas loquitur, inter carnem et spiritum ... divisionem vero statim tum incipere primum ubi a Domino vocatus est, ac spiritu sanctificatus.... Atqui Paulus non hic proponit nudam hominis naturam: verum qualis et quanta sit fidelium infirmitas, sub persona sua describit.[81]

To reiterate the matter, "Porro hic locus palam evincit, nonnisi de piis qui iam regeniti sunt."[82] In short, "tantum de fideli, qui propter carnis reliquias et Spiritus gratiam in seipso divisus est."[83]

According to Calvin's interpretation, by the word "flesh," the Apostle implies not only the somatic body with all its desires and passions, but also, and above all, "omnes humanae naturae dotes, ac omnino quicquid in homine est, excepta spiritus sanctificatione," because "utranque igitur competit."[84]

On the well-known phrase of verse 24 "miser ego," Calvin has the following to say: "Claudit disputationem exclamatione vehementiae plena, qua docet non modo luctandum cum carne nostra esse, sed assiduo gemitu deplorandam apud nos et coram Deo nostram infoelicitatem."[85] The reason why the Apostle here mentions "corpore mortis" is that "perfectissimos quoque, quandiu in carne sua habitant, miseriae esse addictos, quia mortis sunt obnoxii: immo dum se penitus excutiunt, nihil in sua natura praeter miseriam ipsis occurrere."[86] It may safely be said that the anthropology of Calvin, as well as of Oecolampadius, follows the pattern of the *Miteinander* typology of Luther, rather than that of the *Nacheinander*

---

[79]Parker, p. 144, lines 56–57.   [80]Parker, p. 148, lines 94–113.
[81]Parker, pp. 148f, lines 18–33.   [82]Parker, p. 150, lines 81–82.
[83]Parker, p. 151, lines 99–100.   [84]Parker, p. 151, lines 1–6.
[85]Parker, p. 153, lines 86–89.   [86]Parker, p. 154, lines 9–11.

of Augustine, to borrow the distinction proposed by Althaus.[87] There seems to be an unmistakable parallelism between the two Reformers, although it would surely be going too far to say that Calvin wrote his Romans commentary under the influence of Oecolampadius. We should be content with finding a close similarity and resemblance between the two.

IV. The Teaching on Sacraments: Romans 4:11

Because of space restriction, our discussion is confined to Romans 4:11: "He received circumcision as a sign or seal of the righteousness which he had by faith while he was still uncircumcised."

a. *Oecolampadius.* Oecolampadius asks: "Quid opus erat iustificato Abrahae signo?" Circumcision was nothing more than a sign ("signum" or "signaculum," namely, "obsignatio"). All in all, a sacrament is a sign, no more, no less, according to Oecolampadius. He continues to say: "Certitudinem se ex fide iustificatum in praeputio, id est, absque operibus."[88] The necessity of a sign consists, however, in that "Res enim ardua est, et humanum captum transcendens, credere se absque operibus post peccata iustificari."[89]

It is obvious here that the "res" itself, that is to say, the justification by faith alone, and its "signum" are to be clearly differentiated. Thus, for Abraham, circumcision as a sign has double connotation or utility. First, it works in the way "ut fluctuans ipsius conscientia confirmaretur." This might well be designated as the "vertical" use of sacraments between God and men. In contrast, the second may be delineated as "horizontal" among men. Oecolampadius puts it as follows: "Proderat deinde quod iustificabatur apud homines, ... ut declaratus sit pater omnium credentium."[90]

Paraphrasing this duplex relation, Oecolampadius explains: "Idem usus circumcisionis et Iudaeis erat, quia primum pro se credebant se saluari fide in deum. ... Et ita iusti apud deum," while the second use aims at "apud proximos ... quam deus peculiariter tanquam suam et sibi dedicatam hoc signo delectam habere voluit."[91]

This duplex use of circumcision corresponds directly to that of the Christian sacraments, "usus sacramentorum, etiam nostrorum: nempe in baptismo et participatione mensae." Both are useful "nobis et proximis, uel coram deo et proximo." When he says "nobis" [for our own selves], the implication is that "ad pacandas conscientias exercitamento fidei," whereas, when he says "proximis," he

---

[87] Althaus, *Paulus und Luther,* 72 ff.   [88] *Adnotationes,* 38b.
[89] *Adnotationes,* 38b.   [90] *Adnotationes,* 38b–39a.
[91] *Adnotationes,* 39a.

recognizes that "ex confessione ad ecclesiam nos pertinere agnoscant."[92] Fundamentally, however, the signs of the Old Covenant and those of the New are continuous in substance and effects, despite apparent differences in external forms and methods. To cite again Oecolampadius' own explanation on baptism, which "enim certos nos reddit, per fidem in Christum, submersum Pharaonem nihil posse nobis nocere, dum credimus uerbis dei, quae ipse tali signo commendauit. Baptismo testamur etiam aliis admissos nos in ecclesiam."[93]

What, then, can be said regarding the sacrament of the Supper? A natural question may be: "Quid ergo opus participatione mensae, cum iam in conscientia securi sumus propter baptisma: et promixi sciant nos dedisse nomen Christo per baptismum?" The answer is: "[o]pus est et istis discrimine, quantum ad proximum: et noua confirmatione conscientiae, quantum ad ipsos poenitentes."[94] It should be noted that, here also, the duplex structure of "coram deo et proximo" is reiterated.

Oecolampadius employs another terminology, namely, the concept of "mysterium" in order to emphasize the importance of the promise contained in it as well as to avoid the unfortunate confusion of "res" and its "signum." He says: "Confirmantur autem plurimum hoc mysterio, habente promissionem additam signo, quando fide non in aquam, non in panem, non uinum signa ipsa, sed in Christum ipsum intendunt, cuius caro tradita, et sanguis effusus in remissionem peccatorum, iuxta promissionem."[95]

Finally, Oecolampadius points out another cardinal benefit of the participation in the Supper. "Insuper et religionis unitas seruatur hoc symbolo, quo eo Christianos a non Christianis, et membra eiusdem Christi dignoscimus: ut simus omnes infermentatus panis Christi."[96] This is tantamount to saying that the Eucharist serves first to maintain and strengthen the unity and integrity of the believing community, then to distinguish it from the outside world. Thus, it may fairly be said that Oecolampadius affirms three aspects or efficacies in both Baptism and the Lord's Supper, namely, first, the aspect of "coram deo," second, that of "coram hominibus," and last, that of "coram ecclesia," so to speak, since there needs to be a locus where these first two functions operate meaningfully and become effective for salvation. We might see this as a perpendicular or "three-dimensional" interpretation of sacraments, figuratively speaking.

In conjunction with this issue arises the question regarding infant Baptism. We have neither the need nor space to offer a full historical description of baptismal controversies from 1523 on, which occurred first in Zurich, then in many

---

[92] *Adnotationes*, 39a.   [93] *Adnotationes*, 39a.   [94] *Adnotationes*, 39b.
[95] *Adnotationes*, 39b.   [96] *Adnotationes*, 39b.

other Swiss city states, including Basel itself. It will be noted only that the issue was already of pressing concern in Basel by the time of the publication of this commentary. In the same year (1525), Oecolampadius' German booklet *Ain gesprech etlicher predicanten zu Basel gehalten mit etlichen bekennern des widertauffs* was published. It would be reprinted in the following year, as if to reflect the urgency of the matter.[97] To recapitulate the main points of Oecolampadius' sacramental teaching, as far as his annotation on chapter 4 is concerned, we note the parallelism between, and the continuity of the two covenants, and thus the obvious analogy between Israelite circumcision and Christian baptism. It is certain that newborn babies do not understand the mystery of baptism; therefore, the faith to be confessed can be either that of their parents or that of the entire Church. In this respect, Oecolampadius reminds us more of Luther than of Zwingli.

Most characteristic of Oecolampadius, however, is that, in his understanding of sacraments, he put a great deal of emphasis on mutual love, just as he did in his treatment of other major theological loci. His vindication of infant baptism is based on this theme of love, or charity, since it is intended more to be a sign of mutual love toward one's neighbors rather than something which achieves the salvation of baptized infants. Two years after the publication of the Romans commentary, in March of 1527, Oecolampadius wrote to Johann Grel, who was being engaged in the parish ministry in Kilchberg near Basel: "Charitas igitur dictat, ut externis symbolis, quibus eiusdem fidei ac religionis societatem Dominus coadunare voluit, fidem ac charitatem nostram testatur."[98]

So much for these exceptionally lengthy remarks on Romans 4:11 as a clue to the understanding of Oecolampadius' view on the sacraments. Needless to say, almost all that is characteristic of the Reformed view on the sacraments is already unequivocally noticeable, even though sometimes in a primitive or germinal way. By the time of the culmination of the Evangelical Reformation in the city of Basel (1529), Johannes Oecolampadius was, without a doubt, one of the most mature and powerfully influential theological leaders of the Reformed branch in the Protestant Reformation.

b. *Calvin.* Since it is far beyond the scope and essential task of this paper to survey the sacramental teaching of Calvin in any comprehensive manner, we confine our discussion only to his exposition of Romans 4:11, for the purpose of comparing it with that of Oecolampadius.

---

[97] *Oecolampad-Bibliographie,* nos. 114–16.
[98] *Briefe und Akten zum Leben Oecolampads,* ed. E. Staehelin. no. 472.

Calvin begins his arguments by affirming that, although circumcision has by no means a justifying potency, it is nevertheless useful and effective for salvation. Its main raison-d'être is duplex; namely, the usage of sealing the righteousness by faith and that of ratifying the état accompli, so to speak. He says: "non tamen fuisse vanam superfluamque Circuncisionem, tametsi non iustificaret: quandoquidem alium haberet valde praeclarum usum, utpote cuius officium erat iustitiam fidei obsignare, ac veluti ratam facere."[99] One may recall that this term "obsignare" appeared in Oecolampadius in the noun form. The concept of ratification is not totally alien to Oecolampadius, although his use of the word may not be very frequent. There is no entry of this word in the index.

Calvin continues: "Ac tametsi per se nihil iuvant, Deus tamen qui gratiae suae instrumenta esse voluit, arcana Spiritus sui gratia efficit ne profectu careant in electis."[100] Similarly, Oecolampadius has a line that points out the work of the Holy Spirit even in those who are physically sleeping: "Nam et dormientes sancti spiritu non destituti sunt."[101] In particular, Calvin stresses that this working of the Holy Spirit is limited to the elect saints alone. In the final edition of 1556, though not in the earlier versions of 1540 and 1551, Calvin makes the following comments: "Quare maneat hoc fixum, sacra symbola esse testimonia quibus gratiam suam Deus cordibus nostris obsignat."[102]

Together with Oecolampadius, Calvin talks about the "duplicem gratiam" of circumcision; the first part is the promise of God by which the Lord pledged himself to the blessing of Abraham and his descendants, whereas the second concerns itself with the gratuitous redemption free from all human meritoriousness.

Analogously, Baptism symbolizes this duplex grace—a regenerated life and the forgiveness of sin that precedes it. In Calvin's own words: "Duae denique, ut Baptismi hodie sunt, ita olim Circuncisionis erant partes: nempe tam vitae novitatem, quam peccatorum remissionem testari."[103] This clause is, in fact, an addition to the second edition and those that followed. In the final edition, furthermore, Calvin emphasizes that divine grace is the substance (*res*) of the sacraments, and that the accompanying external signs may not necessarily coincide with each other in terms of chronological sequence, because "nequis externis rebus salutem affigeret."[104] At present, it is sufficient to remember that the issue of infant baptism continued to be warmly debated, especially in the Reformed cities of Switzerland, well into the middle of the sixteenth century.

---

[99]Parker, p. 86, lines 34–37.
[101]*Adnotationes*, 40a.
[103]Parker, p. 87, lines 65–67.
[100]Parker, p. 87, lines 43–45.
[102]Parker, p. 87, lines 48–49.
[104]Parker, p. 87, lines 69–70.

V. Appendix: The Reformation Theology of Oecolampadius

1. Christ as the Scopus of Scripture

In the preface to the Romans commentary, Oecolampadius confirms that the "mysterium regni" can only be revealed to the "studiosis et simplicibus," who eagerly seek the glory of Christ by faith alone, because "scopus enim totius scripturae est, vindicare gloriam dei, ut regnet deus in omnibus, maxime autem in cordibus hominum."[105] "Christ as the only scopus of the whole Bible"—this remained the keynote of Oecolampadius' Biblical hermeneutics throughout his Reformation activities in Basel. The following are quotations from his other commentaries along the same line. "Nullis enim aperitur sensus scripturae, nisi iis qui et Christum quaerunt, et quibus se Christus revelat."[106] Similarly, "nam scriptura omnis ad Christum tanquam ad scopum spectat."[107] "Christus scopus est prophetarum omnium."[108] And, from the Ezekiel commentary: "[q]uia verbum Dei a spiritu sancto inspiratum est, non possum non statuere quod in omnibus locis, in Christum Jesum, seu finem et scopum et methodum respiciat spiritus scripturarum."[109]

The Christocentric interpretation of both the Old and the New Testament naturally urges us to pray "ut Christus Iesus glorificetur, laudetur, et colatur ab omnibus."[110] Appropriately, his preface to the Romans commentary closes with:

> Nam ab Adam et a carne, peccatum, seruitus, et mors sunt: a spiritu dei, sanctificatio, libertas, vita, et securitas. Securitatem autem praedestinatione munit: in quibus omnibus gloriam dei praedicari uidebis, quam et per nos sanctificari precemur.[111]

Though this may have been the case, it is a different matter whether he was authentically successful in attaining his objective, as Calvin pointed out in his somewhat critical evaluations.

2. Sola Scriptura as the Formal Principle

The essential activities of Oecolampadius as a Reformation theologian consisted chiefly in his commitment to scriptural exposition. Both in the pulpit, first at St. Martin's, and then later at the Münsterkirche, he preached and lectured assiduously on Scripture. He offered annotations on Genesis, Job, and all the

---

[105] *Adnotationes*, 2b.
[106] *Iesaiam Prophetam Hypomnematon*, 2a (1:1).
[107] *Iesaiam Prophetam Hypomnematon*, 22b (2:1).
[108] *Commentarii omnes in libres Prophetarum*, 73a.
[109] *Commentarii omnes in libres Prophetarum*, 73a-b.
[110] *In Psalmos*, 235 (137:3).   [111] *Adnotationes*, 3a.

books of the Prophets. He also published a significant corpus of New Testament commentaries both on the Gospels and on the Epistles.

When he began his lectures on Isaiah, which literally introduced the Evangelical Reformation into Basel, he made it abundantly clear that one should depend only upon the original text, and reject the falsified authority of the Vulgate and the Septuagint. He says: "Nisi Hebraice legere valuissem Hebraeorumque consuluissem commentarios, ne ausum quidem fuisse illum attingere."[112] This kind of insistence upon the need for linguistic strictness is present, in a substantial way, in his Romans commentary, as has been amply observed in the preceding pages. We have noticed that his Latin rendering of the Greek text is completely free from the dominance of any other then extant authorities including the Vulgate, *Novum Instrumentum,* and others.

Already by August of 1523, Oecolampadius had convincingly asserted the principle of *sola scriptura* in his theses that he posted for public disputation. Thesis 1 reads: "Sicut verba.... spiritus sunt ac vita dicique merentur panis vitae, quo vivant animae, ita omnis mundana philosophia, omnes Pharisaeorum secundariae traditiones, omnis denique humana eruditio caro sunt.... Igitur ut in scholis et templis christianorum solius Christi omne magisterium est, ita ethnicorum philosophorum et omnium aliorum, quanticunque sunt, doctorum, contemptibilis sit authoritas."[113] Also, in his sermon on Psalm 57, he provided the following amplification: "Scriptura non ob id sancta erit, quia ab ecclesia recepta sit, sed ecclesia sacram scripturam recepit, quia sancta et ex Deo est.... Nam ecclesia Biblicos libros recepit ante magna Concilia."[114]

In brief, the regulative authority of Scripture does not rest upon anything human and historical—neither Church, Councils, nor even the Apostles themselves to the extent their work was human. In his exposition on 1 John, he says: "Nonne et apostoli fuerunt homines sicut et nos? Fuerunt quidem et apostoli homines, sed non docuerunt, neque scripserunt humano spiritu, sed divino affluatu: non sua commenta provididerunt, sed quae vel oculis viderant, vel a domino acceperant."[115] Similarly, "Ante omnia enim Christianos persuasum esse oportet, scripturas sacras divinitus inspiritas."[116] Consequently, "necesse est ut corda nostra audiant. Internum magistrum audimus, spiritus sanctum."[117]

It is very clear that the doctrine of the self-sufficiency of Scripture constituted the fundamental premise not only of Oecolampadius' theological construction,

---

[112] *Briefe und Akten,* 1:346, no. 241.
[113] *Briefe und Akten,* 1:245–46, no. 166.
[114] *In Psalmos LXXIIII etc. Conciones* (Basel: 1544), 318.
[115] *In Epistolam Ioannis,* 7b (1:1).   [116] *In Epistolam Ioannis,* 64b (4:1).
[117] *In Epistolam Ioannis,* 100a (5:24).

186   *Akira Demura*

but also of all his work in homiletics and hermeneutics. We have confirmed this through his Romans commentary.

3. *Sola Fide as the Material Principle*

In our section that deals with the Doctrine of Justification, we saw the structure of Oecolampadius' main contentions concerning Law and Grace. According to him, "lex sancta erat et bona. Nostrae autem imfirmitatis erat, quae bono pharmaco deterior fiebat,"[118] for soteriological purposes. There is, therefore, no contradiction between the Law and the Gospel, between Moses and Christ, although, of course, one must add, "Mose Christo ancillabitur." In fact, the truth is, "legem esse spiritus, et legem spiritualem esse,"[119] because "charitatis autem lex, lex est spiritus."[120]

The reason behind the impotency of the Law is the universal and perpetual human sinfulness resulting from the first sin. "In Adam enim omnes peccavimus, non imitatione sola qua sponte peccamus, sed et carnis eius participes facti, in qua habitare ceparat peccatum, contagione quoque infecti sumus."[121] Our predicament is not merely that we "imperfecti fuerunt, neque ad malum propensi sunt: sed, peccaverunt. Agnoscamus ergo nos peccatores."[122] Here we ought to listen to the existential cry concerning his own sinfulness, and with it, the brotherly confession by which he had embraced an unusually deep concern even apart from the Catholic sacrament of penance.

Indeed, the very root of all sins is unbelief. "Incredulitas radix est, et iniustitia dicitur."[123] To cite his annotation on the Gospel of John: "Est igitur perfidia vel incredulitas, vera radix omnium aliorum peccatorum.... Sufficit igitur fides sola, ad delenda omnia peccata."[124] It goes without saying, therefore, that "atqui iustitia nostra vera ex fide est, fidei thesauris peccata redimus."[125] From his commentary on Jeremiah, we quote: "Fides igitur coram Deo iustificamur, ut Paulus manifeste convincit."[126] Again, on Isaiah, Oecolampadius could not be any clearer: "absque nostris operibus sola fide nos salvare."[127] Thus, he could be sure of this principle of *sola fide* even in the Old Testament and, to an even greater degree, in the New Testament. On 1 John, he comments, conclusively: "Quamvis autem charitas

---

[118] *Enarratio in Euangelium Mattaei*, 3a.
[119] *Enarratio in Euangelium Mattaei*, 3a.
[120] *Iesaiam*, 150a (24:5).
[121] *In Librum Iob exegemata*, 80a (14:4).
[122] *Adnotationes*, 33b (3:23).   [123] *Adnotationes*, 30b (3:10).
[124] *Annotationes in Euangelium Ioannis*, 298b (14:9).
[125] *In Danielem Prophetam*, 59 (4:25).
[126] *In Hieremiam Prophetam Commentariorum*, 37b (5:3).
[127] *Iesaiam*, 171a (29:6).

magna sit, non tamen iustificat: quia nemo diligit quantum debet.... fide enim iustificamur, et filii dei efficimur: et charitati non tributur iustificatio."[128]

Oecolampadius could talk about *sola fide* and *sola gratia* in the same breath, precisely because faith itself is a gift from God. In his annotation on John 6:1, he says: "Nam hoc est maximum dei beneficium. ... ut concedat nobis illam fidem, quo credamus illum redemptorem nostrum."[129] Similarly, on Romans 1:21 we find: "Deum glorificare, dei donum est. Nemo enim glorificat, uel gratias agit, nisi in spiritus sancto."[130] Again, "Beneficia quae nobis non cedat Deus, non propter nostram merita, sed propter suam largitatem dat, et ex mera gratia."[131] In his commentary on Lamentation, he offers the following sentence, which reminds us of Augustine: "Profecto ad animum revoco absolutam Dei benignitatem et misericordiam, gratis createm, gratis servantem, gratis reparantem electum suum."[132] Most convincingly, however, his annotation on Romans 1:16 offers the following statement:

> neque iustitia ita tribuitur fidei nostrae, si exacte loquaris quasi operi nostro: hoc enim foret abuti fide, si fide mea uidear fidere, quasi dignum aliquid in me sit quod remuneret: sed ideo tribuitur iustitia fidei, quia fides tribuit totum dei misericordiae,[133]

as if he is guarding himself against the danger of transforming our faith into some kind of human accomplishment, regardless of how praiseworthy such may be.

Finally, we would quote some sentences which were already referred to in our main contention regarding the relationship between justification and sanctification. Oecolampadius admits "concupiscentiam quandiu uiuimus, in nobis relinquit,"[134] as well as "quandiu igitur uiuimus, inhabitamus crasse corpora, atque divina perspicere non possemus."[135] Hence, the necessity of constant efforts toward newness of life, evinced by an expression such as: "Corpus mortuum, non quod affectus mali simul omnes emorientur ... in hac vita: sed, quod perpetuum studium mortificandi affectus malos."[136]

4. Predestination and Prescience

So far, because of time and space limitation, there has been no opportunity to mention the problem of *Praedestinatio, Praescientia,* or *Praedefinitio.* Therefore, a few quotations from the Romans commentary may be appropriate.

---

[128] *In Epistolam Ioannis,* 54a-b (3:10).   [129] *In Euangelium Ioannis,* 110a.
[130] *Adnotationes,* 16b (1:21).   [131] *In Euangelium Ioannis,* 111a (6:5).
[132] *Die klag des heyligen propheten Ieremia...* (Basel: 1527), 269b (3:22).
[133] *Adnotationes,* 12a.   [134] *Adnotationes,* 41a (4:14).
[135] *Adnotationes,* 73a (see n. 74).   [136] *Adnotationes,* 62a–b (8:10)

"Obserua tamen hoc loco," says Oecolampadius on 8:30, "quod praescire non idem quod praecognoscere.... Distinguitur autem a quibusdam praescientia a praedestinatione."[137] He does not fail to mention that the teaching of predestination is closely and inseparably linked, indeed, with that of consolation and consolidation. He says on 9:6: "Nunc consolatur seipsum duobus modis: Primum quod praedestinatio immutabilis mane. Deinde quod promissiones prophetarum non evacuantur: et hoc est quod dicit, Sermo dei excidit. Quod ad praedestinationem attinet."[138] Whether or not Oecolampadius had a full-fledged doctrine of double predestination, like that of the mature Calvin, we are unable to say in any conclusive sense.

Since Oecolampadius left little or no dogmatic or systematic writings, with a few exceptions connected with the Eucharistic controversies, his theological thought can be construed only out of his exegetical works on Scripture. The task remains woefully incomplete. The publication of a modern, critical edition of his major works, except for Ernst Staehelin's pioneer achievements, remains still unaccomplished, or even unattempted. It seems that much remains to be carried out in Oecolampadius studies.

---

[137] *Adnotationes*, 66b.   [138] *Adnotationes*, 70b.

Plaisir des mets, plaisirs des mots: Irdische Freude bei Calvin

Max Engammare[1]

IM JAHRE 1560 ÜBT DER PAPSTTREUE POLEMIKER ANTOINE DU VAL scharfe Kritik an Luther und Calvin hinsichtlich deren Tisch- und Bettfreuden.

> Premierement nous dirons que les Lutheriens et les Calvinistes ensuivent les Nicolaïtes,[2] lesquels furent premiers auteurs de liberté et de dances. Et tout ainsi que ceste secte cy estoit de faire grand chere, et (comme on dict) mener joyeuse vie, sans faire aucune abstinence, ainsi font noz Calvinistes, lesquels (comme on veoit) n'en veulent faire aussi, ne voulans jeusner aucunement. Et tant s'en fault, ils mangent de la chair le Caresme....[3]

Die Kritik verlagert sich alsbald vom Bauch in Richtung Unterleib, denn:

> Calvin dict qu'il ne s'en pourroit passer [de femmes] moins que de manger. Mais je croy, s'il avoit esté quinze jours sans manger, et autant sans femme, qu'il aymeroit mieux l'un que l'autre, et qu'il feroit le contraire de ce qu'il dict. Ne voylà pas la doctrine d'un vray Apostre?[4]

War Antoine du Val von einem Genfer Hedonismus zu Ohren gekommen, als dessen exemplarisches Oberhaupt Calvin galt, der, dem weiblichen Geschlecht und guten Speisen über die Maßen zugetan, uns somit zwingt, das Bild des unerbittlichen Reformators, das uns über Jahrhunderte hinweg von Inschriften allzu

---

[1]Ich danke sehr Frau Christiane Gerheuser für ihre Hilfe in die Übersetzung und die Korrektur meines hier vorliegenden Textes. Der Titel dieser Studie lehnt sich an den Titel an, den Michel Jeanneret seinem Buch über Bankette und Tischgespräche in der Renaissance gab, *Des mets et des mots* (Paris: Corti, 1987).

[2]Eine in der Apocalypse 2:6 und 14–15 erwähnte Sekte, deren Anhängern ein ausschweifendes Leben und der Verzehr von den Götzen geopfertem Fleisch nachgesagt wird. Die Anmerkung in *La Bible qui est toute la saincte Escriture* (Genf: Barbier et Courteau, 1559); Betty Chambers, *Bibliography of French Bibles. Fifteenth- and Sixteenth-Century French-Language Editions of the Scriptures*, Travaux d'Humanisme et Renaissance, 192 (Genf: Droz, 1983), no. 253, note "c," fol. 110v: (NT), präzisiert: "C'estoyent heretiques, lesquels vouloyent que les femmes fussent communes. Ilz furent ainsi appelez de l'autheur de leur secte, nommé Nicolas, qu'on dit [déjà Irénée] avoir esté celuy dont il est parlé au 6e des Actes [v.5, Nicolas d'Antioche], lequel fust esleu entre les diacres."

[3]*Miroer des Calvinistes et armeure des chrestiens pour rembarrer les Lutheriens et nouveaux Evangelistes de Genève: Renouvellé et augmenté de la plus grand part* (Paris: Nicolas Chesneau, en la maison de Claude Fremy, 1560), in octavo, fol. 4v.

[4]*Miroer des Calvinistes*, fol. 8r.

streng überliefert wurde, zu revidieren? Um 1550 hätte jeder Bewohner Genfs, auch wenn er einen Becher Wein in einer Taverne einer Predigt in der Kathedrale vorgezogen hätte,[5] diese Behauptung als übertrieben erachtet. In der Tat bedient sich Du Val einer wohlbekannten Vorgehensweise: er versucht, den Menschen und seine Ideen abzuwerten, indem er ihn moralisch diskreditiert. Ohne mich mit diesen Übertreibungen der Konfessionspolemik im 16. Jahrhundert aufhalten zu wollen, die Du Val, Bolsec und sogar Calvin[6] auf das Privatleben richteten, bleibt jedoch der exzessive Rigorismus, den die Überlieferung Calvin zuschrieb, einer erneuten Betrachtung zu unterziehen.[7] Dieser Rigorismus basiert selbstverständlich auf unzähligen theologischen Betrachtungen: das Elend des Menschen, seine Unfähigkeit, gut zu sein, die Übermacht der Sünde, usw. Seltene, aber präzise Äußerungen des Reformators tragen dazu bei, die verbreiteten Vorstellungen zu korrigieren: sie lassen sogar einen den Freuden des Mahls nicht abgeneigten Menschen zum Vorschein kommen. Ich werde den Beispielen folgen, die das gesamte Werk Calvin durchziehen und anschließend zeigen, daß diese Betrachtungen zu den menschlichen und irdischen Freuden mit einer Schöpfungstheologie und Anthropologie verknüpft sind.

---

[5]Calvin selbst wettert dagegen in einer Predigt im Februar 1555 (die sich auf 1 Tim 5:1–3 bezieht, und auf die Ehrerbietung, die Witwen entgegenzubringen sei): "Quand il est question d'elire et de choisir les magistrats, on devroit estre ici [à Saint-Pierre] pour invoquer le nom de Dieu, afin qu'il presidast au conseil, qu'il donnast esprit de prudence et de droiture. Mais cependant où sera-on? Aux tavernes ou au jeu, et ceux qui ont voix d'elire, ce sont ceux qui frequentent moins les sermons. Il est vray qu'on ne les verra gueres non plus venir les autres jours au temple ... Et d'où sortent-ils? D'un cabaret, au lieu qu'ils devroyent estre ici pour invoquer le nom de Dieu et pour regarder en eux-mesmes." *CO* 53, col. 452.

[6] Man denke u.a. an die Argumentation Calvins und Farels in der Polemik gegen Pierre Caroli: letzterer habe in den Jahren 1523–1524 in Paris eine Prostituierte ausgehalten.

[7]Die Studien von Léon Wencelius, *L'esthétique de Calvin*, Paris (1937; reprint Genf: Slatkine, 1979), von Ernst Pfisterer, *Calvins Wirken in Genf* (Neukirchen: Zeugen und Zeugnisse, 1957), insbes. 64–85, und von Alain Perrot, *Le visage humain de Jean Calvin* (Genf: Labor et Fides, 1986), mit einem Einfühlungsvermögen, das einer Hagiographie nahekommt, oder die neueren Arbeiten von William Bouwsma, *John Calvin: A Sixteenth Century Portrait* (New York: Oxford, 1988), und von Heiko Oberman, insbesondere "The Pursuit of Happiness: Calvin between Humanism and Reformation," in *Humanity and Divinity in Renaissance and Reformation: Essays in Honor of Charles Trinkaus*, hg. von J. O'Malley, Th. Izbicki, G. Christianson, Studies in the History of Christian Thought, 51 (Leiden,: Brill, 1993), 251–83, hinsichtlich irdischer Freuden insbes. 273–74 haben bereits mit Erfolg den Versuch unternommen, ein weniger rigoroses Bild des Reformators zu entwerfen. Zahlreiche detaillierte Studien und Biographien älteren und neueren Ursprungs; François Wendel, *Calvin: Sources et évolution de sa pensée religieuse*, 2d ed. (Genf: Labor et Fides, 1985); Alister E. McGrath, *A Life of John Calvin* (Oxford: Blackwell, 1990–), gehen dagegen nicht auf das Thema der Freude bei Calvin ein, sondern heben stattdessen umso mehr den Einfluß Augustins oder des Stoizismus auf Calvin hervor. Die von Edmond Huguet angeführten Beispiele lassen ihn nur zu dem Schluß kommen, daß "Calvin fait la guerre aux plaisirs de la table"; siehe Edmond Huguet, "La langue familière chez Calvin," *Revue d'Histoire littéraire de la France* 23 (1916): 39.

I. Begriffe für die Freude: Die Terminologie Calvins

Bei Calvin, sowie allgemein in der Sprache des 16.Jahrhunderts deckt das Wort "plaisir" den heutzutage gebräuchlichen Sinn ab: etwas Angenehmes, etwas, was gefällt, manchmal auch mit negativer moralischer Konnotation, d. h. im Sinne von "voluptas" (sinnlicher Lust / Wollust). Zu dieser Bedeutung tritt eine weitere hinzu: "le service" (der Dienst). Freude bereiten bedeutet bereits einen Dienst erweisen.[8]

Sowohl das Konzept als auch der Begriff des "plaisir" gehören der Sprache Calvins an. Sie sind in allen Schriften des Reformators anzutreffen: in der *Institution de la Religion Chrestienne*,[9] in den Kommentaren, den Traktaten, der Korrespondenz, usw. In den Predigten über die Genesis z. B. greift Calvin jeden zweiten Tag auf diesen Begriff zurück.[10] Was Calvin im Französischen positiv mit "plaisir" ausdrückt oder übersetzt, lautet im Lateinischen vor allem "oblectatio" und "oblectamentum"[11] (*IRC* 3:10:1–2; *Commentarii in librum Psalmorum*, Ps. 104, *CO* 32.90–91), aber auch "hilaritas" (*IRC* 3:10:2), "laetitia" (*Commentarii in librum Psalmorum*, Ps. 104, *CO* 32.91), oder "jucunditas." Im negativen Sinn, dessen sich Calvin auch bedient, wird mit "plaisir" das lateinische Wort "voluptas" übersetzt.[12]

Darüber hinaus wird ein Ausdruck, der das Wort "plaisir" enthält, in den Schriften des Reformators bevorzugt verwendet: "le bon plaisir de Dieu" ("Gottes Wohlgefallen"), ein biblischer, insbesondere neutestamentarischer Ausdruck

---

[8]Edmond Huguet, *Dictionnaire de la langue française du XVIe siècle* (Paris, 1965), 6:14–15; Frédéric Godefroy, *Dictionnaire de l'ancienne langue française et de tous ses dialectes du IXe au XVe siècle* (Paris, 1889), 6:191–92; Walther von Wartburg, *Französisches etymologisches Wörterbuch* (Basel, 1959), 9:1–5.

[9]Siehe insbes. Kap. 10 des Buches 3(§ 2 und 3). Ich zitiere l'*Institution de la Religion Chrestienne*, in der Ausgabe von Jean-Daniel Benoît, 5 Bande (Paris, 1957–1963) (abgekürzt *IRC*).

[10]In den Predigten 2, 4–9, 11–14, 16–19, 22, 24, 28, 30–31, 33, 35, 37, 40–41, 50, 53–56, 63, 68–69, 71, 73. Exzesse menschlicher Freude werden selbstverständlich angeprangert; Gottes Wohlgefallen wird regelmäßig erwähnt (Predigt 2, Londres, Lambeth Palace, Ms. 1784, fol. *9a; Predigt 5, ibid. fol. *24b; Predigt 18, Oxford, Bodleian Library, Ms. Bodl. 740, fol. 99a; Predigt 19, ibid. fol. 107a; etc.), aber ebenso eine positive Bewertung der Freude (so in den Predigten 7, Oxford, Bodleian Library, Ms. Bodl. 740, fol. 8b; 8, fol. 16a; 9, fol. 25b; 11, fol. 38b; etc.).

[11] Das Verb "oblecto" und das Substantiv "oblectamen" und "oblectamentum'"gehören der ciceronianischen Sprache an; cf. Cato Major, de senectute 52, 55–56; Epistolae ad Quintum fratrem, 2.12.1; etc.

[12]In *IRC* 1:14:4; oder 2:8:25. "Voluptas" wird im Französischen auch mit "volupté" wiedergegeben; *IRC* 1:15:8; 2:12:1; 2:10:3). Erstaunlicherweise verwendet Calvin das Wort "volupté" in einigen Predigten über die Genesis (9, fol. 24v; 14, fol. 65v; 22, fol. 97r–v) auch in positiver Bedeutung. Der Begriff "delectatio," der in der *IRC* zweimal vorkommt, wird im Französischen nicht mit "plaisir," sondern mit "bien" (2:3:14), bzw. mit einer Periphrase (2:8:50) übersetzt. Der in der *IRC* mehr als hundertmal verwendete Begriff "Libido" umfaßt im Französischen ein immenses semantisches Feld. Allein in Buch 1 der *IRC* wird "libido," z. T. in Verbindung mit einem Adjektiv, mit: "appetit desbordé" (4:1); "appetit" (4:3); "convoitise" (6:3); "fantasie" (11: 8); "necessité" (17:3); "rage" (17:5 et 7); "intemperance" (17:11); "fureur" (18:1); oder "meschante cupidité" (18:4) wiedergegeben.

(Eph. 1:5; Phil. 2:13; etc.), der "voluntas Dei" im Lateinischen, "eudokia" oder "eudokia tou thelématos autou" (Eph. 1:5) im Griechischen und "ratsôn" im Hebräischen (Ps. 30:6[13]) wiedergibt. Dies verdeutlicht, daß eine Reflexion Calvins über die Freude nur im Einverständnis mit Gottes Wohlgefallen zu verstehen ist.

II. Tafelfreuden: "in vino oblectatio"

Bis zur Ausgabe des Jahres 1557 enthielt das letzte Kapitel der *IRC* eine berühmte Passage,[14] die diesem magnum opus dadurch eine unbestreitbare Bedeutung zukommen ließ. Darin unterstreicht der Reformator, daß die Güter dieser Welt nicht nur für unsere nächsten Bedürfnisse erschaffen wurden, sondern auch zu unserer Freude:

> Si nous réputons à quelle fin Dieu a créé les viandes, nous trouverons qu'il n'a pas seulement voulu pourvoir à nostre nécessité, mais aussi à nostre plaisir et récréation. Ainsi aux vestemens, outre la nécessité il a regardé ce qui estoit honneste et décent. Aux herbes, arbres et fruits, outre les diverses utilitez qu'il nous en donne, il a voulu resjouir la veue par leur beauté et nous donner un autre plaisir en leur odeur. Car si cela n'estoit vray, le Prophète ne raconteroit point entre les bénéfices de Dieu que le vin resjouist le coeur de l'homme, et l'huyle fait reluyre sa face (Ps.104:15). L'Escriture ne feroit point mention çà et là, pour recommander la bénignité de Dieu, qu'il a fait tous ces biens à l'homme. Et mesme les bonnes qualitez de toutes choses de nature nous monstrent comment nous en devons jouir et à quelle fin, et jusques à quel poinct.[15]

In dieser Passage hebt Calvin deutlich hervor, daß Nahrung, Wein, Kleidung, ja selbst Blumen uns nicht nur nützlich seien, sondern auch durch ihr Aussehen, ihren Duft und Geschmack Freude bereiteten. Diese Äußerung Calvins ist bei weitem kein *hapax legomenon*, denn sein gesamtes literarisches Schaffen gibt ihm die Möglichkeit, dieser sinnlichen Freude Ausdruck zu verleihen. Sie findet ihre

---

[13]In Ct. 7:11, wird "teshúqâh" (Verlangen) in den Genfer Bibeln des 16. Jh.s, von Olivétan ("appetit" bei Lefèvre d'Etaples) bis in die Jahre 1570 mit "plaisir" übersetzt (dann mit "desir" bei den Pastoren und Professoren Genfs, im Jahre 1588).

[14]Die Passage wurde auch von Hans Helmut Eßer in seinem Vortrag anläßlich des letzten Calvin-Kongresses erwähnt: "Der Eigentumsbegriff Calvins angesichts der Einführung der neuen Geldwirtschaft."

[15]*IRC* 3:10:2. Im Anschluß an diese, seit 1539 in diesem Wortlaut enthaltene Passage greift Calvin das Beispiel der Freude am Duft der Blumen wieder auf und ergänzt es durch die Freude an Farben, Metallen und Edelsteinen. Dieses Kapitel bildete das 21. und letzte Kapitel (das christliche Leben) aller Ausgaben der *IRC* bis 1557. Vgl. hierzu auch das Vorwort zu dem 1535 erschienenen Neuen Testament, "Epître aux fidèles montrant comment Christ est la fin de la Loi," in *Oeuvres choisies*, hg. v. Olivier Millet, Folio classique 2701 (Paris: Gallimard, 1995), 31.

biblische Grundlage im Vers des Psalmisten, ein im wahrsten Sinn des Wortes roter Faden im gesamten literarischen Werk Calvins. Ein roter Faden, dem wir folgen wollen.

"Und das der Wein erfrewe des Menschen Hertz" singt der Psalmist (Ps. 104:15).[16] Dieser Vers ist die bevorzugte Wendung, beinahe die Rechtfertigung für den Ausdruck irdischer Freude bei Calvin. Calvin beruft sich in seinem Kommentar darauf, daß der Wein eine Gabe Gottes sei, die er den Menschen in seiner Freigebigkeit schenkt und ihnen somit über das Notwendige hinaus Genuß und Freude zukommen läßt.[17] Die Menschen müssen sich jedoch coram Deo,[18] im Angesicht Gottes freuen und dabei ihre Begierde zügeln, wie Calvin hinzufügt:

> Il sera utile aux hommes de cognoistre que Dieu leur permet d'user modérément de délices, quand ils en auront la jouissance; autrement ils n'oseront jamais user mesmes de pain et de vin en tranquillité de conscience. Et qui plus est, à la fin, ils feront scrupule de savourer de l'eau; à tout le moins ils ne se mettront jamais à table, sinon en tremblant.[19]

Calvin gesteht nicht nur die Möglichkeit zu, die Genüsse der Tafel in Maßen in Anspruch zu nehmen, er spricht darüber hinaus auch diejenigen frei, die darüber in Gewissensnot geraten. Mann und Frau dürfen in aller Ruhe Wein trinken: das ist keineswegs zu tadeln. Im Angesicht Gottes ist die maßvolle Freude des Menschen rechtmäßig. Im Gegenteil, es ist verwerflich, dem Menschen den Genuß einer solchen Freude abzusprechen. In seinem Traktat gegen die Anabaptisten, in dem er gegen ihre Weigerung, auf die Bibel zu schwören, zu Felde zieht, veranschaulicht Calvin seine Argumentation durch einen Vergleich mit einer anderen Art der Übertreibung:

> L'yvrongnerie, qui est un vice fort deshonneste et villain, regne à present en beaucoup de gens. Si pour reprendre ces abus quelcun condamnoit totalement l'usage du vin et de toutes bonnes viandes, ne seroit-ce pas blasphemer Dieu d'ainsi vituperer et reprouver les bonnes creatures qu'il a destinées à nostre usage?[20]

---

[16]Ich zitiere nach der *Biblia: Das ist Die gantze Heilige Schrifft, Deudsch, Auffs new zugericht. D. Martin Luther* (Wittenberg, Hans Lufft, 1545; Reprint Stuttgart, 1983).

[17]*Commentaires de Jehan Calvin sur le livre des Pseaumes* [1557], Bd. 2 (Paris, 1859), 271–72. *Calvini opera quae supersunt omnia*, 59 Bde. (Brunschwig-Berlin, 1863–1900) (abgek. *Calvini Opera*), Bd. 32, col. 91.

[18]*Calvini Opera*, 32.91. Calvin zitiert hier Mose: Lev. 23:40. In seinem Kommentar zu Levitikus geht Calvin nicht näher auf diese Freude *coram Deo* ein; *Calvini Opera* 24.596.

[19]*Commentaires de Jehan Calvin sur le livre des Pseaumes* [1557], Bd. 2 (Paris, 1859), 272. *Calvini Opera* 32.91.

[20]*Brieve instruction pour armer tous bons fideles contre les erreurs de la secte commune des anabaptistes* (1544); *CO* 7:93.

Klarer kann man es nicht ausdrücken: der Genuß von Wein und guten Speisen ist da von Gott gegeben—vollkommen legitim. Entgegen einer weitverbreiteten Meinung waren darüber hinaus Bankette in Genf nicht verboten. Ihren Ausuferungen waren jedoch Schranken gesetzt. Die Ausrufungen von Mitte Oktober 1558 verurteilten diverse Exzesse bezüglich Kleidung, Frisur und sogar Nahrung: "Daventage que es banquetz n'y ait plus hault de troys venues [Gänge], et à chaque venue plus hault de quatre platz."[21] Keineswegs ein Verbot von Festivitäten, lediglich ein Beschränkung auf 12 Speisen![22]

Diese Toleranz wird von Calvin noch an anderer Stelle thematisiert. In einem Brief an den Herzog von Longueville anläßlich dessen Hochzeit schreibt er:

Je ne suis pas si austere que de condamner ni les festins des princes ni la resjouissance qu'on demeine en leur mariage.[23]

Selbst wenn in dieser knappen Äußerung Hochzeitsfeste den Prinzen vorbehalten zu sein scheinen, tadelt Calvin sie nicht. Seine Ausführungen knüpfen an die maßvolle Freude an, die ein jeder bei Tische genießen kann. Darüber hinaus weiß man, daß sich die Menschen während des Mahles an Musik erfreuen konnten. Eine Musik, die nicht mit sakraler Musik zu vergleichen ist, sondern zur Unterhaltung beiträgt.[24]

Diese sehr positive Auffassung vom Genuß des Weines ist leicht nachvollziehbar, wenn man sich an die Bedeutung des Weins in der Gesellschaft des 16. Jahrhunderts erinnert: als Getränk unbedenklicher als Wasser, war er zudem eine Beigabe zum Gehalt der Minister, sei es in Genf, in Lausanne oder in Straßburg. Zuzüglich zu einem Gehalt in bar erhielt Calvin, ebenso wie die anderen Priester, ein Bezahlung in Naturalien: "douze coppes de froment et deux bossot(s) de vin." Die Veranschlagung für ein "bossot" (oder "bosset') variiert zwischen einem einfachen und einem doppelten und bewegt sich somit zwischen etwa 350 und 700 Litern. In jedem Falle handelte es sich um eine beträchtliche Menge Wein, die

---

[21] *Annales Calviniani*, in: *Calvini Opera* 21.706. Eine von Emil Doumergue äußerst fehlerhaft zitierte Textstelle, in: Emil Doumergue, Jean Calvin. *Les hommes et les choses de son temps*, Bd. 7 (Paris, 1927), 118.

[22] In der Tat stellte ein Mahl mit 12 Speisen nach Sitte der Menschen im 16. Jh. nur ein kleines Bankett dar. Siehe dazu die Bemerkung Jean Boudins von 1574, der Kritik übt an gewöhnlichen dreigängigen Mahlzeiten, wobei bei jedem Gang "encore il faut d'une viande en avoir cinq ou six façons." Zitiert von Barbara Ketcham Wheaton, *L'office et la bouche. Histoire des moeurs de la table en France 1300–1789* (Paris: Calmann-Lévy, 1984), 97.

[23] Brief vom 26. Mai 1559, *Calvini Opera* 17.3060. 532–33.

[24] Calvin macht dazu Andeutungen in seinem "Epistre au lecteur" aus *La forme des prieres et des chantz ecclesiastiques* de 1542, in: *Calvini Opera* 6.169–70: "Et ainsi il y ait grande difference entre la musicque qu'on faict pour resjouyr les hommes à table et en leur maison, et entre les psalmes, qui se chantent à l'église, en la presence de Dieu et de ses anges." Calvin verurteilt diese Praxis nicht.

einen täglichen Konsum von zwei bis vier Litern gestattete.[25] Überdies ist Calvin dem Weinkonsum so wenig abgeneigt, daß er für seinen Freund Jacques de Bourgogne in Erwartung dessen Niederlassung in Genf ein Faß guten Weines kauft.[26] Diese zahlreichen Beispiele[27] zeigen uns, daß der Genuß eines Glases guten Weines oder der Verzehr einer guten Mahlzeit nicht nur zu den von Calvin gestatteten Freuden zählen, sondern daß er auch persönlich in den Genuß dieser Freuden gelangte. Es ist anzunehmen, daß es nicht die einzigen waren. In einer anderen Passage der *IRC* zählt der Reformator weitere irdische Freuden auf:

> Et n'est en aucun lieu défendu ou de rire ou de se souler, ou d'acquérir nouvelles possessions, ou de se delecter avec instrumens de musique, ou de boire vin.[28]

Der Zufriedenheit angesichts eines Glases Wein oder eines Gelages ("se souler," in der Bedeutung des 16. Jahrhunderts) fügt Calvin das Lachen, den Erwerb von Gütern und die Musik hinzu. Im folgenden wollen wir auf diese Freuden sowie auf die des täglichen Lebens, der Familie, der Freundschaft und schließlich des Schreibens näher eingehen.

III. Begriffe, um der Freude Ausdruck zu verleihen

1. *Freude am täglichen Leben*
Calvin hatte einen Sinn für schöne Dinge, waren es Felder in ihrer Farbenpracht oder auch ein schönes Haus:

> Or, quand on entre dans une maison, encores qu'elle soit belle et plaisante, si on n'y void ne table ne buffet, ni rien qui soit, cela est comme deguisé, la vue s'esgare, on n'y prend point plaisir. Mais quand une maison est accoustrée et qu'il y a des meubles et ornemens convenables, alors on la regarde avec plus grande admiration.[29]

---

[25]Gemäß des Registers des Conseil, datiert vom 4. Oktober 1541. Cf. Emil Doumergue, *Jean Calvin. Les hommes et les choses de son temps*, Bd. 3 (Lausanne, 1905), 450, 467–68; J.-F. Bergier, "Salaires des pasteurs de Genève au XVIe siècle," in: *Mélanges d'histoire du XVIe siècle offerts à Henri Meylan* THR, 110 (Genf: Droz, 1970), 159–78, hier 163. Der Weinkonsum in Genf im 16. Jahrhundert belief sich, Schätzungen zufolge, auf bis zu einen halben Liter pro Einwohner. Vgl. Anne-Marie Piuz, Lilianne Mottu-Weber u. a., *L'économie genevoise, de la Réforme à la fin de l'Ancien Régime, XVIe-XVIIIe siècles* (Genf: Société d'Histoire et d'Archéologie, 1990), 307–8.

[26]Brief vom 3. April 1548, ibid., no. 48, S. 194: "J'avoye achepté un bon tonneau de vin, tel qu'il seroit difficile de recouvrer. Mais je m'en suis deffaict sans difficulté, et mesme à requeste." Calvin war zu diesem Zeitpunkt auf der Suche nach einem Haus für Monsieur und Madame de Falais.

[27]Weitere Beispiele hierzu in meinem kurzen Artikel: "Au plaisir de Calvin," *Cahiers protestants*, 1992/3, S. 25–30, hier S. 26f.

[28]*IRC* 3:19:9.

[29]Achte Predigt über die Genesis, Bodleian Library, MS Bodl. 740, fol. 16a.

Calvins Korrespondenz mit Jacques de Bourgogne zeigt darüber hinaus die einzelnen Etappen einer Suche nach einem schönen Haus für diesen grand Seigneur. Calvin steht von menschlicher Hand geschaffener Schönheit so wenig gleichgültig gegenüber, daß man sogar behaupten kann, er habe ein Auge für schöne Kleidung gehabt. Man kennt natürlich seine Predigt aus dem Jahre 1554, die bereits im 16. Jh. veröffentlicht wurde,[30] und die ein Thema wiederaufgreift, das bereits Cyprian und Tertullian behandelt hatten;[31] eine Predigt "où il est monstré, quelle doit estre la modestie des femmes en leurs habillements" (in der gezeigt wird, wie die Bescheidenheit der Frauen in ihrer Kleidung zum Ausdruck kommen muß). Wenn sich jedoch Schlichtheit mit Schönheit vereint, ist Calvin durchaus für geschmackvolle Kleidung empfänglich. Als Beweis für diese Empfänglichkeit Calvins für Mode genügt es, die beiden uns überlieferten zeitgenössischen Porträts Calvins zu betrachten. Zu sehen ist eine schlichte Eleganz der Kleidung, die jedoch durch einen edlen Pelzkragen unterstrichen wird; ohne Pomp und Prunk.[32]

---

[30]Im Jahre 1561. Cf. Jean-François Gilmont und Rodolphe Peter, *Bibliotheca Calviniana* 2, nos. 61/2, 9 (Genf: Droz, 1994): 854–56.

[31]Auszüge aus dem *Liber de habitu virginum* von Cyprian wurden im Anschluß an Calvins Predigt veröffentlicht; die beiden Traktate des *De cultu foeminarum* von Tertullian wurden 1565 von Lambert Daneau herausgegeben und 1580 neuaufgelegt; cf. Olivier Fatio, *Méthode et théologie: Lambert Danau et les débuts de la scolastique réformée*, THR 147 (Genf: Droz, 1976), nos. 2, 3, S. 3*, 4*).

[32]Cf. *IRC* 3:10:3. Darüber hinaus ist nachdrücklich darauf hinzuweisen, daß Calvin, entgegen zahlreichen Behauptungen insbesondere dogmatischer Studien, keine derart negative Haltung gegenüber der Malerei vertrat, auch wenn es stimmt, daß der Reformator jegliche Darstellung des Göttlichen verbot. Cf. Margaret Stirm, *Die Bilderfrage in der Reformation* (Gütersloh: Mohn, 1977), S. 161–223; dieselbe, "Les images et la Bible," in: *Le temps des Réformes et la Bible*, Bible de tous les temps, 5 (Paris: Beauchesne, 1989), S. 683–750, insbes. S. 693–96; oder Jérôme Cottin, *Le regard et la Parole. Une théologie protestante de l'image*, Lieux théologiques, 25 (Genf: Labor et Fides, 1994), insbes. Kap. 12, "Calvin: L'esthétique sans l'image," S. 285–311, v.a. S. 294–96. Sehr oft liest man eine vorschnelle und nicht weiter ausgeführte Beurteilung der Stellung Calvins zur Kunst, wie kürzlich bei Calame: "Calvin va immoler à Genève tous les arts, à commencer bien sûr par l'art sacré," in *Jean Calvin, Anges, diables et péchés*, Vorwort v. Christophe Calame (Paris: La Différence, 1991), S. 11. Aber Calvin verwendet regelmäßig das Bild des Malers; so heißt es in der siebten Predigt über die Genesis: "Car quand un peinctre aura fait une image, il la regarde et considère à veue d'oeil, pour observer toutes les traces qui y sont et pour savoir qu'il y a que redire; autant en est il des autres ouvriers, chacun en son ouvrage ... Quand un peinctre fera un traict de travers, comme il n'y a si bon ouvrier ne si exellent en son art qui ne face quelque coup qui ne viendra pas à propos..."; Oxford, Bodleian Library, Ms. Bodl.740, fols. 12r-v. In seinem Kommentar zum Brief an die Kolosser 2:17, zeigt Calvin darüber hinaus, daß er die Maltechniken kennt, die möglicherweise zur Anfertigung seines eigenen Porträts angewandt wurden: "Car tout ainsi que les peintres ne tirent pas au vif une image du premier trait, et ne luy donnent pas les couleurs vives, mais font premierement un pourtrait grossier de charbon, aussi la representation de Christ n'estoit encore que tracée rudement sans la Loy, et n'avoit encore que les premiers traits, mais en nos sacremens elle est peinte et tirée au vif." *Commentaires de M. Jehan Calvin sur toutes les Epistres de l'Apostre s. Paul* (Genf, Conrad Badius, 1556), 595; *Commentarius in Epistolam ad Colossenses*, CO 52, col. 110–11; *Joannis Calvini opera omnia denuo recognita*, series 2, vol.16, hg. Helmut Feld (Genf: Droz, 1992), S. 434. Diese positiven Erwähnungen der Malerei und des Malers werden an zwei Stellen in der *IRC* bestätigt (1:11:12—l'art de peindre et tailler est un don de Dieu; und 4:12:22—exemple d'un bon peintre).

2. Freude an der Freundschaft

Die Freude über die Schönheit eines Hauses oder über die Qualität eines Gewandes tritt jedoch gegenüber der Freundschaft in den Hintergrund. Die freundschaftlichen Briefkontakte zu Farel, Buzer oder Bèze sind wohlbekannt. Regelmäßig ist zu lesen, daß Calvin den innigen Wunsch äußert, einen Freund wiederzusehen. Im Jahre 1542 beendet Calvin einen Brief an Pierre Viret mit folgendem Ausruf:

Avec quel plaisir je m'entretiendrais avec toi la moitié du jour.[33]

Einige Jahre später vertraut er Jacques de Bourgogne, Seigneur de Falais, an:

Combien j'aurois grand desir, si c'estoit le plaisir de Dieu, d'estre avec vous trois ou quattre jours pour deviser de bouche plustost que d'escrire.[34]

Das Zusammensein mit einem Freund beschränkt sich nicht auf theologische oder politische Gespräche. In einem Brief an Monsieur de Falais aus dem Jahre 1547 teilt Calvin diesem sein Bedauern über dessen Abwesenheit mit:

Il me faict mal que je ne puys estre avecque vous du moings ung demy jour, pour rire avecque vous, en attendant que l'on face rire le petit enfant en payne d'endurer cependant qu'il crye et pleure.[35]

Mit einem Freund stundenlange Gespräche führen, aber auch lachen und ein Glas Wein mit ihm trinken—so wie Luther gerne einen Schoppen Bier mit seiner Frau oder seinen engsten Freunden trank[36]—"faire pleine feste"[37] bereitete Calvin wahre Freude. Ferner ist auch das Lachen und Lächeln eines Lesers zu nennen, das Calvin schätzte, wie aus seinem Vorwort zu den *Disputations chrestiennes touchant l'estat des trepassez* von Pierre Viret hervorgeht.

---

[33]"Libenter tecum dimidium diem confabularer." *Calvini Opera* 11, Nr. 416, 430.

[34]Lettres à Monsieur et Madame de Falais, TLF 404 (Genf: Droz, 1991), no. 14, du 24 janvier 1546, S. 80. Zitiert von Pfisterer, *Calvins Wirken in Genf,* Sp. 74. Leider hat Ernst Pfisterer zu selten die Nummer der Seiten angeführt.

[35] Lettres à Monsieur et Madame de Falais (TLF 404), Genf, 1991, no. 38, du 16 août 1547, S. 166.

[36] Siehe dazu z. B. einen Brief an seine Frau vom 29. Juli 1534, in dem er schreibt: "Gestern hatte ich ein bosen trunck gefasset, Da müst ich singen: Trink ich nicht, das ist mir leid, und thetts so rechte gerne. Und gedacht, wie gut wein und bier hab ich daheyme, da zu eine schone frawen oder (solt ich sagen) herren. Und du thettest wol, das du mir heruber schicktest den gantzen keller voll weyns, und eine pflosschen [=Flasche] deines biers, so erst du kanst, Sonst kome ich fur dem newen bier nicht wider." *WA*, Brief Nr. 2130, S. 91–92. Ich danke meinem Freund Reinhard Bodenmann sehr für diesen Hinweis aus seinem Vortrag anläßlich des Straßburger Kolloquiums über das biblische Zitat (April 1992, die Kolloquiumsbeiträge sollen demnächst erscheinen). S. R. Bodenmann, "La Bible et l'art d'écrire des letters. Pratiques dans l'aire germanique du XVIe siècle," *BSHPF* 141, (1995): S. 357–82.

[37]Ein weiterer, von Calvin in einem Brief an Jacques de Bourgogne verwendeter Ausdruck: "Maistre Guillaume Farel et maistre Pierre Viret on[t] icy esté sept jours. Il n'eust fallu que vous pour faire pleine feste." Ibid. , no. 40 du 29 septembre 1547, S. 170–71.

Bien est vray que la seule doctrine, quand nous la cognoissons bonne et
utile, nous devroit bien suffire.... Mais il y en a plusieurs, et quasi la
plus-part, qui seront beaucoup plus aises qu'on les enseigne avec une
façon joyeuse et plaisante qu'autrement, en sorte que, comme en s'esbatant, ilz profitent et reçoyvent instruction.... Mais d'autant que le subjet
qu'il [Viret] a entreprins de traiter portoit qu'il enseignast comme en
s'esbatant et par forme de risée, il a pretendu à la doctrine comme à son
droit but, meslant cependant avec icelle les faceties, comme un acces-
soire.[38]

Es ist keineswegs abwegig sich vorzustellen, daß Calvin mit seinem Kind oder
mit dem Enkel eines Freundes lachte, so ungewohnt dies auch scheinen mag. Entgegen dem überlieferten Bild von der Kindheit im 16.Jahrhundert (wonach die
Menschen ihren kleinen Kindern wenig Zuneigung entgegenbrachten und ihnen
kaum Aufmerksamkeit schenkten),[39] spricht Calvin häufig von dem Glück, das
Kinder spenden.[40] So bieten sowohl der Kommentar zu Jeremias 16:2 ("Du solt
kein Weib nehmen, und weder Söne noch töchter zeugen, an diesem ort"),[41] als
auch die Predigt über das Deuteronomium 28:47 ("Das du dem Herrn deinem
Gott nicht gedienet hast mit freude und lust deines Hertzen, da du allerley gnug
hattest") die Gelegenheit, den Freuden der Vaterschaft Ausdruck zu verleihen. In
letzterer verwendet Calvin eine sehr beliebte Metapher: Gott ist uns ein Vater.
Dieser Vater wird jedoch wie ein menschlicher Vater beschrieben:

tout ainsi que un pere ne demande qu'à gagner ses enfans, riant avec eux,
et leur donnant tout ce qu'ils desirent. Si un pere pouvoit tousjours rire
avec ses enfans et satisfaire à leurs appetis, il est certain que tout son plaisir seroit là.:[42]

---

[38]Pierre Viret, *Disputations chrestiennes touchant l'estat des trepassez* (Genf: Jean Girard, 1552), S.
3, 5–6. Cf. auch Jean Barnaud, *Pierre Viret, sa vie et son œuvre (1511–1571)* (Saint-Amans, 1911), 269–
70 Barnaud hat bereits einige Zeilen dieses Zitats angeführt. Ich danke Alain Dufour sehr, der mich auf
dieses Vorwort aufmerksam machte.

[39]Cf. Philippe Ariès, *L'enfant et la vie familiale sous l'Ancien Régime*, Points Histoire 20 (Paris,
Seuil, 1975), insbes. S. 236; M. Bethlenfalvay, *Les visages de l'enfant dans la littérature française du XIXe
siècle*, Histoire des Idées et Critique Littéraire, 176 (Genf: Droz, 1979), 15.

[40]Ebenso äußert Calvin Trauer über den Tod von Kindern. Cf. W. Bouwsma, *John Calvin*, 38–39.

[41]Calvin kommentiert: "C'est comme si Dieu disoit: Il ne faut point que personne s'amuse pour
l'advenir à engendrer des enfans ou qu'il en pense avoir quelque plaisir (vel putet hoc sibi fore
jucundum)." *Leçons ou commentaires et expositions de Jean Calvin sur les revelations que sur les Lamen-
tations du prophete Jeremie* (Lyon: Claude Senneton, 1565), S. 364; CO 38, Sp. 239. Diese in der Vernei-
nung formulierte Bemerkung spielt darauf an, daß die Eltern bei der Zeugung in der Regel Freude
empfinden.

[42]*Sermons sur le Deuteronome*, in CO 28, Sp. 441.

Um Vater zu werden, muß man jedoch vorher Geliebter gewesen sein und seine Frau gekannt haben. Calvin wendet sich nie gegen die Sexualität—im Rahmen einer ehelichen Bindung, selbstverständlich;[43] denn: "Dieu permet à une jeune femme de se réjouir avec son mari … bien au contraire il va jusqu'à concéder à son mari et à la femme de s'ébattre ensemble."[44] Die Sexualität und das Vergnügen, das Mann und Frau gemeinsam erleben, gehören zum ehelichen Zusammenleben, sind jedoch nie Selbstzweck, wie aus einer Predigt Calvins hervorgeht:

Car le mariage n'a point esté ordonné de Dieu seullement afin qu'un homme prenne son plaisir et volupté avec sa femme, mais c'est une compaignie à vie et à mort.[45]

3. *Freude am Schreiben*

Calvin ist jedoch darüber hinaus auch ein bedeutender Intellektueller, und sein literarisches Schaffen, sei es in Form freundschaftlicher Briefe, eines systematischen Traktats oder einer Polemik, bereitet ihm wahre Freude. Wie Olivier Millet kürzlich herausgearbeitet hat, bemüht sich der Reformator in seinem Diskurs um eine gewisse ästhetische Schönheit.[46] In einem der Vorworte, die Calvin zur Bible d'Olivetan aus dem Jahre 1535, "A tous amateurs de Jesus-Christ et de son Evangile," verfaßte, werde ich einige Sätze zur Illustration seiner komplexen Kompositionsweise zitieren:

Jésus-Christ s'est asservi pour nous affranchir, il s'est appauvri pour nous enrichir, il a été vendu pour nous racheter, captif pour nous délivrer; il a été défiguré pour nous figurer, il est mort pour notre vie, tellement que par lui rudesse est adoucie, courroux apaisé, ténèbres éclaircies, injustice justifiée, péché empêché, mépris méprisé, crainte assurée, dette quittée, labeur allégé, tristesse réjouie, malheur bienheuré,

---

[43]Vgl. Eric Fuchs, *Le Désir et la tendresse. Sources et histoire d'une éthique chrétienne de la sexualité et du mariage* (Champ éthique 1) (Genf, 1982_, hier S. 136–144.

[44]Calvins Kommentar über das Pentateuch (Dt. 24, 5), *Calvini opera* 24, Sp. 653: "Porro quod novæ uxori permittit Deus se oblectare cum marito … imo ultro concedit, ut maritus et uxor se oblectent." Zitiert von E. Fuchs in *Le Désir* … , S. 139–40; vgl. auch Perrot, *Le Visage humain*, 44.

[45]Vgl. 31. Predigt über die Genesis (6:1–3), vom 14. November 1559 (Oxford: Bodleian Library, Ms. Bodl. 740, Bl. 191v).

[46] Dagegen verhält sich Calvin gegenüber der *delectatio* als rhetorischer Wirkung des Wortes Gottes abweisend; das Konzept einer ästhetischen Freude an Gottes Wort ist a priori ausgeschlossen. Cf. Millet, *Calvin et la dynamique de la parole*, 214, 250, 311. Die Freude der *delectatio* spielt offensichtlich in seiner Konzeption biblischer Redekunst (315) keine Rolle. Die drei Wirkziele der ciceronianischen Rhetorik lauten: *docere, movere* et *delectare*.

difficulté facile, damnation damnée, abîme abîmé, enfer enferré, mort morte, mortalité immortelle.[47]

Es ist unvorstellbar, daß Calvin bei der Ausarbeitung dieser langen Auflistung von Oppositionen, die sich in der Person Christi auflösen, kein intellektuelles Vergnügen empfand. Calvin spielt hier mit der Sprache und verwendet mehrere rhetorische Figuren.[48] Antithese, *figura etymologica* und zum Abschluß ein Oxymoron, indem er zwei unvereinbare Begriffe miteinander kombiniert: unsterbliche Sterblichkeit; ein Oxymoron, das er zwei Jahre später, in *Catéchisme* von 1537, wiederaufgreifen wird.[49]

In den polemischen Traktaten,[50] wie zum Beispiel im Traité des reliques, läßt sich ein ähnliches intellektuelles Vergnügen erahnen. Und die Ironie Calvins ist besonders beißend.[51]

Der Reformator hat, abgesehen davon, seinen Hang zum Schreiben niemals verheimlicht. Wie er 1539 Sadolet gegenüber eingesteht, hätte es seinen Wünschen entsprochen

jouir de loisirs pour les lettres au moyen de quelque condition honnête et libre.[52].Später, im Jahre 1557, vertraut er Conrad Hubert an:

Par nature j'étais assez porté à la poésie, mais je lui ai dit adieu, et depuis vingt-cinq ans je n'ai rien composé, si ce n'est à Worms, à l'exemple de

---

[47]*La vraie piété: Verschiedene Traktate Jean Calvins und das Glaubensbekenntnis Guillaume Farels,* hg. von Irena Backus und Claire Chimelli, Histoire et Société 12 (Genf: Labor et Fides, 1986), 35.

[48]Die grundlegende Studie zum Stil Calvins war lange Zeit diejenige von Francis Higman: *The style of John Calvin in his French polemical treatises* (Oxford, 1967). Die Arbeit von Olivier Millet, *Calvin et la dynamique de la parole.* Etude de rhétorique réformée (Paris: Champion, 1992), hat, ohne die Ergebnisse Francis Higmans zu modifizieren, das Untersuchungsfeld erheblich erweitert.

[49]S. *Opera selecta,* 1:402–3.

[50] Zum Traktat *Des reliques* siehe insbesondere: Jean Calvin, *Three French Treatises,* hg. v. Francis Higman (London: Athlone Press, 1970), 12–16; *La vraie piété,* 155–161, sowie die beiden Beispiele, die ich in "Au plaisir de Calvin," 29, angeführt habe.

[51]Von dieser letzten Polemik an durchzieht diese beißende Ironie das gesamte Werk Calvins. So lehnt er sich in seinem Kommentar zu 1 Cor. 13:13 ("la plus grande des vertus est charité") zunächst an die katholische Auslegung an, um sie daraufhin ins Lächerliche zu ziehen: "Elle [la charité] a plus de vertu à justifier les hommes, pource qu'elle est la plus grande. Il s'ensuyvra donc qu'un roy labourera mieux la terre que le laboureur, il fera mieux un soulier que le cordonnier, pource qu'il est plus noble que tous les deux. L'homme donc courra plus vite que le cheval, il portera plus pesant fardeau que l'elephant, pource qu'il est plus excellent ... (Ergo rex melius terram arabit quam agricola, melius calceum faciet quan sutor: quia nobilior est utroque. Ergo homo celerius curret quam equus, plus oneris portabit quam elephas: quia dignitate spuerat)." *Commentaires de M. Jehan Calvin sur toutes les Epistres de l'Apostre s. Paul* (Genf: Conrad Badius, 1556), 297; *Commentarii in primam epistolam s. Pauli ad Corinthios, CO* 49:516.

[52]Zitiert von Millet, *Calvin et la dynamique de la parole,* 509.

Philipp [Melanchthon] et de Sturm, je fus amené à écrire par amusement ce poème que tu as lu.[53]

Die Verse, von denen Calvin spricht, und die in Wirklichkeit Jesus Christus gewidmet sind, sind sein *Epinicion Christo cantatum*.[54] Einige Jahre zuvor hatte Théodore de Bèze in seinem Vorwort zu Abraham sacrifiant (1550), ein ebensolches Bekenntnis abgelegt:

Car je confesse que de mon naturel j'ay tousjours pris plaisir à la poësie et ne m'en puis encores repentir.[55]

Sowohl Calvin als auch de Bèze blieben trotz allem Humanisten, Gelehrte, die durch die Streitigkeiten innerhalb des Protestantismus daran gehindert wurden, sich ungeteilt ihren natürlichen literarischen Neigungen hinzugeben.[56] Und dennoch hat Calvin einen unbestreitbaren Hang zur literarischen Komposition beibehalten.

4. Freude an Volkstümlichen Redensarten und Sprichwörtern

Als Abschluß dieser Übersicht über die irdischen Freuden bei Calvin möchte ich einen letzten Aspekt näher beleuchten, der bisher noch nicht ausreichend untersucht wurde: Calvins ausufernde Verwendung von Redensarten und volkstümlichen Sprichwörtern. Ich werde diesen Punkt auf dem Umweg über die Predigten zur Genesis, deren Herausgabe ich vorbereite, angehen. Teils mit Humor,

---

[53]"Ad poeticen natura satis eram propensus: sed ea valere jussa, ab annis viginti quinque nihil composui, nisi quod Wormaciae exemplo Philippi et Sturmii adductus sum, ut carmen illud quod legisti per lusum scriberem"; *Thesaurus epistolicus Calvinianus*, CO 16:2632:488; übersetzt von Jean-François Gilmont, *Bibliotheca Calviniana*, 1:163.

[54]Anläßlich des Kolloquiums in Worms im Jahre 1541, unter Einfluß Melanchthons verfaßt. Cf. *Bibliotheca Calviniana* 1:44/8:162–64, und 2:55/4:566–68; E. A. de Boer, *Loflied en hekeldicht: De geschiedenis van Calvijn's enige gedicht: Het Epinicion Christo cantatum van 1 januari 1541* (Haarlem: Acamedia, 1986). Ebenfalls bekannt ist, daß Calvin während seines Aufenthalts in Straßburg (1539) Psalmen in Verse gesetzt hat.

[55]*Correspondance de Théodore de Bèze*, gesammelt von H. Aubert, hg. von F. Aubert und H. Meylan, Bd. 1, Travaux d'Humanisme et Renaissance 40 (Genf: Droz, 1960,), 200. Bèze gab abgesehen davon die Dichtung, selbst die profane, niemals auf. Regelmäßig überarbeitete und erweiterte er seine Poemata, die in den Jahren 1548, 1569, 1576, 1588(?), 1597, 1598, 1599 veröffentlicht wurde. Cf. Frédéric Gardy, *Bibliographie des oeuvres théologiques, littéraires, historiques et juridiques de Théodore de Bèze*, Travaux d'Humanisme et Renaissance, 41 (Genf: Droz, 1960), Nr. 1–12, S. 1–14. Bèze verheimlichte diese Tätigkeit nie. Im August 1576 dankt ihm Rudolf Gwalter, l'*antistes* von Zürich, für die Zusendung der neuen Ausgabe seiner *Poemata*. Cf. *Correspondance de Théodore de Bèze*, gesammelt von H. Aubert, hg. von A. Dufour, B. Nicollier und R. Bodenmann, Bd. 17, Travaux d'Humanisme et Renaissance, 286 (Genf: Droz, 1994), S. 142, und n.1, S. 143–44.

[56]Vgl. einige Jahre später George Buchanan, dessen (sakrales und profanes) poetisches Schaffen von erheblichem Ausmaß war: mehr als vierzig Ausgaben im 16. und 17. Jahrhundert, abgesehen von den Paraphrasen der Psalmen und dem dramatischen Werk. Siehe dazu: John Durkan, *Bibliography of George Buchanan* (Glasgow: Glasgow University Library, 1994), Nr. 168–209, S. 158–93. Vgl. auch I. D. McFarlane, *Buchanan* (London, 1981), chap. 8, "The Profane Poems," S. 287–319.

in jedem Falle aber mit einem geschärften Sinn für Formulierungen schmückt der Prediger Calvin seine Unterweisungen mit unzähligen Sprichwörtern und volkstümlichen Redewendungen. "Mettre la charrue devant les boeufs" (Das Pferd von hinten aufzäumen) (Predigt 55, fol. 380 v), "sauter du coq à l'asne" (vom Hundertsten ins Tausendste kommen) (Predigt 56, fol. 388 v), "estre comme le haut allemand" (so schwierig wie hochdeutsch) (Predigt 67, S. 109 der Ausgabe von 1561) oder mit der Unvereinbarkeit von Feuer und Wasser spielen (Predigt 36, fol. 228v; 50, fol. 341v) sind alte Sprichwörter, die Calvin übernimmt. Aber "estre comme sacz à charbonniers pour noircir l'un l'autre" (wie ein Sack Kohlen sein, der denjenigen, der ihn trägt, sofort verschmutzt) (Predigt 34, fol. 210b; 54, fol. 370b; 60, fol. 419b),[57] "faire acroire que le noir est blanc" (jemandem ein X für ein U vormachen) (Predigt 57, fol. 397 r), "pendre sa conscience au croc" (sein Gewissen an den Nagel hängen) (Predigt 53, fol. 360 a) oder den freien Willen zur "yvrognerie de la papauté" (Trunksucht des Papsttums) machen (Predigt 64, S. 68 der Ausgabe von 1561) sind zeitgenössische—bzw. speziell Calvinsche—Wendungen, "vives images heureusement créées par l'esprit populaire,"[58] die Fragmente Rabelaisscher Derbheit in Erinnerung rufen,[59] da bei Rabelais derartige Redewendungen häufig anzutreffen sind.[60] Selbstverständlich ist die Derbheit Rabelais' anstößiger als diejenige Calvins. Wo Calvin das Wort "vinaigre" (Essig) in Verbindung mit "miel" (Honig) gebraucht—"mesler le vinaigre parmy le miel"—verwendet Rabelais das Wort "pissen": "pisser le vinaigre."[61] Calvin lehnt es allerdings nicht ab, sich auch vulgärer Ausdrücke wie "pisser au benoistier" (in den Weihwasserkessel pissen)[62] zu bedienen. Es wäre übertrieben zu behaupten, Calvin sei

[57]Siehe dazu vier weitere Beispiele bei Edmond Huguet, "La langue familière chez Calvin," *Revue d'Histoire littéraire de la France* 23 (1916): 27–52, hier 29.

[58]Um einen Ausdruck Huguets zu übernehmen, in "La langue familièr," 27.

[59]Einige Ausdrücke, die beiden gemeinsam sind, finden sich bereits in dem schon etwas älteren Werk von Edmond Huguet, *Le langage figuré au XVIe siècle* (Paris: Hachette, 1933), passim, insbes. S. 6 ("usque ad vitulos"); S. 146 ("tout va par escuelles"); S. 150–11 ("avoir un col de grue"); etc. Cf. ders., "La langue familière ...," S. 34 und 51. Cf. auch Higman, *The Style,* Kap. "Imagery," S. 123–52, insbes. 125–27. Cf. auch den neueren Artikel von François Rigolot, "Sémiotique de la sentence et du proverbe chez Rabelais," in *Etudes Rabelaisiennes XIV,* Travaux d'Humanisme et Renaissance, 162 (Genf: Droz, 1977), 277–86.

[60]Cf. "tourner le noir en blanc" (*Tiers Livre,* hg. M. Screech, Textes Littéraires Français 102, Kap. 43, l. 49); "sauter du coq à l'asne" (*Gargantua,* hg. L.-V. Saulnier, Classiques Garnier-Flammarion180, Kap.11, l.43); "devenir plus noir qu'un sac de charbonnier" (*Quart Livre,* hg. Robert Marichal, Textes Littéraires Français 10, Kap. 52, l. 152–53). Darüber hinaus ist bei Calvin (Predigt 32, fol. 197v) und bei Rabelais (*Gargantua,* Kap. 43, l. 34) auch von Menschen die Rede, die "y vont 'à bride avallée'" (die Zügel schleifen lassen); etc.

[61]"et pissa vinaigre bien fort" (*Pantagruel,* hg. J. Boulenger, Bibliothèque de la Pléiade 15, Kap. 19, l. 99). Es handelt sich um eine in der Ausgabe von 1542 hinzugefügte Passage, die in der editio princeps von 1532 (cf. hg. Saulnier, TLF 2, Kap. 13) fehlt.

[62]Cf. E. Huguet, "La langue familière, 32; ein aus den Predigten über den Brief an die Korinther (Predigt 8, *Calvini opera* 49. 677) und über den zweiten Brief an Thimotheus (Predigt 7, *Calvini opera* 54. 81) entnommenes Zitat.

von Texten Rabelais beeinflußt oder habe vor dem Einschlafen einige Seiten in Pantagruel gelesen.[63] Aber beide Autoren verwenden eine Umgangssprache, die es ermöglicht, den Leser oder Zuhörer durch treffende Formulierungen zum Lächeln oder Lachen zu bringen. Angesichts dieser Verwendung umgangssprachlicher Redewendungen wird man darüber hinaus an Luthers Übersetzungsanweisung erinnert,[64] die die Aufforderung enthält, der Sprache des Volkes Aufmerksamkeit zu schenken. Und wir können sicher sein, daß sich sowohl Calvin als auch Rabelais an derart witzigen Redensarten und volkstümlichen Sprichwörtern ergötzten.

5. Schöpfungstheologie und christliche Anthropologie

Die irdischen Freuden, denen sich Calvin hingab, waren zweifellos zahlreicher als es das Bild, das uns die strenge calvinistische Tradition überliefert, vermuten läßt: ein Glas guten Wein trinken oder mit Freunden ein Trinkgelage veranstalten, geschmackvolle Kleidung tragen oder in einem schönen Haus leben, sind empfehlenswerte materielle Freuden; ebenso die Wahrnehmung der Schönheit der Bäume und des Blumendufts oder die Freude an sakraler oder profaner Musik. Ein Kind zum Lachen zu bringen oder stundenlange Gespräche mit einem Freund zu führen, sind wahre Freuden des Menschen als geselliges Wesen; Calvins literarische Freuden bleiben dahingegen diejenigen eines Humanisten, der der klassischen Literatur zugetan und darüber hinaus ein Schöpfer scharfsinniger Polemiken und ein gewandter Rhetoriker ist.

Täuschen wir uns indes nicht: diese Zitate Calvins über die Freude sind bei weitem seltener als die langen Ausführungen über das Elend des Menschen, über seine Unfähigkeit, gut zu sein oder über die Kasteiung des Fleisches, die uns bekannt sind.[65] Calvin hat nie ins Auge gefaßt, ein De oblactamente zu schreiben, in dem er uns seine Ansichten über die irdischen Freuden offengelegt hätte,[66]

[63]Calvins Angriffe gegen Rabelais in seinem Traktat *Des Scandales* von 1550 sind bekannt. Cf. die Ausgabe von Olivier Fatio, TLF 323 (Genf: Droz, 1984), 138 und n. 248.
[64] Cf. "Ein Sendbrief vom Dolmetschen" (1530), in *Martin Luther Werke* 30/2, S. 627–46. In diesem Text, in dem Luther das Einfügen des Wortes "allein" in seine deutsche Übersetzung des Briefes an die Römer 3,:28 rechtfertigt, formuliert er einige Übersetzungsanweisungen, ausgehend von dem Beispiel "der Baur bringt (allein) korn und kein geld," S. 637: "Das ist ein vollige Deutsche klare rede wird, den man muss nicht die buchstaben inn der lateinischen sprachen fragen, wie man sol Deutsch reden, wir diese esel [seine Gegner, u. a. Hieronymus Emser, Johann Faber, Johannes Cochlaeus] thun, sondern, man mus die mutter ihm hause, die kinder auff der gassen, den gemeinen man auff dem marckt drumb fragen, und den selbigen auff das maul sehen, wie sie reden, und darnach dolmetzschen, so verstehen sie es den und mercken, das man Deutsch mit in redet."
[65]Dieses einzige Beispiel ist einer Predigt vom 16. November 1550 entnommen, der 37. über die Apostelgeschichte (7:38–42): "Car les choses qui nous plaisent à l'oeil nous doibvent estre suspectes et à bon droit" (Genf, BPU: Ms. fr. 25, fol. 310b).
[66]Man darf niemals außer acht lassen, daß sich Calvin von 1536 an konstanter Polemik ausgesetzt sah. Er konnte sein Denken nie positiv und in Ruhe entwickeln, sondern immer nur in Form von Reaktionen.

doch der aufmerksame Leser entdeckt im Verlauf des 30jährigen mannigfaltigen literarischen Schaffensprozesses ausreichende Betrachtungen zur Freude des Menschen—ergänzt durch eine regelmäßige praktische Realisierung—um sich nach ihrer Bedeutung zu fragen. Ohne vorschnell diese irdischen Freuden vergeistigen zu wollen,[67] sind diese Überlegungen des "Calvin of the labyrinth" noch in den von "Calvin of the abyss" begründeten, vorherrschenden theologischen Diskurs einzufügen.[68]

Zunächst ist hervorzuheben, daß zahlreiche Äußerungen und Gewohnheiten Calvins an diejenigen Erasmus' oder Thomas Morus' erinnern.[69] Es handelt sich um humanistische Standpunkte, die jegliche Übertreibung ablehnen: weder Schlemmerei noch Enthaltsamkeit, wie es die antike Weisheit (Cicero, Seneca, oder Plinius) bereits wiederholt formuliert hat.[70] Calvin nennt es mit seinen eigenen Worten "tenir le moyen."[71]

Die Freuden der Nahrung verweisen auf eine wohlgesonnene und gefällige Natur, die Gott für das Wohl des Menschen erschaffen hat. (*IRC* 3:10:2; Predigt 45 über die Genesis; Kommentar zu Psalm 104).[72] Das menschliche Geschöpf hätte sich mit Brot und Wasser begnügen können (*IRC* 3:10:1; Kommentar zu Ps. 104:15),[73] aber Gott zeigte sich ihm gegenüber großmütig und freigebig,

---

[67]Ich schließe mich den Überlegungen H. Obermans an, in "The pursuit of happiness," 272–73. Ich hätte die Passagen hervorheben können, die fast immer auf die von mir zitierten Beispiele folgen, in denen Calvin von Mäßigung, von Kasteiung des Fleisches, von der Überlegenheit des Geistes über das Fleisch und auch von Enthaltsamkeit spricht.

[68]Diese Bipolarität verweist natürlich auf die Analyse von Bouwsma, *John Calvin*, 45–48, 231. Siehe dazu auch Heiko Oberman, der den Begriff wiederaufgreift, und zwar in seinem Werk *Initia Calvini: The matrix of Calvin's Reformation*, Koninklijke nederlandse Akademie van Wetenschappen, Mededelingen van de Afdeling Letterkunde, Nieuwe Reeks, Deel 54, no. 4 (Noord-Hollandsche, Amsterdam, New York, Oxford, Tokyo, 1991), S. 20–28.

[69]Zu humanistischen Freuden der Nahrung siehe Franz Bierlaire, "Erasme, la table et les manières de table," in *Pratiques et discours alimentaires à la Renaissance*, hg. v. Jean-Claude Margolin u. Robert Sauzet (Paris:, 1982), 147–60; zur Freundschaft bei Erasmus, vgl. André Godin, "Les amitiés d'Erasme de Rotterdam," in *Mélanges de la Bibliothèque de la Sorbonne offerts à André Tuilier*, 8. Bd. (Paris, 1988), 123–40.

[70]Vgl. Cicero, *Laelius de amicitia*; Seneca, *Epistolæ ad Lucilium* 3 u. 9. Plinius hat ein Buch seiner *Historia naturalis* (14) der Weinrebe und dem Wein gewidmet. Er verurteilt jeglichen Mißbrauch (xxviii (22), § 137–141). Z.B. schreibt er, daß der Wein "neque viribus corporis aliud neque voluptatibus pernciosius si modus absit"; Kap. vii (5), §58.

[71]Vgl. sein Vorwort zu den *Disputations chrestiennes* von Pierre Viret, *Disputations chrestiennes*, S. 4–5: "Ainsi de tenir le moyen, c'est de savoir bien à propos, et avec grace et par mesure, parler joyeusement pour recréer tellement qu'il n'y ait rien d'inepte, ou jetté à la volée, ou débordé, ce n'est pas une vertu commune ou vulgaire."

[72]Vgl. Pierre Gisel, *La création. Essai sur la liberté et la nécessité, l'histoire et la loi, l'homme, le mal et Dieu* (Genf: Droz), 1980; zu Calvin insbes. S. 225–237.

[73] Vgl. Erasmus, in einem Brief (1524) an Joost Vroye (Gaverius): "Et juvenis cibum ac potum semper ita sumpsi ut pharmacum; et saepenumero doluit non licere sine cibo potuque perpetuo degere." *Opus epistolarum Des. Erasmi Roterodami*, hg. v. Perry S. Allen, 5. Bd. (Oxford, 1924), Nr. 1347, S. 249, 349–50, ins Französische übersetzt u. zitiert v. F. Bierlaire, *Erasme, la table*, 147.

indem er ihn über das Notwendige hinaus überreichlich beschenkte. Im Gegenzug ist es die Aufgabe des Menschen, ihn als Schöpfer anzuerkennen (*IRC* 3:10:3). Ursprünglich gereichte die gesamte Schöpfung dem Menschen allein zur Freude. Selbst die Arbeit, die Adam und Eva vor dem Sündenfall verrichteten, war nur ein "labeur de plaisir" (eine freudvolle Arbeit),[74] ein "esbat de plaisir" (eine fröhliche Ausgelassenheit).[75]

Selbstverständlich vergißt Calvin so gut wie nie zu präzisieren, daß diese Freude nur als eine maßvolle und zudem coram Deo, im Angesicht Gottes, als eine durch Mäßigung, Enthaltsamkeit und das Bedürfnis der anderen in Schranken gehaltene zu verstehen ist. In der Tat führt die Maßlosigkeit dazu, daß man Gott vergißt und seinen Nächsten verachtet.[76] Wir können uns nicht freuen, wenn unsere Brüder im Elend sind und leiden, verkündet Calvin im Jahre 1560 von der Genfer Kanzel von Saint-Pierre herab, wobei er an die Franzosen denkt, die Opfer ihres Glaubens werden.

De nous resjouir, quand nos freres sont ainsi en destresse, ce seroit une cruauté trop brutale à nous.[77]

Bei Calvin verweisen die irdischen Freuden allerdings nicht nur auf eine Theologie der Schöpfung, sondern auch auf eine Anthropologie, auf die ich jetzt noch in Kürze eingehen werde, um anschließend die Diskussion in unserem Seminar zu eröffnen.

Die *imago Dei* in der Seele des Menschen, sowie—da Gott Fleisch geworden ist—die *imago Christi* in seinem Körper, verleihen der menschlichen Existenz und somit auch den irdischen Freuden einen besonderen Wert. Man kann natürlich entgegensetzen, daß das Elend des Menschen ein Klagegesang ist, den Calvin häufiger anstimmt als das Lied von der Erhabenheit des Menschen. Doch trotz allem bleibt die menschliche Natur als etwas grundlegend Gutes bestehen.

Wenn also zu einer Erfahrung oder zu einem naturgegebenen Wissen ein Vernunftelement ("en raison evidente") und die Bestätigung durch einen Bibeltext hinzukommen, so erachtet Calvin diese Triade als ausreichende Bestätigung für

---

[74]Predigten über die Genesis: 9, Oxford, Bodleian Library, Ms. Bodl. 740, fol. 25b und 27a; 18, fol. 97b.

[75]Predigt 18 über die Genesis, Oxford, Bodleian Library, Ms. Bodl. 740, fol. 95a.

[76] "Brief, que si nous voulons estre recongnuz pour enfans de Dieu, qu'en toute prosperité nous aprenions, quoy qu'il en soit, de nous retenir, afin de ne point abuser en intemperance des biens que Dieu nous fait. Que nous prenions et vin et viande seulement pour en estre soutenuz, sachant que tout est dedié à nostre usage, et que nous soyions sur nos gardes, pour n'estre point raviz de folle joie." Predigt 30 über die Genesis, Oxford, Bodleian Library, Ms. Bodl. 740, fol. 186a.

[77]Predigt 72 über die Genesis (15:11–14), vom 19. März 1560, Oxford, Bodleian Library, Ms. Bodl. 740, fol. 462a.

die Richtigkeit einer Beweisführung.[78] Es scheint bisweilen, als ob die dem Menschen zueigene vernunftgelenkte Intuition—wenn sie im Einverständnis mit der Lehre der biblischen Offenbarung ist—von der Sünde verschont würde.[79]

In einer erstaunlichen Passage der Predigt über die Gen. 15:1–4 behauptet Calvin darüber hinaus, daß der Glaube auch einen gealterten Menschen nicht gänzlich bessere, da "il faut qu'il y ait quelque chose de l'homme" (etwas vom Menschen bleiben soll).

Ainsi donc ne trouvons point estrange qu'Abram ait ainsi repliqué. Vray est qu'il se devoit tenir à ce qui avoit desja esté prononcé une fois, mais, comme j'ay desja dit, la foy n'aneantit point du tout nos affections naturelles, nos souciz et nos desirs. Il faut qu'il y ait quelque chose de l'homme. Il est bien vray que la foy corrige bien tout ce qui est excessif en nous, car, quand nous appetons quelque chose, nous avons une fin oblique et tortue, pour nous destourner de Dieu. Et puis nous avons nos passions qui nous transportent. La foy corrige ces vices là, et elle nous admenne à Dieu, et fait qu'il soit tout nostre but. Et puis elle nous retient à ce que nous n'aions point une impetuosité trop grande pour vouloir assujectir Dieu à nos souhaitz. Quoy qu'il en soit il y demeure tousjours quelque desir. Et cela est exprimé en ce mot dont use Abram: "Seigneur, dit il, je chemyne solitaire."[80]

Dieser Text ist erstaunlich, doch er basiert auf einem biblischen Vers, der eine solche Auslegung ermöglicht: "Ich gehe dahin on Kinder" (Gen. 15:2). Calvins Übersetzung lautet: "Je chemyne solitaire" (ich gehe einsam dahin). Was der Mensch auch unternimmt, er bleibt einsam, seiner Natur und seinen eigenen Wünschen unterworfen, denn: "tousjours les fideles tiennent de l'homme, et il y aura quelque foiblesse et quelque tardiveté"[81] (die Gläubigen bleiben immer Menschen, schwach und schwerfällig). Wie dies bei Calvin oft der Fall ist, ergeben sich aus dem Zusammenhang, der dem Diskurs zugrunde liegt, unerwartete Entwicklungen. Diese erstaunliche Textpassage schlägt vielleicht eine Bresche in

---

[78]So in seinem Traktat gegen die Freidenker ("libertins spirituels"), in einer Passage, in der die Medizin als eine Gabe Gottes erachtet wird: "Une telle congnoissance naturelle, qui gist en raison evidente et est approuvée par l'Escriture saincte, doit elle estre tenue pour enchantement ou illusion de Sathan?" (*CO* 7, col. 245).

[79]Cf. dazu die Beispiele, die Francis Higman, "Calvin et l'expérience," in *Expérience, Coutume, Tradition au temps de la Renaissance*, hg. von M. T. Jones-Davies (Paris: Klincksieck, 1992), 245–56, insbes. seine Schlußbemerkung, 255–56, anführt.

[80]Predigt 66 über die Genesis, fol. 444b.

[81]Predigt über die Genesis 15:8–10, vom 18. März 1560, Oxford, Bodleian Library, fol. 446v. In der gleichen Bedeutung zitiert Calvin Markus 9:24 in der *IRC*, um zu bekräftigen, daß eine Perfektion im Glauben auf der Erde nicht zu erlangen sei; *IRC* 4:14:7.

Irdische Freude bei Calvin 207

unser Verständnis des Glaubens bei Calvin.[82] So als ob sich die Auflösung des gealterten Menschen, der menschlichen Leidenschaften und des irdischen Verlangens als unmöglich herausstellte,[83] und insofern lediglich eine Besserung unserer Neigungen vorstellbar wäre;[84] so als ob der Kampf gegen das Fleischliche, den ein Christ laut Calvin[85] bestehen muß, immer verloren wäre; so als ob neben der Vernunft eine andere dem Menschen innewohnende Beschaffenheit, sein Gemeinschaftssinn, nicht ganz von der Sünde verdorben wäre; so als ob die globale Offenbarung durch die Schöpfung ("revelatio generalis") sich nicht völlig in der Offenbarung durch Christus ("revelatio specialis") vollzöge; so als ob die imago Dei, unabhängig von einer Zustimmung oder einer Absage der revelatio specialis, einen allen Menschen gemeinsame Spur hinterlassen hätte.[86] Diese ursprüngliche Reinheit, die noch in einigen Betrachtungen des Humanisten zum Vorschein

---

[82]Ich übersehe nicht, daß das Denken des Reformators kontextuell zu sehen ist.

[83]Man halte sich die Bedeutung vor Augen, die dem Konzept der "delectatio" im Denken Thomas von Aquins zukommt. P.e. *Summa theologiae*, 1a 2ae, q. 11, 1 ad 3; q. 31, 1 c ad 2; q. 34, 1c; 9.35, 1c; q. 43, 1.2; etc. "Delectatio est in appetitu sensitivo et in appetitu intellectivo": 1 a 2ae, q. 30, 1c; q. 31, 4; q. 35, 1 c. Die Freude stellt eine Dimension der menschlichen Wirklichkeit dar.

[84] Calvin, sowie nach ihm Montaigne, ist sich der Unbeständigkeit des Menschen bewußt. Cf. Bouwsma, *John Calvin*, 230.

[85]Cf. *IRC* 3:2:17; 3:3:10; 3:20:46; 4:15:11; etc.

[86]In der *IRC* 2:2:12–13, mit einem von Augustin (De natura et gratia 3:3; 19: 21; 20:22) beeinflußten, von Petrus Lombardus, *Sentenciae*, Lib. 2, dist. 25, cap. 8, rezipierten Zusatz von 1559/1560, unterstreicht Calvin zunächst, daß "les dons naturels ont esté corrompus en l'homme par le péché, et les surnaturels ont esté du tout abolys (naturalia dona fuisse corrupta in homine per peccatum, supernaturalibus autem exinanitum fuisse).... Pareillement aussi l'intégrité de l'entendement et la droiture du coeur nous ont esté ostées (rursum sanitas mentis et cordis rectitudo simul fuerunt ablata)." Im folgenden mildert Calvin jedoch sein Urteil: "Car combien qu'il nous reste quelque portion d'intelligence et de jugement avec la volonté, toutesfois nous ne dirons pas que l'entendement soit sain et entier, estant si débile et envelopé en beaucoup de ténèbres.... (Nam etsi aliquid intelligentiae et judicii residuum maneat una cum voluntate, neque tamen mentem integram et sanam dicemus, quae et debilis est, et multis tenebris immersa).... Puis donc que la raison par laquelle l'homme discerne d'entre le bien et le mal, par laquelle il entend et juge, est un don naturel, elle n'a peu estre du tout esteinte (Quum ergo ratio qua discernit homo inter bonum et malum, qua intelligit et judicat, naturale donum sit, non potuit in totum deleri)." Im folgenden Absatz hingegen gesteht Calvin dem menschlichen Verstand wesentlich umfassendere Fähigkeiten zu: "Toutesfois quand l'entendement humain s'efforce à quelque estude, il ne labeure pas tellement en vain qu'il ne profite aucunement, principalement quand il s'adresse à ces choses inférieures, combien qu'il vaque négligemment à les chercher des choses supérieures, combien qu'il vaque négligemment à les chercher (Neque tamen ita conatus eius semper in irritum cedunt, quin aliquid assequatur, praesertim ubi seipsam ad inferiora ista intendit. Quinetiam non ita stupida est quin exiguum quiddam et de superioribus delibet, utcunque negligentius illis percontandis vacet)...." Calvin behauptet schließlich, daß "nul n'est destitué de la lumière de la raison quant au gouvernement de la vie présente (in huius vitae constitutione, nullum destitui luce rationis hominem)." Eine Äußerung über die Verderbtheit der natürlichen Gaben findet sich bereits etwas weiter oben in der *IRC*, in 2:2:4.

kommt, findet in den Freuden dieser Welt eine Ausdrucksmöglichkeit, die Calvin, demjenigen des Labyrinths, in seiner "pursuit of happiness,"[87] wohlbekannt war.

[87]Um den Titel der sehr anregenden Studie von Heiko Oberman, art. cit., aufzugreifen, mit dessen Ergebnissen wir weitgehend übereinstimmen, unter dem einzigen Vorbehalt, daß das imago Dei doch einen Bestandteil der natürlichen menschlichen Struktur darstellen könnte (cf. 271), und daß die religiöse Angst/Furcht nicht völlig aus den Predigten Calvins ausgeschlossen ist (cf. 278). Cf. dazu meine Studie "Le paradis à Genève: Comment Calvin prêchait-il la Chute aux Genevois?" *Etudes théologiques et religieuses* 69 (1994): 329–47.

Varied Themes in Calvin's 2 Samuel Sermons and the Development of His Thought

Douglas Kelly

UNTIL WELL ON INTO THE TWENTIETH CENTURY, Calvin's preaching, and in many respects his work as commentator, tended to be neglected in the study of his theology and influence. Rodolphe Peter, Thomas H. L. Parker, Thomas F. Torrance, R. S. Wallace, and more recently Brian Gerrish and many others have helped to redress this imbalance. The remark of Thomas F. Torrance states the position well:

> One of the calamities of traditional exposition and interpretation of Calvin's theology has been, by means of arid logical forms, to make Calvin's own distinctions too clean and rigid. This has resulted in an oversimplification which has obscured the flexibility as well as the range and profundity of his thought. There is no doubt that Calvin was at times guilty himself of this procedure, particularly in his more systematic treatises when he was engaged in debate, as in regard to the problems of predestination and providence, but in the vast bulk of his work where he sticks closely to the Scriptures there is much profound theology that has never been sufficiently brought to light.[1]

Just the sheer massiveness of the preaching done by Calvin would indicate that he held the task of the pulpit in highest regard, and indeed, as the center of his pastoral activity. His introduction to the various editions of his *Institutes* make it clear that he considered them primarily as a guide to help the flock understand the Scriptures. Hence the *Institutes* were subsidiary to the Scriptures, not the Scriptures to them.

Rodolphe Peter estimated that Calvin preached well over three thousand sermons during his ministry in Geneva and Strasbourg, and of these we possess nearly fifteen hundred. Calvin spent far more time and energy on his preaching than on writing and revising his *Institutes* and various tracts, treatises, and letters (crucial as these are). Therefore, for a fuller understanding of his thought, we must look at Calvin's preaching as well as his commentaries.

---

[1]Thomas F. Torrance, *Calvin's Doctrine of Man* (London,1947), 7,8.

I. Calvin's Activity as a Preacher

Calvin had done some preaching before he came to Geneva in 1536, but we have very little information about it. For all practical purposes, his preaching ministry begins in earnest in late 1536 as "reader in Holy Scripture" and later as "Pastor and Doctor in the Church." We are not certain how often Calvin preached nor precisely what books of Scripture he may have preached through during his first Genevan stay. After his banishment by the town council of Geneva, he was pastor of the French Church in Strasbourg from 1538 to 1541, when he was recalled to be chief pastor of Geneva. At Strasbourg Calvin lectured or preached nearly every day and preached twice on Sundays. Among many other duties there, he preached through Romans, St. John's Gospel, and 1 Corinthians.

After his return to Geneva in 1541, Calvin again began his expository preaching (starting with the very next verse following the one he had last preached on before his banishment in 1538—the better to show the nature of his ministry as a mere servant of the Word of God written). From 1541 until his death in 1564, Calvin preached effectively and voluminously, apparently considering the pulpit as the heart of his ministry.

Upon his return, he seems to have preached twice on Sundays and once every Monday, Wednesday, and Friday. In the words of Parker:

> But in the autumn of 1542 some who appreciated his preaching urged him to preach more frequently, "which" he says, "I have already commenced and shall endeavor to do until the others have become more acceptable to the people" (*Calvini Opera* 11:417, Herminjard 8:79). But this proved too heavy a burden and after two months the council released him from preaching more than once a Sunday (*CO* 21:302). In October 1549, however, sermons were ordered for every day of alternate weeks as well as twice on Sundays.
>
> His custom was to expound the Old Testament on weekdays, the New on Sundays, although sometimes he gave up Sunday afternoons to Psalms. We have little evidence as to what books he expounded or even what individual sermons he preached before 1549. Certainly he was preaching through Hebrews until August 1549, and it would therefore seem that he began that book in 1548. At some time probably between 1546 and 1548 he was expounding on Sunday afternoons the metricized psalms in the service book. Since he did not preach on Romans, St. John's Gospel, Philippians, Colossians, and the Catholic epistles after 1549, we may conjecture that he preached on them earlier.[2]

---

[2]Thomas H. L. Parker, *John Calvin* (Herts: Berkhamstead, 1975), 108, 109.

It is much easier for us to trace the details of Calvin's preaching after 1549, for in that year the French emigrants to Geneva hired an able professional scribe, Denis Raguenier (who used a system of shorthand), to record, transcribe, and bind in sets all of Calvin's sermons (usually around six thousand words in length). We refer again to Parker:

> And so we can trace him preaching on Sundays with one hundred and eighty-nine sermons on the Acts between 1549 and 1554, a shorter series on some of the Pauline letters between 1554 and 1558, and the sixty-five on the harmony of the gospels between 1559 and 1564. During this time the weekdays saw series on Jeremiah and Lamentations (up to 1550), on the minor prophets and Daniel (1550–52), the hundred and seventy-four on Ezekiel (1552–54), the one hundred and fifty-nine of Job (1554–55), the two hundred of Deuteronomy (1555–56), the three hundred and forty-two on Isaiah (1556–59), one hundred and twenty-three on Genesis (1559-61), a short set on Judges (1561), one hundred and seven on I Samuel and eighty-seven on II Samuel (1561–63) and a set on I Kings (1563–64).[3]

II. Some Characteristics of Calvin's Preaching

Calvin's preaching was expository, based on a methodology of going through books of the Bible passage by passage, seeking to understand their original meaning, and then applying them to the life of the congregation. Zwingli in Zurich preached directly through books of the Scriptures in an expository manner; in so doing, he was following such great Church Fathers as John Chrysostom and Augustine as well as the more allegorical Origen. Calvin broke with the elaborate medieval forms of allegorical preaching in favor of straightforward explanation of the text plus direct and relevant application to life in his own day.

In the plainest expository manner, whether preaching from Old or New Testament, Calvin subjected himself to the message of the particular text with which he was dealing, without importing into every text the entirety of systematic theology. It was Calvin's desire to follow the thrust of the passage rather than fit the passage into a preconceived theological mold: "I do not willingly accept interpretations which can only be fitted to the words by twisting the words to them" (CO 49:384–85). To avoid such twisting, Calvin laid heavy emphasis on the context of the verse and passage. What Parker says about Calvin's methodology in his commentaries is equally true of his sermons:

[3]Ibid., 109.

The context is all-important. Individual words or clauses are not allowed any eccentricity; they are controlled by the context. Conversely, the meaning of the context is understood by the interrelationship of the meanings of the individual parts. Hence these parts are to be interpreted only in relationship to the other parts. This is illustrated by Calvin's practice in the sermons, where he will not single out for special treatment some sublime verse, far less a clause, but builds up the meaning of the passage from a patient explanation of the members.[4]

After deriving the meaning of the historical document for its own time, Calvin then relates its lessons to the contemporary world, often with remarkable insight but never at the expense of dehistoricizing the document. Parker has summarized this movement very clearly:

> Hence for Calvin, the historical document is of prime importance; it cannot be dispensed with; it cannot be left aside in favor of the substance that is extracted from it: in brief, it must never cease to be a historical document. But then, this document is seen as addressed to all men of every age, to be for every age God's message, meaning life or death for every man. Nothing therefore, could be of more concern than this document. It is not right to treat it as history unrelated to every generation. The unrelieved tension between history and contemporaneity is reflected in Calvin's commentaries in the way that the scene continually shifts from the first to the sixteenth century, from the third person to the first person plural, and back again. We almost forget which century we are in; we hardly know whether the participants are they or we. We are talking about the Judaizers in Galatia—no, we are not, they are the Romanists in France and Switzerland—indeed, we are not talking about the Judaizers at all, we are joining in the controversy, we are taking sides, entering into an engagement that will certainly change the outward course of our lives. Or St. John is speaking; but as we listen, his Greek strangely becomes the sort of Latin or French with which we are familiar and we find to our surprise that he knows about our modern problems and says the definitive thing about them.[5]

Thus Calvin seeks to understand the message of the ancient text and then to apply it to modern life. His sermons do not have what we would consider today a formal outline of let us say three or four parts with an introduction and conclu-

---

[4] Thomas H. L. Parker, *Calvin's New Testament Commentaries* (London: SCM, 1971), 80.
[5] Ibid.

sion. Yet these homilies are not totally without form. They are essentially a running commentary plus application on the various parts of a passage. Elsewhere Parker gives a "'typical" outline of a sermon by Calvin:

> Having established the meaning of a verse, he applies it to the congregation and exhorts them to follow its teaching. Assuming a verse consisting of two members, we might reconstruct a typical sermon as follows:
>
> 1. Prayer
> 2. Recapitulation of a previous sermon
> 3. (a) Exegesis and exposition of first member
>   (b) Application of this, and exhortation to obedience or duty
> 4. (a) Exegesis and exposition of second member
>   (b) Application of this, and exhortation to obedience or duty
> 5. Bidding to prayer, which contains a summary of the sermon[6]

Yet, as he says,

> There might of course, be considerably more than two main headings, and sometimes he digressed from his text, thought rarely from his subject; but the structure of the sermon remains the same.[7]

In another place, Parker notes:

> The form of his sermons is determined by the exposition. In theory it follows the pattern of explanation of a clause or sentence and its application to the people, sometimes in the context of an immediate situation. In practice, the form is flexible, even loose. It is saved from being rambling by his capacity for keeping to the point and breaking the material up into short sections, usually with some formula as "so much for that point" or "so you see what the prophet (or apostle) meant to say."[8]

Calvin employed very few anecdotes and personal references, but did often paint vivid scenes and engaged the Biblical characters (or modern sinners and saints) in imaginary dialogues in order to bring home the point of the text. In these vivid scenes Calvin was somehow able to enter into the very mind and soul of the Biblical characters and "make them talk" so that they reveal to us our own inner motives and moral character. The late Ford Lewis Battles has depicted this aspect of Calvin's preaching and exegetical work:

---

[6]Thomas H. L. Parker, *The Oracles of God* (London: Lutterworth, 1947), 70.
[7]Ibid., 71.
[8]Parker, *John Calvin*, 110.

His exegesis strangely enters the personal experience of Biblical characters, in whom he finds a reflection of his own. In the Psalms of David he
finds "an anatomy of all the states of the soul." Here is an experiential
approach to Biblical exegesis through biographical identification with
Old Testament personages strikingly similar to that of Martin Luther (cf.
C. W. Hovland, "Anfechtung in Luther's Biblical Exegesis," in Franklin H.
Littel, ed., *Reformation Studies*) and not unrecognized by all authentic
preachers. Elsewhere (cf. *The Piety of John Calvin*) I have discussed the
"imitatio Davidis," so frequently met with in Calvin' writings—especially in the *Institutes* and in the *Commentary on the Psalms.* Frequently
he prefers to let David speak for his own spiritual condition....[9]

Calvin preached without notes, but not without careful preparation. He
apparently preached directly from the original Hebrew and Greek texts. Calvin
had, of course, written his own commentaries on many of the books from which
he preached and never ceased to study the commentaries of the Church Fathers,
medieval scholastics, Jewish rabbis, and fellow reformers (such as Bullinger,
Bucer, and Melanchthon). He did careful work in the best editions of his time on
Hebrew and Greek grammar, history, customs, and geography. And obviously he
thought out ahead of time the specific lessons which the text contained for the
lives of the people. He then went to the pulpit with all of these matters stored in
his powerful mind.

III. The Sermons on 2 Samuel and Development of Calvin's Wider Thought

The series on 1 and 2 Samuel was preached at the peak of Calvin's career. He finished them just one year before his death in 1564, and thus they represent much of
his most mature thinking. By selecting a few varied themes from his 2 Samuel sermons, we may consider how they fill out matters discussed in other realms of his
writing, such as the *Institutes*, and a few of his commentaries as well as his *Tracts
and Treatises.* (We are taking only a small, but I hope, representative sample of this
material.)

I agree with those who assess Calvin's thought to have been very consistent
throughout his career. Taking that for granted, it is my impression that these sermons on 2 Samuel do not introduce much new material or diversity of thought
from his earlier work (with a possible exception concerning the right of resistance
to evil government). Rather, the great value of these sermons lies in their filling

---

[9]Ford Lewis Battles, *Analysis of the Institutes of the Christian Religion* (Grand Rapids: Baker,
1980), 17.

out with pastoral fullness important matters that are dealt with only briefly elsewhere. This greater richness of pastoral application is no small benefit to the church in any age. In addition to that, a larger pastoral passage can illumine a brief statement, which may have been deemed inappropriate to enlarge in another more formal theological context.

1. General Themes in the Sermons on 2 Samuel

I have chosen at random a few varied themes for discussion along these lines: warfare, child rearing, the right of resistance of evil government, God's guidance to his people, the connection of Old and New Testaments, worship, sacraments, and prayer.

a. *Warfare.* Before addressing these matters, it is important to note that in addition to appropriate passages in his commentaries, Calvin's *Letters* supply much information concerning his hatred of warfare. What he says about 2 Samuel is not—to the best of my knowledge—different, but it is fuller.

As would be expected in a book such as 2 Samuel, which deals extensively with battles and warfare, Calvin has much to say on the subject of war. What might not be expected is that Calvin, who has been thought of by many as a bellicose Reformer eager for holy war, paints a realistic picture of the horrors of war and thus insists on the moral necessity of negotiation—even, where possible, with religious enemies. This he states at some length in sermon 6:

> Let us thus learn that God will punish any pride that strengthens our cruel passions so that we have no pity on men, but expose them to butchery like calves or sheep. That is an enormous vice to which we must give serious consideration. I speak to those who have power of some sort for one sees how earthly princes only rejoice when they fill the fields with dead bodies. There will be many poor widows and orphans as victims of their greed. That to them is only a pastime; it is of no more concern than wiping their mouths. Well, since God has declared a manifest judgment on them, they will in no way escape giving an account for their cruelty....
>
> [The fact that 360 men were killed in the battle between Joab and Abner] shows us even more how horrified we should be over shed blood of the faithful and of those who are joined to us in the name of God. In general one cannot kill a man without the image of God being violated. And that is why Scripture says that a man, being created in the image of God, cannot be killed without the offence being against God himself, who has stamped his image in our nature. It is a crime because everyone should see himself in his neighbor. We are worse than savage beasts when

we are thus burning to destroy one another. And there is in particular a sacred bond among those who claim to be the people of God—as it was formerly among the whole family of Abraham, so it is today in the Church. That is why, therefore, even though there were only three hundred and eighty men killed among all who were defeated, it is still said that the battle was hard.

That is for our instruction. Thus when we see that in Christendom people are tearing one another up, let us realize that this is being taken into account by God, and even if men harden themselves, God does not change his mind. We have already seen battles over such a long time. There is no end to them. And even apart from battles we have seen how many people have been killed by wars. This has not been the case merely in one place and in a single army, but it has gone on among princes who claim to be Christians and Catholics—and yet they are killing an infinite number of people. One sees poor people dead among the bushes, and others who are left have to endure hunger and thirst, and heat and cold, and many deprivations—to such a degree that if you cut their throat, you would do them a favor. For they are suffering and will die ten times, so to speak, before death strikes the final blow. Now that is nothing to us because we have become too used to it....

Not only is it those who attack one another in a diabolical rage, but also the adherents of Christianity are thus embittered against one another. Notice the extremity of the situation, that the bond (as I have said) of our union consists in the call that God has given to us to be his people, and yet we come to the point of breaking and dismembering it. Well, under the shadow of the name of God, under the shadow of the pure religion which ought to keep us united in one body, under the shadow of our Lord Jesus Christ who is our head, if we are in strife and contentions, what will be the outcome?

Calvin goes on to say in this sermon that neutrality is not always possible or moral, and that fighting can be imperative. Nevertheless, Calvin teaches that insofar as it is possible, we should try to emulate what Joab did in showing mercy to his enemies in this religious/civil war:

Nonetheless, let us try to carry on peaceably as far as we can and to pursue brotherhood as far as possible. For the love of Joab is shown here to be worthy of praise, when he had compassion on his unfortunate brethren. Even though those people in history, with the exception of the tribe of Judah, were his enemies, he nevertheless treated them kindly, keeping in mind the fact that God had chosen them to be his heritage along with the others. When he took that into consideration, he was moved with pity towards them. Therefore, even when we do battle for the cause of God, we should still seek reconciliation when it is genuine, but not such hollow reconciliations (i.e. as that of Abner and Joab).

In sermon 30, Calvin shows that there are occasions when it is wise and proper to negotiate alliances with open pagans. He speaks of this as he comments on 2 Samuel 10:1–4, where King Hanun abused the ambassadors of King David.

> Well, because the outcome was not good, and because Hanun turned the friendship that David had for him to mockery and shame, some think that God wanted to chastise him for having thus sought fellowship with unbelievers. It is true that the Ammonites are kept back and banished from the church by law. But nevertheless it is not said that David could not act kindly toward them. For he is not rebuked for having had an alliance with King Hiram, and yet Hiram was an idolater. We see also that Abraham had an alliance with those who had nothing in common with him as far as religion is concerned. It is not said in Scripture that one should not seek such alliances, but according as God presents occasions for them, sometimes one is constrained to form them. For when Abraham was dwelling in the midst of the unbelievers, what could he have done, and especially when he sees that he cannot achieve peace otherwise, unless he has a mutual promise? And when the king of the Philistines comes to him, he must also swear and promise to be loyal to him.

What is even more noteworthy in Calvin's teaching about war than his insistence on negotiation and treaty, is his insight into the frequent economic motivation of war. Since the nineteenth-century Marxist attempts to examine the economic motivations of society and statecraft, we have become familiar with discussions of the economic foundations of national and international conflict (from both conservative and liberal viewpoints). It is perhaps surprising that in the sixteenth century, Calvin—from a Biblical viewpoint—uncovered the sinful greed and vainglory that lie behind so much warfare. He says in sermon 31 that there are such things as just wars: "if the honor of God is procured and the rulers have regard to the peace and general condition of the people." But he goes on to say in this sermon (and in others in the series) that most wars in fact are undertaken from dishonorable motives:

> We see many people who will argue in a good cause, and indeed will seem to be motivated by nothing but zeal, and yet when we look at them

more closely, we will discover that under the pretext of the honor of God and the public good, they are actually seeking an occasion to enrich themselves. For instance, in these troubles that we see today, how many are there who are fighting under the very shadow of the banner of Jesus Christ, making profession of the Gospel, and yet in actuality are addicted to pillaging and plundering, and sing of nothing but their purse and grab money wherever they can get their hands on it?

And why? ... Now if it is really only a matter of marching and doing their duty, and of procuring the honor and service of God without any profit in it, very soon their zeal will become as cold as ice. But if it is simply a question of gathering into the coffer and cabinets, now they are the greatest zealots in the world.[10]

In sermon 30, Calvin speaks at greater length of how most wars come from the economic and power ambitions of the ruling classes:

Now here are the only two just causes of war: the good and common salvation of the people and the honor of God, which is mentioned in this text (i.e. 2 Samuel 10:12) in the second place. Not that God's honor should be considered of least value, but the main thing is often placed at the end and at the tail, as it weighs the most.... Yet if we consider the opposite which has always caused wars, we will find that the greatest part has come from avarice and ambition.

Here, for instance, is a prince who undertakes war. And why? He wants to be great. He has no other goal; or he is insatiable as the pit of hell. He wants to get everything for himself, and it seems to him that his income will not be sufficient for him. Now that is the source of wars. Distrust is also mixed in with these motives. For when a prince will have a strong enemy, he will say: "If I advance myself, I will be first." Therefore he concludes: "It is necessary to wage war, and when I gain the advantage, I will profit all the more from it...." And yet where is the common good? A prince will have his poor subjects. He must raise his taxes and rates, and does this without end or measure. And he will shed human blood. It will not bother him to make many widows and orphans, and for many houses to be burnt and for all their goods to be taken as prey, and for all that one is accustomed to do in time of war to happen....

Today the Venetians will say that it is for the civil good when they trouble the world with their enterprises, but it is certain that it is nothing

---

[10]This quotation is taken from Sermon 31, which deals with the text in 2 Sam. 10:10–14.

but the avarice and ambition to be great and to become famous which pushes them to make war.... It is the same with the Romans. For the fact that they stirred up and whipped the whole world was only for their grandeur and in order to acquire fame and renown, more and more, and then riches also set them on fire.

Calvin's concern for a godly, just social order does not stop with exposing the evil economic motivations of ruling classes who are eager to start wars. In tones not unlike those heard in many industrialized countries today, he laments the damage a dishonest bureaucracy can do, and calls for honest public servants. In Sermon III (on 2 Samuel 2), Calvin describes the situation;

> It is the honor of a good prince to relieve his subjects. This must be carefully noted, for it is a thing very rare. Today the princes do nothing but draw to themselves everything they can, and then they support these raving wolves who never have enough to fill their appetite. For when one enters the court, instead of serving his prince, he tries to make himself important. One will use his pen to get into the rank of the brave, another to be debauched, another to be a cook, another for this or that. They will not be satisfied to remain in a low degree, but one by using this person or that person will acquire some lordship or the rent of fifteen thousand francs....
>
> And at whose expense? Of the poor people, who are skinned alive; who are eaten and ravished on every side. But it is necessary nevertheless that the mouth be politely closed when my lord speaks. This is how princes are stunned after this rabble despoil their impoverished subjects in order to adorn themselves sumptuously.

b. *Child Rearing.* In a somewhat more positive, though slightly sarcastic vein, Calvin mentions the "almost angelic reformation" that would occur if kings—like David—would choose godly and just civil servants and officers (in sermon 28, on 2 Samuel 8).

In addition to the wars in which David was involved, 2 Samuel paints a realistic picture of his family life with both its joys and disasters. Calvin is not slow to take up this subject and make strong applications from it to the family responsibilities of the people of God in every age. In sermon 28 (on 2 Samuel 8), Calvin speaks of how we should face the frustrations involved in rearing good children. After commenting on 2 Samuel 8:18, which asserts that David's sons were priests, Calvin goes on to explain the apparently unusual usage of "priest" here:

In sum, David's children could never have been priests, because that would have been an abomination to God. What this expression really means is that David took pains to have them instructed and taught in the requirements of the law. So we must conclude that they are considered excellent persons who were eminent among the people. But this passage extended their excellent reputation in one area by analogy to another area; as though it were saying they were sacred persons. Still these words show us that David attempted to make his children worthy, so he might have good and faithful successors who could train the people in righteousness and maintain them in integrity. That is why he did not bring up his children only in pompous show, but gave them personal excellence so they might know what it is to govern and might be trained in it for the future. This shows us that he was not merely content with doing his duty during his life, but that he wanted a well-regulated state to continue even after his death.

He took great pains to carry this out, but was frustrated in his attempt. It is true that God raised up Solomon to succeed him as he had promised, but what about Absalom and all the others? Why were they so disorderly?

Although kings may seriously attempt to have their children trained to govern themselves properly, yet they will not always be successful. This principle applies to everyone. Fathers, for instance, often try to train their children properly, and yet they do not get the fruit they hoped for. This is not meant to make them lose courage, as though we were saying: "Why worry ourselves about this matter, since those who are so concerned to guide their children properly are only wasting their time? Thus we must leave them alone, since God has promised to take care of them."

On the contrary, this is the conclusion we should draw: "Since those who take such pains and spend so much to have their children properly taught, are still frustrated in their hopes, what terrible things will happen if I care nothing about it, and put the reins in their hands so they will have freedom to become degenerate?" The sad experience of David teaches fathers to strive harder to instruct their children.[11]

Calvin then gives some practical advice to fathers on how to avoid frustration in raising their children:

[11]The preceding quotations are taken from sermon 28, which deals with the text in 2 Sam. 8.

Fathers are further instructed by this principle to commend their children to God, asking him to instruct them by his Spirit. They must realize that all their labor, industry and vigilance will be useless unless it is blessed by his Spirit. Even when fathers spare neither gold nor silver, even when they send their children to school, and give them good examples and keep them under a firm hand of leadership—still their whole duty has not been discharged. They can do all of that, and still miss the main thing, which is to call upon God and recognize their dependence upon him to prosper the instruction of their children.[12]

In the passage dealing with David's failure to punish Amnon for his violation of Tamar, Calvin advises the timely punishment of erring children:

Now it is not that David applauded Amnon, nor that he approved, but that he was lax and did not sue severity and rigor as he should have done. This, therefore is the evil which David did.

Now we are taught in this passage that it will not be enough for evil to displease us, unless we correct it, or at least unless we make the effort as far as we are able. We must, I say, exterminate the evil and force ourselves to do it. We will not be let off for saying, "I wish it had not been done; I am perplexed over it; it displeases me." When we have made all these impressive protestations, it is certain that we will not fail to be condemned before God. Above all, fathers are instructed here. When they see that their children have done wrong, it is not enough to be angry, but to use such correction that the child may be brought back to the right path, and may have no occasion to let himself go astray—but that he may be kept in control....

In fact, what follows this story shows that David was chastised as he deserved, when he failed to punish Amnon. If David had done his duty, he could have prevented this very enormous homicide which occurred; the wrath of Absalom would have been appeased.[13]

In an interesting passage addressed to what we call today working class parents, Calvin speaks encouragingly of their opportunities for successful child rearing:

This passage [i.e. 2 Samuel 8] warns us that it is a very rare thing for the children of princes to bear good fruit, even though they have been

[12]Ibid.
[13]The preceding quotations are from sermon 42 on 2 Sam. 13.

instructed in their childhood and youth … let us not be surprised today if the children of rulers are so disorderly, and are more like savage beasts than reasonable creatures.

How are they instructed? People simply make idols of them, and they think that the world is created for them.…

This warns all those whom God keeps in a low condition in society to realize that it is to their advantage when they can govern their families peacefully, and help their children to live in a modest way, and can earn their living honestly by their labor. We see in fact how those who have more status or money, even thought they are neither princes nor kings, cannot get along with their own children when they grow up. Their children unconsciously become presumptuous and proud. They think, "My father is rich, why should I not be treated as my rank demands?" Then they want to act brazenly and cannot be kept in line. They even despise work and want to live off their rents. Moreover, they heedlessly consume everything.

Yet as I have said, those to whom our Lord has given nothing of official authority, nor lordships, nor great riches, should recognize that he does this for their good and profit. Hence they ought to be content with their estate and stay in their small position, but at the same time rejoice as they teach their family to live properly and see their children trained in the fear of God and kept in modesty, as they faithfully earn their living. Thus they can rejoice because their children are not inflated with pride and presumption, and are not rude, as many are who would like to be on top and climb over others.[14]

c. *Obedience to God's Will in Daily Life.* In these two subjects we have chosen for discussion from the sermons on 2 Samuel, warfare and family life, we find a twofold emphasis running all through them (as indeed it runs all through practically every major subject Calvin tackles in the series): the necessity of obedient, godly action on the one hand, and constant trust in the providence of God on the other. Perhaps enough has been quoted to indicate Calvin's emphasis on the necessity of intelligent, practical obedience to God's will in daily life. We shall conclude this study by referring to a passage in sermon 36, where through all the responsibilities and difficulties of life, Calvin inculcates deep, continual trust in the providence of the God who can turn all the evil that comes across the paths of his children into good:

[14]From the sermon 28 on 2 Sam. 8.

What should happen if the wicked and even the devil, who is their father, could do something of themselves without the allowance and permission of God? What would our condition be? Here we are surrounded by so many thieves and all sorts of people who seek only to devour us. Now the devil is a roaring lion, who only roams here and there, seeking prey; and would he not have soon swallowed us up? If, therefore, the devil were not held in control, and all the wicked were not governed by the counsel and secret and incomprehensible virtue of God, then where would we be? Hence, let us realize that when the wicked are in control over us, and trouble us, although they do it unjustly, still God is over it, and we must return to that fact, and we will never know how to profit from it while we endure it, unless we accept this principle: that is, when the wicked pursue their disordered lusts—yet God is still guiding them.

Of course it is true that they do not look at it this way. And that is why also they are never credited with serving God. For they did not want to do it, as Scripture says of Sennacherib, King of the Assyrians, who chastised the people of God by his commandment. Now he did not think of it that way at all, and God compares him to an axe, for he was a tyrant to the fullest degree. God says, "I hold him in my hand like an instrument in order to lop off bad branches." Certainly Sennacherib did not look at it in this way, yet God shows by these words that Sennacherib will be condemned, and yet God will not fail to be a just judge.

Let us learn then to discern that however much men remain confused in their iniquities, and in the evil that they commit against the Law (which ought always to be detested), yet God does not fail to exercise his justice in such a way that the evil is turned into good. That is to say, as far as he is concerned, he knows so how to use evil beyond our thoughts that he converts it into good; that is, to a good end, in such a way that he will not only always remain just, but we shall have occasion all the time of our life to glorify him everywhere in every way.[15]

If these few selections that I have taken from several of Calvin's 2 Samuel sermons have served to give us fuller and richer insight into various aspects of the theology of the great Reformer, then it is to be hoped that the publication of the entire series will encourage a widespread study of his preaching and a better understanding of the breadth and depth of his pastoral theology.

---

[15]Sermon 31.

Calvin's Understanding of *Pietas*

Sou-Young Lee

I. General Introduction to Calvin's use of Pietas

The whole life of Christians ought to be a sort of practice of godliness [pietas]....[1]

These words of Calvin succinctly show how important pietas is in his life and theological thought. This can be affirmed by his commentary on 1 Timothy. As he interprets 1 Tim. 4:7–8, he states:

It is as if he had said, "There is no reason why you should weary yourself with other matters to no purpose. You will do the thing of greatest value, if with all your zeal and ability you devote yourself to godliness alone."[2]

Godliness is the beginning, middle and end of Christian living and where it is complete, there is nothing lacking....Thus the conclusion is that we should concentrate exclusively on godliness, for when once we have attained to it, God requires no more of us....[3]

Reflecting upon the amount of meaning Calvin pours into pietas, we may find it a bit surprising that he did not put aside a special chapter specifically to deal with pietas among the eighty chapters of his major work, *The Institutes of the Christian Religion*. However, when we discover that he deals with pietas throughout the entire book instead of in a single chapter in *The Institutes*, we need not be surprised. The Prefatory Address to King Francis I, which Calvin prefixed to successive publications of the book, begins like this:

When I first set my hand to this work, nothing was farther from my mind, most glorious King, than to write something that might afterward be offered to Your Majesty. My purpose was solely to transmit certain rudiments by which those who are touched with any zeal for religion might be shaped to true godliness.[4]

---

[1] *Institutes*, 3.19.2.

[2] Comment on 1 Tim. 4:7. In David W. and Thomas F. Torrance, eds., *Calvin's New Testament Commentaries: The Second Epistle of Paul the Apostle to the Corinthians, and the Epistles to Timothy, Titus and Philemon*, trans. Thomas A. Smail (Grand Rapids: Eerdmans, 1964), 243. (Hereafter cited *Calvin's NT Commentaries*.)

[3] Comment on 1 Tim. 4:8, *Calvin's NT Commentaries*, 244.

[4] *Institutes*, 3.19.9.

And in the first Latin edition (1536) and the first French edition (1541) of the *Institutes*, he attached the full titles of the books as follows, respectively:

> Christianae religionis institutio totam fere pietatis summam et quidquid est in doctrina salutis cognitu necessarium complectens, omnibus pietatis studiosis lectu dignissimum opus ac recens editum.[5]

> Institution de la religion chretienne: en laquelle est comprinse une somme de pieté, et quasi tout ce qui est necessaire a congnoistre en la doctrine de salut.[6]

Does not this show that whatever he discusses, "instruction unto pietas" is the ultimate concern that governed and permeated his thought and theological efforts? It could be said that pietas was his entire theological direction and goal, rather than merely one theme in his theology.

Even though Calvin places much importance on pietas, it is difficult for us to find any trace that he attempted to describe pietas systematically. We catch only a glimpse of his understanding and thoughts on pietas scattered throughout his writings. Nevertheless, even though his references to pietas are not systematic but sporadic, not synthetic but fragmentary, we can ascertain that the content is a mass of highly clear and consistent thinking.

II. THE PRIMARY (NARROW) MEANING OF PIETAS

Whenever we are faced with Calvin's references to pietas, we can find there a series of terms consistently related to the word "pietas." These terms play the decisive role in providing an understanding of the meaning of pietas as Calvin understands it, who just provides several explanations regarding pietas but never attempts to give a clear, synthetic, and decisive definition of it. We can find a considerable number of these words simply in the following two quotations:

> For not only does piety beget reverence toward God, but the very sweetness and delightfulness of grace so fills a man who is cast down in himself will fear, and at the same time with admiration, that he depends upon God and humbly submits himself to his power.[7]

---

[5] See *Joannis Calvini Opera Selecta*, ed. P. Barth, vol. 1, p. 19, where the title page of the *Institutes* is reproduced.

[6] See Rodolphe Peter and Jean-François Gilmont, *Bibliotheca Calviniana: Les Oeuvres de Jean Calvin publiées au XVIe siècle*, Travaux d'Humanisme et Renaissance, no.255 (Geneva: Droz, 1991), 96, where a photocopy of the original title page of 1541 is provided.

[7] *Institutes*, 3.2.23.

Luke counts the fear of God and prayer as fruits and proofs of piety and the worship of God, and he is quite right. For religion cannot be torn away from the fear and reverence of God, and nobody can be considered godly unless he knows God as both Father and Lord, and yields himself to him. But let us realize that what is commended here is spontaneous fear, when those who truly think over in their own minds what is due to God, submit themselves to him gladly and from the heart.[8]

We can see that Calvin intimately connects pietas with fear of God, reverence for (toward) God, submission (or yielding ourselves) to God, worship of God, prayer, and so forth. It would not be easy to contrast the differences, to figure out the interrelationships, or to establish the appropriate chronological sequence amongst the meanings of these concepts. The important thing is to know that these concepts are the core elements of true pietas.

1. *Fear of God*

It may be that Calvin mentions the fear of God most often when he talks about pietas. When he explains the meaning of pietas or lists its key elements, it often appears in the first place: "en vraye piété, c'est à dire en la crainte de son nom, en sa fiance, en saincteté de vie...."[9]

Sometimes he refers to pietas and the fear of God side by side, almost as if they are synonyms, as in the following two passages: "ceux qui ne sont touchez d'aucune crainte de Dieu, ou de sentiment de piété"[10] and "we are not conformed to the fear of God and do not learn the rudiments of piety, unless we are slain by the sword of the Spirit...."[11]

When he wrote *vera pietas*[12] in the Latin edition, he expressed this as "la piété et crainte de Dieu" in the French version. Also by translating "cum pietate" in Latin to "avec la crainte de Dieu" in French,[13] and in turn, "serio Dei timore" in Latin to "en vraye piété" in French,[14] he shows that these two words can be used interchangeably. Thus, "fear of God" is an important part of the meaning of pietas in Calvin's understanding.

2. *Reverence toward God*

In Calvin's references to pietas, the word that often appears together or side by side with "the fear of God" is "reverence." In the *Institutes* 1.2.1–2, Calvin presents a lengthy discussion in reference to the pious mind, and follows this by say-

---

[8]Commentary on Acts 10:2. In *Calvin's NT Commentaries*, 6:284.
[9]*Institutes*, 1.14.4. [10]*Institutes*, 3.2.8. [11]*Institutes*, 3.3.8.
[12]*Institutes*, 2.8.51. [13]*Institutes*, 4.3.11. [14]*Institutes* 4.16.32.

ing: "Here indeed is pure and real religion: faith so joined with an earnest fear of God that this fear also embraces willing reverence, and carries with it such legitimate worship as is prescribed in the Law."[15]

While explaining ungodliness (*impietas*) in his commentary on Titus 2:12, he speaks of it as whatever is contrary to "fear and reverence toward God sincerely from the heart."[16] Calvin elsewhere explains the meaning and interrelationship of the two words of "fear of God" and "reverence toward God":

> Now, "the fear of the Lord"—to which all the saints give witness—and which is in some places called "the beginning of wisdom" [Ps. 111:10; Prov. 1:7], in other places "wisdom itself" [Prov.15:33; Job 28:28]— although one, yet derives from a double meaning. For God has in his own right the reverence of a father and of a lord. Therefore, he who would duly worship him will try to show himself both an obedient son to him and a dutiful servant. The Lord, through the prophet, calls "honor" that obedience which is rendered to him as Father. He calls "fear" the service that is done to him as Lord. "A son," he says, "honors his father; a servant, his lord. If, then, I am a father, where is my honor? If I am a lord, where is my fear?" [Mal. 1:6].[17]

However he may distinguish them, we see how he fuses together the two terms. "Therefore, let the fear of the Lord be for us a reverence compounded of honor and fear."[18]

3. Submission to God

Another very important element which helps us understand Calvin's teaching on pietas is seen in his urging us to submit (yield) ourselves to, or obey, God. And we should take careful note that Calvin repeatedly emphasized that as the fear of God should be spontaneous, so reverence should be willing submission, which is also to be done gladly (*libenter*) and from the heart (*ex animo*).[19]

4. Worship of God

In understanding Calvin's pietas, the most important concept is perhaps worship. The reason is that fear, reverence, and submission to God blossom and ripen into the fruit of worship. To say that worship is the flower of the life of pietas, and pietas reveals and proves itself just through worship, would probably not have any

---

[15]*Institutes*, 1.2.2.
[16]Comment on Titus 2:12, in *Calvin's NT Commentaries*, 373; cf. *Institutes*, 3.7.3.
[17]*Institutes*, 3.2.26.   [18]*Institutes*, 3.2.26.
[19]Comment on Acts 10:2, in *Calvin's NT Commentaries*, 284.

problem in being acknowledged in Calvin's thoughts. In his explanation of the Apostle's statement, "Ananias, a devout man according to the Law (Acts 22:12)," in his commentary on Acts, such as, "Therefore he [Paul] asserts that he [Ananias] worshipped God 'according to the Law,' and that his piety was known...," and also in the following quotations it is clearly shown that pietas and worship have an inseparable relationship in Calvin's thinking:

Here indeed is pure and real religion: faith so joined with an earnest fear of God that this fear also embraces willing reverence, and carries with it such legitimate worship as is prescribed in the law.[20]

Therefore the (first) substance of the precept will be that true piety— namely the worship of his divinity—is pleasing to God....[21]

... there was to be a stated day for them to assemble to hear the law and perform the rites, or at least to devote it particularly to meditation upon his works, and thus through this remembrance to be trained in piety.[22]

The moral law (to begin first with it) is contained under two heads, one of which simply commands us to worship God with pure faith and piety....[23]

The second advantage is the preservation of *godliness*, that is, when magistrates undertake to promote religion, to maintain the worship of God and to require reverence for sacred things.[24]

In the same manner that Calvin spoke about fear, reverence, and submission, he repeatedly emphasized that worship also must be "according to the Law" (Comm. Acts 22:12), "legitimate as prescribed in the Law" (*Institutes*, 1.2.2), or "sincere and from the heart" (Comm. Acts 13:50), and "spiritual and with a pure conscience."

By the word "godliness" he means the spiritual worship of God which is found only in a pure conscience....[25]

5. *Prayer*

Prayer is also an element which cannot be omitted from Calvin's understanding of pietas. For him, pietas and worship have an inseparable relationship, and as

---

[20]*Institutes*, 1.2.2.   [21]*Institutes*, 2.8.8.
[22]*Institutes*, 2.8.28.   [23]*Institutes*, 4.20.15.
[24]Comment on 1 Tim. 2:2, in *Calvin's NT Commentaries*, 207 ff.
[25]Comm. 1 Tim. 4:7, in *Calvin's NT Commentaries*, 243.

he himself states, "the worship of God is proved by prayer": "Luke counts *the fear of God and prayer* as fruits and proofs of piety and the worship of God, and he is quite right" (Comm. Acts, 10:2).

> Moreover, because a large part of the world adulterates and perverts the worship of God with fictitious nonsense, Luke is justified in adding that Cornelius prayed continually. By that he means that not only did he show his piety by external ceremonies, but he also worshipped God spiritually, whenever he exercised himself in prayer. At the same time the assiduousness of his prayer must also be noted, for from that we gather that he did not go through with the duty of prayer coldly, as is usually done, but that he exerted himself seriously in prayer, as the constant blessings of God invite and prompt us to do, and the power of faith ought to reveal itself in that. Accordingly let each one of us take the example of Cornelius and encourage himself to persevere in prayer.[26]

> ... godliness includes not only a good conscience towards men and reverence for God, but also faith and prayer. (Comm. 1 Tim. 4:8)

6. *Knowledge*

Besides these major elements of Calvin's understanding of pietas, even simple reference to the quotations above such as "trust in God," "dependence upon God," and "admiration" can be regarded as the elements to explain the meaning of pietas. However, there is a more basic element that truly makes all the elements of pietas possible. That element is none other than "knowledge." True knowledge is the beginning point and also the foundation for pietas. From the beginning, without knowledge, pietas would not even be possible. The following writings of Calvin demonstrate this fact:

> Knowledge is the basis of life and the first doorway to godliness. None of the spiritual gifts can be of any use for salvation until we are enlightened with the knowledge of God by the teaching of the Gospel.[27]

> Under ungodliness I include not only the superstitions in which they had erred, but the irreligious neglect of God that prevails among men until they have been enlightened into the knowledge of the truth. (Comm. Titus, 2:12)

---

[26]Comment on Acts 10:2, in *Calvin's NT Commentaries*, 285.
[27]Comment on 2 Pet. 1:3, in *Calvin's NT Commentaries*, 329.

Besides, while some may evaporate in their own superstitions and others deliberately and wickedly desert God, yet all degenerate from the true knowledge of him. And so it happens that no real piety remains in the world. (*Institutes*, 1.4.1)

... let us realize that the truth and the sound teaching of the Word of God is the rule of piety, so that there may be no religion without the true light of understanding. (Comm. Acts 17:4)

In Calvin's understanding of pietas, we catch a glimpse of the importance of knowledge by seeing that he paraphrases "ad pietatem" in the Latin version of *The Institutes* (4.16.32) into "en la crainte et discipline de sa Loy, et en la cognoissance de son Evangile" in the French version.

Then, for Calvin, what kind of knowledge is the foundation, the starting point, the absolute necessity of pietas to which he refers? If we express Calvin's thought about this most concisely and to the point, it is to know God as the Lord and Father. This knowledge of God corresponds to the twofold knowledge (*cognitio duplex*) of knowing God as the creator and savior, and expresses it most concretely, and explains it most significantly. The twofold knowledge of understanding God as the Lord and Father, as well as creator and savior, is the basis for explaining the difference between the meanings of fear and reverence within pietas. This view of knowledge is the source from which all elements of pietas originate and which makes them genuine. Especially, God who is our father in Christ and brings us salvation with such love, concern, and care as the Father has for his children seems to be the essence of Calvin's understanding of God as we see it.

... nobody can be considered godly unless he knows God as both Father and Lord, and yields himself to Him. (Comm. Acts 10:2)

Only let the readers agree on this point: let the first step toward godliness be to recognize that God is our Father to watch over us, govern and nourish us, until he gathers us unto the eternal inheritance of his Kingdom. (*Institutes*, 2.6.4)

A little more concrete thought on the knowledge of pietas can be found in Calvin's following remarks from his commentary on Luke 2:25 where he describes Simeon's pietas: "The evidence of his piety lay in his expectation of the consolation of Israel, for God is not properly served without the confidence in salvation, which depends both on faith in His promises, and particularly in the restoration promised in Christ." That is to say, the knowledge to become the foundation and starting point of genuine pietas is none other than to be confident of, and long for, God's having given the promise of comfort, salvation, and restoration in Christ with great conviction and eager anticipation.

The following two paragraphs show Calvin's even more detailed explanation on the knowledge which makes genuine pietas possible:

> Moreover, although our mind cannot apprehend God without rendering some honor to him, it will not suffice simply to hold that there is One whom all ought to honor and adore, unless we are also persuaded that he is the fountain of every good, and that we must seek nothing elsewhere than in him. This I take to mean that not only does he sustain this universe (as he once founded it) by his boundless might, regulate it by his wisdom, preserve it by his goodness, and especially rule mankind by his righteousness and judgment, bear with it in his mercy, watch over it by his protection; but also that no drop will be found either of wisdom and light, or of righteousness or power or rectitude, or of genuine truth, which does not flow from him, and of which he is not the cause. Thus we may learn to await and seek all these things from him, and thankfully to ascribe them, once received, to him. For this sense of the powers of God is for us a fit teacher of piety, from which religion is born. I call "piety" that reverence joined with love of God which the knowledge of his benefits induces. For until men recognize that they owe everything to God, that they are nourished by his fatherly care, that he is the Author of their every good, that they should seek nothing beyond him—they will never yield him willing service. Nay, unless they establish their complete happiness in him, they will never give themselves truly and sincerely to him. (*Institutes*, 1.2.1).

For, to begin with, the pious mind does not dream up for itself any god it pleases, but contemplates the one and only true God. And it does not attach to him whatever it pleases, but is content to hold him to be as he manifests himself; furthermore, the mind always exercises the utmost diligence and care not to wander astray, or rashly and boldly to go beyond his will. It thus recognizes God because it knows that he governs all things; and trusts that he is its guide and protector, therefore giving itself over completely to trust in him. Because it understands him to be the Author of every good, if anything oppresses, if anything is lacking, immediately it betakes itself to his protection, waiting for help from him. Because it is persuaded that he is good and merciful, it reposes in him with perfect trust, and doubts not that in his loving-kindness a remedy will be provided for all its ills. Because it acknowledges him as Lord and Father, the pious mind also deems it meet and right to observe his authority in all things, reverence his majesty, take care to advance his glory, and obey his commandments. Because it sees him to be a righteous judge, armed with severity to punish wickedness, it ever holds his judgment seat before its gaze, and through fear of him restrains itself from provoking his anger. And yet it is not so terrified by the awareness of his judgment as to wish to withdraw, even if some way of escape were open. But it embraces him no less as punisher of the wicked than as benefactor of the pious. For the pious mind realizes that the punishment of the impious and wicked and the reward of life eternal for the righteous equally pertain to God's glory. Besides, this mind restrains itself from sinning, not out of dread of punishment alone; but, because it loves and reveres God as Father, it worships and adores him as Lord. Even if there were no hell, it would still shudder at offending him alone.

Here indeed is pure and real religion: faith so joined with an earnest fear of God that this fear also embraces willing reverence, and carries with it such legitimate worship as is prescribed in the law." (*Institutes*, 1.2.2)

7. Summary.

Now, depending on these two quotations above, and referring to all the other quotations listed up to this point, we reach the stage where we can attempt to define the synthetic meaning of pietas that Calvin tries to understand and explain. We conclude as follows:

Pietas according to Calvin is:

(1) To recognize that there is only one true God;

(2) To know God as he manifests himself;

(3) To know God as creator, sustainer, ruler, guide, protector, and the judge of the universe in his might, wisdom, goodness, mercy, righteousness, and judgment.

(4) To know God as our father and lord via Christ Jesus;

(5) To know God as the author and fountain of every good;

(6) To know that we owe everything to him;

(7) To know that we must seek and await all things and seek help only from him;

(8) And, with this knowledge, to fear and revere God;

9) To submit ourselves to and depend upon God;

10) To trust in and pray to God;

11) To thank and adore God;

12) To worship God;

13) To love and to serve God; and,

14) To do all of the above, sincerely and gladly from the heart.

III. The accompanying (extensive) meaning of Pietas

When we put together these descriptions or the components of pietas, it becomes evident that pietas relates to one's attitude toward God. Indeed, can we say that pietas for Calvin is confined only to the vertical relation with God? Are those components mentioned above all that Calvin says in connection with pietas? For Calvin, does pietas have nothing to do with the horizontal relations between humans? To find an answer, we must note that Calvin several times mentions the two tables of the Law when talking about pietas.

> Piety and righteousness relate to the two tables of the Law: so integrity of life consists in these two parts. (Comm. Luke 2:25)

> But it amounts to this, that Cornelius excelled in the virtues in which the integrity of the godly consists, so that every aspect of his life was ordered according to the rule which God lays down for us. But because the Law is contained in two tables, in the first place Luke commends the piety of Cornelius, and then he proceeds to the second part, his exercising the duties of charity towards men. (Comm. Acts 10:2)

> But as the exercises of godliness depend on the first table of the Law, so.... (Comm. Titus 2:12)

First, we ascertain that Calvin relates pietas to the first of the two tables of the Law, consequently distinguishing pietas from "righteousness" or "exercising the duties of charity towards men" that are related to the second table. Calvin's attempt to understand pietas as something toward God and the conception restricted only to the relation with God comes to light more obviously in his remarks as follows:

> Godliness is religion in relation to God, whereas righteousness is exercised towards men. (Comm. Titus 2:12)

> Now we can understand the nature of the fruits of repentance: the duties of piety toward God, of charity toward men, and in the whole of life, holiness and purity. (*Institutes*, 3.3.16)

1. *Pietas Inseparable from Charity toward Men*

In understanding the meaning of the word pietas, we should keep in mind that Calvin's intention to distinguish pietas from righteousness or charity does not mean separation from either of them. Just as two tables of the Law have facets distinct from each other but at the same time they cannot be separated, altogether constituting one entity of Law of God, and as in Christian life the love of God and the love of men cannot be separated, so "pietas toward God" and "righteousness and charity toward men" cannot be separated. Therefore, we should think that when Calvin distinguishes the meanings of both of them, it is not for separating the two ideas, but for emphasizing the intimate and inseparable relation between them. In the commentary on Acts 10:2, Calvin's intention is to reveal the relation and continuity rather than the difference between them.

> But it amounts to this, that Cornelius excelled in the virtues in which the integrity of the godly consists, so that every aspect of his life was ordered according to the rule which God lays down for us. But because the Law is contained in two tables, in the first place Luke commends the piety of Cornelius, and then he proceeds to the second part, his exercising the duties of charity towards men.... Accordingly, in ordering life properly, let faith and religion be fundamental, for if these are taken away all the remaining virtues are nothing else but illusions. (Comm. Acts 10:2)

Here, what Calvin tries to reveal emphatically are, first, that love, righteousness, and all other kinds of virtues toward humans should be based upon true faith and pietas and proceed from them, so that they may be true and worthy, and second, that true pietas necessarily proceeds to righteousness and the service of love toward men and proves itself through them and otherwise there can be no integrity of the pious. In the next two quotations, we can find the same idea.

> Nous voyons comment la bonne conscience et la foy, c'est a dire en un mot, la piété et crainte de Dieu, est mise au dessus, comme au chef; et de là apres est deduite la charité. (*Institutes*, 2.8.51)

> The moral law (to begin first with it) is contained under two heads, one of which simply commands us to worship God with pure faith and piety; the other, to embrace men with sincere affection. Accordingly, it is the true and eternal rule of righteousness, prescribed for men of all nations and times, who wish to conform their lives to God's will. For it is his eternal and unchangeable will that he himself indeed be worshipped by us all, and that we love one another. (*Institutes*, 2.20.15)

For our piety ought to break out to men so that we testify that we do fear God by the practice of kindness and uprightness (*iustitiam*). Since the word alms (*eleemosyna*) is properly speaking mercy (*misericordia*), an inner feeling of the heart, it has been transferred to the outward services by which we help the poor. (Comm. Acts 10:2)

… godliness includes not only a good conscience towards men and reverence for God, but also faith and prayer. (Comm. 1 Tim. 4:8)

2. *Pietas Related to the Entire Life*

The fact that Calvin considers pietas in an intimate, inseparable relation with righteousness and charity among humans (*inter homines*) ultimately shows that for him pietas is related to a Christian's entire life. In truth, he says, "godliness is the beginning, middle, and end of Christian living" (Comm. 1 Tim. 4:8), and he thinks of pietas in association with "integrity of life" (Comm. Luke 2:25), and regards it as "ordering life properly" (Comm. Acts 10:2). The following passages clearly show that pietas for him is related to our entire life.

The whole life of Christians ought to be a sort of practice of godliness, for we have been called to sanctification. (*Institutes*, 3.19.2)

… as soon as he [Peter] has made mention of life he immediately adds godliness as if it were the soul of life. (Comm. 2 Peter 1:3)

But it amounts to this, that Cornelius excelled in the virtues in which the integrity of the godly consists, so that every aspect of his life was ordered according to the rule which God lays down for us. (Comm. Acts 10:2)

He now lays down the rule by which we may order our lives well, and tells us that we ought to begin by renouncing our former way of life, two features of which he mentions—ungodliness and worldly lusts. (Comm. Titus 2:12)

In this context, we find that the concept of pietas is naturally related to that of holiness.

en vraye piété, c'est à dire en la crainte de son nom, en sa fiance, en saincteté de vie…. (*Institutes*, 1.14.4)

… godliness, which joins us in true holiness with God when we are separated from the iniquities of the world. (*Institutes*, 3.7.3)

The whole life of Christians ought to be a sort of practice of godliness, for we have been called to sanctification." (*Institutes*, 3.19.2)

IV. THE ORIGIN, OR SOURCE, OF PIETAS

It will not be meaningless to examine briefly how Calvin thinks pietas comes about. First, he thinks that pietas cannot arise from the human nature, but it is given only to the believers chosen by God in Jesus Christ.

> From it one may easily grasp anew how much this confused knowledge of God differs from the piety from which religion takes its source, which is instilled in the breasts of believers only. (*Institutes*, 1.4.4)

> Peter is not speaking here about the natural gifts of God, but he is describing only those which he bestows particularly on his elect over and above the common natural order. Since everything that makes for godliness and salvation is reckoned to be included among ... the supernatural gifts of God, men must learn not to claim as of right, but humbly to ask from God whatever they seem to need, and to give credit to Him whatever blessing they receive. By claiming the whole total of godliness and all the helps to salvation as originating in the divine power of Christ, Peter here removes them from the corrupt nature of man, thereby leaving us without the merest scrap of any virtue. (Comm. 2 Peter 1:3)

Second, once pietas is given like this, it is natural for Calvin to say that it comes from the Holy Spirit.

> ... we are not conformed to the fear of God and do not learn the rudiments of piety, unless we are violently slain by the sword of the Spirit and brought to nought. (*Institutes*, 3.3.8)

> ... the advancement of every man in godliness is the secret work of the Spirit. (*Institutes*, 2.24.13)

Third, if pietas comes from the Holy Spirit, we can estimate well enough that it cannot be separated from the Word of God. This came to light apparently in the fact that having written "ad pietatem" (*Institutes*, 4.16.32) and "a pietate" (4.20.32) in the Latin edition of *The Institutes*, he replaces them respectively by the remarks "en la crainte et discipline de sa Loy, et en la cognoissance de son Evangile" and "de sa sainte parolle," in the French edition, and also in the following remark:

The truth and the sound teaching of the Word of God are the rule of piety, so that there may be no religion without the true light of understanding. (Comm. Acts 17:4)

V. Pietas and Faith

When we consider the relation between pietas and faith, we can easily grasp that what Calvin defines as pietas and its related matters is in accord with what he says concerning faith. For Calvin, the words "faith" and "religion" are used interchangeably; even while he is discussing pietas, faith or religion and sometimes both of them together are used in the place of "pietas" (e.g., Comm. Acts 10:2; 17:4; *Institutes*, 1.2.1–2). Of course, now and then, there appear such expressions as "piety, from which religion is born" (*Institutes* 1.2.1) or "the piety from which religion takes its source" (*Institutes* 1.4.4), or "godliness includes not only ... but also faith and prayer" (Comm. 1 Tim. 4:8), but it does not mean they let us inquire into the causal relationship between them or whether large or small in concept. In most cases these words are understood to be used simply side by side or interchangeably.

The moral law (to begin first with it) is contained under two heads, one of which simply commands us to worship God with pure faith and piety.... (*Institutes*, 4.20.15)

You see how conscience and sincere faith are put at the head. In other words, here is true piety. (*Institutes*, 2.8.51)

Institutes	Latin Edition	French Edition
3.24.13	"in pietate"	"en foy et en piété"
4.14.19	"vera pietas"	"piété et religion"
4.1.4	"ad verae pietatis cultum"	"au service de Dieu et a la vraye religion"
1.8.9	"omnia pietatis principia"	tous les principes de religion"

Is pietas merely a word that is no different in meaning than "faith" and "religion"? Or does it retain its own distinct role in Calvin's theological thought? Calvin himself did not prescribe strictly the difference of meaning and reciprocity between "pietas" and "faith."

As mentioned, Calvin's explanation of faith and his references to pietas are in accord in content and even in the words used. Nevertheless, if there is one difference, it is just that while Calvin intends to distinguish "pietas toward God" from "righteousness and love toward men," there can be found no trace of such a distinction in his understanding of faith. If we borrow Calvin's way of explanation, we can safely say that it is Calvin's idea that while faith is concerned with both tables of the Law, pietas is related especially to the first table of the Law. Even though Calvin distinguishes between pietas toward God and righteousness and charity toward men (*inter homines*), and at the same time intends never to separate them, but to unite them more closely, such a distinction is the only element to distinguish between pietas and faith. It can be explained as the following diagram.

God	First Table of the Law	Pietas	
Man	Second Table of the Law	Righteousness (Charity)	Faith

We can conclude that Calvin considered pietas as a facet toward God of faith, the essential element making faith the true faith, and the generative power warranting the real meaning and worth of all virtues of a believer's life.

Some might ask whether pietas thus conceived is a general or Old Testament pietas instead of the Christian or New Testament pietas? Such an unfortunate conclusion can be avoided by the reminder that for Calvin God is always a trinitarian God, that "God our Father and our Savior in Jesus Christ" is the essential and central point of his understanding of God (*Institutes* 2.6.1). This understanding should be considered as a firm presupposition of all of his mentions of true pietas and faith.

Book of the Ritter von Turn. Five-year-old Daniel lays bare the false witness of the two priests who had brought about the condemnation to the stoning of Susanna.

Kirche als unabhängige Institution in Genf 1536–1538

Márkus Mihály

DIE VORGÄNGE UM DIE ENTLASSUNG CALVINS in Genf im Jahre 1538 sind bekannt. Guillaume Farel, Calvin, und der blinde Prediger Elias Courault müssen die Stadt verlassen, weil sie sich weigerten, zu Ostern der Gemeinde das Abendmahl auszuteilen. Es war letztlich ein Akt der Kirchenzucht. Ihre Einführung war in Genf gescheitert und um ihretwillen schritten die Prediger zu dieser in der Kirchengeschichte wohl einmaligen Tat. Mit einer allgemeinen Sittenzucht durch den Rat wollten sie sich nicht zufrieden geben. Sie wollten eine strenge kirchliche Zucht. Die Unabhängigkeit und Selbständigkeit der Kirche war gefordert, wenngleich nur auf diesem einen speziellen Gebiet.

Wie sah Calvin diese Unabhängigkeit? Die Antwort, es habe damals in Genf wie fast überall in Europa eine Staatskirche bestanden und diese habe keine kirchliche Selbständigkeit zugelassen, ist zu einfach. Natürlich unterstanden die Pfarrer in Genf dem Rat, der sie berief, bezahlte und entlassen konnte. Calvin war ein realdenkender Mensch, der um die Gegebenheiten genau wußte. Er war aber auch ein bibelgebundener Theologe, der seine Glaubenserkenntnis nicht einfach den örtlichen Gegebenheiten unterordnete, sondern sich verpflichtet wußte, sie—falls notwendig—zu ändern. Wie verstand er das Verhältnis der Kirche zum Staat und umgekehrt? Es liegt nahe, eine frühere ausführliche Quelle zur Beantwortung heranzuziehen, die Institutio 1536. In ihr formuliert er seine Erkenntnis unabhängig von einer bestimmten örtlichen Situation, in genauem Hinhören auf die Heilige Schrift. Seine Darstellung ist—wie nicht anders zu erwarten—zeitgebunden, durchbricht aber die gängige Lehrmeinung.

Er behandelt das Thema Unabhängigkeit der Kirche in der Institutio 1536, wenn er im vorletzten Kapitel die beiden verschiedenen Regierungen (regimen duplex), nämlich die kirchliche Vollmacht (potestas ecclesiastica) und die Verwaltung des Staates (administratio politica), ausführlich erörtert. Dieses Problem war durch den alten Streit zwischen Papst und Kaiser präsent, jedoch konkreter noch durch die Machtansprüche der römischen Bischöfe. Wie äußert sich Calvin über beide Regierungen? Es sind von diesen Texten her Schlüsse auf seine grundsätzliche Einstellung und auf seine Haltung in seiner ersten Genfer Zeit 1536 bis 1538 möglich.

Wir folgten der Einteilung Calvins und diskutierten im Seminar jeden Abschnitt gesondert.

I. R*egimen* D*uplex* (*OS* 1:232-233; S*piess* 337-338[1])

Auffallend ist die Bezeichnung "doppelte Regierung im Menschen." Das duplex regimen ist faßbar und konkret, denn es wird volkstümlich nicht unzutreffend die geistliche und die nur eine Zeit während Rechtsprechung (iurisdictio) genannt, meint Calvin. "Im Menschen" darum, weil die geistliche Leitung (so ist wohl besser zu übersetzen) sich auf das "Leben des Seele" erstreckt und sich ausdrücklich auf die "innerliche Seele" bezieht; die staatliche Leitung ordnet die "äußerlichen Sitten." Daraus ist jedoch nicht zu schließen, daß sich nur die geistlich Leitung auf Herz und Gewissen ("im Menschen") bezieht, der staatlichen Leitung aber dieser Rang nicht zukommt. Die politische Leitung betrifft die "Pflichten des menschlichen und bürgerlichen Lebens" und regiert ebenfalls "im Menschen," das heißt, sie betrifft die inneren Regungen des Menschen, wenngleich sie nur "temporal" ist. Calvin will keine Leitung der anderen über- oder unterordnen. Ausdrücklich wünscht er keinen "Streit" gegen die staatliche Regierung. Eine erste Klärung, auch in Bezug auf die Ereignisse des Jahres 1538, ist damit gegeben.

Calvin wendet sich vielmehr gegen die Bischöfe ("Hirten der Kirche"), die die Christen mit ungeistlichen Gesetzen grausam bedrücken; gemeint sind etwa die selbsterfundenen Buß-, Beicht- und Ablaßgesetze. Sie sind gegen die "Regierung Christi" gerichtet. Ein neuer, wichtiger Begriff taucht damit auf.

II. P*otestas* E*cclesiastica* (*OS* 1:234, 235–237; S*piess* 339–40, 343–46)

Calvin will abseits des bischöflichen Anspruches eine biblisch-begründete "kirchliche Vollmacht" entwickeln. Läßt man alle Polemik und Abgrenzung gegen Rom beseite, so ergibt sich: Die kirchliche Vollmacht beruht darauf, daß im Neuen Bund "Christus uns mit der Predigt seines Evangeliums erschienen ist" (*OS* 1:236) und er Matth.28 den Auftrag gegeben hat, allen Völkern zu lehren, was er selbst befohlen hat (*OS* 1:234, 237). Diese Reihenfolge muß unbedingt eingehalten werden: "Christus allein, meine ich, muß reden, während die anderen schweigen" (*OS* 1:237). "Im Namen und durch das Wort Gottes" ist dann aber den Beauftragten eine Vollmacht (potestas) gegeben, zu befehlen, zu lehren oder zu raten (*OS* 1:234). Calvin betont die "Begrenzung dieser Vollmacht" durch das Wort Gottes (*OS* 1:237).

Zweierlei fällt auf: Erstens, aus dem Lehramt Christi (magisterium) ergibt sich der Dienst am Worte Gottes (ministerium verbi). Die Vollmacht ist alleine an die Predigt gebunden. Calvin kennt nur ein einziges Amt oder besser: einen einzigen Dienst. Zweitens spricht Calvin nur akthaft von Aufgaben und Tätigkeiten,

---

[1]Bernhard Spieß, *Unterricht in der christlichen Religion von 1536* (Wiesbaden, 1887). Die Klammern zeigen jeweils die Texte an, die im Seminar behandelt wurden.

nicht seinshaft von Vollmacht, Rang und Zuständigkeiten. Nur einmal betont Calvin, daß Ansehen und Würde "den Menschen nicht als solchen verliehen ist, sondern dem Amt (ministerium), dem sie vorstehen, oder um es noch einfacher auszudrüken: dem Wort Gottes, zu dem sie berufen sind" (*OS* 1:234). Selbst an dieser Stelle spricht er im Nachssatz und sonst durchgehen sogleich wieder von der aufgetragenen Tätigkeit, das heißt, von der Funktion, zu der berufen wird. Diese akthafte Ausdrucksweise ist charakteristisch für die Institutio 1536. Eine Ämterlehre kennt er noch nicht, nur eine Gebundenheit der Predigt an einen Auftrag. Die Lehre vom allgemeinen Priestertum aller Glaubenden wäre eine mögliche Konsequenz dieses Denkens, aber Calvin teilt sie bekanntlich nicht. Der Verkündigungsauftrag Christi richtet sich an einen bestimmten Personenkreis, der aber keinen Status hat, sondern in einem aufreibenden, unermüdlichen Dienst steht. Das akthafte, funktionale Denken Calvins verdient mehr Aufmerksamkeit in der Forschung.

III. Administratio Politica (*OS* 1:258–60, 264; Spiess 383–89, 393–94)

Zuerst wendet sich Calvin gegen "einige Fanatiker" (*OS* 1:259)—zweifellos sind die Wiedertäufer in Münster gemeint—die keine Obrigkeit und Gesetze über sich dulden wollen und ein "Christus alleine" proklamieren. Erstaunlich ist, daß Calvin sie bezichtigt, alles abzulehnen, was ihrer Freiheit (libertas) entgegensteht. Hat Calvin von den libertinistischen Ausschreitungen in Münster gewußt? Calvin proklamiert einen für unser Thema relevanten Grundsatz, wenn er äußert, das geistliche Reich Christi und die bürgerliche Ordnung seien zu trennen, aber die in Christus zugesagte Freiheit sei mit den ihr gesetzten Grenzen zu verbinden (*OS* 1:259). Gemeint ist die bürgerliche Ordnung.

Fragt man nach den Pflichten des Staates gegenüber der Religion, so äußert sich Calvin eher zurückhaltend: Unterdrückung des Götzendienstes, der Lästerung des Namens Gottes, der Schmähung der Wahrheit Gottes und anderer öffentlichen Ärgernisse gegen die Religion. Das Gewicht liegt auf der Sorge der Obrigkeit für Menschlichkeit und öffentlichen Frieden.

Calvin entwickelt fraglos eine Zwei-Reiche-Lehre. Aber es ist zu beachten, daß er zwar von einem duplex regimen spricht, beide Regierungen aber nicht parallel setzt. Aus dem Reich Christi wird eine kirchliche Vollmacht (potestas ecclesiastica) abgeleitet, dem Staat wird jedoch keine (göttliche) Vollmacht zugesprochen, sondern ihm wird nur eine politische Verwaltung (administratio politica) zugewiesen. Die Konsequenz könnte letztlich doch eine Abwertung des Staates sein, verglichen mit der Kirche.

Exkurs: Die Staatsform

Die Geschichte hat den "Calvinismus" mit der "Demokratie" unlösbar verbunden. Calvin selbst gebraucht das Wort "Demokratie" nicht. Das Wort findet sich erst in der Übersetzung von B. Spieß, 392:

> Vom Königtum zur Tyrannis (Gewaltherrschaft eines Einzelnen) unvermerkt überzugehen, ist nur ein Schritt auf abschüssiger Bahn; doch ebenso leicht setzt sich die Gewalt der Optimaten (Edelen) in die Oligarchie (Partei weniger Gewalthaber) um; bei weitem am leichtesten vollends geht die Volksherrschaft (Demokratie) in Empörung (Ochlokratie) über.

Calvin schreibt jedoch:

> Proclivis est a regno in tyrannidem lapsus; sed non multo difficilior, ab optimatum potestate in paucorum fractionem, multo vero facillimus a populari dominatione in seditionem. (*OS* 1:263)

Calvin gibt also keine Stellungnahme ab, weder für eine bestimmte Staatsform, noch dagegen. Die Staatsform ist keine "theologische" Frage. Die Überschrift "De administratione politica" steht immerhin im Kapitel "Über die christliche Freiheit."

IV. CONFRONTATIO MAGNA

Es ist nicht problemlos, einen früheren Text auf ein späteres Ereignis, die Abendmahlsverweigerung im Jahre 1538, zu beziehen. Doch soll dies mit aller Vorsicht geschehen.

Calvin gibt nach seiner Vertreibung aus Genf an, die Prediger hätten vor der Gemeinde klar ausgesprochen, "wir hätten das Sakrament entweiht, wenn das Volk nicht würdig dazu sei. Wir wiesen auf die Unordnung und Sünden hin, die bis heute noch in der Stadt herrschen, in freventlichen Lästerungen und Spottreden gegen Gott und sein Evangelium, wie auch in Unordnung und Parteiungen und Spaltungen. Denn öffentlich, ohne Bestrafung fielen Tausende von Spöttereien gegen Gottes Wort und selbst gegen das Abendmahl vor" (*CO* 10B, 189) Demnach richtete sich der Akt der Abendmahlsverweigerung gegen den Rat, der seine religiöse Pflicht vernachlässigt hat. Denn die von Calvin erhobenen Vorwürfe deken sich mit den in der Institutio 1536 aufgezählten Aufgaben des Staates gegenüber der Religion. Die Erwähnung des Abendmahls geht vielleich über die oben erwähnte Auflistung der Pflichten hinaus. Nach Calvins Ansicht, haben also die Prediger mit ihrem spektakulären Schritt nur den Rat auf seine Pflicht hingewiesen.

Aber dieser Hinweis geschah nicht verbal vor dem Rat, sondern durch Verhängung des kleinen Kirchenbanns, nämlich durch den Ausschlußes vom Abendmahl. Dem Rat und dem Volk wird die Unabhängigkeit der Kirche bzw. ihrer Hirten von der Obrigkeit in einer Staatskirche demonstriert. Das regnum Christi und die sich aus ihr ergebenden potestas ecclesiastica werden der staatlichen Gewalt übergeordnet. Die Ereignieße am Ostersonntag 1538 in Genf sind ein Akt der Unabhängigkeit der Kirche vom Staat.

Betrachten wir daraufhin noch einmal die oben erwähnten Abschnitte aus der Institutio 1536. Einerseits besteht die Freiheit des Evangeliums nur in den vom Staat gesetzten Grenzen. Calvin hatte in der Institutio keinen Grund gesehen, warum beide Regimente nicht ohne Konflikt nebeneinander bestehen könnten. Zwei Jahre später brach dieser Konflikt jedoch aus. Andererseits ist zu beachten, daß Calvin schon in der Institutio 1536 die Aufgabe der Prediger in der Weise beschreibt, daß sie notwendig mit einer Staatskirche bzw. mit der sie leitenden Obrigkeit in Konflikt kommen mußte:

> Mit dieser Vollmacht müssen die Hirten der Kirche ... ausgestattet sein, nämlich daß sie mit dem Wort Gottes, zu dessen Diener und Verwalter sie bestellt sind, zuversichtlich alles wagen, daß sie alle Kraft, Herrlichkeit und Erhabenheit der Welt zwingen, seiner (des Wortes) Majestät zu weichen und zu gehorchen, daß sie mit diesem Wort allen Menschen, vom höchsten bis zum letzten, gebieten, daß sie das Haus Christi erbauen, des Satans Herrschaft stürzen, die Schafe weiden, die Wölfe töten, die Gelehrigen ermuntern und unterweisen, die Widerspenstigen und Verstockten überführen, anfahren, widerlegen, lossprechen und binden, schließlich blitzen und donnern: aber alles in (der Vollmacht) durch das Wort Gottes. (*OS* 1:237)

V. Schlussfolgerungen

Calvin versucht beide Regierungen nebeneinander bestehen und wirken zu lassen, indem er ihnen verschiedene Aufgaben zuweist. Er will in der Institutio keine der anderen vor- oder nachordnen. Die Aufgaben der Prediger sind aber schon in der Institutio so umfassend, daß ein Zusammenstoß mit dem Rat zu erwarten war. Dieser erfolgt am Osterfest 1538, als die Prediger die Unabhängigkeit und Selbständigkeit der potestas ecclesiastica zeigten und vor Augen führten.

Es stellt sich die Aufgabe, zu untersuchen und aufzuzeigen, wie Calvin in der Folgezeit das Verhältnis von Staat und Kirche neu bestimmt.

Lucas Cranach, *Saint Peter with Keys to the Kingdom.*

Scholasticism in Calvin: A Question of Relation and Disjunction

Richard Muller

I. The Problem of Calvin's Relationship to Scholasticism

1. *Patterns in Scholarship*

The name of John Calvin and the term "scholasticism" have seldom been stated positively in the same breath. The reasons for assuming a profoundly negative relationship between Calvin and the scholastic doctors of the Middle Ages literally abound on the pages of Calvin's *Institutes*. Nonetheless, Calvin's theology—whether from the perspective of its methods or from the perspective of its contents—did not arise in a sixteenth-century vacuum. Not only did Calvin formulate his theology in distinct opposition to elements of late medieval and early sixteenth-century Roman Catholicism, he also quite subtly felt the influence of the medieval as well as the patristic past. It is worth recognizing from the outset that the Reformation altered comparatively few of the major *loci* of theology: the doctrines of justification, the sacraments, and the church received the greatest emphasis—while the doctrines of the God, the trinity, creation, providence, predestination, and the last things were taken over from the tradition by the magisterial Reformation virtually without alteration. In addition, many of the differences between the theological methods of the Reformation and those of the Middle Ages can be attributed to the development of logic and rhetoric and their impact on the relatively stable *disputatio* rather than to a vast rebellion in academic approach.[1]

---

[1]Cf. John Schneider, *Philip Melanchthon's Rhetorical Construal of Biblical Authority* (Lewiston: Edwin Mellen, 1990), 73–75, with Willem Van 't Spijker, *Principe, methode en functie van de theologie bij Andreas Hyperius*, Apeldoornse Studies, 26 (Kampen: J. H. Kok, 1990); Ian McPhee, "Conserver or Transformer of Calvin's Theology? A Study of the Origins and Development of Theodore Beza's Thought, 1550–1570" (Ph.D. dissertation: Cambridge University, 1979), xv–xviii; John Patrick Donnelly, *Calvinism and Scholasticism in Vermigli's Doctrine of Man and Grace* (Leiden: Brill, 1975), 193; Peter Fraenkel, *De l'écriture à la dispute: Le cas de l'Académie de Genève sous Théodore de Bèze* (Lausanne: Revue de Théologie et de Philosophie, 1977), 5–7, 36–39; Irena Backus, "L'enseignement de la logique à l'Academie de Genève entre 1559 et 1565," *Revue de Théologie et de Philosophie* 111 (1979): 153–63; William T. Costello, *The Scholastic Curriculum at Early Seventeenth-Century Cambridge* (Cambridge, Mass.: Harvard University Press, 1958), pp. 15–35; Mark H. Curtis, *Oxford and Cambridge in Transition, 1558–1642: An Essay on Changing Relations between the English University and English Society* (Oxford: Clarendon Press, 1959), 96; and with Stephen Spencer, "Reformed Scholasticism in Medieval Perspective: Thomas Aquinas and François Turrettini on Incarnation" (Ph.D. dissertation, Michigan State University, 1988), 88–95.

The frequently cited dissertation of Armand Aime LaVallee,[2] largely confines itself to an analysis of Calvin's criticism of the scholastics and comes to the still useful conclusion that Calvin perhaps "did not think of the Scholastics in terms of schools of thought" and that the generalized "scholastic theologian" of Calvin's critique is more likely than not a variety of late medieval nominalists such as Calvin might well have encountered around the edges of his education in Paris.[3] In addition, LaVallee concluded that the scholastic theologian of Calvin's critique is very much "the reversed image" of Calvin, very much a foil for Calvin's positive exposition of the teachings of the Reformation—and he also offered a critique of the editorial practice of citing various scholastics in the apparatus of the *Institutes* without any clear indication that Calvin had read their works.[4] The more subtle question of continuities between Calvin's thought and medieval scholastic theology—particularly in those places where Calvin does not offer negative comments about the older theology, but simply formulates a doctrinal point—was addressed in a massively erudite manner by Karl Reuter, who points quite convincingly to elements of late medieval Scotistic and Augustinian thought, specifically in the works of John Major and Gregory of Rimini, that are parallel to Calvin's teaching.[5] Reuter's detailed study of the medieval background of Calvin's thought has, however, been criticized for its reliance on the assumption that Calvin studied theology in Paris under John Major and, therefore, had direct and positive access to late medieval scholastic theology from the beginning of his intellectual career. As LaVallee argued and as Alexandre Ganoczy has clearly demonstrated, not only is it impossible to determine that Calvin studied with Major (indeed, the evidence points in the opposite direction); it is also not clear that Calvin's earliest theology evidences the direct influence of scholastic thought and method.[6] Reuter's response to Ganoczy has been subjected to almost microscopic scrutiny by Lane—with the result that the views of LaVallee and Ganoczy have been confirmed.[7] Thus, despite its insight into the positive relationship between Calvin's teaching and that of the medieval doctors, Reuter's work may not be able to identify either the definitive source of Calvin's inherent scholasticism or their precise trajectory in and through Calvin's thought. Similarly, Thomas F. Torrance's occasionally insightful essay on Calvin's "hermeneutics" assumes as a basic premise of

---

[2]Armand Aime LaVallee, "Calvin's Criticism of Scholastic Theology" (Ph.D. dissertation: Harvard University, 1967).

[3]LaVallee, "Calvin's Criticism," 237.   [4]LaVallee, "Calvin's Criticism," 237–41.

[5]Karl Reuter, *Das Grundverständnis der Theologie Calvins* (Neukirchen: Neukirchner, 1963), 35–36.

[6]LaVallee, "Calvin's Criticism," 242–49; Alexandre Ganoczy, *Le Jeune Calvin: Genèse et évolution de sa vocation réformatrice* (Wiesbaden: Steiner, 1966); in translation, *The Young Calvin*, trans. David Foxgrover and Wade Provo (Philadelphia: Westminster, 1987), 173–78.

[7]Cf. Karl Reuter, *Vom Scholaren bis zum jungen Reformator* (Neukirchen: Neukirchner, 1981); with A. N. S. Lane, "Calvin's Use of Bernard of Clairvaux," in *Bernard von Clairvaux: Rezeption und Wirkung im Mittelalter und in der Neuzeit,* ed. Kaspar Elm (Wiesbaden: Harrassowitz, 1994), 303–32.

its argument the early positive connection with scholasticism by way of Major, with the result that the modified scholastic background and framework that it constructs for Calvin's theory of knowledge and interpretation lacks clear and precise contact with Calvin's own work.[8] The scholastic influences remain, but their source or sources are obscure: whereas it is quite instructive to identify scholastic distinctions in Calvin's thought and then inquire into their medieval background, it is not useful—indeed, as Torrance's work demonstrates, it is quite perilous to assume a particular late medieval scholastic background and to understand Calvin's thought through its detailed and often technical language.

Recent essays by David Steinmetz, Susan Schreiner, John Thompson, Heiko Oberman, and Jelle Faber have looked in detail at aspects of the scholastic background and at Calvin's dialogue with it.[9] On the one hand, all of these scholars have taken up the question of Calvin's encounter with several themes from Scotist and nominalist theology—notably the distinction between *potentia absoluta* and *potentia ordinata*—against a background of recent reappraisal of Scotism and nominalism, in which a theme of divine transcendence has been emphasized at the same time as the claim (found in older scholarship) that the language of *potentia absoluta* indicated an utterly arbitrary God.[10] On the other hand, all four

[8]Thomas F. Torrance, *The Hermeneutics of John Calvin* (Edinburgh: Scottish Academic Press, 1988); cf. Alister E. McGrath, "John Calvin and Late Medieval Thought: A Study in Late Medieval Influences upon Calvin's Theological Development," *Archiv für Reformationsgeschichte* 77 (1986): 58–78, for an attempt to balance Reuter's and Torrance's approach with Ganoczy's findings by hypothesizing a somewhat generalized, early influence of the *via moderna* and what McGrath calls a *schola Augustiniana moderna* on Calvin's thought. McGrath's argument in effect supports Reuter's and Torrance's without recourse to John Major's; see the trenchant critique of McGrath in Heiko A. Oberman, *Initia Calvini: The Matrix of Calvin's Reformation* (Amsterdam: Koninklijke Nederlandse Akademie van Wetenschappen, 1991), 14.

[9]David C. Steinmetz, "Calvin and the Absolute Power of God," in *Journal of Medieval and Renaissance Studies* 28 (Spring 1988): 65–79; idem, "Calvin among the Thomists," in *Biblical Hermeneutics in Historical Perspective* (Grand Rapids: Eerdmans, 1991), 198–214; Susan E. Schreiner, "Through a Mirror Dimly: Calvin's Sermons on Job," in *Calvin Theological Journal* 21 (1986): 175–93; idem, "Exegesis and Double Justice in Calvin's Sermons on Job," in *Church History* 58 (1989): 322–38, and idem, *Where Shall Wisdom Be Found? Calvin's Exegesis of Job from Medieval and Modern Perspectives* (Chicago: University of Chicago Press, 1994); John L. Thompson, *John Calvin and the Daughters of Sarah: Women in Regular and Exceptional Roles in the Exegesis of Calvin, His Predecessors and His Contemporaries* (Geneva: Droz, 1992); idem, "The Immoralities of the Patriarchs in the History of Exegesis: A Reappraisal of Calvin's Position," in *Calvin Theological Journal* 26 (1991): 9–46; and idem, "Patriarchs, Polygamy and Private Resistance: John Calvin and Others on Breaking God's Rules," in *Sixteenth Century Journal* 25 (1994): 3–28; Oberman, *Initia Calvini*, 13–15; Jelle Faber, "Nominalisme in Calvijns preken over Job," in *Een sprekend begin*, ed. R. ter Beek, et al. (Kampen: Uitgeverij Van den Berg, 1993), 68–85.

[10]Cf. ,e.g., Paul Vignaux, "Nominalisme," s.v. in *Dictionnaire de théologie catholique*, 2.1, cols. 717–84; idem, *Justification et prédestination au XIVe siècle: Duns Scot, Pierre d'Auriole, Guillaume d'Occam, Grégoire de Rimini* (Paris: Letouzey et Ane, 1934); and idem, *Nominalisme au XIVe siècle* (Montreal: Institute d'études médiévales, 1948); Heiko A. Oberman, *Archbishop Thomas Bradwardine: A Fourteenth-Century Augustinian: A Study of His Theology in its Historical Context* (Utrecht: Kemiak E Zoon, 1958); *The Harvest of Medieval Theology: Gabriel Biel and Late Medieval Nominalism*, revised ed. (Grand Rapids: Eerdmans, 1967); idem, *Masters of the Reformation: Emergence of a New Intellectual Climate in Europe*, trans. Dennis Martin (Cambridge: Cambridge University Press, 1981); and idem,

have noted that, despite the significant impact of Scotism on Calvin, the Reformer also distanced himself at crucial points from the older theology and rejected not only interpretations or abuses of scholastic distinctions, but some of the distinctions themselves.[11] Schreiner and Steinmetz have also indicated similarities and differences between Calvin's interpretation of select passages in Scripture and the Thomistic literal trajectory in medieval exegesis.[12] Actual sources have remained obscure while, at the same time, a predominantly "Scotist-nominalist" background to Calvin's assumptions concerning divine transcendence and hiddenness has been identified alongside what can be called the "Thomistic" trajectory of literal exegesis. (We remember, of course, that the Franciscan Nicholas of Lyra also stands in this trajectory.[13]) In addition, more subtle relationships than scholarship has previously recognized have been outlined between Calvin's use, acceptance, or rejection of the terms and concepts from earlier theological tradition and their use by medieval theologians and exegetes.[14]

2. The Identification of "Scholasticism"

The problem of the relationship of scholasticism to Calvin (and to later Calvinism as well) is complicated, moreover, by the tendency of much twentieth-century Protestant theology and historiography to view scholasticism as a highly speculative and rationalistic system of thought bound to Aristotelianism and to certain specific theological and philosophical conclusions, characteristic of the thirteenth, fourteenth, and fifteenth centuries, the primary goal of which was to

---

"Some Notes on the Theology of Nominalism with Attention to Its Relation to the Renaissance," in *Harvard Theological Review* 53 (1960): 47–76; Francis Oakley, "Pierre D'Ailly and the Absolute Power of God: Another Note on the Theology of Nominalism," in *Harvard Theological Review* 56 (1963): 59–73; and William J. Courtenay, "Nominalism in Late Medieval Religion," in Trinkhaus and Oberman, eds., *The Pursuit of Holiness,*. 26–59; and idem, "The Dialectic of Omnipotence in the High and Late Middle Ages," in Rudavsky, ed., *Divine Omniscience and Omnipotence in Medieval Philosophy,* 243–69; cf. the collection of Courtenay's essays, *Covenant and Causality in Medieval Thought: Studies in Philosophy, Theology, and Economic Practice* (London: Variorum Reprints, 1984).

[11]Cf. Steinmetz, "Calvin and the Absolute Power of God," 77–79, with Faber, "Nominalisme in Calvijns preken over Job," 84–85.

[12]Susan E. Schreiner, "'Through a Mirror Dimly': Calvin's Sermons on Job," in *Calvin Theological Journal* 21 (1986): 175–93; idem, *Where Shall Wisdom Be Found?* 91, 152–55, et passim; and David C. Steinmetz, "Calvin among the Thomists," in *Biblical Hermeneutics in Historical Perspective* (Grand Rapids: Eerdmans, 1991), 198–214.

[13]On Lyra's exegesis, its place in the development of the Biblical commentary, and its significant use of Aquinas' exegetical work, see Ceslaus Spicq, *Esquisse d'une histoire de l'exégèse latine au moyen âge* (Paris: J. Vrin, 1944), 335–42, with F. Vernet, "Lyre, Nicolas de," s.v. in *Dictionnaire de théologie catholique,* 11/1, cols. 1410–22.

[14]Cf. Oberman, *Initia Calvini,* 117–21, with Schreiner, *Where Shall Wisdom Be Found?* 106, 115.

produce a synthesis of Christian theology and Greek philosophy.[15] When, however, scholasticism is rightly defined as a dialectical method of the schools, histor-
ically rooted in the late patristic period, particularly in the thought of Augustine,
and developed throughout the Middle Ages in the light of classical logic and rhetoric, constructed with a view to the authority of text and tradition, and devoted
primarily to the exposition of Scripture and the theological topics that derive
from it using the best available tools of exegesis, logic, and philosophy,[16] a rather
different picture emerges. In other words, if we oblige the understanding (characteristic of generations of scholarly study of medieval thought) of "scholasticism"
as a method that, in itself, did not necessarily prejudice theological conclusions,
we are pressed to offer a series of qualifications. Some distinction becomes necessary between the relationship of the substance of Calvin's thought to aspects of
older theology (method notwithstanding) and the relationship of Calvin's expository methods to the methods used by the older theology.

So too, the relationship between ideas and method must not be overlooked:
recourse to the ideas of a particular thinker or thinkers may result, if only mini-
mally, in some acceptance of the method through which the ideas were con-
veyed—or *vice versa*. One of the points of overlap between these issues of method
and content is, of course, the use of distinctions: the scholastic method resolved
problems and seeming contradictions by generating distinctions—and the use of
these distinctions in turn affected the content of theology. Nonetheless, the caveat
remains in force here as well: the acceptance of distinctions (like those between
absolute and ordained power, proper and alien work, the decree and its execution,
the sufficiency and efficiency of Christ's death) does influence content, primarily
in terms of patterns of exposition and the identification of various sub-issues as
identified by the distinction, but it does not determine the final result of an argument. All of the distinctions just noted fit as easily into semi-Pelagian as into strict
Augustinian argumentation or, in the era of the Reformation, into Arminian as
well as Reformed theology.[17]

[15]Cf. Brian G. Armstrong, *Calvinism and the Amyraut Heresy: Protestant Scholasticism and
Humanism in Seventeenth Century France* (Madison: University of Wisconsin Press, 1969), 32; idem,
"The Changing Face of French Protestantism: The Influence of Pierre Du Moulin," in *Calviniana: Ideas
and Influence of Jean Calvin*, ed. Robert V. Schnucker (Kirksville, Mo.: Sixteenth Century Journal Pub-
lishers, 1988), 145–49; S. van der Linde, "Het 'Griekse' Denken in Kerk, Theologie en Geloofspraktijk,"
Theologia Reformata 28 (1985): 260.

[16]Cf. David Knowles, *The Evolution of Medieval Thought* (New York: Vintage Books, 1962), 87;
with James A. Weisheipl, "Scholastic Method," in *NCE* 12, p. 1145; G. Fritz and Allen Michel, "Scholas-
tique," in *DTC*, 14/2, col. 1691; and Armand Maurer, *Medieval Philosophy* (New York: Random House,
1962), p. 90.

[17]Cf. Oberman, *Thomas Bradwardine*, 101–2, 120; idem, *Harvest of Medieval Theology*, 30–56,
96–105; idem, "Some Notes on the Theology of Nominalism," 56–68; Richard A. Muller, *God, Creation
and Providence in the Thought of Jacob Arminius: Sources and Directions of Scholastic Protestantism in
the Era of Early Orthodoxy* (Grand Rapids: Baker Book House, 1991), 184–85, 190–91, 202–5, 228–29.

II. Scholasticism in Calvin: Relation and Disjunction

According to Ganoczy's measured conclusions, "the first edition of the *Institutes* reveals only a very limited and superficial knowledge of scholastic theologians," as indicated by Calvin's very unsystematic and polemical use of Lombard and Gratian. At an early stage in his development, Calvin evidences no knowledge of major scholastic theologians like Aquinas, Duns Scotus, Occam, Gregory of Rimini, or Pierre d'Ailly and, indeed, no knowledge of the thought of John Major.[18] Ganoczy also argues that, both in style and in content, this use can be traced to Calvin's study of Luther, particularly of the German Reformer's *Babylonian Captivity of the Church*, rather than to a detailed study of Lombard and Gratian. At an early stage in his thought, Calvin most probably "assimilated—without knowing it—diverse elements of the scholastic system" through his reading of Luther. In addition, the scholastic philosophy, to which Calvin was most surely introduced in the basic course of study at the Collège de Montaigue, "contributed to the dialectical structure of Calvin's thought and indirectly to the elaboration of his theological doctrine." At the same time, however, "his conscious position was characterized from the start by an indignant refusal to accept this 'theology of the sophists.'"[19] To this we may add that the study of philosophical matters by the identification of topic or locus, prevalent after the fifteenth-century work of Rudolf Agricola, together with the determination of conclusions through the process of academic disputation, also, surely, had its impact on Calvin. LaVallee has quite convincingly hypothesized that Calvin studied scholastic theology privately after his conversion and that much of what Calvin knew came from contemporary Roman Catholic commentaries on the *Sentences* (in which, presumably, the opinions of major teachers of previous centuries were summarized).[20] In addition, Calvin most certainly read medieval theology after 1536 and, we may hypothesize, he read more fully in the work of Biblical commentators like Nicholas of Lyra and Denis the Carthusian than he did in the dogmatic writings of the period.

1. *Calvin's Polemics against Scholasticism: Indications of Relationship, Positive and Negative*

Calvin's polemical references to the scholastics or, as he also identifies them, the sophists, are nearly all general attacks which, except for the occasional reference to Lombard, seldom identify the scholastic theologians to whose teaching

---

[18]Ganoczy, *Young Calvin*, 176; cf. LaVallee, "Calvin's Critique," 237–41.

[19]Ganoczy, *Young Calvin*, 177–78.

[20]LaVallee, "Calvin's Criticism," 249. One such work was Gabriel Biel's *Collectorium*, but (as LaVallee noted) we have no evidence that Calvin ever examined it. The difficulty with the hypothesis, obviously, lies in the identification of the work or works that Calvin read.

Calvin objects. In some cases, Calvin appears to attack as "scholastic" views not held by the major medieval doctors—and, after his attack, to adopt positions that actually reflect teachings of the medieval scholastics. Quite notable among Calvin's mature attacks on scholasticism is his sharp declamation against the distinction between *potentia absoluta* and *potentia ordinata*, and his related attack on the use of this and similar distinctions to define the divine transcendence as *ex lex*.[21] In the sermons on Job (the original of which exists in French only), Calvin speaks of the teaching of "the doctors of the Sorbonne" as "a devilish blasphemy forged in Hell"[22] because it identifies the "absolute" power of God as "lawless"— indeed, because it violates the fundamental assumption of the inseparability of the divine attributes.[23] What is notable here is not only the specification of "Sorbonistes," and the association of their theology with a notion of God as *ex lex* (not characteristic of the theology of the great scholastics of earlier times), but also the fact that Calvin opposes this particular "scholastic" or Sorbonnistic teaching with equally "scholastic" assumptions concerning the divine simplicity and the essential identity of the divine attributes.

Similarly, Calvin had little sympathy with traditional distinctions between God's positive will and God's permissive willing, although his critique of such distinctions not only placed him clearly in the tradition of medieval Augustinianism but also drew positively on other scholastic distinctions, such as those concerned with the hidden and manifest will or wills of God (*voluntas Dei beneplaciti / signi*). Thus, Calvin can insist that "though to our apprehension the will of God is manifold, yet he does not in himself will opposites, but, according to his manifold wisdom, transcends our senses, until such time as it shall be given us to know how he

---

[21]*Institutes*, 3.23.2: "Neque tamen commentum ingerimus absolutae potentiae: quod sicuti profanum est, ita merito detestabile nobis esse debet. Non fingimus Deus exlegem, qui sibi ipsi lex est.... Dei autem voluntas non modo ab omni vitio pura, sed summa perfectionis regula, etiam legum omnium lex est"; cf. the discussion by Steinmetz, "Calvin and the Absolute Power of God," 65–79. On the history of the concept, see: William J. Courtenay, *Capacity and Volition: A History of the Distinction of Absolute and Ordained Power* (Bergamo: P. Lubrina, 1990). Cf. Jean Calvin, *Sermons sur le Livre de Iob*, in *CO* 34:331–44; cf. John Calvin, *Sermons of Maister Iohn Calvin, upon the Book of Iob* (London, 1574), especially sermon 88 (pp. 412–16); and see the discussion in Schreiner, *Where Shall Wisdom be Found?* 110–20.
[22]Calvin, *Sermons sur le Livre de Iob, CO* 34, col. 339: "Et de fait, quand ces docteurs Sorboniques disent, que le Dieu a une puissance absolue, c'est blaspheme diabolique qui a esté forgé aux enfers"; cf. Calvin, *Sermons on Job*, col. 415:44–45.
[23]Calvin, *Sermons sur le Livre de Iob*, in *CO* 34, col. 336: "Or en cela Iob blaspheme Dieu: car combien que la puissance de Dieu soit infinie, si est-ce que de la faire ainsi absolue, c'est imaginer en luy une tyrannie, et cela est du tout contraire à sa maiesté, car nostre Seigneur ne veut point estre puissant qu'il ne soit iuste: et ce sont choses inseparables, que sa iustice et sa puissance"; cf. Calvin, *Sermons on Iob*, col. 414:2–5.

mysteriously wills what now seems adverse to his will."[24] Calvin also notes how Scripture in general and the book of Job in particular keep us "humble" by noting the theme of the hidden will of God.[25] And whereas Calvin typically objected to the standard distinction between positive and permissive willing falls short inasmuch as nothing can happen "without the will of God"—he could, if pressed, accept the Augustinian qualification that the permission of God must be understood as a "willing" rather than an "unwilling" permission.[26] Calvin's assault on scholastic distinctions, therefore, often occurs within the bounds of rather traditional constructions that he shared with many medieval theologians.

His discussion of the object of faith, perhaps more than any other place in the *Institutes*, evidences an unwillingness to deal with the details of scholastic theology. Calvin writes,

> When faith is discussed in the schools, they identify God as the object of faith *simpliciter*, and by a fleeting speculation ... lead miserable souls astray rather than direct them to a definite goal. For, since "God dwells in inaccessible light" Christ must become our intermediary.... This evil, then, like innumerable others, must be attributed to the Schoolmen, who have, as it were, drawn a veil over Christ to hide him. Unless we look straight toward him, we shall wander through endless labyrinths.[27]

On the one hand, Calvin's point that scholastic theology drew attention away from Christ, is a truism of Reformation era polemic—on the other, it falls considerably short of being a description of scholastic theology either in general or in particular. Few medieval scholastics claimed, without qualification, that God is the object of faith.

---

[24]*Institutes*, 3.24.17: "quamvis multiplex sit Dei voluntas quoad sensum nostrum, non tamen eum hoc et illud in se velle, sed pro sapientia sua varie multiplici ... attonitos reddere sensus nostros, donec cognoscere nobis dabitur mirabiliter eum velle quod nunc videtur esse voluntati eius adversum."

[25]*Institutes*, 1.17.2: "sed ... arcanam Dei providentiam reverenter suspicere jubeat. Hujus quoque altitudinis elogium ponitur in libro Job, quod mentes nostras humiliet."

[26]*Institutes*, 1.18.1, 3: "Tergiversando itaque effugiunt, Dei tantum permissu, non etiam voluntate hoc fieri....[3] Unde [Augustinus] exclamat: magna opera Dei, exquisita in omnes voluntates eius (Ps. 111:2); ut miro et ineffabili modo non fiat praeter ejus voluntatem quod etiam contra ejus fit voluntatem: quia non fieret si non sineret; nec utique nolens sinit, sed volens, nec sineret bonus fieri male, nisi omnipotens etiam de malo facere posset bene."

[27]*Institutes*, 3.2.1–2: "Imo quum in scholis de fide disputant, Deum ejus objectum simpliciter vocando, evanida speculatione ... miseras animas rapiunt transversum magis quam ad scopum dirigant. Nam quum Deus lucem inaccessam habitat, Christum occurrere medium necesse est.... Ergo hoc malum, ut alii innumera, Scholasticis acceptum referri par est, qui velut obducto velo Christum texerunt, in cujus intuitum nisi recta intenti simus, per multos labyrinthos semper vagari continget"; cf. 2.6.4

The theological tradition of the Augustinian order, as presented in the work of Giles of Rome and Gregory of Rimini, came very close to Calvin's perspective when it identified the *obiectum theologiae* as *Deus creator et redemptor* of *Deus creator, redemptor, et glorificator*. Not only do these latter definitions have a clear affinity with Calvin's insistence that faith looks to God in Christ, they also most surely, point directly toward Calvin's theme of the twofold knowledge of God, the so-called *duplex cognitio Dei*, according to which God is known primarily as Creator and Redeemer. On this issue, then, we may fairly ask whether Calvin knew of the variety of scholastic formulation—or whether he ignored it for the sake of polemic. If the *duplex cognitio Dei* offers any indication of an answer, we may hypothesize here that Calvin knew and, very quietly, without citation, drew on scholastic views of the *obiectum theologiae*, and then turned about to polemicize broadly about what he knew to be either a caricature or a minority opinion. Perhaps, too, the polemic was more pointed and specific than Calvin's Latin "*scholastici*" indicates: the 1560 French text offers "théologiens Sorboniques."

Similarly, Calvin accuses the scholastics of "wearing down all the force of faith and almost annihilating it by their obscure definition."[28] Here too, the point is generalized and overstated for the sake of polemical rhetoric—at the same time that Calvin's own definition of faith carries with it clear reflections of traditional, scholastic definition. Indeed, Calvin's inclusion of *fiducia* in his definition (particularly given his typical identification of "heart" as the will) places him in direct accord with most scholastic definitions, where, quite typically, faith is distinguished into a twofold act of intellect (knowledge of a truth and the judgment that it is indeed true) and an act of the will (assent to or apprehension of the truth for one's self). Thus, Aquinas distinguishes "between faith and all other intellectual operations" on the ground that, whereas the intellect "first conceives a simple meaning" and then, in an "act of judgment," recognizes the meaning to be either true or false, faith consists in this but also in something more, an assent of the will to the truth. "The author of faith," Aquinas writes,

> is he who produces the believer's assent to the truth declared. Mere hearing is not a sufficient cause. The assent is caused by the will, not by any necessity of reason. And therefore a preacher or herald cannot produce faith. God is the cause of faith, for he alone can alter our wills.[29]

---

[28]*Institutes*, 3.2.2: "Praeterquam vero quod calignosa sua definitione totam vim fidei deterunt ac fere exinaniunt...."

[29]Thomas Aquinas, *De Veritate*, 1 and 3, ad. 12, translated in *St. Thomas Aquinas: Theological Texts*, selected and translated with notes by Thomas Gilby (Durham, N.C.: Labyrinth Press, 1982), 195, 198.

As Augustine, Lombard, Aquinas, and virtually all the scholastics comment, it is one thing to "believe concerning God (*credere Deo* or *de Deo*)," another to "believe God (*credere Deum*)," and yet another to "believe in God (*credere in Deum*)"— which is to say, to believe that what is said about God is true, to believe that God exists (both of which levels of belief are found in good and evil people alike), and to believe in or cling to God in love, which last is the character of the faith that jus-tifies.[30] Calvin's generalized polemic against scholasticism and the "scholastics," therefore, frequently points in two directions—toward a strong distaste for spe-cific scholastic formulae, but also toward an appropriation of other elements of medieval scholastic theology, often as the means by which elements of scholastic thought viewed by Calvin as problematic might be refuted.

These (and other) significant discrepancies between Calvin's claims in his cri-tiques of *scholastici* and the actual teachings of the "scholastics" raise the historical and analytical question of how literally we ought to understand Calvin's terms. On the one hand, some license must be granted to his polemic—and, on the other, some insight may be provided by Calvin's French usage: in the 1560 French *Institutes* and in Calvin's French sermons, the target of his critique is often identi-fied, not as the "scholastici," but, with considerably greater specificity, as the *théo-logiens Sorboniques*.[31] Indeed, when one examines the texts of the 1559 and 1560 *Institutes*, a surprising difference of usage appears. Calvin refers to the "scholas-tici" twenty-six times in the edition of 1559; all of the instances of the word in the 1539 edition passed over into 1559 and have their parallels in the French of 1560.[32] Of the twenty-six (or, if we include the "quae in scholis" = "sorbonistes" of 3.2.8, twenty-seven) references to "scholastici" found in the Latin text of the 1559

---

[30]Peter Lombard, *Sententiae*, III, d.23, c.4, s.1, citing Augustine, *In Ioannem*, 29.6: "Aliud est enim credere in Deum, aliud credere Deo, aliud credere Deum. Credere Deo, est credere vera esse quae loquitur: quod et mali faciunt; et nos credimus homini, sed non in hominem. Credere Deum, est cre-dere quod ipse sit deus; quod etiam mali faciunt. Credere in Deum, est credendo amare, credendo in eum ire, credendo ei adhaerere et eius membris incorporari"; cf. the variant form of the statement in Thomas Aquinas, *Summa theologiae*, IIa IIae, q. 2, a. 2.

[31]On the "théologiens Sorboniques" see James K. Farge, *Biographical Register of Paris Doctors of Theology, 1500–1536*, Subsidia Medievalia, 10 (Toronto: PIMS, 1980), and idem, *Orthodoxy and Reform in Early Reformation France—The Faculty of Paris, 1500–1536* (Leiden: E. J. Brill, 1980).

[32]Cf. LaVallee, "Calvin's Criticism," 267–69, where the author offers a collation of translations showing the "interchangeability of terms" such as *adversarii* and *Papistes*, *scholastici* and *Sorbonnistes* in Calvin's *Institutes*. In the above analysis I also rely on John Calvin, *Institutes of the Christian Religion of John Calvin: 1539, Text and Concordance*, ed. Richard F. Wevers, 4 vols. (Grand Rapids: Meeter Center for Calvin Studies, 1988); *Institutio christianae religionis* (1559), in *Ioannis Calvini opera quae supersunt omnia*, 59 vols., ed. Guilielmus Baum, Eduardus Cunitz, and Eduardus Reuss (Brunswick: Schwetschke, 1863–1900), vols. 29–30; *Institution de la religion chrestienne de Calvin*, texte originel de 1541, réimprimé sous la direction de Abel Lefranc par Henri Chateain et Jacques Pannier (Paris: Librairie Honoré Champion, 1911); idem, *Institution de la religion Chrestienne* (Geneva: Crespin, 1560), and I have also consulted *Institution de la religion chrétienne*, 4 vols. (Geneva: Labor et Fides, 1955–58).

Institutes, fifteen are rendered precisely as "scolastiques" in the 1560 *Institutes* while twelve are altered in their passage into the French of 1560. Of these twelve Latin references to "scholastici," one is rendered "théologiens romanistes," two are translated as "sophistes," and the remaining nine appear as "théologiens sorboniques" or "sorbonistes." There are also noted the four references to the Sorbonne and its teachers found in the 1539 *Institutes*: All carry over verbatim into the French in 1541 and are retained in 1559 and 1560.[33]

The polemic against the Sorbonne, therefore, although resident in Calvin's Latin text from 1539 onward, intensifies in the French of 1541 and retains that intensity in subsequent French editions through 1560. It is, therefore, principally a polemic directed toward the French audience: the rendering of "scholastici" as "théologiens sorboniques" represents a reading characteristic of Calvin's movement from Latin to French, as seen from the texts of the 1539 and 1559 *Institutes* and is largely focused on materials found in book 3 of the *Institutes*. Calvin also never moves from the Latin "sorbonistae" to a French "scolastiques" or some other equivalent. Thus, the word "scholastici" does not appear at all in *Institutes*, book 1 (despite the several attacks on medieval theology and philosophy) and the references to "scholastici" in book 2 are all rendered "scolastiques." It is in book 3, however, that the term "théologiens sorboniques" appears, with the result that of the fifteen Latin references to "scholastici," eight are rendered "théologiens sorboniques," one (3.4.26) alters syntax and renders "universi scholastici" as "toutes leurs écoles," and two are rendered "sophistes"—leaving only three references to "scolastiques" in the French. In the Latin of book 4, there are five references to "scholastici," two appear in French as "scolastiques," one as the synonymous construction "docteurs de l'école," one as "théologiens romanistes," and one as "théologiens sorboniques."

Beyond these variations, two other stylistic features characteristic of the translation process should be noted. First, in all cases where Calvin's Latin reference is to Peter Lombard and other (unidentified) scholastics—2.2.4; 2.2.16; 2.17.6; 3.4.26–the French translation gives "scolastiques." The single exception to this generalization appears to be *Institutes*, 3.3.43, where Lombard's teaching is mentioned, but then contrasted with the greater abuses of the later schools: here, "in scholis" is rendered "ez escolles des Sophistes, c'est à dire Sorboniques." And, second, in the few cases in which Calvin's reference to "scholastici" is not entirely negative—his reference to scholastic use of Augustinian definition (2.2.4), the two references to "saniores scholastici" (2.2.6 and 3.14.11) and one to a more "mod-

---

[33]I.e., *Institutes*, i.e. 2.3.13; 3.15.7; 3.18.8; 3.18.9. There is also the "ineptos istos rabulas, sorbonistas et canonistas" that occurs in the 1543–59 Latin (4.19.24) and carries over into the 1545–60 French as "ces badaux de theologiens Sorboniques & Canonistes."

est" formulation of the scholastics (4.17.13)—he translates "scholastici" as "scolastiques," never as "sorbonistes." When Lombard's formulations are cited and, therefore, when the older scholasticism is identified in debate, Calvin typically uses "scholastici" or "scolastiques." In cases where Lombard is not mentioned, and potentially where a more recent scholastic abuse is indicated, Calvin's French quite frequently specifies the theology of the Sorbonne. Thus, while "scholastici" can occasionally function as a neutral term, "théologiens sorboniques" is invariably a term of reproach.

We have already noted the concentration of the French usage "théologiens sorboniques" in book 3 of the *Institutes*. It is also the case that the usage is largely confined to the discussions of faith (3.2), repentance, confession, and penance (3.4), righteousness and justification (3.11.15; 3.14.11–12; 3.17.15), and one reference in the discussion of the relationship between predestination and sin (3.23.6). Even so, three out of the four references to the Sorbonne that carry over from 1539 into the later editions (i.e., 3.15.7; 3.18.8; 3.18.9) indicate a similar pattern of reference. If we add to this list the numerous references in the sermons on Job—where the issue is the problem of divine transcendence and the ramifications of speculation on the *potentia absoluta* for the discussion of divine and human righteousness—it becomes possible to identify, in the midst of Calvin's seemingly unspecified attacks on "scholastici" and, in particular, in several places where the general language and argument of the Latin *Institutes* could be faulted for imprecision, a rather pointed and precise attack *not* on the older scholastic tradition but on a strain of contemporary scholastic theology viewed by Calvin as especially problematic in view of its extreme nominalism.

What is significant here is that a large number of the references to "sorbonistes" in book 3 of the *Institutes* are not the result of Calvin's heated dispute with the Paris doctors over the articles drawn up by the Sorbonne at the behest of Francis I (to whom Calvin had dedicated the first edition of his *Institutes*). The articles appeared in 1543 and Calvin responded with his *Articuli a facultate sacrae theologiae Parisiensi determinati super materiis fidei nostrae hodie controversis: Cum antidoto* in 1544.[34] Most of the polemic against the Sorbonne in *Institutes*, book 3, originated in the 1539 Latin and was intensified in the 1541 French translation. (The added polemics of the 1543–59 Latin and 1545–60 French text, largely belonging to *Institutes*, book 4, with their references to "les sorbonistes" can surely be traced to the debate over the condemnatory articles.) Calvin's distaste for the Sorbonne arose, therefore, before his major conflict with the Paris doctors: it may

---

[34]*CO* 7, cols. 1–44. Calvin's text contains the articles of the Sorbonne doctors. Also see the French in the *Recueil des opuscules*, cols. 531–71, and cf. the discussion in de Greef, *Writings of John Calvin*, 159–60.

be related to his earlier conflict with the sometime Reformer and sometime apostate, Pierre Caroli, beginning in 1536: Caroli had a doctorate from the Sorbonne.[35] There was, certainly, an intensification of Calvin's problems with the Sorbonne after 1543--and his French usage then, certainly, takes on the accents of what Oberman has identified as the "refugee" mentality and the theology of an "underground" church,[36] for it was on the ground of the royally sanctioned Sorbonne articles that many of Calvin's French associates and students were executed for heresy. What we cannot conclude, however, is that the distaste for the Sorbonne was a later phenomenon caused by the articles of 1543. For his French audience, Calvin early on portrayed the Sorbonne as the extreme and abusively scholastic adversary, and he specifically linked his polemic to certain doctrinal issues.

2. *Calvin's Positive Appropriation of Scholastic Distinctions in the Institutes and Treatises and Commentaries*

Of course, once the "scholastic" opponents are specified in this manner, Calvin theology appears less overtly antagonistic to medieval scholasticism in general. Indeed, by way of contrast with the preceding examples, we can look to a wide variety of elements of Calvin's theology as indicators of the positive side of his relationship to scholastic theology. Thus, while Calvin's identification of Christ as Mediator according to both natures appears quite contrary to traditional Catholic doctrine, it also contains echoes of the medieval discussion of the problem of mediation, particularly among the Franciscan doctors: Bonaventure could, for example, declare "verumtamen *mediator* esse non posset, nisi est *medius*," and that Christ was *medius* by reason of the union of the two natures.[37] Scotus offers much the same argument.[38] The *medium*, argues Biel, has something in common with two extremes: to this concept the term *mediator* adds the idea of an *officium reconciliationis*. Christ is thus *medium* between extremes "per paticipationem utriusque nature divine & humane" but "Est autem mediator: quia existens medium officium reconciliationis exhibuit secundum naturam humanam tantum...."[39] Calvin's Christology reflects the medieval discussion by pressing the question of

[35]See Richard C. Gamble, "Calvin's Theological Method: The Case of Caroli," in *Calvin: Erbe und Auftrag. Festschrift für Wilhelm Heinrich Neuser zum 65. Geburtstag*, ed. Willem Van 't Spijker (Kampen: Kok Pharos, 1991), 130–37

[36]Oberman, *Initia Calvini*, 39–43.

[37]Bonaventure, III *Sent.* d. 19, a. 2, q. 1, ad. 1.

[38]Duns Scotus, III *Sent.* d. 19, q. unica: "unde tandem concludit quod Christus dicitur mediator non secundum divinam sed secundum humanam in qua illa suscepit quibus nos toti trinitati reconciliat ut passionem mortemque..." but "quod mediatoris officio congruit cum medium sapiat proprietatem utriusque extremorum."

[39]Biel, *Collectorium* III, d. xix, q. unica, art. 3, dubium 4.

Christ's median status to the point that he could conclude that Christ must be understood as mediator according to both natures.[40] Similarly, Calvin's way of arguing the sufficiency of Christ's merit on the ground of the divine decree may be an extension of the Scotist critique of Anselm's satisfaction theory: whereas Scotus had argued that Christ's merit could not be infinite because it rested on the obedience of the human nature and God merely accepted it as payment, Calvin appears to argue that the payment was infinite because God decreed that it would be so.[41]

There are also numerous instances in which Calvin either appropriates a scholastic distinction without comment and incorporates it into his own theology or identifies the distinction as belonging to the older theology and its method and acknowledges its correctness and its usefulness to his own thought. Thus, the distinction between the eternal decree and its execution in time occupies a fairly prominent place in Calvin's discussions of the relationship between God and world and is used both in the commentaries and in the *Institutes* as a way of focusing attention on God's revelation rather than on God *in se.*[42] So too, in his discussions of providence and of the divine-human person of the Mediator, Calvin reflects on scholastic distinctions between levels of necessity.[43] In the former instance, he notes the difference between "necessity *secundum quid*" and "absolute necessity" or between "consequent necessity" and a "necessity of the consequence." Calvin notes, "that which God has determined, though it must come to pass, is not, however, precisely, or in its own nature, necessary." By way of example, Calvin argues that John 19:33 and 36 should be understood to mean that God made Christ's bones breakable, like all human bones, but "in reference to the necessity of his counsel," God "exempted them from actual fracture." It was neither an absolute necessity nor a necessity of the consequence that Christ's bones were not broken, but a necessity *secundum quid*, a consequent necessity resting on a specific divine willing and not on the nature of the bones themselves. There is, Calvin concludes, "good ground for the distinction which the Schoolmen made" between different kinds of necessity.[44] Similarly, Calvin notes that there was no

---

[40]Cf. *Institutes*, 2.14.3, 6 with Joseph Tylanda, "Christ the Mediator: Calvin versus Stancaro," in *Calvin Theological Journal* 8 (1973): 5–16, 131–57.

[41]Calvin, *Institutes*, 2.17.1; cf. Wendel, *Calvin*, 227–32.

[42]*Institutes*, 1.16.8; cf. 3.21.7; and note Commentary on Romans 11:34, *CO* 49, 231: "Tenenda vero est quam nuper attuli distinctio inter arcanum Dei consilium et voluntatem in scriptura patefactam"; Commentary on Eph. 3:11, *CO* 51, 183: "fuisse aeternum semperque fixum decretum, sed quod debuerit in Christo sanciri, quia in ipso statutum erat"; Commentary on John 6:40, *CO* 47, 147: "Quod si Deus fide servari vult quos elegit et aeternum suum decretum hoc modo sancit ac exsequitur, quisquis non contentus Christo de aeterna praedestinatione curiose inquirit, quantum in se est, praeter Dei consilium salvus esse appetit. Electio Dei per se occulta est et arcana: eam Dominus vocatione qua nos dignatur patefacit"; and the Commentary on John 10:16, *CO* 47, 244: "Nam arcanum Dei consilium, quo ordinati sunt ad vitam homines, tandem suo tempore patefacit vocatio."

[43]*Institutes*, 1.16.9; 2.12.1.*1*   [44]*Institutes*, 1.16.9, cited above.

"simple or absolute" necessity that the Mediator be both divine and human but that the constitution of the Mediator "flowed from the divine decree on which the salvation of man depended"—in other words, a necessity of the consequence.[45] Here, Calvin certainly echoes the Scotist critique of Anselm's *Cur Deus homo*— specifically to the point that God must not be understood as subject to necessity. It is not the nature of the problem of human sin that dictates the nature of the Mediator, albeit the suitability of the Mediator to the work of redemption: rather it is the divine will that the Mediator be the God-man that provides the necessity of the incarnation.[46]

Given the formal and methodological importance of the exegesis of Scripture both to the genesis of medieval scholastic theological system and to the creation of Calvin's *Institutes*, we turn to several examples of the Biblical or exegetical founda-tions of theological loci treated by Calvin and by the medieval scholastic doc-tors.[47] First, Calvin's reading of Exodus 3:14, both in the *Institutes* and in his commentary on the text, falls precisely into the traditional, "essentialist," reading of the text and indicates Calvin's continuity with both the patristic and the medi-eval past: God's "eternity and self-existence are announced by that wonderful name," declares Calvin in the *Institutes*.[48] He elaborates at considerable length on this issue in his commentary, noting the future tense of the divine declaration, "I will be what I will be," but arguing that its meaning differs little from the usual translation into the present, except insofar as the future tense even more forcibly "designates the perpetual duration" of God. Calvin also assumes that God here "attributes to himself alone divine glory, because he is self-existent and therefore eternal." Further Calvin concludes that God "gives existence and subsistence to every creature" while at the same time retaining his own distinct predicates or attributes: "eternity is proper to God alone." Thus, "all things in heaven and earth derive at his will their essence or subsistence from the One who truly is."[49] Parallel

---

[45]*Institutes*, 2.12.1: "De necessitate si quaeritur, non simplex quidem (ut vulgo loquuntur) vel absoluta fuit: sed manavit ex coelesti decreto, unde pendebat hominum salus."

[46]Cf. Reinhold Seeberg's analysis of Scotus' argumentation, *Textbook of the History of Doctrines*, tr. Charles Hay, 2 vols. (Grand Rapids: Baker, 1977), 2:156–57.

[47]See Pieter A. Verhoef, "Luther's and Calvin's Exegetical Library," in *Calvin Theological Journal* 3 (1968): 5–20; cf. Steinmetz, "John Calvin on Isaiah 6," 160–63.

[48]*Institutes*, 1.10.2: "Ubi animadvertamus ejus aeternitatem και αυτουσίαν, magnifico illo nomine bis repetito"; cf. *Institutes*, 1:13:23, of Christ: "Nam quum ubique ponatur nomen Jehovae, sequitur deitatis respectu ex se ipso esse."

[49]John Calvin, *Mosis reliqui libri quatuor in formam harmoniae, digesta a Ioanne Calvino: Cum eiusdem commentariis*, in *CO* 24, col. 43–44: "Futurum verbi tempus legitur Hebraice: Ero qui ero: sed quod praesenti aequipollet, nisi quod designat perpetuam durationis tenorem. Hoc quidem satis liquet, Deum sibi uni asserere divinitatis gloriam, quia sit a se ipso ideoque aeternus: et ita omnibus creaturis det esse, vel subsistere. Neque enim vulgare quidquam vel commune aliis de se praedicat, sed aeternitatem vendicat propriam solius Dei, idque ut pro sua dignitate celebretur. Proinde continuo

understandings of the text can be found in Thomas Aquinas, Bonaventure, and Duns Scotus.[50]

Calvin also knew and accepted, with limitation, the medieval distinction between the "sufficiency" of Christ's satisfaction for all sin and its "efficiency" for the "elect" or "believers" alone. (We do not raise, at this point, the perennial question of whether or not Calvin held a doctrine of "limited atonement"—we only illustrate one of the difficulties involved in coming to grips with Calvin's use of scholastic distinctions.) In commenting on the text of 1 John 2:1–2, Calvin recognized that verse 2, "and not for ours only, but also for the sins of the whole world," raised the question of the universality of Christ's satisfaction. The text does not indicate universal salvation resting on the infinite value of the sacrifice: even so, in order to "avoid this absurdity," the exegetical tradition had often resolved the problem of this and similar texts with the time-honored distinction that "Christ suffered sufficiently for the whole world, but efficiently only for the elect." "This solution," Calvin adds, "has commonly prevailed in the schools."[51] Calvin pro-

---

post neglecta ratione grammaticae, idem verbum primae personae loco substantivi usurpat, et verbo tertiae personae annectit: ut admiratio subeat animos, quoties incomprehensibilis essentiae fit mentio. Etsi autem de hac aeternitate magnifice disserunt philosophi, et Plato constanter affirmet, Deum proprie esse τò ὄν, hoc tamen elogium non scite neque ut decet, in suum usum accommodant, nempe unicum esse Dei absorbeat quascunque imaginamur essentias: deinde ut accedat simul summum imperium et potestas gubernandi omnia.... Ergo ut solide apprehendamus unum Deum, scire primum necesse est, quidquid in coelis est vel in terra, precario suam essentiam vel subsistentiam ab uno qui solus vere est, mutuari. Ex illo autem esse nascitur et posse: quia si Deus omnia virtute sustinet, arbitrio quoque suo regit"; cf. *CTS Harmony* 1:73–74; and note the similar comments in Zwingli's *On the Providence of God*, 147.

  [50]Aquinas, *Summa theologiae*, I, q.2, a.3: "Sed contra est quod dicitur, Exodi 3,14, ex persona Dei: *Ego sum qui sum*"; cf. Aquinas, *Summa contra gentiles*,1.23.9–10: "Deus autem est primum ens, quo nihil est prius. Dei igitur essentia est suum esse. [10] Hanc autem sublimem veritatem Moyses a Domino est edoctus: qui cum quaeret a Domino, *Exod*. 3:13–14, dicens, *Si dixerit ad me filii Israel, Quod nomen eius? quid dicam eis?* Dominus respondit: *Ego sum qui sum; sic dices filiis Israel: Qui est misit me ad vos*, ostendens suum proprium nomen esse QUI EST. Quodlibet autem nomen est institutum ad significandum naturam seu essentiam alicuius rei. Unde relinquitur quod ipsum divinum esse est sua essentia vel natura." See also Bonaventure, *Itinerarium mentis in Deum*, 5:2, 8; trans. José de Vinck in *The Works of Bonaventure*. 5 vols. (Paterson: St. Anthony Guild, 1960), 5: 43, 46; and John Duns Scotus, *A Treatise on God as First Principle*, trans. Allan B. Wolter (Chicago: Franciscan Herald Press, 1966), 1:1: "Dominus Deus noster, Moysi servo tuo, de tuo nomine filiis Israel proponendo, a te Doctore verissimo sciscitanti, sciens quid posset de te concipere intellectus mortalium, nomen tuum benedictum reserans, respondisti: EGO SUM, QUI SUM. Tu es verum esse, tu es totum esse."

  [51]Calvin, *Commentarius in Iohannis Apostoli epistolam, CO* 55, col. 310: "Qui hanc absurditatem volebant effugere, dixerunt, sufficienter pro toto mundo passum esse Christum: sed pro electis tantum efficaciter. Vulgo haec solutio in scholis obtinuit"; CTS, 173; cf. Lombard, *Sententiae in IV libris distinctae*, III, d. xx, c. 5.1: "Christus ergo est sacerdos idemque hostia et pretium nostrae reconciliationis, qui se in ara crucis non diabolo, sed Deo Trinitati obtulit, pro omnibus quantum ad pretii sufficientiam, sed pro electis tantum quantum ad efficaciam, quia praedestinatis tantum salutem effecit." Also note the *Glossa* on Heb. 5:9, *causa salutis aeternae omnibus obtemperantibus sibi*: "Tantum enim valet eius passio quod omnibus sufficit ad salutem" in *PL* 192, col. 438 B. See further, Landgraf, *Dogmengeschichte*, 2/2, 329–58.

ceeds to indicate that the proffered solution does not apply to this particular text, while at the same time indicating the theological correctness of the distinction: "Though then I allow that what has been said is true, yet I deny that it is suitable to this passage, for the design of John was no other than to make this benefit common to the whole church."[52] Calvin, thus, accepts the standard scholastic distinction, but indicates that the distinction could not be applied to this particular text. So too, in his comments on Isaiah 28:22, Calvin has simply reflected, without editorial comment or polemic, the medieval tradition of understanding here a necessary distinction between the divine *opus proprium* and *opus alienum*. The scholastic or medieval exegetical tradition and its understanding of problems and seeming contradictions as distinctions has in fact set the agenda for Calvin's comments on the text.[53]

Calvin's later exegetical work, some of which had an impact on the 1559 *Institutes*, and some of which was done so late in his career that it did not, was largely devoted to the exposition of the Old Testament—Genesis, the Harmony of the Pentateuch, Psalms, the Prophets. Here, Calvin experienced, as he surely did not experience in his interpretation of the New Testament, great theological problems involving the status of the literal meaning of the text and its relation to the doctrines of God, creation, and providence. As Schreiner has shown, this problem is evident in the sermons on Job,[54] and we have seen it also from the vantage point of the commentaries on Exod. 3:14 and Isa. 28:22. Calvin certainly examined the commentaries of Nicholas of Lyra, and in so doing drew on a digest of scholastic opinion extending back to Thomas Aquinas, much of whose thought had been incorporated into Lyra's commentary. And it was perhaps here, apart from the polemical context of debate, that Calvin encountered both many of the traditional scholastic distinctions and the rationale, in the Biblical text, for their enunciation by the medieval doctors.

3. Some Conclusions

It often appears from the *Institutes*, commentaries, treatises, and sermons that Calvin held a fundamentally negative view of scholastic theology, at times to the point of caricature, at the same time that his theology contained a measure of

---

[52]Calvin, *Commentarius in Iohannis Apostoli epistolam, CO* 55, col. 310: "Ego quamquam verum esse illud dictum fateor: nego tamen praesenti loco quadrare. Neque enim consilium Iohannis, quam toti ecclesiae commune facere hoc bonum" (CTS, 173).

[53]John Calvin, *Commentarii in Isaiam prophetam* 28:22, in *CO* 36, col. 479: "*Alienum* hoc opus dici ideo nonnulli putant, quod nihil magis Dei proprium sit, quam miseri atque ignoscere peccatis nostris ... alienamque veluti personam et naturae ipsius adversam induere"; *CTS* 2:298–99).

[54]See Schreiner, "Through a Mirror Dimly," 179, 186; idem, "Exegesis and Double Justice," 327, 329, 331, 337–38; cf. Steinmetz, "John Calvin on Isaiah 6," 159, 61.

positive allusion to and indirect reliance on scholastic formulations. In several of the cases noted, the appearance of caricature may be related to the disparity between Calvin's Latin and French usage: many of the places in which Calvin's critique of *scholastici* seems exaggerated or misapplied give a rather different impression when the target of the critique is understood as the *théologiens Sorboniques* identified by Calvin's French text. The hypothesis that "scholastici" and "théologiens Sorboniques" are not simple equivalents and that the latter term is more precise and specific than the former is confirmed to a certain extent by Calvin's consistent rendering of phrases like "Petrus Lombardus et Scholastici," "Magister sententiarum et scholastici," and "saniores scholastici" with precise verbal equivalents and by the probable target of Calvin's most bitter attacks on extreme aspects of late medieval nominalism. Indeed, if the language of the French text is accepted as Calvin's meaning, the critiques are often quite specific and, indeed, quite contemporary—and no longer directed against such luminaries of the scholastic past as Bonaventure, Aquinas, or Duns Scotus. In addition, Calvin clearly tended to reserve his most angry and specified polemic for his French audience.

Calvin's knowledge of scholastic theology certainly also increased as he prepared his lectures on Scripture, his commentaries, and the successive editions of the *Institutes*. It may well be the case that his more positive use of scholastic distinctions arose by way of his encounter with them as explanations of difficulties and seeming contradictions in the Biblical text, an encounter largely related to his reading of major medieval commentators in preparation for his writing of lectures and commentaries on Scripture. This hypothesis is supported by the findings of Steinmetz, Schreiner, and Thompson and accounts for his continuing negative assessment of scholastic theological system, his fairly consistent but also rather vague reflection of the scholastic tradition in many of his central arguments (such as his discussion of the merit of Christ and his great theme of the twofold knowledge of God), his occasional misunderstanding or intentional distortion of the import of a scholastic argument, and his increasing nonpolemical notice of scholastic distinctions in his writings. In addition, with a view toward scholarly writing on the subject, the way of framing the problem permits Reuter's massively learned correlation of Calvin's views with those of the medieval scholastics to be held in tension with the problem of Calvin's access to their thought: the relation and disjunction between Calvin's theology and medieval scholasticism reflects the variegated process by which Calvin assimilated their ideas—polemically through explicit negative reference in the writings of predecessors like Luther and Bucer who were learned in the older theology, positively but vaguely and without reference to specific scholastic thinkers (or even to scholasticism as such) through the reading of these same works, and more dialogically (with clearer reference to the sources of the concepts) through the reading of medieval commentators. We are also able to accept and refine many of LaVallee's arguments, particularly his conclusions concerning the identity of the "scholastici" as "théologiens sorbo-niques"—but now in only certain of Calvin's most concentrated polemical arguments. This understanding leads, in turn, to the possibility of finding a place in Calvin's developing thought for the positive impact of earlier strains of medieval thought and even for Calvin's participation in the long-term development of a doctrinal theme, as in the Christological examples we have noted.

In short, Calvin's overtly negative reaction to "scholastici" conveys only a small part of his relationship to medieval scholastic theology, its method, its themes, and its distinctions. Alongside the rejection, there is also appropriation, sometimes explicit, often unacknowledged. There are also parallels in method and intention, notably between Calvin's approach to system and commentary and the approach of Peter Lombard—and, finally, there is the exegetical tradition to which Calvin became increasingly attentive and through which he received the insights both of the patristic and of the medieval periods. It is to this latter investigation, the detailed relationship between Calvin's exegesis and the western exegetical tradition, that study will need to turn in order to clarify fully the relation and disjunction between Calvin's theology and the thought of the medieval doctors.

Albrecht Dürer, *Saint Paul in His Study*

The Reception of Calvinism in Britain

Andrew Pettegree

I. The Problem of British Calvinism

Anyone coming to this subject for the first time might notice at once the reluctance of many British scholars active in the field to acknowledge the Anglican church of the sixteenth century as fully Calvinist. True, all specialists who have devoted themselves to the doctrine and practice of the English church will acknowledge that Anglicanism had Calvinistic features, not least a personal affection for Calvin's writings and a general fidelity to the reformer's theology; nevertheless most argue that the particular features of English Anglicanism are sufficient to deny it full membership in the family of European Calvinist churches.

One of the best examples of this style of argumentation can be found in Patrick Collinson's elegant article on England and International Calvinism in the collected volume on International Calvinism edited by Menna Prestwich.[1] His careful, subtle formulation makes an excellent starting point for this discussion. By the 1580s, Collinson contends:

> Calvinism, if it meant anything, no longer signified Geneva and the churches that looked to Geneva for guidance, but a loose and free alliance of churches, universities, academies and other intellectual, political and spiritual resources located in France, the Netherlands, South-West Germany, England and Scotland, not to speak of more distant outposts. … All of this must be borne in mind as we concede that the Church of England was putting down its anchors in the outer roads of the broad harbour of the Calvinist or (better) Reformed Tradition.[2]

Note the extreme caution of this formulation: "outer roads"; "Calvinist (or better) Reformed tradition." But Collinson's formula probably represents as close as we will get to a consensus position. The Anglican church of the Elizabethan period was essentially Calvinistic in doctrine, so much so that it is customary to talk of the "Calvinist consensus" of the Elizabethan church, a consensus fundamentally challenged only in the 1620s.[3] Nevertheless its aberrant position on

[1] Patrick Collinson, "England and International Calvinism, 1558–1640," in Menna Prestwich, ed., *International Calvinism, 1541–1715* (Oxford: Oxford University Press, 1985), 197–223.
[2] Ibid, 215.
[3] For the "Calvinist consensus" see Nicholas Tyacke, *Anti-Calvinists: the Rise of English Arminianism*, rev. paperback ed. (Oxford: Oxford University Press, 1990); Peter G. Lake, "Calvinism and the English Church, 1570–1635," *Past and Present* 114 (1987): 32–76.

church discipline, and its affection for bishops, makes it something less than a fully Calvinist church.

There are several aspects of this construction that are worth testing. For anyone standing somewhat outside the intricacies of the debate, the insistence on the distinctiveness and separation of the English church can be somewhat puzzling. For despite Collinson's caution, the general stress on the peculiarity of English Calvinism carries with it the implication that, England apart, Calvinism was a quite clearly defined system, into which a number of the main continental Calvinist churches can comfortably be placed. Yet from the perspective of scholars whose primary focus has been on these continental churches, it is clear that the individuality which British writers claim for Anglicanism, allegedly taking it away from the Calvinist mainstream, was every bit as characteristic of other European churches.

For instance, those familiar with recent writings on Dutch Calvinism know that much scholarly debate has concentrated on the question of whether the Dutch Reformed Church, as it emerged in the new free northern state, was not characterized by such variety of belief and practice, that to speak of it as "Calvinist" is inappropriate.[4] Certainly if discipline is to be regarded as the touchstone of a fully Calvinistic system, then the Netherlands can hardly be made to qualify, since fewer than 15 percent of the population ever became full confessing members of the church.[5]

Similarly in the French church, an assumption of allegiance to Genevan practice and doctrine is more a function of the comparatively underdeveloped state of research, and poor survival of sources than a reflection of historical reality. Ministers trained in Geneva dominated in the larger city churches; elsewhere men from a bewildering variety of backgrounds intruded themselves into a ministry which the Calvinist synodical structure struggled to control. And even when most of its energies were necessarily bent towards a struggle for physical and political survival, as in the 1560s, the French church was still riven by fundamental divisions over doctrine and church practice, as in the long-running controversies raised by the writings of Jean Morély.[6]

---

[4]Willem Nijenhuis, "Variants within Dutch Calvinism in the Sixteenth Century," *Low Countries History Yearbook* 12 (1979), 48–64. Alastair Duke, "The Ambivalent Face of Calvinism in the Netherlands, 1561–1618," in Prestwich, *International Calvinism*, 109–34.

[5]A. Th. van Deursen, *Bavianen & Slijkgeuzen* (Assen: Van Gorcum, 1974); idem, *Plain Lives in a Golden Age: Popular Culture, Religion and Society in Seventeenth-Century Holland* (Cambridge: Cambridge University Press, 1991), 260–79. Joke Spaans, *Haarlem na de Reformatie* (The Hague, 1989).

[6]Robert M. Kingdon, *Geneva and the Consolidation of the French Calvinist Movement* (Geneva: Droz, 1967). Philippe Denis and Jean Rott, *Jean Morély (ca. 1524–ca. 1594) et l'Utopie d'une démocratie dans l'église* (Geneva: Droz, 1993). For a commentary on the poor survival of sources for French Calvinism see the introduction to Alastair Duke, Gillian Lewis, and Andrew Pettegree, eds., *Calvinism in Europe: A Collection of Documents* (Manchester: Manchester University Press, 1992).

A scholar of these continental churches coming fresh to a consideration of English Anglicanism might justly observe that if the Anglican church were entitled to withdraw on the grounds of variety of practice and doctrine, little would remain of International Calvinism. Even Scotland, which is often regarded as the most perfect model of a Calvinist polity outside Geneva, had several idiosyncratic features.

Certainly Calvin himself, in his theological considerations of what constituted a true church, imposed no such demanding tests of total conformity. If we look at Calvin's writings to establish his view of this question, we will see that his own perspective was remarkably relaxed.[7] The visible church comprised, in his opinion, the "whole multitude of men spread over the earth who profess to worship one God and Christ." He did not expect such churches to achieve perfect conformity in ceremonies, and he warned that "we must not thoughtlessly forsake the church because of any petty dissensions."[8]

His actions and counsel to other churches demonstrate that such convictions did inform Calvin's actions in practice as well as theory. When in 1553 the new French-speaking refugee congregation in Lutheran Wesel was ordered to conform to the local ceremonies, their ministers' first inclination was to refuse and seek a more hospitable refuge elsewhere. But Calvin, to their surprise, advised them to put aside their scruples and rather conform "in all those ceremonies, which do not have a decisive influence on our faith, so that the unity of the church is not disturbed either by our excessive severity or timidity."[9]

Calvin clearly regarded the churches of other Protestant confessions as true churches. His definition of the indispensable characteristics of a true church— pure preaching of the Word and administration of the sacraments—was almost certainly influenced by his desire not to put up barriers against ecumenical overtures towards the German Lutherans. If Calvin regarded the exercise of congregational discipline as in practical terms highly desirable, then it was only later writers who added this as an indispensable third mark. This is something worth bearing in mind as we consider the later presbyterian assault on the Anglican church, "but half reformed."

What then are we to make of English Calvinism in this context? What I propose here will address the question from a somewhat different angle from that of most of the writers who have concerned themselves with analyzing the theological nature of sixteenth-century Anglicanism. For rather than address this question

---

[7]This paragraph follows the crisp survey of this question by Alastair Duke in the introduction to Pettegree, Duke, and Lewis, eds., *Calvinism in Europe*, 2.

[8]*Institutes*, p. 1026.

[9]Duke, *Calvinism in Europe*; cf. Pettegree, "The London Community and the Second Sacramentarian Controversy, 1553–1560," *Archiv für Reformationsgeschichte* 78 (1987): 223–52.

through analysis of texts, and testing the theological formulas found therein against this or that test of Calvinist orthodoxy, I will offer a series of observations from a rather different perspective. What follows is divided into three parts. First, I offer a consideration of the Elizabethan settlement of 1559, the crucial events of which decisively established the essential pattern from which English worship would not then substantially deviate. Second, I present some thoughts on the influence and importance of Calvin's writings in England, based on data from surviving books lists and testamentary material. Finally, I offer some briefer reflections on the knotty problem of discipline.

II. Calvin and the Elizabethan Settlement.

If we are to take the temperature of English Protestantism in the Elizabethan period, there is no denying that the religious settlement of 1559 represents the crucial defining event. English Protestants were not to know that this would be the final state of official religion, from which the queen was not to be moved forward to a church settlement in total conformity with the best continental practice; but that indeed proved to be the case. That being so, it is important to establish a view of what Elizabeth and her close advisors were intending during the complicated parliamentary maneuvers from which the Acts of Supremacy and Uniformity finally emerged.

Given the importance of the issues at stake, it is not surprising that these matters have been the subject of intense historical debate.[10] For most of the period since the sixteenth century, indeed from the first decades of the Elizabethan period until the 1950s, writers who commented on the settlement were content with a pleasingly obvious explanation, that a Protestant queen enacted a Protestant settlement over the determined opposition of those most wedded to Marian Catholicism, principally the bench of bishops. In the 1950s, however, this view was turned on its head by an influential article by the distinguished parliamentary historian John Ernest Neale.[11] According to Neale, the settlement which emerged at the conclusion of this troubled parliament was far from what the queen had originally intended. Elizabeth's personal preference had been for something far more moderate and less decisively Protestant. The Royal Supremacy would be assumed once more, but religious observance would be patterned according to the first (and therefore to Catholics more acceptable) Edwardian Prayer Book of 1549. It was opposition from a determined Protestant pressure group in the House of

---

[10]The literature on the Elizabethan Settlement is well reviewed in Norman L. Jones, *Faith by Statute. Parliament and the Settlement of Religion 1559* (London: Royal Historical Society, 1982).

[11]J. E. Neale, "The Elizabethan Acts of Supremacy and Uniformity," *English Historical Review* 65 (1950): 304–32.

Commons that eventually drove Elizabeth into accepting a more radical settlement, based on the more fully Protestant second Edwardian Prayer Book of 1552. The final shape of the Elizabethan settlement could, in this reading, be attributed to the effective marshalling of parliamentary force to persuade a reluctant queen to move beyond her own more conservative inclinations.

The significance of this proposed reinterpretation is immediately obvious, for if Neale's view is accepted, the fault line around which the battles of the later Elizabethan period were fought, between Elizabeth and her later puritan critics, was established right from the beginning of the reign. But recently the tide has shifted against Neale, notably with the publication in 1982 of Norman Jones' painstaking reconstruction of the events of the parliament. Jones, in effect reinstates the received view: that the settlement of 1559 was by and large that which the queen and her close advisors intended.[12]

Jones's arguments carry considerable weight. Neale never presented his reconstruction as anything more than an hypothesis, and on several critical points his evidential base has been found to be weak. Most critical writing has concentrated its fire on Neale's postulation of an organized "puritan" lobby in the House of Commons, but two other crucial aspects of his argument fail to stand up to scrutiny: his assumption of the queen's innate conservatism and his suggestion that the earlier Edwardian Prayer Book of 1549 was ever seriously canvassed as an option in 1559. Here Neale's evidence is a mixture of conjecture and a somewhat bizarre identification of the 1549 Prayer Book with the Lutheran Confession of Augsburg, for which Elizabeth occasionally expressed a rather vague affection. There was little more to this than diplomatic camouflage, of the sort the queen later proved herself a master; in England in 1559 the only realistic options were the later Prayer Book of 1552 and the more radical continental church orders canvassed by returning exiles.[13] Nor is there any real evidence that the queen herself would have favored a return to anything akin to Henrician Catholicism. By background, personal history, and kinship, Elizabeth was firmly wedded to Protestantism, as all contemporary commentators immediately realized.[14]

If Neale's thesis must therefore largely be consigned to oblivion, the question still remains to be answered why Elizabeth ultimately drew back from the full reform agenda being urged on her by exiles returning from the Protestant cities of

[12]Jones, *Faith by Statute.*
[13]I develop this argument more fully in Andrew Pettegree, "'The Marian Exiles and the Elizabethan Settlement," in my *Marian Protestantism: Six Studies,* St. Andrews Studies in Reformation History (Aldershot: Scolar Press, 1996).
[14]See, for instance, the comments of the Spanish ambassador at the beginning of the reign. *Calendar of State Papers; Spanish, 1558–1567,* p. 7. Protestant observers were equally confident of the queen's instinctive allegiance to their cause.

Europe. Here Calvin's personal role and reputation in England at this time become relevant, and in some respects, it may be argued, played a decisive role. This is clear if one attempts a brief reconstruction of events from Calvin's own point of view. In company with all other continental Protestant reformers, Calvin welcomed Elizabeth's accession as a providential liberation from the Roman tyranny of her sister; one of a sequence of providential events in this remarkable year which undoubtedly proved God's favor for the Protestant cause.[15] And the Genevan reformer did not neglect necessary practical steps to encourage the new queen along the paths of righteousness. On 15 January 1559 (the date of Elizabeth's coronation), he sent her a copy of his Isaiah commentary, together with a letter dedicating the work to her. Reminding her of the excellent work accomplished in the reign of her brother Edward VI, Calvin urged Elizabeth to raise up the poor persecuted flock of Christ, to receive back the exiles scattered abroad, and ultimately to ensure that true religion was quickly restored to its former splendor.[16] Two weeks later a further letter to William Cecil, Elizabeth's new first minister, reinforced this message with a new admonition to unflinching pursuit of the paths of righteousness.[17]

Calvin was due a rude awakening. A second letter to Cecil later in this crucial spring period is very different in tone: at once aggrieved, defensive, and conciliating. It is worth quoting here:

> The messenger to whom I gave in charge my commentaries upon Isaiah to be presented to the most serene Queen brought me word that my homage was not kindly received by her Majesty, because she had been offended with me by reason of some writings published in this place. He also repeated to me, most illustrious sir, the substance of a conversation held by you, in which you seemed to me more severe than was consistent with your courtesy, especially when you had been already assured by my letter how much I promised myself from your regard towards me.[18]

The point at issue here, as Calvin's letter goes on to acknowledge, was John Knox's notorious *First Blast of the Trumpet against the Monstrous Regiment of Women*, published in Geneva with ghastly and quite unprovidential timing just

---

[15]Jean-Daniel Benoit, "L'année 1559 dans les annales calviniennes," *Revue d'Histoire et de philosophie religieuses* 39 (1959): 103–16.

[16]*Joannis Calvini commentarii in Isaiam prophetam* (Geneva, Crespin, 1559). Rodolphe Peter and Jean-François Gilmont, eds., *Bibliotheca Calviniana*, vol. 2: 1555–1564 (Geneva: Droz, 1994), 59/1.

[17]*CO* 17:418–20.

[18]*CO*, 17:490–92. The translation is from *Letters of John Calvin*, ed. Jules Bonnet, 4 vols. (Edinburgh: Constable / Philadelphia: Presbyterian Board of Publication, 1855–58,) vol. 4: no. 538.

before Elizabeth's accession.[19] Calvin denied having any knowledge of its publication, but for Elizabeth the name of the Genevan reformer was indelibly associated with this most unfortunate production of the Genevan press.

How damaging this might be for exponents of the Genevan reform, Calvin was immediately aware; hence his hurried (and rather unconvincing) attempts to distance himself from Knox's book. But the scale of Elizabeth's anger only becomes clear if we take into account the evidence of another contemporary source, a letter previously buried in the archives of the north German town of Emden and, therefore, not known to other scholars who have worked on the Elizabethan settlement.[20] The author, Anthony Ashe, had recently arrived in London as the delegate of the refugee congregation in Emden. He had been sent to negotiate the reopening of John a Lasco's London foreign congregations, which had been shut up during Mary's reign. As his letter makes clear, this proved to be a more arduous negotiation than had first been anticipated. Right up until the last moment the full settlement of religion for which Protestants so ardently hoped still hung in the balance, as optimistic hopes of a smooth return to godly worship were frustrated by bitter parliamentary opposition. Further there were worrying indications that the godly were drifting out of favor, apparently largely as a reaction to Knox's book. Ashe reports that a house to house search had been initiated to track down copies, and three of the godly had even been arrested. The designation "extreme predestinarians" hints at the extent to which Geneva, Knox, and the defining doctrine of the Genevan reform had become associated in the eyes and minds of the Council.

The evidence from Ashe's letter is, I think, helpful in understanding why Calvin's personal relationship with Elizabeth got off to such a shaky start. And it may offer the key to understanding why Elizabeth, having set in train an essentially mainstream Protestant settlement, nevertheless made a point of insisting on a more conservative rubric on ceremonies and ecclesiastical accoutrements. For all her personal allegiance to Protestantism, Elizabeth was clearly determined to preserve independence and freedom of action in matters of church government. Her perverse insistence on items of ecclesiastical furniture which gave pain to her loyal Protestant admirers was one way of emphasizing that she would not be dictated to by the continental centers of reform; that their practice should not be prescriptive for England. Many of the later disputes which rent the Anglican church might have been avoided if the godly had had the insight to perceive that

---

[19]John Knox, *First Blast of the Trumpet against the Monstrous Regiment of Women* (Geneva, J. Poullain and A. Rebul, 1558 [STC 15070])
[20]The full text is published in English translation in Pettegree, "Marian Exiles and the Elizabethan Settlement."

Elizabeth's attachment to conservative ceremonial usage was in this sense largely symbolic.

III. CALVIN AND THE THEOLOGY OF THE ANGLICAN CHURCH

1. *Calvin's Writings in England*

In personal terms Calvin may therefore be said to have made a shaky beginning to the new reign; so much so, in fact, that the new minister of the French church in London, Nicholas des Gallars, could frankly warn his mentor in Geneva that the mention of Calvin's name would undoubtedly harm the church in any sensitive negotiations with the English administration.[21] If this was the case, how then did Calvin's reputation recover from this early battering; and indeed recover so effectively that later writers talk not of "extreme predestinarians" in the negative sense indicated by the letter of Ashe quoted above, but of the Anglican church being dominated by a "Calvinist consensus"?

Clearly the influence of Calvin's writings and theology was not slow to penetrate England; but just how rapidly, and with what effectiveness is again a somewhat debated question. The most common approach is to acknowledge Calvin's great influence in England as a writer, but to argue that Calvin was in effect no more than the first among equals: that what was transmitted into English thought and theology was not pure Calvinism but a more variegated and attenuated "Reformed" tradition. This is a solution which of course has the great advantage of preserving the individuality to which English writers are so firmly wedded.

The core of this argument is the belief that English writers and theologians looked upon Zurich and its reformers as providing theological guidance as authoritative as that of Calvin and his heirs: hence diluting the influence of "pure" Genevan theology. Examples of this style of argumentation can be found in the works of the several leading authorities on English Protestantism in this period. Thus Christopher Mattinson Dent, in his study of theology in Oxford:

> For the first two decades of the reign, Oxford men viewed Zurich as a centre of reform at least as significant as Geneva. The writings of Calvin and his successor, Beza, had by no means achieved the total dominance in English minds claimed by those who equate the influence of the continental reformed tradition with the dissemination of Calvin's Institutes, catechisms, and commentaries.[22]

---

[21]Patrick Collinson, *Archbishop Grindal: The Struggle for a Reformed Church* (London: Jonathan Cape 1979), 132.

[22]C. M. Dent, *Protestant Reformers in Elizabethan Oxford* (Oxford: Oxford University Press, 1983), 74.

And here is Collinson in similar vein.

The student who has only heard of "Calvinism" must learn that English theologians were as likely to lean on Bullinger of Zurich, Musculus of Berne, or Peter Martyr as on Calvin or Beza.[23]

Statements of this sort, even from such a distinguished source, deserve a degree of analytical testing. One's suspicions are somewhat aroused by the fact that subsequent argumentation seldom demonstrates convincingly and specifically how the theological variety alleged to have dominated the reading of English divines actually influenced their own doctrinal views on, say, grace and predestination. Dent's evidence of the continuing influence of Zurich in Elizabethan Oxford consists mostly of personal contacts, rather than theological influences. There is also a real danger of reading the controversies of the early seventeenth century back into the sixteenth century, and by implication enrolling Bullinger and the Zurich writers as honorary Arminians. This would be perverse, not least in view of Dent's argument that the influence of Zurich was in any case waning by the 1580s.

Let us try to shed a little light on this question by quantifying what English readers actually read. To approach this matter I have conducted an analysis of the data presented in Elisabeth Leedham-Green's two-volume survey of books recorded in the wills of Cambridge testators.[24] This is extremely valuable information because very often the whole of a testator's collection was inventoried, along with titles and prices. This material is much more valuable as an index of what continental literature was actually penetrating England than, for instance, the holdings of College libraries, since libraries had the tendency constantly to replace popular books with later editions, thus distorting the historian's view of their sixteenth-century holdings. As Dent points out, the fact that several of the Oxford college collections contain no copies of sixteenth century editions of Calvin's works will indicate that these were used and replaced, rather than that none were bought.[25]

Testamentary evidence is not, of course, without its own difficulties. In this particular sample the presence of a larger number of collections inventoried in the 1580s accounts for a bulge in that decade in virtually every author's totals. Inventories are also more likely to record individually large expensive books than small

[23]Collinson, "England and International Calvinism," 214.
[24]Elizabeth S. Leedham-Green, *Books in Cambridge Inventories: Book-Lists from the Vice-Chancellor's Court Probate Inventories in the Tudor and Stuart Periods*, 2 vols. (Cambridge: Cambridge University Press, 1986).
[25]Dent, *Protestant Reformers*, 93.

FIG. 1. COPIES OF WORKS LEFT IN CAMBRIDGE WILLS, 1540–1610

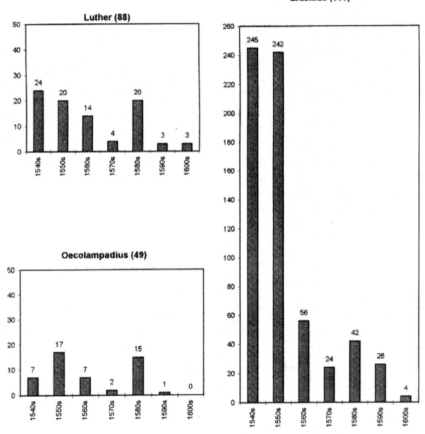

Fig. 1 (CONTINUED)

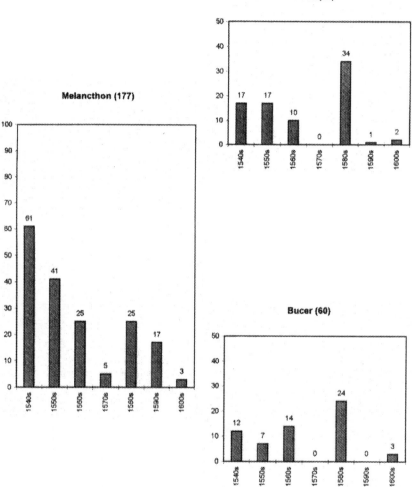

FIG. 1 (CONTINUED)

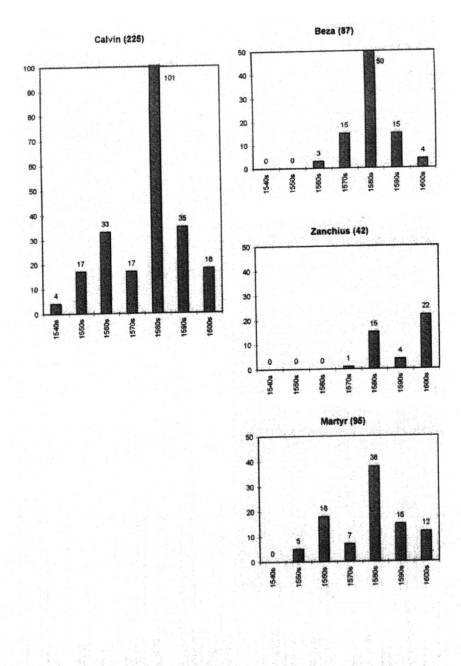

FIG. 1 (CONTINUED)

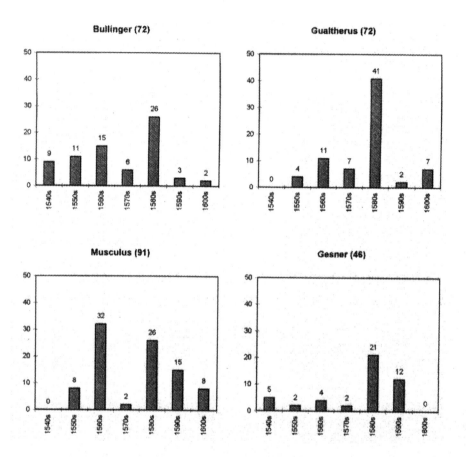

volumes, and thus there will be a bias towards Latin works over the vernacular. The Cambridge provenance of these wills increases the bias towards scholarly and Latin works. And the astonishing near absence of some books known to be popular from other sources—as for instance John Foxe's *Acts and Monuments*—suggests that wills cannot be a wholly reliable guide to what English Protestants were actually reading.[26] In the case of Foxe, a book which achieved almost canonical status in Elizabeth's reign, scholars were presumably making use of college copies for what was in any case a costly book for personal purchase.

Nevertheless the results of this survey are quite suggestive. They confirm, firstly, the preeminent position of Calvin as the dominant theological influence in Elizabeth England. The total number of editions of Calvin's works left in these wills easily outstrips all other continental contemporaries, a supremacy reinforced if one removes the first two columns (which reveal the rather surprising early popularity of Melanchthon's works). Of the other "Genevans'" the figures highlight the gradual emergence of Beza, the rapid increase in popularity of Zanchius's writings towards the end of the century, and the continued interest in England in the writings of Peter Martyr Vermigli. On the Swiss-German writers the evidence is more ambiguous. Bullinger, Musculus and Rudolph Gualter were all much read in Elizabethan England, but these figures tend to confirm Dent's suggestion of a sharply declining popularity in the 1590s and early seventeenth century.

The German Lutheran authors were not left without a voice, mainly because of the continued interest in the writings of Brenz; but Luther himself was apparently not much read in England in the second half of the sixteenth century.[27] Overall Brenz proved as popular an author as Beza, but declining in influence through the reign, whereas all the Genevans were on a strongly upward curve. By the 1580s all the writers of the first generation had effectively been superseded, with the exception of Calvin. In this context it is interesting to note the enormous but sharply declining popularity of Erasmus. Clearly he was the man primarily for an age of uncertainty.

One striking feature of these lists is the fact that English authors are scarcely represented. These Cambridge inventories list only eleven copies of books by William Perkins, and five by Thomas Cartwright. One could argue that as a sample of English reading such a survey is unfair. Wills are bound to have a bias against English books, since small cheap books tended to be grouped together at the end

---

[26]The Cambridge inventories list only three copies of John Foxe, *Acts and Monuments*.

[27]Continuing demand for works by Lutherans scholars in England is also revealed by the surviving booklist of an Emden publisher serving the English market. See Andrew Pettegree, "Emden as a Centre of the Sixteenth-Century Book Trade: A Catalogue of the Bookseller Gaspar Staphorst," *Quaerendo* 24 (1994): 114–35. This list, too, suggests the dominant place in the market of Reformed theology.

of inventories instead of being individually listed; this is particularly the case in a scholarly community like Cambridge. But if we turn to different data concerned exclusively with vernacular editions the dominance of Calvin, even as an English author, is hardly disturbed.

2. Sixteenth-Century Translations of Calvin's Works

Figure 2 reproduces graphically Francis Higman's analysis of Calvin's works in translation, using data gathered by Jean-François Gilmont for his revised Calvin bibliography.[28] England, on this evidence, was far and away the biggest market for Calvin's works in translation; and it is worth bearing in mind that these editions were very often substantial tomes, such as the near complete edition of Calvin's biblical commentaries published in English in the 1580s.

3. English Translations of Works of Continental and Leading English Authors

Calvin's eminence remains unchallenged even if one introduces English authors into the equation. In terms of editions, and here relying on data from the revised *Short Title Catalogue of Books Printed in England, 1475–1640*, English editions of Calvin's works easily outstripped all other continental writers, and dwarfed the production of native English theologians (figure 3). One is tempted to argue that continental theology had established as dominant a position in the market in the sixteenth century as has Japanese technology in the twentieth.

4. The Influence of Calvin's Writings and Theology

To sum up: the evidence from the diverse, if somewhat unusual, measures of popularity and influence presented here suggests that whatever measure one employs Calvin emerges as the dominant force in the theology of the Elizabethan church. Whether one judges from the books collected by learned Cambridge divines, or the English translations published for the wider market, Calvin reigns supreme: and indeed, to judge by the comparison with other nations suggested by Francis Higman's figures, English readers had a particular affection for the Genevan reformer. Higman goes on briefly to analyze the translators and patrons of Calvin's English works, concluding that they included in roughly equal measure figures from the theological mainstream of the English church and members of the self-consciously godly.[29] That may indeed have been the secret of Calvin's success: the ability to appeal simultaneously to both the Elizabethan establishment

[28]Francis Higman, "Calvin's Works in Translation," in Pettegree, Duke, and Lewis, *Calvinism in Europe*, 82–99.
[29]Higman, "Calvin's Works in Translation," 88–99.

FIG. 2. SIXTEENTH CENTURY TRANSLATIONS OF CALVIN'S WORK INTO
FOREIGN VERNACULARS

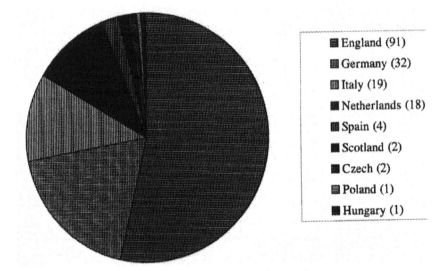

- England (91)
- Germany (32)
- Italy (19)
- Netherlands (18)
- Spain (4)
- Scotland (2)
- Czech (2)
- Poland (1)
- Hungary (1)

FIG. 3. EDITIONS IN ENGLISH OF WORKS BY CONTINENTAL REFORMERS
AND LEADING ENGLISH AUTHORS

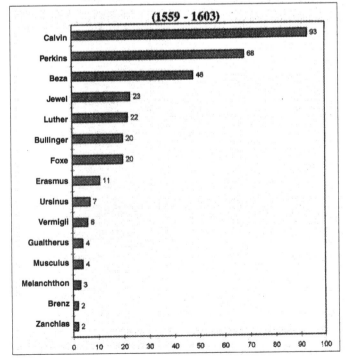

and the emerging radical opposition. In this crucial respect, the "Calvinist consensus" of the Angelical church did remain largely intact.

IV. DISCIPLINE.

Of course there was more to the making of the Elizabethan church than this. To say that members of the Elizabethan establishment and their critics both honored the Genevan reformer, is not to say that they were necessarily agreed on the extent to which Genevan precepts for church organization and community life should be followed in practice. Here we may with profit refer to a useful distinction proposed by a number of writers on English Calvinism, who while acknowledging the general acceptance of the Calvinist theology of salvation suggest that it could be interpreted in radically different ways, and with important results for the writers' views of the developing Anglican church. Thus R. R. Kendall and Peter Lake both postulate a clear line of division between what they call "credal" and "experimental" predestinarians.[30] Credal Calvinists, while they might agree wholeheartedly with the formal content of Calvinist predestinarianism, had no impulse to take the doctrine into the popular pulpit, or to derive a view of the Christian community from it. Experimental predestinarians, in contrast, wanted to place their view of predestination, election, and assurance at the center of their practical divinity, to erect a style of piety on the foundations provided by a Calvinist doctrine of predestination, and to define the godly community in terms of those who both understood the doctrines and acted upon them.

As with most aspects of this subject this distinction has by no means won general acceptance, and there is no doubt that such hard and fast positions bear only a tenuous relationship to the more subtle realities of Elizabethan ecclesiastical politics, where the ground of public debate was constantly shifting in response to swings of opinion at court and, perhaps more compellingly, external events. But it does draw attention to one undoubted truth, that it was possible to share in the wide-ranging theological consensus which underpinned the Elizabethan church and still be deeply disappointed at the practical consequences of reform.

The greatest area of disappointment was undoubtedly connected with matters of church organization and ecclesiastical discipline. As Collinson has put it, "Calvinist doctrine was far from shaping the institutional fabric of the English church."[31] This was certainly the point at which the English church most conspicuously failed to measure up to continental archetypes. English reformers concerned at the queen's unaccountable affection for certain conservative traditions

---

[30]Lake, "Calvinism and the English Church," 39–40. R. T. Kendall, *Calvin and English Calvinism to 1649* (Oxford: Oxford University Press, 1979).
[31]Collinson, "England and International Calvinism," 217.

at the beginning of the reign were in for a further rude awakening in 1563, when a comprehensive scheme of ecclesiastical reform was brutally arrested by an indignant royal veto.[32] Hereafter the history of organized pressure for further reformation, be it in church government or ecclesiastical ornaments, was one of the progressive alienation of those who would not accept the English church "but half reformed." The favorers of discipline were driven increasingly to the margins, forced to content themselves with informal structures patterned on continental models and providing the intellectual leadership grievously neglected by the hierarchy, the prophesying movement of the 1570s, and the puritan conferences of the 1580s.[33]

Now in all of this there was a good deal of truth. It is certainly the case that those marginalized by the Elizabethan establishment looked to Geneva for models and inspiration. The most outspoken manifesto of the earnest parliamentary pressure of the first half of the reign, the *Admonition to Parliament*, put the question quite simply: "Is a reformation good for France? and can it be evil for England? Is discipline meet for Scotland? and can it be unprofitable for this realm?" Exponents of the Reformed church orders eagerly drew attention to the example of the stranger churches in the capital, which lived out their own versions of Reformed church life in the midst of the citadel of Anglicanism. In this connection it is highly relevant that the *Admonition to Parliament* was published only after the failure of a parliamentary bill which would have legalized the use of the stranger churches' liturgies in parish churches.[34]

1. The School of Christ in Geneva

Thus, increasingly, English reformers tested the English settlement against the paradigm of Geneva, and found it wanting. The favorers of further institutional change hurled Calvin back in the face of members of the Establishment who they knew honored the man and read his works. Criticism of the state of English church life and morals was almost inevitably spiced with routine praise of the contrasting state of affairs in Geneva. John Reynolds, preaching in Oxford in the mid 1580s, compared the state of Oxford unfavorably with the School of Christ in Geneva. In Oxford there should be no drunkenness, beggars, whoring, or dancing: but all was not well. The implication was clear: none of this would be tolerated in the city of Calvin and Beza.[35]

---

[32]William P. Haugaard, *Elizabeth and the English Reformation: The Struggle for a Stable Settlement of Religion* (Cambridge: Cambridge University Press, 1970).

[33]Patrick Collinson, *The Elizabethan Puritan Movement* (London: Jonathan Cape, 1967).

[34]Patrick Collinson, "The Elizabethan Puritans and the Foreign Reformed Churches in London," *Proceedings of the Huguenot Society* 20 (1964): 518–55.

[35]Dent, *Protestant Reformers*, 182.

But was this denigration of English morals and church order, set against a demanding standard of continental perfection, really fair? As before, I wish to enter a number of qualifications which would militate against too absolute a separation between the developing values of English Anglicanism and the continental Calvinist mainstream. Firstly, one must question the purity of orthodox Calvinist criticism where it relates to English episcopacy. Although critics of the Elizabethan church settlement inevitably came to see bishops as a principal obstacle to change, Calvin himself had no prescriptive view on the question. As the *Institutes* make clear, Calvin was quite comfortable with a variety of forms of church organization, and his views on the government or the church were no more prescriptive than on secular authority. It was Beza who first introduced a strong exception to episcopacy. As Collinson has pointed out, one may trace very effectively in Beza's correspondence his movement from a cautious familiarity with the English bishops at the beginning of the reign, to a largely negative appraisal of English conditions, in particular a hardening contempt for diocesan episcopacy as lordly dominion. But even Beza was not necessarily prepared to express such views directly to members of the English establishment; he was too much of the ecclesiastical politician for that.[36] But the movement in Beza's views does make the point that the increasingly negative assessment of English church government was not fundamental to Calvinism, but a reaction to a developing sense of disappointment.

The same point could be made in relation to English presbyterianism, and the presbyterian assault on English church government. Presbyterian critics of the English church identified the root cause of the failure to combat both structural problems in the church and a widespread moral failure within the population with the defective scheme of congregational government, in other word the failure to institutionalize Calvinist church structures. But within this criticism lay a slightly misinformed view of the Genevan model. English presbyterianism was a later variation, as becomes clear if one examines a statement of presbyterian goals. According to Lake's definition, presbyterianism was a form of church government which vested ecclesiastical power first in the individual congregation, and then in a hierarchy of synods. The congregation was ruled by ministers and elders, and served by deacons collecting for their poor, all of which officers were elected by the congregation. The system was predicated on a sharp division between civil and ecclesiastical power, the discipline effectively excluding the lay power from the day-to-day running of the church.[37]

[36]Collinson, "England and International Calvinism," 210–11.
[37]Peter Lake, *Anglicans and Puritans? Presbyterian and English Conformist Thought from Whitgift to Hooker* (London: Unwin Hyman, 1988), 1–2.

This was a demanding standard to which Geneva itself could hardly match up. Geneva, in fact, left an extensive role for the magistrates in church affairs. This was something which harassed city governments would occasionally throw back in the faces of ministers who they thought had overreached themselves. When in 1576 the States of Holland and the local Reformed ministers were in dispute over who should elect ministers in the new state churches, the States wrote into their draft preamble a lengthy statement in which they pointed out that it was their proposed model, and not the autonomous congregational model proposed by the ministers, which in fact reflected the Genevan practice.[38]

This was more than just a debating point. It demonstrated that the foreign admirers of the Genevan polity were to a large extent attempting to impose on their own local conditions a highly idealized view of the Genevan system, and one which distorted crucial elements to their own advantage. Geneva was a "perfect school of Christ's church" only in John Knox's nostalgic imagination. One only has to read some of Calvin's sermons, in which he denounces the inadequacies of the local population in the most pungent terms to realize this. "The world is so disorderly that the impiety I can see in Geneva today is of such enormity that it is like seeing down a chasm into the very mouth of hell."[39] That was Calvin's own view of the "perfect school of Christ." It is ironic that the time when English presbyterians were attempting to build their idealized Geneva was precisely when Geneva itself was receding in influence, and the Genevan church polity was itself increasingly under strain.[40]

2. Critics of the English Church

Critics of the English church particularly regretted that in the absence of an effective congregational discipline the enforcement of a strict morality became well nigh impossible. Denunciations of moral degeneracy rife among the broad mass of the population became a commonplace in Elizabethan England, though one would think hardly more so than in other places in the Reformation century. But just as new work has suggested the essential unfairness of Calvin's designation of his domestic opponents as "libertines," reluctant to accept his own stricter concept of discipline,[41] it seems now that contemporary English critics who lamented the absence of a Genevan discipline grossly exaggerated the contrast between this

---

[38]C. Hooijer, *Oude Kerkordeningen der Nederlandsche Hervormde Gemeenten* (1563–1638), 121, 126–31. Cf. the translated extracts in Duke, Lewis and Pettegree, *Calvinism Documents,* here at 179.

[39]Duke, Lewis, and Pettegree, *Calvinism Documents,* 33.

[40]Gillian Lewis, "Calvinism in Geneva in the Time of Calvin and Beza, 1541–1608," in Prestwich, *International Calvinism,* 39–70.

[41]William Naphy, *Calvin and the Consolidation of the Genevan Reformation* (Manchester: Manchester University Press, 1994).

and a truly Reformed society. A recent study of attitudes to sexual disorder and incontinence in Elizabethan England by the social historian Martin Ingram has called attention to the remarkable similarity between the social values which existed in this society and in congregations governed by a Genevan-style consistory. It appears that English communities were governed, as one might expect, by a widespread consensus condemning illicit sexuality, and neighborly pressure could be exerted very effectively against those who infringed commonly held standards of decency.[42]

Equally, contemporary critics of English society did less than justice to the extent to which Calvinist preaching exercised an effective influence on wide areas of social behavior. In this respect the watershed decade seems to have been the 1580s, for it was then that apparently "Puritan" attitudes to important social institutions began to become generalized through society. One can identify the effects of this creeping influence on literature, drama, in attitudes to religious art and popular religious culture, and in increasingly rigorous attitudes to the Sabbath.[43] In fact the English Sunday was a much more rigorous affair than in many apparently more fully Calvinistic societies, such as the Netherlands. English visitors to the Netherlands frequently commented with surprise on the extremely relaxed Dutch attitude to sabbath observance, though this was not a situation of which the Reformed *predikanten* would have been proud. But all their sermons, petitions, and threats were in vain: the magistracy turned a deaf ear, and the shops and taverns remained open.[44]

3. Discipline and Scottish Calvinism

This introduces one final point: the question of whether consistorial discipline was necessary for the promotion of Calvinistic social values. Alongside a recognition of the progress made by the godly in inculcating their views on proper social relations and correct forms of sociability, must be placed a much less romanticized view of the real effectiveness of consistorial discipline in promoting general obedience to Calvinist moral values. The best laboratory for such an

---

[42]Martin Ingram, *Church Courts, Sex and Marriage in England, 1570–1640* (Cambridge: Cambridge University Press, 1987).

[43]Patrick Collinson, *The Birthpangs of Protestant England: Religious and Cultural Change in the Sixteenth and Seventeenth Centuries* (Houndmills: Macmillan, 1988). Tessa Watt, *Cheap Print and Popular Piety, 1550–1640* (Cambridge: Cambridge University Press, 1991). Kenneth L. Parker, *The English Sabbath* (Cambridge: Cambridge University Press, 1988).

[44]For English comment on the disorderly Dutch Sunday see the diary of Fynes Moryson, quoted in Martin A. Breslow, *A Mirror of England: English Puritan Views of Foreign Nations, 1618–1640* (Cambridge, Mass.: Harvard University Press, 1970), 92–93. Andrew Pettegree, "Coming to Terms with Victory: The Upbuilding of a Calvinist Church in Holland, 1572–1590," in Pettegree, Duke, and Lewis, *Calvinism in Europe*, 160–80.

investigation is probably Scotland, not least because its honored place as a mainstream Calvinist system has never seemed in much doubt. Certainly the leaders of the Scottish kirk had an opportunity which their Dutch brethren would have envied to subject the whole of their population to Calvinist moral regulation, acting in consort with a lay power which did not, as in the Netherlands, limit the effective control of the discipline to a small minority who became full confessing members of the church. In this respect Scotland had a real opportunity to be the nation state most nearly in tune with the Genevan model of a close cooperation of church and state to impose a strict Calvinist morality.

But that is not how it turned out. Scotland was undoubtedly formed and marked by its experience of Calvinism; but not without the ministers having made real compromises in order to secure the cooperation of the lay power. The principle of an indifferent justice without respect for persons and social status was one which was necessarily speedily sacrificed in order to reconcile the local laird to what would otherwise have been a highly intrusive form of social regulation.[45]

In the same way, Calvinism in Scotland proved itself in at least one respect highly adaptable to local cultural forms, in order to win an influential role in a highly traditional society. I am thinking here primarily of Calvinism in the Highlands, the Celtic speaking Gaidhealtachd, so elegantly surveyed in a recent article by Jane Dawson.[46] Not only did the Calvinist missionaries find ways to inculcate loyalties to the new church in an essentially nonliterate culture, largely by shrewd alliances with clan leaders, they also soothed the misgivings of local folk by accepting parts of the local culture which one would normally have expected to be abhorrent to right-thinking Calvinists. These included a variety of supernatural practices which Gaelic Calvinist ministers accepted as deeply ingrained, and as a not particularly harmful or threatening part of local cultural observances.

It is a remarkable story and brings us face to face with the flexibility of a system which is sometimes unfairly characterized as rigid and dogmatic. Perhaps contemporaries understood better than have modern historians, that differences of custom and practice did not necessarily take churches such as the English Anglican church out of the Calvinist family. The fact that English preachers

---

[45]Michael Graham, "Social Discipline in Scotland, 1560–1610," in Raymond A. Mentzer, ed., *Sin and the Calvinists: Moral Control and the Consistory in the Reformed Tradition*, Sixteenth Century Essays and Studies, 32 (Kirksville, Mo.: Sixteenth Century Journal Publishers, 1994); idem, "The Civil Sword and the Scottish Kirk, 1560–1600," in W. Fred Graham, *Later Calvinism. International Perspectives*, Sixteenth Century Essays and Studies, 22 (Kirksville, MO: Sixteenth Century Journal Publishers, 1994). Graham's work offers a substantially less generous view of the effectiveness of discipline in Scotland than that of Geoffrey Parker, "The 'Kirk by Law Established' and Origins of 'The Taming of Scotland': Saint Andrews, 1559–1600," also in Mentzer, *Sin and the Calvinists*, 159–97.

[46]Jane Dawson, "Calvinism and the Gaidhealtachd in Scotland," in Pettegree, Duke, and Lewis, *Calvinism in Europe*, 231–53.

lamented the imperfections of their own church, as is the proper function of preachers in any age, should not be read as a sweeping condemnation of English Anglicanism, nor as a negation of its essential Reformed, Calvinistic roots. Loyalty and affinity can be expressed in various ways, some not always well understood in ages with different social mores. But when the cause of International Calvinism on the continent of Europe seemed to be under threat, it was to England that the brethren looked for assistance, counsel, and prayers, and with a certain confidence that their hopes would not be rebuffed.[47] It is in these circles and connections that the true nature of European Calvinism is to be found, a strongly bonded affinity from which the English church should not be discounted.

---

[47]Collinson, "England and International Calvinism," 203–10. Ole Peter Grell, *Dutch Calvinists in Early Stuart London: The Dutch Church in Austin Friars, 1603–1642* (Leiden: Brill, 1989), 176–223.

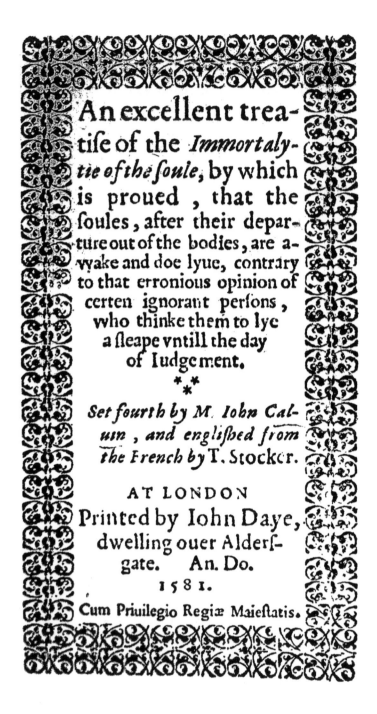

An excellent trea-
tife of the *Immortaly-*
tie of the foule, by which
is proued , that the
foules , after their depar-
ture out of the bodies, are a-
vvake and doe lyue, contrary
to that erronious opinion of
certen ignorant perfons ,
who thinke them to lye
a fleape vntill the day
of Iudgement.

**

Set fourth by M. Iohn Cal-
uin , and englifhed from
the French by T. Stocker.

AT LONDON
Printed by Iohn Daye,
dwelling ouer Alderf-
gate.   An. Do.
1581.
Cum Priuilegio Regiæ Maieftatis.

Karl Barth as Interpreter of Calvin's *Psychopannychia*

Hans Scholl[1]

I. The Theses of the Psychopannychia and their Assessment

Calvin wrote the Psychopannychia[2] in the fall of 1534, shortly before he left France for good. In the late summer a manuscript of some one hundred pages was ready for the printer; its preface was addressed "To a certain friend" (*Ad quendam amicum*), and Orleans is indicated as the place of publication. The booklet never appeared in this first version; hence its title, too, is rather uncertain. In his correspondence Calvin once referred to a manuscript on the immortality of the soul, which was ready for publication.[3] When in 1542 the manuscript was published for the first time at Strasbourg it was entitled, "The souls of those who have died believing in Christ live with Christ and do not sleep" (*Vivere apud Christum non dormire animis sanctos qui in fide Christi decedunt*). The title succinctly summarizes the content of the tract. At issue is the state of the souls of believers in Christ after their death. This formulation is a subheading of the general topic on immortality of the soul. An answer to the question is given within the parameter of the Christian life [*vita christiana*]: i.e., to live with Christ [*vivere apud Christum*]. Rejected are two teachings which claim (a) that after death souls sleep until the Last Judgment and (b) that at the moment of physical death the soul also dies and will be raised together with the body at the time of the Last Judgment.

At first glance Barth appeals to our own sensitivities when he speaks of the "arbitrary remoteness"[4] of the topic or when he asserts that "we can read the entire tract, and still shake our head just as much as when we read the title only."[5]

---

[1]I am grateful to E. J. Furcha, Faculty of Religious Studies, McGill University, Montreal, who translated the text into English; see also Hans Scholl, ed., *Karl Barth und Johannes Calvin: Karl Barths Göttinger Calvin-Vorlesung von 1994* (Neukirchen: Neukirchener Verlag, 1995), 155–71.
[2]For the full text of the *Psychopannychia* see *CO* 5.165–232. See also, *Quellenschriften zur Geschichte des Protestantismus*, ed. Carl Stange, vol. 13, *Psychopannychia*, by John Calvin, ed. Walther Zimmerli (Leipzig: A. Deichertsche, 1932), 108 pp. The title *Psychopannychia* appears only in the second edition, Strasbourg, 1545. It is likely not Calvin's title, but that of the printer/publisher and is best translated as "the wakefulness of souls." Since this was misunderstood later, the term was translated by "soul sleep." On this see ibid., 10.
[3]See *CO* 10:2:52, Calvin to Christoph Faber, 3 September 1535.
[4]Barth uses the term "arbiträre Abgelegenheit."
[5]Karl Barth, *Die Theologie Calvins 1922*. Karl Barth Gesamtausgabe, 2 (Zurich: TVZ, 1993), 194–95.

Wolfgang Capito, probably after having consulted with Martin Bucer, recommended as late as 1535 against publication, because there were weightier matters to be dealt with at the moment.[6] It must also be said that Barth's further comments on the *Psychopannychia* show that the topic merely appears to be arbitrary. How, after all, could the subject of death be arbitrary unless we repress it? And that is precisely what Calvin, in the tradition of Psalm 90, did not wish to do.[7] And so we find that the theme of the *Psychopannychia*, as soon as we go below the surface, is not at all far fetched, and is certainly not just a mere recounting of "eschatological whims."[8] Rather, the theme points up certain aspects which give it some relevance and urgency, especially in the early sixteenth century.

First, the theme must be viewed against the background of the renewed dispute in the fifteenth century between the Platonic and the Aristotelian traditions and their influence on theological thinking. Here the problem of the soul, in other words, the question regarding the immortality of the soul or its transience and entanglement with matter, is merely one of the many aspects in the dispute.[9] The nature of universals, too, continues to be debated and continues in part in the intra-reformatory conflict regarding the Lord's Supper.

And is the burning issue of that day—the selling of indulgences—perchance far removed from the theme of the *Psychopannychia*, namely from its concern over life after death? More forcefully than Barth was aware of, the question concerning the state of the soul after death was being discussed in the decades prior to the Reformation. Jung-Uck Hwang was able to cite a long list of ecclesiastical decrees and contemporary tracts on the topic, among which the *Psychopannychia* must be numbered.[10] We should also note in this context that Calvin's voice is significantly anticipated by Heinrich Bullinger and Ulrich Zwingli.[11] To drive home my point

[6]See *CO* 10:2:45–46.

[7]See *CO* 31: 840 on Ps. 90:12, "Ut numeremus dies nostros sic scire fac, et adducemus cor ad sapientiam: nemo composita mente vitam instituet, nisi qui cognito vitae fine, hoc est morte ipsa, ad considerandum vivendi scopum deductus fuerit, ut ad palmam supernae vocationis pergat."

[8]Barth, *Calvin*, 207.

[9]On the "Battle of the Traditions" (Platonists/Aristotelians) in the course of the fifteenth and sixteenth centuries see W. Windelband, *Lehrbuch der Geschichte der Philosophie*, ed. H. Heimsoeth (Tübingen: J.C.B. Mohr [Paul Siebeck], 1957), 15: 306–314. See also F. Copleston, *A History of Philosophy*, vol. 3, parts 1, 2 (New York: Image Books, 1963).

[10]See Jung-Uck Hwang, *Der junge Calvin und seine Psychopannychia* (Ph.D. dissertation, Wuppertal, 1990; published Frankfurt: Peter Lang, 1991). Note esp. the excursus "Verfechter der Lehre vom Seelenschlaf vor 1534"—defender of the doctrine regarding soul sleep, before 1534; 118–127.

[11]In a letter to Paul Beck written in the summer of 1526 (HBBW, 2:127–33), Henry Bullinger was the first to challenge the doctrine of soul sleep. On this cf. Heinold Fast, *Heinrich Bullinger und die Täufer*, Schriftenreihe des mennonitischen Geschichtsvereins, no. 7 (Weierhof: Pfalz, 1959), 26–28. Subsequently Zwingli too opposed the doctrine in *Catabaptistarum strophas elenchus* (1527); see Z VI 1:188–89, and in *Fidei Expositio*, see Z VI 5:126.8–9 (July 1531), and earlier still in 1523 in his exposition of the 37th article (Z 2:430–31) and during the Second Zurich Disputation of October 1523 against Hofmeister (Z 2:782–83).

in the shortest and most pleasant manner, may I refer you to Umberto Eco who, as you know, uses medieval sources in the most graphic manner. In his well-known novel, *The Name of the Rose*, the righteous Benedictines—platonically turned toward the world above—are annoyed with their pope. He is carved from a totally different block of wood, namely an Aristotelian piece—wholly this-worldly in outlook. A full two hundred years before the Reformation he shocked the righteous people of his day. Calvin also mentions the same pope, Pope John XXII.[12] Eco spins the following tale:[13]

> "He?" Ubertino interrupted him. "Why, you do not yet know his follies in the field of theology! ... He is planning some mad if not perverse propositions that would change the very substance of doctrine and would deprive our preaching of all power."

Brother Berengar goes on to elaborate on this:

> "It is a murky and almost incredible story," Berengar said. "It seems John is planning to declare that the just will not enjoy the beatific vision until after Judgment." ... "And more, it seems that he wants to go further and assert that hell too will not open before that day, not even for the devils."

> "Lord Jesus, assist us," Jerome cried. "And what will we tell sinners then, if we cannot threaten them with an immediate hell the moment they are dead?"

> "We are in the hands of a madman," Ubertino said. "But I do not understand why he wants to assert these things...."

> "The whole doctrine of indulgences goes up in smoke," Jerome complained, "and not even he will be able to sell any after that. Why should a priest who has committed the sin of bestiality, pay so many gold pieces to avoid such a remote punishment?"

> "Not so remote," Ubertino said firmly. "The hour is at hand."

> "You know that, dear brother, but the simple do not know it. This is how things stand!" cried Jerome in agitation. "What an evil idea; those

---

[12]See *CO* 5:171–72, "Et aliquanto post tempore, Ioannem episcopum romanum, quem schola parisiensis ad palinodiam adegerit."

[13]Umberto Eco, *The Name of the Rose*, trans. William Weaver (New York: Warner Books, 1984), 355–58, abbreviated (a German translation was made by B. Kroeber and published in Munich/Vienna in 1982; the cited passage there is on pp. 378–82).

preaching friars [Aristotelians! H.S.] must have put it into his head....
Ah!" And he shook his head.

The fictitious narrator, Adson, a novice, says somewhat later that the dogmatic
advance of John XXII was exactly along the lines which his own mentor William
of Canterbury had predicted.

> My master was truly very sharp. How could he foresee that in four years'
> time, when John was first to pronounce his incredible doctrine, there
> would be an uprising on the part of all Christianity? If the beatific vision
> was thus postponed how could the dead intercede for the living? And
> what would become of the cult of the saints? It was the Minorites them-
> selves who would open hostilities in condemning the Pope and William
> of Occam would be in the front rank, stern and implacable in his argu-
> ments. The conflict was to last for three years until John, close to death,
> made partial amends. Years later I heard him described as he appeared in
> the Council of December 1334,... and how with a pale and gaunt face he
> declared.... We confess and believe that the souls separated from the
> body and completely purified are in heaven, in paradise with the angels
> and with Jesus Christ, and that they see God in his divine essence, clearly,
> face to face ... and then after a short pause—it was never known whether
> this was due to his difficulty in breathing or to his perverse desire to
> underline the last clause as adversative—"to the extent to which the state
> and condition of the separated souls allow." The next morning, a Sunday,
> he had himself laid on a long chair with reclining back, and he received
> the cardinals who kissed his hand, and he died.

As you can see, as far as Eco is concerned our topic touches on the concerns of the
times.

But we have no need to roam into Ecoesque distant horizons. One of the
major references Calvin uses against any kind of soul sleep of the righteous may be
found in the Confession of Faith all of us share: after his death on the cross Jesus
descends into the domain of the dead and preaches to the righteous of every age.[14]
Together with the Lazarus account[15] and the Pauline desire to depart and be with
Christ,[16] the *descensus ad inferos* is a major argument Calvin uses in support of the
wakefulness of the soul after death. Even when in some details Calvin fails to find
the scope of the Scripture passage he cites—more often than not he misses—he
nonetheless has to this day, as Barth emphasizes, by and large sound scholarship
on his side. Joachim Jeremias, quite apart from Calvin's first tract, sums up the

---

[14]See *CO* 5:185–86.   [15]See *CO* 5:187–88.   [16]See *CO* 5:197.

findings of New Testament scholarship in an article on Hades: The notion of soul sleep is as alien to the entire New Testament as it is to late Judaism. The image of sleep is ... merely a euphemism to indicate death.[17]

But is Calvin's tract also relevant as Reformed testimony? If we take it in its definitive version of 1542 this question can be answered easily in the affirmative. Even the preface of 1536, *Lectoribus*, has Reformed overtones. The question is less clearly answered in view of the very first version of 1534 which is of special interest to us. There we actually find nothing in the significant Preface *Ad quendam amicum* that would point us in a Reformed direction. This much must be preliminary considerations and should be said at the outset:

(1) At first glance the theme of the *Psychopannychia* in itself does not fall back on any basic themes of the Reformation. Had it been argued in a Reformed mode, a negative mention of the teaching regarding purgatory would have been inevitable.

(2) By contrast to the aggressive, revolutionary Cop speech of November 1533—if it was indeed Calvin's—the *Psychopannychia* strikes up a different note. It picks up on a topic that was debated in the catholic scholastic theology of the late Middle Ages. The *Psychopannychia* advocates and defends, as did the Sorbonne two hundred years earlier, the dogma of the wakefulness of the soul after death.[18]

(3) As I stated earlier, the preface of 1534 appears not to have been influenced by Reformed ideas. The antagonists, too, whom he probably aimed at in the *Psychopannychia*, and who held some notion of soul sleep or death of the soul in whatever form, do not direct the tract toward basic questions of the Reformation. Hwang reaches the following conclusion after a thorough overview:[19] In Calvin's day this teachings was held—first by Pomponazzi, restorer of philosophical Aristotelianism; second, by the humanist circle around Margaret of Navarre, along with the lutheranizing Bishop Briçonnet of Meaux near Paris, who, of course, distanced himself from everything "heretical" at the first encounter of difficulties with the Reformation or simply with reform-minded people in France; third and finally, by Luther and Karlstadt. This insight, too, makes it difficult to assess the *Psychopannychia* as a Reformation writing of the allegedly greatest disciple of Luther.

Scholarship up to most recent times had nothing to present that was very enlightening on the subject. Even the Wuppertal thesis, "Young Calvin and His

---

[17]J. Jeremias, "Hades" in the New Testament: 1. Its link to Judaism," in *ThWNT*, 1:148.
[18]See n. 11 above regarding the affair surrounding Pope John XXII; Hwang, *Psychopannychia*, 161–64. Further, N. Tylenda, "Calvin and the Avignon Sermons of John XXII," *Irish Theological Quarterly* 41 (1974),: 37–52, and Heiko A. Obermann, "Initia Calvini" in *Calvinus sacrae scripturae professor.* Papers Presented at the International Congress for Calvin Research, 1990 at Grand Rapids, MI, ed. W. H. Neuser (Grand Rapids: Eerdmans, 1994), 140–52.
[19]See Hwang, *Psychopannychia*, 123.

Psychopannychia," completed some years ago by Hwang, has its strength in specific observations rather than in its attempts at a comprehensive interpretation.
Now, however, Karl Barth's Calvin lecture has been aroused from its seventy-year
sleep by the Kirchliche Hochschule Wuppertal. In this work by the young Barth
Calvin scholarship is forcefully reminded that in order to understand Calvin this
text must, of necessity, be interpreted and understood comprehensively. Barth
himself made every effort in this his first historical lecture to achieve a break-
through. With a great touch of irony he wrote his friends in Switzerland that he
had just presented a brilliant hypothesis[20] about the *Psychopannychia* which naturally had waited specifically for him, Barth, to be interpreted correctly.[21] Barth's
incredible theological sensitivity in grasping historical texts allows us to anticipate
something very illuminating. Here then are some aspects of his "brilliant hypothesis."

II. BARTH'S EMPHASIS OF THE ETHICAL MOMENT

The years 1530 to 1540 are the great, hopeful years of Reformation history. In Germany they seem to lead the Reformation to victory. In France too the Reformation
gains ground from year to year, from day to day. Everything seems to breathe the
morning air of the Reformation. Just as ten years earlier the peasants in Germany
wrote "freedom" on their flags under the impact of the reformatory message, so a
sense of freedom gripped "la douce France" as well. The justification of the sinner
rooted in the freedom of a Christian, and firmly and bindingly laid down for the
first time in the *Confessio Augustana* of 1530, through social criticism found
immediate expression in France as well. Not the peasants (they had to wait until
1789), but the future-oriented bourgeoisie of intellectuals and tradespeople, the
upholders of culture at the time, sensed liberation from the scourge of conservative ecclesiastical tutelage. Humanists like Bonaventure Des Periers and Etienne
Dolet did not stop their criticism even in face of positive representatives of the
Christian religion and their dogmas. The medical student Michael Servetus developed the plan of a sharp attack on the current doctrine of the trinity, first in the
childlike sense of discovery of a youthful humanist, and then incognito as physi-
cian and secretary of the bishop of Lyon. More effective still and fully informed by
the problems of the times was the critique of François Rabelais, who surrendered
scholastic society and church to the ridicule of the day in his utopian novel
Gargantua & Pantagruel.[22] And did not the humanistically enlightened despot

---

[20]Unpublished letter of 30 May 1922 (now located in the Karl Barth Archiv, Basel) to his brother,
Peter Barth.
[21]See Bw.Th. 2:9.
[22]On Calvin and Rabelais see Johann Bohatec, *Budé und Calvin-Studien zur Gedankenwelt des
französischen Frühhumanismus* (Graz, 1950), especially pp. 214–231.

Francis I have his fun with Rabelais and his like *joyeuse liberté?* Here Reformation is understood as license to engage in moral libertinism.[23] This danger was particularly real in easygoing France. A reaction or, to say it better, a clarification regarding the true meaning of the doctrine of justification had to come if the Reformation in France was not to disqualify itself from its very onset; if the "happy exchange"[24] of the freedom of a Christian was not to degenerate into the *joyeuse liberté* of dissolute humanists.

Barth's image of the young Calvin and with it the interpretation of his first publication, the *Psychopannychia*, must be understood wholly in this context. The Reformation faces the inevitable turnabout from faith in justification to the doctrine of sanctification. Only the romantics of the early Reformation, the gnesio-Lutherans, could miss this inevitability. Barth draws a line from the Cop speech of 1 November 1533 to the *Psychopannychia* of the summer of 1534. Along with conservative scholarship he takes the Cop speech to be an authentic Calvin text.[25] Although Calvin follows in part at least a Luther original fairly closely, the text is clearly given a different nuance: Luther's trust in Christ alone is (in the Cop speech) equated with *solam Dei gloriam quaerere.* The notion in Luther that God demands that our heart be reshaped (without the author's awareness of it) into the somewhat different notion that it is God who demands our heart. In this way it becomes a compelling appeal to renounce all other things in order to be able to stand before the judgment throne of Christ.[26] From there, in other words, from the necessary ethical starting point of the time, Barth draws a line to the *Psychopannychia.*

But there seem to be a number of things that speak against a Reformed interpretation of the *Psychopannychia.* The very fact that until recently Calvin scholars ignored this early Calvin text points to the difficulty of a meaningful interpretation and classification. The very theme of the tract, "On the Immortality of the Soul" speaks against its being interpreted as a polemical writing of the Reformation.

The most recent and to this day the most comprehensive work on the *Psychopannychia,* the Wuppertal dissertation of the Korean church historian Jung-Uck Hwang, *Der junge Calvin und seine Psychopannychia* (The Young Calvin and His *Psychopannychia*), tries to show that in this work Calvin has entered an internal

---

[23]Bohatec, *Budé und Calvin,* 199; "joyeuse liberté" is the "exlex licentia" and "cupiditas," (falsely) attributed to the Protestants by Budé.
[24]The term was used by Martin Luther in "Freedom of a Christian" of 1520; WA 7.26. For an English translation, see *Luther's Works,* vol. 31 (Philadelphia: Mühlenberg, 1957).
[25]On the question of the authorship of the speech see H. Scholl, *Calvin-Studienausgabe,* 1/1, ed. E. Busch et al. (Neukirchen: Neukirchener Verlag, 1994), 1–9.
[26]Barth, *Calvin,* 189.

catholic debate representing here the teaching of a conservative catholic school. And indeed some passages of the *Psychopannychia* can be readily understood that way.[27]

Hwang reads the 1534 preface to the *Psychopannychia* and by implication the entire writing as non- and pre-reformatory, since a preface, after all, indicates the major content and direction of a text. On this point Hwang is greatly influenced by Alexandre Ganoczy's view of Calvin. Ganoczy states, "When one reads this small booklet (namely the *Psychopannychia*) one is surprised to find not a single anti-Catholic charge, indeed, not even a hint in that direction."[28]

However much this argumentation seems to contradict Barth's suggested interpretation, it does not on its part solve all problems of interpretation of Calvin's novice theological work.

The *Psychopannychia* was written in 1534 and was prepared for printing in Orleans, but it was not published. After Calvin's flight from France to Basel, the tract was reworked there, given a new preface in 1536, but again not published. Only in 1542, after Calvin's first stay in Geneva, was the tract finally published in Strasbourg in its 1536 version. Hwang himself points out, on the basis of good supportive evidence, that the small booklet was rewritten in 1536 but that its content remained the same.[29] Calvin merely changed the structure and undertook a few stylistic refinements. While the 1534 tract begins rather polemically with a sharp settling of accounts with the defenders of the doctrine of soul sleep, placing Calvin's own positive exposition second, the revised work is structured in reverse order.

When finally in 1542 the small booklet appeared Calvin had already risen to the position of Reformer; indeed, he had become the quiet leader of the entire Reformation, praised by Luther, recognized by Bucer, and on friendly terms with Philip Melanchthon. Now we cannot assume that he would at this stage have published a white elephant from his pre-Reform days had the work (whose content did not change from the time of its creation in 1534), not had reformatory relevance for him? The absence in the *Psychopannychia* of anti-Roman polemics cannot be explained as a fallback to the pre-Reform level of Calvin's early works, as Ganoczy and Hwang would have it. We alluded earlier to the reformatory-ethical dimension of the *Psychopannychia*, which Barth recognized and stressed. However, in Barth's exposition, too, there is a lacuna in his questions regarding

---

[27]See Hwang, *Psychopannychia*, 262, n. 314.

[28]"En lisant ce petit livre, on est frappé de ce qu'il ne contient aucun excurs antiromain, et même pas d'allusion de ce genre"; Alexandre Ganoczy, *Le jeune Calvin* (Mainz: F. Steiner, 1966), 77.

[29]See J Hwang, *Popannychia* 178–84. For the publication history of the *Psychopannychia* see W. Zimmerli, *Psychopannychia*, 6–13.

the unreformed content of the *Psychopannychia*: Ganoczy and Hwang put their finger on the absence of an anti-Roman polemic and the apparent acceptance of catholic scholastic positions. Barth speaks of a method of proceeding which at first glance appears to be arbitrary—the replacement of one eschatological whim by another.[30] Not one of them mentions, however, that the doctrine of the immortality of the soul experienced a significant replenishing in medieval theology, as did the entire aggregate: purgatory, prayer for the dead, indulgences, and so on. In no way could Calvin have strengthened classical catholic scholastic theology with his *Psychopannychia*, had he not been prepared to take a positive stand on purgatory and indulgences. His silence on the matter is an indirect, if not a direct, attack on catholic teaching on the question of life, and the status and activity of the soul after death.[31]

III. Is the *Psychopannychia* an intra-Protestant Polemic?

As indicated above, the very identification of Calvin's first antagonists in the *Psychopannychia* represents the crux of its interpretation. In his minute analysis of the 1534 preface, Hwang said everything that can be said on the matter.[32] Calvin himself has built some of the confusion into his text. He writes against antagonists whom he does not know personally or whom he knows at best through hearsay.[33] Without giving specific reasons, he identifies the advocates of the doctrine of soul sleep with the Anabaptists without specifically knowing them.[34]

Furthermore, in 1534 Calvin had encountered Michael Servetus, whose medically oriented teaching on soul sleep resonates in the *Psychopannychia* and is rejected there.[35] Granted Servetus opposed infant baptism, but he does not identify with the Anabaptists in the narrower sense of that term. The circle around Servetus is made up mostly of Italian humanists who belong to the school of neo-

---

[30]Barth, *Calvin*, 207.

[31]On the medieval notions regarding the other world, see the most recent informative and comprehensive catalogue of the Schweizerischen Landesmuseum by P. Jezler, prepared for the exhibit Himmel-Hölle-Fegefeuer (Heaven-hell-purgatory), Zurich/Cologne, 1994. In this compendium volume Kathrin Utz Tremp demonstrates in "Waldenser und Wiedergänger—Das Fegefeuer im Inquisitionsregister des Bischofs Jacques Fournier von Pamiers (1317–1326)," that besides the Waldensian refusal to swear oaths, it was specifically their rejection of the notion of purgatory which led to the Waldenses being condemned to death in this heresy trial; see especially 125–34.

[32]See n. 17 above.

[33]See CO 5:169–70: "Nondum enim quidquam ad me perlatum erat, praeter murmura et raucos strepitus."

[34]See CO 5:171–72: "Verum saeculis aliquot sopitum, nuper per aliquot ex Anabaptistarum faece excitatum, scintillas emisit."

[35]See CO 5:177: "Alii nihil minus quam substantiam esse [animam] concedunt: sed vim duntaxat vitae esse aiunt, quae ex spiritu arteriae, aut pulmonum agitatione ducitur: et quia sine corpore subiecto subsistere nequit, ideo una cum corpore interit et evanescit [1545: interire et evanescere fingunt]: donec totus homo suscitetur." The heart-lung circulation of the blood discovered by Servetus appears to me to be in the background here, combined with a clear Aristotelian doctrine of the soul.

Aristotelians and who more or less fit the image of the antagonists Calvin had in mind.[36] There must surely have been some Anabaptists who around 1534 advocated a doctrine of soul sleep; however, the notion was not genuinely Anabaptist. It should be noted in addition that the doctrine of soul sleep was explicitly rejected by exponents of the Zurich Reformation, first by Bullinger and then by Zwingli,[37] approximately eight years before the *Psychopannychia*. Here too, similar to what happened in Calvin's case later, the antagonists of the Zuricher remain unnamed.[38] While Calvin could hardly have known Bullinger's letter to Paul Beck, he might well have read Zwingli's *Elenchus* in 1534. In his analysis of the 1534 preface by Calvin, Hwang convincingly resolves the question regarding the antagonists: Calvin's tract of 1534 is not at all, or at best by implication, directed against specific antagonists. Rather, he attacks a doctrine or a dogma, which is in the air.[39] Just because the question regarding Calvin's antagonists was anything but clear in 1534, if the *Psychopannychia* was to have a future; it was to begin soon.

Guillaume Farel, who since 1537 was fighting Anabaptists in Neuenburg, called for a French translation of the *Psychopannychia* of 1536/42 which could be understood by the people.[40] Somewhat later Calvin writes explicitly in French against the Anabaptists.[41] It is true that this tract contains passages from the *Psychopannychia*; but obviously the *Psychopannychia* itself is not easily suited for disputes with the Anabaptists.

More important still is a second trail. As early as 1534 or 1535 Calvin had sent the *Psychopannychia* to the Strasbourg reformers, likely with the intention to have it published there. He receives Wolfgang Capito's reply: Apart from the total illegibility of Calvin's handwriting, Capito finds the tract too harsh. It should be reworked into a milder form since the tract could easily disturb the peace of the church.[42] Calvin reacts immediately to these reservations by Capito. On the one hand, he reports in the new preface, written at Basel in 1536 on the reshaped form

[36]See Hwang's argument in Hwang, *Psychopannychia*, 122–23, and Timothy George, "Calvin's Psychopannychia: Another Look," in Edward J. Furcha, ed., *In Honour of John Calvin*. Papers from the 1986 International Calvin Symposium, McGill University. ARC Supplement 3 (Montreal: Faculty of Religious Studies,, 1987): 297–329, especially 306–7.
[37]See n. 11 above.
[38]In his letter to Beck of 1526, Bullinger does not mention the Anabaptists. Only in *In catabaptistarum strophas elenchus* of 1527 (Z VI/I, pp. 1–196), especially p. 188, does Zwingli establish a link between the Anabaptists and the defenders of the doctrine of soul sleep. Bullinger later follows him in this.
[39]See J. Hwang, *Psychopannychia*, 108–9; Hwang underscores the frequent designation of the teaching on soul sleep as "dogma;" he identifies this as a characteristic of the preface of 1534.
[40]Cf. *Guillaume Farel 1489–1565. Biographie nouvelle* (Neuchatel/Paris: Comité Farel, 1930), 536.
[41]Cf. *CO* 7:45–142, "Briefve instruction pout armer tous bons fideles contre les erreurs de la secte commune des Anabaptistes," 1544 (within this text pp. 114–39 is an excerpt from the *Psychopannychia*).
[42]Wolfgang Capito to Calvin in *CO* 10/2 pp. 45–46.

of the tract; on the other hand, however, he stresses rather forcefully that the topic is serious and central and that the "brothers" have every reason in as important a matter as this "to cling always to the mouth of the Lord" and not to add or take anything away from his wisdom, which can be found only in Scripture. Such conduct alone will guard against heresy and preserve the unity of the church and the common weal.[43] In other words, Calvin had touched a festering boil within the Reformed camp with the preface of 1536, which was clearly addressed to his Strasbourg friends. Not primarily the simple Anabaptists, but the circle of Wittenberg Reformers held to some sort of teaching regarding soul sleep. In 1523 Carlstadt, in agreement with Luther on this point, wrote a tract against prayers for the dead and indulgences and he substantiated the impossibility of this catholic teaching with the notion of soul sleep.[44] Luther fought the fifth Lateran Council of 1512 and its dogma of the immortality of the soul on philosophico-theological grounds.[45]

In 1922, Barth did not as yet have a clear understanding of the Lutheran teaching on soul sleep; but he felt instinctively that a decisive front of the *Psychopannychia* manifested itself here. The doctrine of justification, the *sola gratia* of the first hour of the Reformation, can be misunderstood not only from the left, but also from the right. It offers too weak a starting point for the development of ethics. The Reformed doctrine of justification could contain or develop a strong quietistic element: "Be satisfied and hold still"[46] is the song of later Lutheran orthodoxy, "...let God do it." Resting in God's justifying activity could take on mystical-quietist overtones even with Luther. Barth interprets correctly when he states: "The teaching regarding soul sleep ... could appear in formulations which seemed to resemble closely the reformed insight of the path from life to death, as Luther had taught it."[47] After 1530 the conflict over the place of the law in Lutheranism demonstrated that many Lutherans had developed into genuine romantics (something Luther never was) regarding the doctrine of justification. I should like to remind you here of the poignant statement by Nicholas of Amsdorf in the Majorist controversy, that good works are detrimental to salvation.[48] It is

---

[43]Cf. *CO* 5:175–76; see also Hwang, *Psychopannychia,* 158–60 (comparison of the prefaces of 1534 and 1536).

[44]Cf. Hwang, *Psychopannychia,* 119, n. 112, on Carlstadt's tract: Andreas Bodenstein von Karlstadt, "Ein sermon vom stand der Christglaubigen Seelen von Abrahams Schoss und Fegefeuer der abgeschyden seelen 1523" (Wittenberg, 1523).

[45]Cf. *WA* 20:162–63, and George, *Calvin's Psychopannychia,* 10.

[46]Paul Gerhardt, 1607–1676. "Gib Dich zufrieden und sei still" is quoted from *Gesangbuch der evangelisch-reformierten Kirchen der deutschsprachigen Schweiz* (1952), hymn no. 277.

[47]Barth, *Calvin,* 200; note there the quotes from Luther.

[48]On the so-called Majorist controversy see B. Hägglund, *Geschichte der Theologie: Ein Abriss,* 2d ed. (Munich, 1990), 213.

evident that Calvin had touched a sore point and that, when seen in this light, the *Psychopannychia* had evolved into an intra-Protestant polemical writing. Justification without sanctification encroached on God's business as much as the late medieval notion of sanctification without justification had. Barth: "It simply could not be that the gospel which Luther had proclaimed should be perceived as signalling an inactivity which would dishonor God anew and worse than before. There was to be no such thing as a lazy, idle eternity."[49] There was to be no religious siesta between justification and sanctification.

Today we see clearer than Barth did in 1922 that the *Psychopannychia* has to be interpreted within this range of questions. We can leave aside for the moment whether in 1534 Calvin had his antagonists clearly in view. In 1536 he does, and according to the respective preface he knows that the *Psychopannychia* has the task of calling to reason good people who speak of soul sleep (as for example Luther's camp). What may have been correct in the first hour of the Reformation in its battle against purgatory and indulgences had, in its second hour, to be more carefully thought through and formulated more in keeping with the Word of God. This could only happen in the direction that the state of the Christian person's soul at peace had to be understood not as the sleep of the soul but as the peace of the living, the *pax viventium*.[50] If the soul has something to do with Christ and vice versa then it could only be that this poor little whorish[51] soul, freed from its constant limpness and sleepiness, should become the wide-awake, living bride of Christ. For, so Calvin later: "Faith (in justification) is the resurrection of the soul,"[52] to immortality, of course, and not to the sleep of the soul.[53]

That this total ethical dimension and purposing of the *Psychopannychia*, which Barth demanded, is correct is evidenced by its subsequent publication history: In 1536 the revised *Psychopannychia* was again not published. At this point Calvin is engaged in debate with the Strasbourger regarding the necessity of such a publication. These, however, traumatized by the conflict regarding the Lord's Supper, are not at all keen on pouring oil on the fire of the tensions between Wittenberg and Upper Germany with the new discussion topic "soul sleep." Calvin, however, was not intent on conflict, but on a better, well-founded peace. He is intent on a Reformation which will satisfy the demands of the Reformation even after 1530. Even Bucer sees this more and more clearly. Beginning in 1538 he too

---

[49]Barth, *Calvin*, 202.   [50]*CO* 5:190.   [51]See n. 23 above.

[52]*CO* 7:599: "Fides est animae resurrectio" (Interim adultero-germanum: cui adiecta est Vera christianae pacificationis et ecclesiae reformandae ratio [1549]).

[53]Cf. Barth, *Calvin*, 201: "It is not by accident that in more than one instance he has difficulties in distinguishing convincingly the state of departed believers from that of believers still living. The righteous person in the bosom of Abraham who anticipates the last things is Calvin's righteous person, regardless of whether in this life (*in hac vita*) or after this life (*post hanc vitam*)."

demands its publication. In 1542, then, the time has come for the *Psychopannychia* to appear in Strasbourg, without offending the Lutherans, but rather to instruct them quietly, not only through a piece of good theology, but through a tract which is generally important and foundational to understanding the Christian life. Meanwhile Calvin fully took into account in his French Psalter what was important to Luther as the certainty of faith, especially with *Simeon's Thanksgiving*, and he expressed it wonderfully without using the ambiguous Lutheran metaphor of soul sleep:

> Maintenant, Seigneur Dieu
> as donne, en moi lieu
> a ta sainte promesse
> puisque ton serviteur
> sortir des tout malheur
> en bon repos tu laisses.[54]

With the ethical interpretation of the *Psychopannychia* Barth located its *Sitz im Leben* within the intra-Protestant debate regarding the indissoluble interrelationship of justification and sanctification. Much, but by no means everything that is essential about its interpretation, has been said with this.

IV. THE *PSYCHOPANNYCHIA*—THE WAKEFULNESS OF THE SOUL—AS A FOUNDATIONAL STARTING POINT FOR THEOLOGY AND THE CHRISTIAN LIFE IN CALVIN

Slowly but surely, the *Psychopannychia* found its *Sitz im Leben* in the years of its history of publication between 1534 and 1542 in the inevitable ethicizing of foundational Reformed insights. But in relegating it to its place Barth's interpretation is not fully exhausted. As important to an understanding of the *Psychopannychia* and its significance for a general understanding of Calvin is the other focal point, which Barth refers to under the belated heading "time and eternity."[55] It is not quite correct, of course, when Barth states that the topic of soul sleep is not relevant in 1534. "An attack from the other side, a refutation from Anabaptist circles, which might possibly have defended the teaching of soul sleep was according to Calvin's own testimony demonstrably lacking."[56] More recent scholarship has

---

[54]Markus Jenny, *Luther, Zwingli, Calvin in ihren Liedern* (Zurich: Theologischer Verlag, 1983), 258–59. Simeon's Thanksgiving was part of the regular Sunday worship service since the first edition of the Geneva liturgy of 1542. Cf., by contrast, Luther's "In Peace and Joy I now Depart ... death is become my slumber"; ibid., 57. Luther narrows (different from Calvin), the song of faith of Simeon to a funeral hymn. It was indeed included in a collection of funeral hymns published at Wittenberg in 1542. For an English translation of the hymn, see *Luther's Works* (Philadelphia: Fortress Press, 1965), 53:247.
[55]Barth, *Calvin*, 203–6. [56]Barth, *Calvin*, 203.

shown that the topic of soul sleep—not lastly in connection with the teachings on indulgence and purgatory which the Reformation fought—proved to be somewhat relevant after all. The opinion of valiant Capito, which Barth quotes, that Calvin, the neophyte in the Reformed camp, had better find a more convincing topic, was certainly not everyone's opinion.[57] I mentioned earlier the opinions of Bullinger, Zwingli, Carlstadt, and Luther. But Barth's suggestion that the *Psychopannychia* somehow contains the essential Calvin goes to the heart of the matter: "If we wish to understand the origin of Calvin's starting point we should rush decidedly less quickly past it, as Calvin scholarship has done thus far."[58]

What then, in addition to the polemical-ethical dimension, makes the *Psychopannychia* of the young Calvin tick? What is the starting point of his theology, its message, its core?

Every favorably inclined reader of Barth's lecture on Calvin recognizes immediately that he wrote the section on the *Psychopannychia* with special delight. There is a climax here. With the catchwords "time and eternity"[59] Barth drives his exegetical shafts deep into the *Psychopannychia,* thus uncovering important layers of the starting point of Calvin's theology.

For one, there is the comparison between Platonism and Christianity which Barth discovers and underscores in Calvin. Both accept an anthropologically constitutive immortality of the soul which for Christians is seen as the bearer of godlikeness and for that reason is accountably within the light realm of creation, which has nothing to do with the so painfully burdened earth remnant of the night. That life cannot be an inert festive night, either for light-filled antiquity—which Calvin loves—or for Calvin himself, or for any form of genuine Christianity, Barth clearly emphasizes.

More important than this tentative comparison with Plato is Barth's reference to the eschatological dimension of the doctrine of soul sleep and of Calvin's theology as such: "The real life for Calvin is the future or eternal life, in a more pregnant, more sharply pronounced sense than for Luther. We could formulate this in a different way, as follows: when he visualized the salvation store which became clear to him through Luther's teaching on faith and justification, he linked it more immediately than Luther himself to the thought of death and the life to come."[60] We would certainly have to ask whether Barth reads the expressionist conception of time of the early dialectical theology into the *Psychopannychia* when after having stressed ethics, in other words, this world, he describes Calvin's turn to the other world, to the thought about death, always in a somewhat anti-Lutheran

---

[57]Cf. Barth, *Calvin,* 204, commenting on *CO* 10:2:45.
[58]Barth, *Calvin,* 207.   [59]Barth, *Calvin,* 203–7.   [60]Barth, *Calvin,* 205.

front, as follows: "The thought of eternity [is] captured very succinctly; eternity is thought of as the negation which stands over against all time, as the position which establishes all time."[61] We may ask, I maintain, whether this terminology adequately measures up to Calvin's very much simpler way of saying things. We cannot deny, however, that Barth succeeds in this way finally to bring Calvin's eschatology to prominence. From the very first moment of his theological work Calvin comprehends life as reflection on the future life (*meditatio futurae vitae*). Thus the ethical dimension which we stressed thus far in Calvin's theology should be protected against any type of moralistic misunderstanding.

But with this insight Barth has not yet reached the profoundest point of his interpretation of Calvin. We must still take hold of the sentence regarding Barth's understanding of time, which we partially quoted earlier. Unabridged it reads as follows:

The notion of eternity, clearly stated: eternity envisaged as the negation which stands over against all time, as the position which establishes all time, in other words, being at no moment in time as something second-ary, an other, that which stands aside. Rather, the primally-ultimate of every moment in time, its meaning, its transcendental content, this notion of eternity will never devalue or empty time. Better still, it emp-ties and devalues [time] totally in order thus to fulfill it totally. [This notion of eternity] takes time fully seriously, wholly important, as the training ground on which nothing, absolutely nothing is eternal, but on which everything, everything because of its relation is directed to and determined by the eternal—full of meaning and full of tasks.[62]

Barth grasps the wonderful flexibility of Calvin's thought which after a sur-prising turn from ethics to eschatology returns equally surprising to this world. From this world to the other world and back, or to use a term which Barth happily borrowed from Ernst Troeltsch, "The strength of this world is the other world."[63] A rigorous glimpse of eternity and a rigorous serious acceptance of the temporal are one and the same for him, two sides merely of the same thing.[64] This is Calvin's message of the wakefulness of the soul, which Barth in 1922 worked out in all clarity as the starting point of Calvin's theology. That he himself was an heir of this Calvinian wakefulness of the soul and became so more and more, is shown by Barth's position in the *Kirchenkampf* [church struggle]. Over an offer he received in 1935 to teach the *Psychopannychia* in Bonn came the deportation

---

[61]Barth, *Calvin*, 205.   [62]Barth, *Calvin*, 205.
[63]Barth, *Calvin*, 206 n. 34. [64]Barth, *Calvin*, 206, n. 34.

order to leave Germany after he had awakened many sleepers through the Barmen declaration. To this event his famous quip applies, "The Lutheran church slept and the Reformed church stayed awake." We now know that in the final stages of formulating the Barmen theses Barth kept himself awake by smoking cigars and drinking coffee while the two Lutherans, Asmussen and Breit, probably after a German Pils, gently nodded off for an afternoon snooze.[65]

Enough of Barth's historical fun. When we attempt to interpret the *Psychopannychia* and its wakefulness of the soul, Barth's lecture has much that is enlightening. Nonetheless, I believe that we must add a few new accents today which go beyond Barth's interpretation. Eberhard Jüngel emphasized in an article on the occasion of Barth's death that the notion of a Christian yearning after death, as Philippians suggests, seems to have been excluded from Barth's work.[66] But it is these very passages in Paul's epistles which are given close attention in Calvin's *Psychopannychia* and which identify Calvin as a Pauline theologian even before his Commentary on Romans of 1539; however, communion with Christ being a prominent motif. On the basis of Phil. 1:23 Calvin knows how to see death in a different light: Paul points to the fact that his better part is chained by the body but will be liberated through death. But this is not, Calvin stresses, the aim of Paul's thought, but rather, "It would be beautiful to be with Christ who surrendered his [earthly] life" [*Pulchre vero esset cum Christo, qui desineret vivere vitam suam*]. Beautiful indeed it would be to live with Christ, who surrendered his earthly life.[67] This and many similar passages give Calvin's early work its ultimate depth and meaning. They awaken the immortal soul. The creationlike dimension of the soul as bearer of Godlikeness should of course be reason enough for its wakefulness,[68] but deeper still than this truth, this wakefulness is guaranteed through the christological-pneumatological union of Christ and his members. The christological union with Christ is the key to understanding the *Psychopannychia* and the starting point of Calvin's theology as such. Over against this, Barth's interpretation of 1922 not only remains on a purely eschatological level but narrows it down philosophically when in interpreting the *Psychopannychia* he speaks of eternity as the transcendental content of time. Only at a later stage does Barth shed these philosophical eggshells and finally pay attention to Phil. 1:23 along

---

[65]For this entire episode, see C. Nicolaisen, *Der Weg nach Barmen: Die Entstehungsgeschichte der Theologischen Erklärung von 1934* (Neukirchen: Neukirchen Verlag, 1985), 29.

[66]"Paul's desire to depart was alien to him," so E. Jüngel in *Neue Zürcher Zeitung* (2 March 1969); reprinted in E. Jüngel, *Barth Studien*, (Zurich: Theologischer Verlag, 1982), 15.

[67]Cf. *CO* 5:194, 197. See also the comments by Hwang, *Psychopannychia*, 219–24, and George, *Calvin's Psychopannychia*, 317–18.

[68]Cf. for instance, *CO* 5:177–78: "Nos vero et substantiam esse ipsam (animam) contendimus, et vere post corporis interitum vivere, sensu videlicet et intelligentia praeditam: ac utrumque evidentibus scripturae testimoniis nos probaturos recipimus."

with Calvin as he speaks theologically of the wakefulness of the soul by translating, even slightly correcting the platonizing Calvin, not at all resigned, "longing to depart in order to be with Christ," but messianically active, "to make a move in order to be with Christ."[69] At this point Barth has caught up with the content of the *Psychopannychia*, namely the christological communion with Christ. In other words, it has become clear to him that Calvin's theology, even that of the very young Calvin, can genuinely and effectively be opened up only from the third article. Calvin is first and last pneumatologist. In 1542 Calvin finally had his *Psychopannychia* published. Meanwhile its reformed content is no longer in doubt. Even the vexatious question regarding its antagonists has been resolved. Now he knows them. In 1543 Calvin undertakes a thorough revision of his *Institutio*. He expands its ecclesiology. In this edition he arrives at an explicit settling of accounts with the Renaissance papacy. But when looked at more closely it is a settling of accounts with the spirit of the age in general which is characterized by a hidden skepticism whose theme song is: "Let us eat and drink, for tomorrow we shall be dead."

Calvin's *Institutio* (1543) 6.7.27: "But why do I name three or four Popes. As if there were any doubt what kind of religion the Popes and their entire college of cardinals have confessed for some time now and still confess to this day. For the chief article of their hidden theology which is prominent among them is this: 'There is no God.' And the second is: 'Everything that is written and taught about Christ is a lie and deception.' And the third: '*The doctrine of a future life and of the final resurrection* [emphasis added] is a fairy tale.'"

There is a state of church and society which represents nothing other than a denial of all three articles of faith. Young Calvin was especially sensitive to this disregard of the third article in his own time and through his time.

V. Conclusion

Let me summarize and conclude.

1. Barth's interpretation of the *Psychopannychia* as an ethico-eschatological tract helps us to understand it in the context of the problem of the Reformation as it had evolved around 1530. The *Psychopannychia* is a Reformation tract.

2. In his attempt at interpretation Barth did not fully succeed in recognizing the actual *Calvinian Proprium*, the hermeneutical key as it were, in the Paulinian eschatological communion with Christ. But if this interpretation of Calvin's starting point is correct, then we can state that:

3. The *Psychopannychia* is an ecumenical tract. Its topic is not pre-reformatory, but reaches beyond the Reformation. The matter of the wakefulness of the

---

[69]K. Barth, *Kirchliche Dogmatik*, 4.3.1062–1069.

soul is a universal Christian topic on which Calvin could make common cause with the Sorbonne, even when it was prepared to bring the Pope up to scratch when he had missed the right understanding of the wakefulness of the soul. More than that, the *Psychopannychia* with its theme of the immortality and wakefulness of the soul is a tract which concerns all of humankind. In the year 1564, the year Calvin died, the poet was born who in one of his tragedies encapsulates the message and concern of the *Psychopannychia* in a secular but incredibly compact and succinct statement; it is Shakespeare in *King Lear*. "Ripeness is all" —to be ready, to be awake, is all![70]

[70] W. Shakespeare, *King Lear* V.2.11 (New York: St. Martin's Press, 1992). See on the matter, W. Naumann, *Die Dramen Shakespeares* (Darmstadt: Wissenschaftliche Buchgesellschaft, 1978), 342–43: "The aphorism reads like a synopsis of Montaigne's essay, 'To philosophise is to learn how to die....' Shakespeare's power of expression is shown in his ability to transmit in short poetic aphorisms the much more diffuse expositions of reflective literature." To complete the circle we must remember that Montaigne's essays could not be understood apart from Huguenot history and tradition, at the outset of which we have Calvin's *Psychopannychia*.

Calvin's Exhortation to Charles V (1543)

J. J. Steenkamp

I. Introductory Remarks

CHARLES V,[1] POSSIBLY THE MOST TRAGIC FIGURE OF THE REFORMATION period, endeavored to defend a lost post by his attempts to hold the medieval Roman Empire of the German Nation together.[2] His efforts to keep the *corpus christianum* from falling apart were the means by which he expected to realize his ideal of a united Europe. Most essential to his thinking were: (1) the rebuilding of the empire; (2) the unity and the expansion of the Roman Catholic Church; (3) the defense of Europe (Christianity) against the Turkish invasion.[3]

The emperor was well aware of many evils in the Roman Catholic Church. Although he regarded the Protestants as heretics, the fact that they ignored the papal bull *Exsurge Domine* persuaded him to accept the fact that not the pope, but a general council would be able to heal the split in the church. And from 1521 onwards he also became increasingly convinced that only a general council would be able to reform the Roman Catholic Church and rid it of its evils. He expected mainly four results from a general council: (1) the reformation of the Roman Catholic Church, (2) the redress of the grievances of the Protestants; (3) the destruction of the so-called Lutheran heresy; (4) the legal and moral justification for military action against the Protestants, if that should become necessary.[4]

Charles V was honest in his attempts to persuade the successive popes to hold a general council. In the beginning this was also true of his negotiations with the Protestants. Apart from the fact that he needed them to wage war against France and the Turks, he recognized the danger they presented to the unity of the Roman Catholic Church. And being a strict and religious, practicing Roman Catholic, to his mind there could be but one church: the Roman Catholic Church as presented by its clerical hierarchy. It was a matter of medieval perceptions dominating his

---

[1]The most important sources used in this study are: (1) Calvin to Melanchthon, 21.04.44, *CO*6, no. 544; (2) Calvin to Myconius 24.06 44, *CO* 6, no. 561; (3) Calvin to Antoine Fumee, Jan. 1545, *CO*6, no. 610; (4) Bucer to Calvin 23.10.43, *CO* 11, 633–635; (5) Myconius to Calvin, 23.11.43, *CO* 11:519; (6) Metzer Edikt 13.10.43 *CO* 11:635–638; (7) Hubert Jedin, "Die Paepste und das Konzil in der Politik Karls V," in: *Kirche des Glaubens, Kirche der Geschichte,* Bd. 2 (Freiburg, Basel, u. Wien, 1966), 156–157; (8) *Supplex exhortatio ad Caesarem et principes 1543, CO* 6:525– 534.

[2]Otto Habsburg, *Karl V* (Wien: Verlag Herold, 1967), 285.

[3]Karl Heussi, *Kompendium der Kirchengeschichte,* 13. Auflage (Tübingen: JCB Mohr [Paul Siebeck], 1971), 271.

[4]Alfred Kohler, hrsg., *Quellen zur Geschichte Karls V.* (Darmstadt: WBD, 1990), 137–38.

thought. Therefore he rejected out of hand the proposals[5] of the diets of Nürnberg 1522 and 1524 should the pope decide not to agree to hold a general council. In contrast with the French monarch, who was not overly concerned with a general council because of his fortunate position on account of the 1516 concordat with the Roman Catholic Church, it was never Charles' intent to question the authority of the Roman See. Consequently, a national council, without the pontiff presiding, would never have met with his approval.

Being continually hampered in his attempts by both the pope and Francis I, later on he used the promise of a national council as a *politicum* to mollify the Protestant princes, dishonestly gaining their support. While continuously referring their case to a general council of the church, he held them to the Nürnberg agreement of 1532 (*Nürnberger Anstand*), which was in effect a political decree. The result was that the Protestants would always end up with contravening the imperial law while propagating the gospel according to their confession.

Since the general council, which was planned to be held in 1537 in Mantua, was postponed because of the third war between Charles V and Francis I, and since the prospects for another council seemed nonexistent, Charles staged the well-known series of religious discussions that took place between 1539 and 1541. Thereby he could avoid the antagonism of the pope and still hold on to the Protestants, whom he needed desperately for another campaign against the Turks as well as against Francis I, who had made common cause with them.

The discussion in Worms in 1540 was postponed to concur with the diet at Regensburg in 1541. This diet concluded: (1) to refer all religious differences to a general council; (2) that if a General Council was impossible, then a national council would be held; (3) failing that, such differences would be dealt with by the following diet; (4) in the meantime, the stipulations of the Nürnberg agreement of 1532 were to be obeyed by all.[6]

Charles V stressed in a declaration that the Nürnberg agreement forbade the Protestants from attempting to persuade the Roman Catholics to their point of view.[7] Thus by promising a council, Charles secured the support of the Protestants while simultaneously restricting the expansion of the Reformation.

By the end of the fourth decade the Protestants were divided among themselves about the prospects of the success of a general council and about whether they should attend or not. The Wittenberg and Strassburg theologians were not convinced that a council would be successful, but were of the opinion that it could be used as a forum to propagate their cause. Others, like the Hessen theologians,

---

[5]Kohler, hrsg., *Quellen*, 155.
[6]The Regensburger Reichsabschied in Kohler, *Quellen*, 261–62.
[7]CO 4:623–25.

the elector of Saxony, and the magistrates of Konstanz, did not want to attend at all and even entertained the idea of holding a contra-council summoned by the Protestants.[8] Because of the religious discussions, however, this seemed to be a relatively peaceful time, but when the Schmalkaldic League attacked and ejected Henry, duke of Brunswick, in 1542, Charles decided to take military steps against the League for having transgressed the imperial order.

The diet of Spires in 1542 addressed only the Turkish question, and it was not before the diet of Spires 1544 that Charles V could be present so that the religious questions could be attended to. However, during 1543 Charles V enforced the stipulations of the Nürnberg agreement wherever Protestant preaching endangered the cohesion of the Roman Catholic Church. This was also the case in Metz. Guillaume Farel arrived in Metz on 19 August 1542 and remained there until 25 March 1543. He preached in the castle of Montigny, and the Protestants came to an agreement on 16 March 1543 with the magistrates that henceforth one church building would be made available to the Protestants and that they could have the services of one minister. But on 21 March 1543, Gaspard de Heu, the Protestant magistrate who had favored them in the negotiations, was ousted in the elections. On 25 March 1543 the Protestants were attacked by soldiers of Lorraine under the leadership of François de Guise, and they were driven from Metz, with Farel hiding among them.[9] On 15 October 1543 an imperial decree was published in Metz, enforcing anew the Nürnberg agreement.

Under these circumstances, Martin Bucer had requested Calvin and Farel to write an apology to the emperor. Since the first letter that Bucer is supposed to have written[10] is lost, it is not quite clear exactly what it was that he had wanted to be communicated to Charles V. This request resulted in Calvin's *Supplex Exhortatio.*

II. Conclusions

1. *Calvin's Purpose for the Exhortation*

Calvin wished to give a concise exposition of the *notae ecclesiae,* and to give a concise exposition of the evils affecting the church. He wanted to urge the emperor, the princes, and the other states to hold a German national council to reform the church in lieu of a general council convened by the pontiff and to stiffen the resolve of the German Protestant princes to uphold the reformation in the face of the menacing attitude of the Emperor. The *Exhortation* was a plea for

---

[8]*Archiv für Reformationsgeschichte* 73 (1982): 43–145.
[9]Doede Nauta, *Guillaume Farel* (Amsterdam: Ton Bolland, 1978), 97–100.
[10]Aime-Louis Herminjard, *Correspondance des Réformateurs dans les pays de langue française...* (Genève u. Paris, 1866–) 9, 86:4

the Emperor not to resort to violence in his dealings with the Protestants. By doing all of this, Calvin hoped to spare the French Protestants the wrath of their monarch.

2. Reasons for Calvin's Reluctance to Write the Exhortation

Calvin did not put much faith in the ability or the resolve of the aristocracy either to uphold or reform the church. Rather, he relied on the effectiveness of the preaching of the Word of God and on the protection of the Lord. It could be speculated that he had feared that his interference in German politics could jeopardize the position of the French Protestants vis-à-vis their own monarch.

3. The Theological Contents of the Exhortation

As noted above, the *Exhortation* should be seen as a concise exposition of Calvin's ecclesiology. Two issues are very notable: (1) Calvin constantly refers to *the* church, thus giving a glimpse of his view on the catholicity of the church as well as the nature of the church as a *universum*. As such, the *Exhortation* touches on almost every aspect of Calvin's theology, albeit very briefly (2) The *Exhortation* touches upon Calvin's view of the validity of a provincial council's resolutions and thus the Christocracy in the order of the church.

4. Calvin's Style in the Exhortation

The *Exhortation* was written in a very uncomplicated way, thereby expressing Calvin's anxiety to be well understood by nontheologians. No plausible solution could be found for the fact that Calvin repeated himself three times in the *Exhortation*. The *Exhortation* should be seen as the second stage in Calvin's dealings with the German emperor— the first being his reactions to the Frankfurt talks. The third stage was his answer to the *Interim* of 1547.

Although Calvin always treated the aristocracy with respect, the *Exhortation* made it clear that a certain distance was developing between Calvin and the aristocracy (emperor). This was confirmed by his sharp criticism of the *Interim*. In the *Exhortation* he was still treating the emperor with due respect, but not with his previous confidence in the latter's diligence.

5. The Result of the Exhortation

No effect of the *Exhortation* on the aristocracy either at the diet of Spires or thereafter was recorded. The *Exhortation* was applauded and welcomed by the Protestant theologians as a true exposition of the ecclesiology of the reformation. Willem F. Dankbaar suggested that the *Supplex Exhortatio* might have caused Charles V to promise a national council at the diet of Spires in 1544, and that this promise had in turn resulted in Paul III's summoning the Council of Trent. This was presumably because the pontiff feared the consequences of a German national council.[11] But such an ironic consequence of Calvin's exhortation doesn't seem very likely, at least not as a result of the diet of Spires. This doubtful honor should rather be reserved for the Peace Treaty of Crespy, 18 September 1544, and especially for the Secret Treaty of Meudon between Charles V and Francis I, 19 September 1544.

The diet of Spires declared the French monarch to be the common enemy of Christianity, on a par with the Turkish invader.[12] And as Calvin had expected, the diet was prevented from achieving a solution for the religious differences. A discussion of these issues was postponed, to be dealt with either by a German national council or a general council. Since a German national council was not viewed to be very opportune at that moment and as the convocation of a general council by the pontiff seemed to be a very dubious matter, the religious differences were referred to the next diet.[13]

The conclusion of the fourth war between Charles V and Francis I by the Peace Treaty of Crespy, just three months after the diet of Spires, changed these views drastically. The Treaty of Crespy referred to the religious differences only in general terms, namely, that the emperor and the king would pursue the best ways to heal the breach in the church.[14] However, the next day, 19 September 1544, the two traitors concluded the Secret Treaty of Meudon in which their real intentions were stated. The important issues of this treaty were: (1) The king of France would help the emperor to resolve the religious difficulties in Germany in any way which the emperor might deem feasible; (2) this goal would be achieved by persuasion at first, and in case of failure, by force. To this end, the troops lent to the emperor to be used against the Turks, would be used against the Protestants instead; (3) a general council would be convened "by the emperor" in either Trent, Cambrai, or Metz (in this regard it is very important to note that the pontiff was by no means involved, not even mentioned, thus indicating a very decisive change in the attitude of the emperor vis-à-vis the primacy of the pontiff); (4) should peace be achieved with the duke of Savoy, he would be helped to obtain Savoy as well as such of his previous possessions as were held by Bern and Freiburg. These would be led back to the Roman Catholic Church "as well as the city of Geneva."[15]

---

[11]Willem Frederick Dankbaar, *Calvijn: Zijn weg en werk* (Nijkerk: G. F. Callenbach NV. 1957), 158.

[12]*Cf.* the *Speyrer Reichsabschied,* in Kohler, *Quellen,* 302.

[13]Ibid., 304–305.

[14]Cf. *Friede von Crespy,* in Kohler, *Quellen,* 309.

[15]Cf. the *Geheimvertrag zum Friede von Crespy,* in Kohler, *Quellen,* 315–17.

It seems impossible to determine whose influence it was that decided the emperor to stage his own general council: Calvin's or Francis' or even the influence of both. The fact that the city of Geneva was singled out to be led back to the Roman Catholic Church might be an indication that Calvin's influence was not predominant.

In any event, the Secret Treaty of Meudon put an end to the politics of the pontiff to divide and to rule over the French king and the emperor. Although it could not be proved *expressis verbis* by this study, the deduction might well be justified that the emperor's decision to hold a general council, at which the king of France had promised to be present, was directly responsible for the convocation of the Council of Trent by the pontiff. It was his only option to retain some of the erstwhile power of the Vatican over the church in Germany.

"The Progress of the Kingdom of Christ" in Calvin's Exposition of the Prophets

Peter Wilcox

THE VIEW THAT THE WRITINGS OF THE REFORMERS afford "exceedingly little" evidence of any concern for "the progress of the preaching of the Gospel through the world"[1] rests, in Calvin's case, upon an assumption that he was "a man of one book,"[2] whose thought is comprehensively expressed in the *Institutes*.[3] But if it is true that the *Institutes* includes little which amounts to a theology of mission, it is also true that at this point the work fails to convey the full scope of its author's thought. Elsewhere, Calvin propounded a doctrine of Christ's Kingdom and in particular of "the progress of the Kingdom," which is vigorous and full of missionary imperatives. The aim of this seminar is to examine the doctrine as it appears in Calvin's exposition of the prophets, and to consider how it relates to the evangelistic activity in which he himself was engaged at the time when these expositions were produced.

I. THE KINGDOM OF CHRIST IN CALVIN'S OLD TESTAMENT EXPOSITIONS

Between 1557 and 1565, commentaries by Calvin were published on all the prophetic books of the Old Testament. In fact, only two of these seven publications (the Commentary on the Psalms, and the revised Commentary on Isaiah) are commentaries in the sense of being continuous expositions of the Biblical text, written or dictated by the author himself. The remaining works are transcripts of lectures Calvin gave in the school at Geneva and were prepared for publication by his friends.[4] There are other parts of Calvin's corpus in which the doctrine of the progress of the Kingdom of Christ appears (such as his commentaries on the

---

[1]Stephen Neill, *A History of Christian Missions* (Harmondsworth: Penguin, 1964), 222.

[2]Cited by Emile Doumergue, *Jean Calvin: Les Hommes et les choses de son temps,* 7 vols. (Lausanne, 1899–1917), 4:1.

[3]"The whole of Calvinism is in the *Institutes,*" Pierre Imbart de la Tour, *Calvin et l'Institution Chrétienne* (Paris, 1935), 55; "[The *Institutes*] present a synthesis of Calvinist thought [which] is sufficient in itself," François Wendel, *Calvin: The Origins and Development of His Religious Thought* (London: Collins, 1963), 111. But cf. Thomas H. L. Parker, *Calvin's New Testament Commentaries* (London: SCM Press, 1971), 1–5, for an explanation of the deliberate complementarity of the *Institutes* and Calvin's commentaries.

[4]Thomas H. L. Parker, *Calvin's Old Testament Commentaries* (Edinburgh: T. & T. Clark, 1986), 20–21.

Gospels, for instance) but these five publications are of particular interest for the study of Calvin's views on evangelization, for two reasons.

First, they date from a time when Calvin's horizons moved beyond Geneva, to the propagation of the reformed faith throughout western Europe. Between 1555 and 1564, several hundred envoys were sent out from Geneva on assignments to nascent reformed congregations, especially in France, but also to cities such as Turin, Antwerp, and London.[5] Although almost all of these assignments took place within the borders of Christendom, it is clear that those who were involved in them regarded them as truly "evangelistic" endeavors. Their purpose was to propagate the Gospel and to establish an effective Christian witness where none was believed to exist.

Second, these five publications represent the single most important element in the theological training that the missionary envoys received. Calvin's lectures had a very specific vocational purpose. They were delivered to a mixed audience of "students, ministers, and other hearers,"[6] three groups which were fully committed to the progress of the reformed church. Many of the students who enrolled in Geneva between 1555 and 1561 were despatched to serve as pastors in France even before Calvin died in 1564. Again, many of those who were already ministers in Geneva before 1555 were sent out as envoys to France during the next ten years. Most of the "other hearers" were religious refugees who had fled France, Italy, England, and Scotland, and who wished to see the reformed church established in the countries from which they had come. If it was for missionaries in training, envoys on furlough in Geneva, and other interested parties that Calvin's lectures were intended, might we not profit by reading them in this light?

The principal theme of these expositions is "the progress of Christ's Kingdom." The subject enjoys a prominence and a breadth of treatment in these works which it is not given in the *Institutes*. However, what is distinctive about this concept as it appears in these expositions is not simply its prominence, but the way that it functions as a framework for the rehearsal of salvation history.

---

[5]Robert M. Kingdon, *Geneva and the Coming of the Wars of Religion in France, 1555–1563* (Geneva: Librairie Droz, 1956). See also Pete Wilcox, "L'envoi de pasteurs aus Eglises de France," *Bulletin de la Société de l'Histoire du Protestantisme Français* 139 (1993): 347–74.

[6]Nicolas Colladon, "Vie de Calvin," *CO* 21:71. The *CO* references are to line, page and volume. Translations are my own. For Calvin's expositions of the prophets, an additional reference is given to the somewhat unreliable CTS.

II. The Progress of the Kingdom of Christ and Salvation History[7]

The characteristic mark of Calvin's exposition of the prophets is his view that prophecy has a triple reference. He maintains that it refers first to an imminent historical event (such as the return of the people from exile); second, to Christ (by which he can mean the "incarnation," "the ascension," or even "the apostolic era and the preaching of the Gospel"; and third, to the whole course of history up until the Last Day (on which grounds he applies them to the sixteenth century church). As Calvin formulates it, the doctrine of Christ's Kingdom functions as a framework for his exposition of salvation history. He construes the history of God's people, at least from the time of the return of the people of Israel from exile, as the history of the Kingdom of Christ. Calvin proposes, for example, in a lecture on Ezek. 17:22 given in 1564, that: "When the Kingdom of Christ is under discussion, we must take its beginning to be the building of the temple when the people returned to their homeland after seventy years. Then, we must take its consummation to be, not at the ascension of Christ, nor even in the first or second centuries, but in the whole progress of his Kingdom until he appears at the Last Day."[8]

The comment is typical of the interpretative scheme which Calvin consistently brought to bear on the prophetic books, and illustrates the degree to which he is able to locate Christ's Kingdom in history. From the perspective of the sixteenth century he can look back at its beginnings, and forward to its consummation; between these two points, he can chart its inexorable progress. Calvin frequently suggests that a particular prophecy relates "to the whole course of the Kingdom of Christ, from its beginnings right up to its end." Such phrases are repeated so often in these lectures on the prophets that they acquire the character of a refrain.

1. *The Beginnings of the Kingdom of Christ*

Of course Calvin acknowledged that there were differences between the Old Testament and the New; but his perception of Christ as the substance of the Covenants and the scope of the Scriptures led him to emphasize not only the theological continuity between the Old Testament and the New, but their historical continuity, too. Calvin saw no neat break at the crucifixion between the Old Covenant and the New. Instead, he viewed the exilic and postexilic periods of the Old Testament as an interval which belonged both to the Old Covenant and to the New, and yet fully to neither. This case may be overstated; but the conclusion is

---

[7]See Thomas Palmer, "John Calvin's View of the Kingdom of God" (Ph.D. thesis, University of Aberdeen, 1991).

[8]Comm. Ezek. 17:22, *CO* 40:417:31–37, CTS, 2:207–8.

warranted by the fact that Calvin regarded the exile as an interruption of the covenant[9] and the return from exile as a new beginning, "the second birth of the
Church."[10] He considered the deliverance effected by God for Israel at the end of
the exile to be an "anagoge" of the deliverance which Christ came to accomplish.[11]
Since a course of redemption began at that point which continued right down to
the end of the Kingdom of Christ, its beginning may be considered to date from
the end of the exile.

Yet, on the other hand, Calvin commonly distinguishes between the end of
the exile, which was an immediate fulfillment of the prophets' oracles, and the
Kingdom of Christ (which was their ultimate referent). The end of the exile was
only the beginning of Christ's Kingdom in the sense of being a prelude to what
was to follow.[12] The "proper" inauguration of the Kingdom of Christ only took
place at the coming of Christ. Calvin does not mean that Christ's Kingdom began
at his nativity (a "senseless" idea),[13] but when he ascended into heaven.[14] Even
this is not to be thought of as a momentary event, since the means by which the
ascended Christ established his reign was the promulgation of the Gospel. For this
reason Calvin also identifies the beginning of Christ's Kingdom with the apostolic
era, or with "the preaching of the Gospel which was begun under Caligula, Clau-
dius, Nero, and their successors."[15]

2. The Consummation of the Kingdom of Christ

On occasions, however, Calvin also speaks as if the apostolic era was the
period in which the Kingdom of Christ attained its consummation. This is the
case especially when he expounds prophetic texts that refer to the rule of God over
"the nations," and the extension of worship "to the ends of the earth." He interprets these as prophecies of the Kingdom of Christ, fulfilled during the lifetimes of
the apostles. For example, the text of Jer. 49:6 prompts Calvin to consider the
connection between the Kingdom of Christ and the calling of the Gentiles. He
suggests:, "The prophet had respect to the Kingdom of Christ here. There is no
doubt that the promise extended right up to his coming, for he is speaking about
the calling of the Gentiles, which God deferred until he manifested his Son to the
world."[16]

---

[9]Comm. Ezek. 11:17, *CO* 40:241:21, CTS, 1:369; Comm. Zech. 2:12, CO 44.165.4–5, CTS, 5:77.
[10]Comm. Dan. 8:1, *CO* 41.87, CTS, 2:80.
[11]Comm. Hag. 2:7–10, *CO* 44.107.56, CTS, 4:363.
[12]Comm. Jer. 3:17–18, *CO* 37:566:24, CTS, 1:186.
[13]Comm. Dan. 2:44, *CO* 40.606.18, CTS, 1.186.
[14]Comm. Dan. 7:8, *CO* 41:50:12–35, CTS, 2:26–27; Comm. Dan. 7:13, *CO* 41:60:41, CTS, 2:42.
[15]Comm. Dan. 7:8, *CO* 41:50:45, CTS, 2:27; Comm. Mic. 4:3, *CO* 43:348:3, CTS, 3:265.
[16]Comm. Jer. 49:6, *CO* 39:352:29–33, CTS, 5:.63.

For Calvin, the calling of the Gentiles was the means by which the Kingdom of Christ was extended to the ends of the earth,[17] and was a process which took place at the time of Christ's coming. He saw the apostolic era as a "Golden Age," in which the propagation of the Gospel within a short period of time was incredible, and the progress which accompanied it was equally extraordinary.[18] "It was a time, when God suddenly became known everywhere, through the Gospel.... For we know that Christ penetrated at great speed, from east to west, like a flash of lightning, in order to bring Gentiles into the Church from all sides."[19] The phrase "through the Gospel" is significant. It is a shorthand expression, meaning "through the preaching of the Gospel in the apostolic era". Thus, Calvin observes that a particular prophecy "should be extended up to the preaching of the Gospel. For although Christ was born about one generation before that time, he only shone out to the world when he became known through the Gospel."[20] It is in his attempt to convey the ultimate significance of Christ's coming, that Calvin sometimes creates the impression that his Kingdom is already complete.

On the other hand, Calvin also affirms that "the Kingdom of Christ has not yet been completed,"[21] and that its consummation will occur only at the Last Day. "When Christ ascends his judgment seat to judge the world, then that which began to take place at the inauguration of the Gospel ... shall be fully accomplished."[22] By "the Kingdom of Christ," Calvin means "not only that which is begun here, but that which shall be completed on the Last Day."[23]

3. The Progress of the Kingdom of Christ

For Calvin, the character of the present moment, and of the whole of salvation history, is determined by the fact that it falls between the beginning of Christ's Kingdom, and its consummation. It is this which gives Calvin's theology its eschatological cast and orientation to the future. He perceives an uninterrupted "course" from the beginning of the Kingdom of Christ until its consummation (*ab initio regni Christi usque ad finem*) such that the period between these two moments is essentially one of progress.

---

[17]Comm. Ps. 47:10, *CO* 31:471:5–9, CTS, 2:214.
[18]Comm. Ps. 87, Argumentum, *CO* 31:799:53–57, CTS, 3:395.
[19]Comm. Ps. 22:28, *CO* 31:235:29–35, CTS, 1:386.
[20]Comm. Dan. 11:45, *CO* 41:285:42–43, CTS, 2:367.
[21]Comm. Isa. 60:18, *CO* 37.368.27, CTS, 3:296.
[22]Comm. Isa. 45:23, *CO* 37:150:12–15, CTS, 3:428.
[23]Comm. Zeph. 3:16–17, *CO* 44:73:31–37, CTS, 4:305–306.

III. The Progress of the Kingdom of Christ and the Reformation

As it appears in these expositions, then, the notion of the progress of Christ's Kingdom functions for Calvin as a framework for the exposition of salvation history. Caught in the interval between Christ's two advents, the Church participates in the inexorable progress of his Kingdom. Since Calvin considered this progress to have begun at the preaching of the apostles, and to be consummated only at the Last Day, it is no surprise to find him making explicit in his comments what these views imply: that the progress of Christ's Kingdom is manifest in the events of the mid-sixteenth century. "The Kingdom of Christ began in the world when God commanded the Gospel to be proclaimed everywhere, and even today its course has not yet reached completion."[24] Or again: "Whenever the prophets speak of fulfillment under the Kingdom of Christ, we should not restrict what they say to one day or a short time. Instead, we ought to include its whole course from beginning to end. For the Lord will carry through to the end what is now making constant progress, until it is completed."[25]

1. *The Progress of the Kingdom of Christ and the Reformed Church*

Calvin identifies the Kingdom of Christ with the Church. He can assert without qualification that "the Church is Christ's Kingdom".[26] Furthermore, this identification is of the Kingdom of Christ not with "the elect" (the invisible Church), but with the institutional (or visible) Church. This is no more than one would expect, given the degree to which Calvin is concerned with the progress of the Kingdom within history. When Calvin speaks of the Church as Christ's Kingdom in this way, he means that it is not only the realm over which Christ reigns (which exists by hearing the Word), but the agency through which he exercises his reign (which exists to proclaim the Word). The function of the Church corresponds to its form. Thus when Calvin comments that "Christ has entrusted to his ministers his Gospel, which is the scepter of his Kingdom, and has committed it, as it were, to their keeping" he means that Christ's scepter is not simply held over the Church, to exact its obedience; it is also held by the Church. Or rather, this scepter is entrusted to the Church, in the form of the Gospel, but continues to be held by Christ. Furthermore "Christ, by his ministers, has subdued to his dominion the whole world, and has erected as many principalities under his authority as there have been churches gathered to him in various nations by their preaching."[27]

---

[24]Comm. Mic. 4:3, *CO* 43:348.3–6, CTS, 3:265.
[25]Comm. Zech. 14:21, *CO* 44:390:51–391:3, CTS, 5:454–55.
[26]Comm. Amos 9:13, *CO* 43:172:53–55, CTS, 2:410, and often in the *Institutes* and in the Isaiah Commentary.
[27]Comm. Ps. 45:16, CO 31:453:29–34, CTS, 2:193.

The significance of this latter quotation is twofold. First, it confirms that for Calvin, Christ has extended his Kingdom through the ordinary ministry of the Church: the preaching of the Gospel was not entrusted to the Apostles alone. Secondly, it suggests that he equated the extension of the Kingdom with the establishment of churches. Calvin's exposition of the Lord's Prayer in the final edition of the *Institutes* is worth noting in this context. He suggests that when we pray "thy Kingdom come," "we must daily desire that God gather churches unto himself from all parts of the earth [and] that he spread and increase them in number."[28]

It remains to be shown that Calvin considered the pastors despatched from Geneva to France (as well as ministers and magistrates committed to the reformed cause elsewhere) to be engaged in the establishment of "true" churches, by the preaching of the Gospel, and thus to be contributing to the propagation of Christ's Kingdom.

2. *The Progress of the Kingdom of Christ and Reformed Ministers*

In this context it is particularly illuminating to bear in mind the nature of Calvin's audience. It has already been suggested that even if not all of those who attended Calvin's lectures were missionaries in training, the majority were caught up with him in an evangelistic enterprise. Explicit references to this enterprise are rare in these expositions; but they are common in Calvin's correspondence. His letters leave no doubt that he understood his own ministry and that of his colleagues in the reformed Church, as furthering the progress of Christ's Kingdom.

This comes across most clearly in the letters Calvin wrote between 1555 and 1564, concerning individual envoys who were being despatched to France from Geneva. For example, in recommending a new pastor to the Church in Dieppe in 1558, Calvin refers to "the zeal he has to advance the Kingdom of Jesus Christ."[29] The labors of Beza, Fornelet, and de Passy in France, and of others elsewhere, all contribute to the promotion of Christ's Kingdom.[30] On the other hand, "nothing hinders the progress of Christ's Kingdom so much as the paucity of ministers."[31] In remarks such as these, Calvin has in mind the ordinary ministry of the Church. Just as it was by the preaching of the Gospel that the Kingdom of Christ was inaugurated by the apostles, so it is by the preaching of the Gospel that it makes progress until it attains its consummation.

---

[28]*Institutes* 3:20:42, 905; *OS* 4:353.8–10.
[29]Ep. 2787, *CO* 17:9: Calvin aux freres de Dieppe (1558).
[30]Theodore Beza: Ep. 3663, *CO* 19:197: Calvin à la Reine de Navarre (1561); Fornelet: Ep. 3381, *CO* 18:439: Calvin aux Ministres de Neuchâtel (1561); de Passy: Ep. 3702, *CO* 19:263: Calvin à M. de Passy (1562); des Gallars: Ep. 3199, *CO* 18:88: Calvinus Grindallo (1560); Lismann: Ep. 2110, *CO* 15:424: Calvinus Bullingero (1555); à Lasko: Ep. 2744, *CO* 16:673, Calvinus Utenhovio [1557].
[31]Ep. 3737, *CO* 19:328: Calvinus Bullingero (1562).

IV. Conclusion

It has been suggested that the distinctive feature of the concept of the Kingdom of Christ as it appears in Calvin's expositions of the prophets, is the way that it provides a framework for the exposition of salvation history. It is the coherence as much as the prominence of this concept in these lectures which is striking, and which makes its absence from the *Institutes* all the more remarkable.

Calvins Uminterpretation Cyprians bei der Beantwortung der Fragen: Auf wen ist die Kirche gegründet und Von wem wird der Bischof gewählt?

Anette Zillenbiller

IN WEIT GRÖSSEREM UMFANG ALS LUTHER RÄUMT CALVIN den Äußerungen der Kirchenväter in seinem Werk einen bedeutenden Platz ein. Besonders in der dritten Ausgabe der *Institutio*, die im Jahre 1543 in Straßburg erschien,[1] bereichert er seine Ausführungen mit den Zeugnissen der Väter. Neben Augustinus und Chrysostomus nimmt Cyprian von Karthago, der nordafrikanische Bischof des dritten Jahrhunderts, eine wichtige Stellung ein.

Erstaunlich häufig und bisweilen sogar als Hauptzeugen bezieht sich Calvin in seinen Ausführungen zur Kirche auf Cyprian, wobei er sich auf wenige Originaltexte beschränkt, die er aber dafür mehrmals in die Diskussion einbringt. Calvin entnimmt sie sowohl dem *Decretum Gratiani* als auch einer Werkausgabe des Erasmus, allerdings ohne eigens auf die Art seiner jeweiligen Quelle hinzuweisen.

Die herausragendsten Themen, bei denen der Reformator Cyprian als willkommene Argumentationshilfe heranzieht, sind die Auseinandersetzung zum Primatsanspruch des Papstes sowie die Darlegung der guten Organisationsstruktur der frühen Kirche und hier speziell des Wahlverfahrens der Amtsträger.

Calvin entnimmt die betreffenden Texte dem Briefkorpus und in extenso der Schrift *De catholicae ecclesiae unitate*[2] des karthagischen Bischofs. Verständlicherweise wählt er die für sein Anliegen günstigsten Aussagen Cyprians aus, genauso wie es seine Zeitgenossen im reformatorischen und im sogenannten römischen Lager praktizierten. Doch Calvin begnügt sich nicht mit dieser selektiven Rezeptionsweise, sondern geht noch einen Schritt weiter. Die Texte werden von ihm teils durch Hinzufügen, teils durch Weglassen von Begriffen in seinem Sinn uminterpretiert. Wie dies geschieht, soll am Beispiel eines in der *Institutio* zweimal vertre-

---

[1]Der Titel lautet: *Institutio Christianae Religionis nunc vere demum suo titulo respondens. Authore Ioanne Calvino....* Argentorati per Wendelinum Rihelium. Mense Martio. Anno M.D.XLIII.

[2]Es handelt sich dabei vor allem um das fünfte Kapitel. Die Schrift war bis ins Jahr 1561 in einer Version zugänglich (Vgl. dazu Anm. 6). Erst durch die Werkedition des Manutius wurde sie zur Bereicherung der Polemik über das Petrusamt.

tenen Textes aus *De unitate* und an den Texten zum Wahlverfahren verdeutlicht werden.

Als Voraussetzung für eine Beurteilung der Rezeption ist es jedoch unabdingbar, zunächst Cyprians Meinung zu den in Frage stehenden Themen auf dem Hintergrund seiner Äußerungen genauestens in Augenschein zu nehmen. Deshalb werden wir im folgenden in einem ersten Schritt jeweils untersuchen, auf wen Cyprian die Kirche gegründet sah, und wie er die Wahl des Amtsträgers beschreibt,[3] bevor wir jeweils in einem zweiten Abschnitt nach der Rezeption durch Calvin fragen.

I. AUF WEN IST DIE KIRCHE GEGRÜNDET?

1. *Cyprians Sicht*

Schon aus dem Exil während der Decischen Christenverfolgung (250/51) formuliert der Bischof von Karthago seine Ansicht, die er dann in seiner Schrift *De unitate* ausführlicher darlegt und auch später immer wieder in den Briefen einbringt.[4] Die Anfangssätze des *Exilbriefs 33* sollen uns zunächst einen Einblick in das Denken Cyprians zu diesem relativ frühen Zeitpunkt seines Episkopats vermitteln.

Dominus noster, cuius praecepta metuere et servare debemus, episcopi honorem et ecclesiae suae rationem disponens in evangelio loquitur et dicit Petro [Mt. 16,18–19]. Inde per temporum et successionum vices episcoporum ordinatio et ecclesiae ratio decurrit ut ecclesia super episcopos constituatur et omnis actus ecclesiae per eosdem praepositos gubernetur. … Cum hoc ita divina lege fundatum sit, miror quosdam audaci temeritate sic mihi scribere voluisse ut ecclesiae nomine litteras facerent, quando ecclesia in episcopo et clero et in omnibus stantibus sit constituta.[5]

Als erstes spricht Cyprian hier ausgehend von dem Jesuswort aus Mt. 16, 18–19 davon, daß die Kirche auf Petrus gegründet sei, durch die im Laufe der Zeit erfolgte *successio* im Amt aber auch auf die Bischöfe, denen aus diesem Grund ihre Leitung obliegt. In der Folge erweitert er jedoch den Kreis derer, auf die die Kirche gegründet ist, indem er nun den Klerus und die Gläubigen neben die Bischöfe stellt.

---

[3]Als Grundlage hierfür werden wir unter anderen auch jene Texte in den Mittelpunkt stellen, denen später durch Calvin dieser Platz zugewiesen wurde.
[4]Ich zitiere im folgenden nach dem *CSEL,* in dem Cyprian die Bände 3:1–3 einnimmt.
[5]Vgl. Ep. 33, 1: *CSEL* 3:2:566.

Hier lassen sich schon zwei schwer miteinander zu vereinbarende Seiten seines Kirchenverständnisses erkennen. Denn einerseits gesteht Cyprian dem Bischof eine monarchische Stellung zu, andererseits aber räumt er dem Klerus und sogar dem Volk einen erstaunlich wichtigen Stellenwert innerhalb der Kirche ein, die er immer zuerst als Ortskirche versteht.

Ein zweites Beispiel findet sich vor allem in den beiden Versionen des vierten Kapitels seiner Schrift *De unitate*, und dann noch einmal im fünften Kapitel.[6] Die ersten Sätze des vierten Kapitels haben in beiden Versionen den gleichen Wortlaut. Christus, der durch seine Worte, die er zuerst an Petrus richtete, seinen Willen offenbarte, steht für Cyprian am Anfang. Nicht nur das Schriftzitat von Mt. 16, 18–19 erinnert an den oben erwähnten Brief. Auch hier ist es ihm (wie schon im Brief 33 durch die Formulierung *"cum hoc ita divina lege fundatum sit"*) sehr wichtig festzuhalten, daß das Amt durch göttlichen Willen besteht. Die sich daran anschließenden Ausführungen Cyprians dazu seien auszugsweise nebeneinandergestellt.[7]

PT:

Super illum aedificat ecclesiam et illi pascendas oves mandat et, quamvis apostolis omnibus parem tribuat potestatem, unam tamen cathedram constituit et unitatis originem adque rationem sua auctoritate disposuit. Hoc erant utique et ceteri quod fuit petrus, sed primatus Petro datur et una ecclesia et cathedra una monstratur; et pastores sunt omnes, sed grex unus ostenditur qui ab apostolis omnibus unianimi consensione pascatur.

TR:

Super unum aedificat ecclesiam et, quamvis apostolis omnibus post resurrectionem suam parem potestatem tribuat [Joh. 20:23 ff.] tamen, ut unitatem manifestaret, unitatis eiusdem originem ab uno incipientem sua auctoritate disposuit. Hoc erant utique et ceteri apostoli quod fuit Petrus, pari consortio praediti et honoris et potestatis, sed exordium ab unitate proficiscitur ut ecclesia Christi una monstretur.

---

[6]Mit Maurice Bévenot gehe ich davon aus, daß der kürzere Text der ältere ist, also nach der Rückkehr aus dem Exil angesichts des Schisma des Novatian in Rom und des Maximus und des Fortunatus in Karthago entstand. Wegen des darin verwandten Begriffes *primatus* wird er als Primacy Text (PT) bezeichnet. Der längere wird Textus Receptus (TR) genannt. Dieser war auch Calvin bekannt (Hrsg.)(Vgl. dazu oben Anm. 2). M. Bévenot, *De lapsis/De ecclesiae catholicae unitate*, Oxford Early Christian Texts (Oxford, 1971). Zur Bedeutung und Wertung des »*primatus Petro datur*« schließe ich mich ebenfalls der Meinung M. Bévenots an, der schreibt: "Cyprien et ses comtemporains n'en [premier Concile du Vatican et … ses définitions de la primauté et de l'infaillibilité du Pape] avaient pas connaissance, et il serait impardonnable de leur attribuer des idées et des préoccupations que seule la vie de l'Église au cours des siècles, après tant d'hérésies et des bouleversements à l'extérieur comme à l'intérieur, devait expliciter, et qu'elle ne connaissait pas encore." Vgl. M. Bévenot "Épiscopat et primauté chez S. Cyprien" in: *Ephemerides theologicae Lovanienses* 42 (Louvain, 1966): 177.
[7]Vgl. *CSEL* 3:1:212 ff.

In PT fällt zunächst der enge Bezug auf Petrus ins Auge, der als erster Inhaber des Bischofsamtes ganz im Mittelpunkt des Interesses steht, ohne daß die Rolle der übrigen Apostel verschwiegen wird. In TR dagegen wird die Rolle der Apostel durch Einfügen der Schriftstelle Joh. 20: 23ff. und durch die Formulierung "pari consortio et honoris et potestatis" hervorgehoben.

Cyprian betont, es werde nur eine Herde gezeigt, und sie soll eins bleiben. Dennoch sind alle Apostel deren Hirten. In einem Atemzug spricht er also von der gesamten Herde—und er meint damit die *ecclesia catholica* als *ecclesia universalis* —und ihren vielen Hirten. Aus seiner Betonung der *ecclesia una* und der *cathedra una* auf der einen und der Aussage, daß alle mit der gleichen Macht ausgestattet sind, auf der anderen Seite, entsteht die Spannung, die es im Laufe der Jahrhunderte den Rezipierenden und Interpreten ermöglichte, den Autor bald als Papalisten, bald als Episkopalisten darzustellen—ein anachronistisches Unterfangen, dem Cyprian sich in Wirklichkeit entzieht.

Allerdings begegnet man diesem Tenor auch im folgenden fünften Kapitel. Die wichtigsten Aussagen seien hier zunächst zitiert: "Quam unitatem firmiter tenere et vindicare debemus, maxime episcopi qui in ecclesia praesidemus, ut episcopatum quoque ipsum unum atque indivisum probemus.... *Episcopatus unus est, cuius a singulis in solidum pars tenetur.* Ecclesia una est, quae in multitudinem latius incremento foecunditatis extenditur."[8]

Bei den darauf folgenden bildhaften Vergleichen mit der Quelle des Wassers bzw. des Lichtes und dem Baum mit den vielen Zweigen wechselt Cyprian, was die Entsprechung der Quelle bzw. des Baumes anbelangt, immer wieder zwischen dem Herrn und dem Bischofsamt und legt sich somit nicht fest. Daher konnten sich in unterschiedlichen Zeiten verschiedene theologische Ansätze auf diesen Text berufen.

Angesichts der gravierenden Mißverständnisse im Zuge der Überlieferung und Rezeption dieser Gedankengänge kann man m. E. nicht oft genug daran erinnern, daß Cyprians Anliegen darin bestand, das Bischofsamt im allgemeinen und sein eigenes im besonderen zu stärken, mußte er doch dieses Amt gegen die Gegenbischöfe in Karthago bzw. Rom als Amt der Einheit in der einen Kirche verteidigen. Cyprian geht es also um die Einheit des Bischofsamtes und um die Einheit der Kirche, die damit steht und fällt.

Sein dahingehendes Bemühen bringt ihn später dazu, diese seine Anschauung noch pointierter zu formulieren. Im bereits während des Episkopats des Stephanus von Rom verfaßten Brief an Puppianus schreibt er wieder in

---

[8]Vgl. *De unitate* c. 5: CSEL 3:1:213–14. Dieser Text ist in den beiden Versionen der Schrift wieder identisch. Bei dem kursiv hervorgehobenen Satz handelt es sich, wie wir weiter unten noch sehen werden, um einen der bevorzugten Cypriantexte Calvins.

Zusammenhang mit der Schriftstelle aus dem Matthäusevangelium: "Unde scire debes episcopum in ecclesia esse et ecclesiam in episcopo et si qui cum episcopo non sit in ecclesia non esse … quando ecclesia quae catholica una est scissa non sit neque divisa."[9]

Undurchtrennbar ist das Band, das den in der Sukzession stehenden Bischof und die Kirche verbindet. Wenn man so will, ist der Bischof sogar der Garant der so wichtigen sichtbaren und erfahrbaren Einheit. Diese Feststellung soll uns vorläufig genügen. Sie wird im nun folgenden Blick auf Calvin ein Kriterium für die Beurteilung seiner Rezeption bilden.

2. Calvins Sicht

Den für unseren Vergleich in Frage kommenden Text Cyprians aus *De unitate* rezipiert Calvin zweimal in der *Institutio* an unterschiedlichen Stellen, wobei er beim ersten Mal seinen Standpunkt darlegt, beim zweiten Mal eine Polemik gegen die Ansprüche der römischen Kirche auf den Primat führt.[10]

Hatte Cyprian den Satz "Episcopatus unus est, cuius a singulis in soldium pars tenetur," jedoch noch ganz auf die konkrete kirchliche Struktur bezogen, so geschieht durch Calvins Bearbeitung dieses Textes eine Akzentverschiebung, die den Blick in eine andere Richtung lenkt.

So schreibt er als Hinführung zu dem dann folgenden langen Zitat des fünften Kapitels der Schrift *De unitate* an der ersten Stelle: "Paulum quoque sequutus Cyprianus, totius ecclesiasticae concordiae fontem *ab unico Christi episcopatu* ducit."[11]

Weiter unten im Rahmen seiner Zurückweisung des römischen Primatsanspruchs referiert Calvin zunächst die Behauptung Roms, daß die Einheit der Kirche nur erhalten werden könne, wenn auch auf Erden ein oberstes Haupt vorhanden ist, dem dann alle Glieder gehorchen sollen.[12] Aus diesem Grunde habe Christus dem Petrus und danach auch kraft des Rechtes der Sukzession dem römischen Stuhl den bis zum Ende verbleibenden Primat gegeben. Dies sei von Anfang an so gewesen.[13]

---

[9]Vgl. Ep. 66, 8; *CSEL* 3.2.733.

[10]Vgl. *CO* 1:556 bzw. 606. Ähnlich ausführlich zitiert und den gleichen Themen zugeordnet findet sich der Text außerdem in der *Supplex exhortatio* von 1543 (*CO* 6:522–23) und den *Articuli a facultate Parisiensi* von 1544; *CO* 7:38. Zur Auswahl der unterschiedlichen Quellen vgl. A. Zillenbiller: *Die Einheit der katholischen Kirche*, VIEG 151 (Mainz: Ph. v. Zabern, 1993), 114 ff., 146 ff.

[11]Vgl. *CO* 1:556. Der Entsprechende Satz in der *Supplex exhortatio* lautet: "Nam ubi ecclesiasticae concordiae fontem constituit *in solo Christi episcopatu*," Vgl. *CO* 6, 522–23.

[12]Vgl. u.a. J. Eck: *De primatu Petri*. Lib.1. c.1. 3 fol. 19 r.

[13] Vgl. *CO* 1:605: "Quum itaque suum illud axioma iactant, non aliter contineri ecclesiae unitatem posse, quam si unum sit in terris supremum caput cui membra omnia pareant, ideoque Dominum Petro, et deinde successionis iure sedi romanae dedisse primatum, ut in ea usque ad finem resi-

In seiner Zurückweisung dieses Anspruchs fügt Calvin dem wörtlichen Zitat des fünften Kapitels als Erklärung bei: "Vides ut *Christi unius episcopatum* universalem faciat, … illius partes in solidum *ab omnibus* teneri dicat qui hoc capite episcopatu funguntur."[14] Hier erreicht der Autor zum einen durch den Zusatz des Wortes *Christi* die Veränderung der Blickrichtung nach oben, durch die Änderung der Wendung *a singulis* in *ab omnibus* andererseits eine breitere Streuung der Sicht.

Mit diesen Eingriffen in den Originaltext betont Calvin die alles dominierende Stellung des Herrn über die Kirche, deren Glieder ihre Einheit nicht in Abhängigkeit von einer irdischen Instanz, sondern von ihrem göttlichen Haupt wer definieren müssen.

Unbestreitbar entfernt er sich durch diese Manipulation aber von Cyprians Aussage in entgegengesetzter theologischer Richtung. Denn der karthagische Bischof hatte ja vorrangig das konkrete von Menschen ausgefüllte Amt im Blick.

Ob und wie Calvin beim zweiten angesprochenen Thema die Treue zur Vorlage beibehält, wird ein Blick auf seine Erläuterungen zum Wahlverfahren der kirchlichen Amtsträger zeigen. Doch vorher sei aus den genannten Gründen die Meinung seines Zeugen genauer untersucht.

II. Von wem wird der Bischof gewählt?

1. *Cyprian zum Wahlverfahren*

"A primordio episcopatus mei statui nihil sine consilio vestro et sine consensu plebis, mea privatim sententia gerere," [15] schreibt Cyprian aus dem Exil an seine Presbyter und Diakone und bittet sie anschließend um Verzeihung, weil er sich einmal nicht an diesen Grundsatz gehalten hat. Sowohl der Rat des Klerus als auch das Einverständnis des Kirchenvolkes sind für den monarchischen Bischof also unverzichtbar.

Doch dies muß nur auf den ersten Blick überraschen. Denn konsequenterweise schreibt der Bischof Karthagos auch bei der Wahl des Bischofs neben dem Klerus dem Volk eine wesentliche Rolle zu. Den hierfür relevanten Text findet man in seinem 67. Brief. Die wichtigsten Aussagen seien im folgenden zunächst zitiert:

---

deat: asserunt id fuisse ab initio semper observatum." Die römische Argumentation kann sich hier zumindest im Ansatz auf Cyprians Ep. 33 stützen. Allerdings hätte der Bischof des 3. Jahrhunderts folgerichtig in jedem Bischof einen Papst der entsprechenden Ortskirche erkannt.

[14]Vgl. *CO* 1:606. Vgl. auch zu den *Articuli*: "Videmus ut *Christi unius episcopatum* faciat universalem, … cuius partes *a ministris* eius teneri docet"; *CO* 7:38.

[15]Vgl. Ep. 14, 4 *CSEL* 3:2:512–13.

Propter quod plebs obsequens praeceptis dominicis, et deum metuens a peccatore praeposito separare se debet, nec se ad sacrilegi sacerdotis sacrificia miscere, cum ipsa maxime habeat potestatem vel eligendi dignos sacerdotes, vel indignos recusandi. Quod et ipsum videmus de divina auctoritate descendere, ut sacerdos plebe praesente sub omnium oculis deligatur et dignus adque idoneus publico iudicio ac testimonio conprobetur, sicut in Numeris....[16] Coram omni synagoga iubet Deus constitui sacerdotem, id est instruit et ostendit ordinationes sacerdotales non nisi sub populi adsistentis conscientia fieri oportere, *ut plebe praesente vel detegantur malorum crimina vel bonorum merita praecidentur et sit ordinatio iusta et legitima quae omnium suffragio et iudicio fuerit examinata....* Propter quod diligenter de traditione divina, et apostolica observatione servandum est et tenendum, quod apud nos quoque et fere per provincias universas tenetur.[17]

Dreimal betont Cyprian in diesem Text, daß das beschriebene Vorgehen bei der Wahl des höchsten Amtsträgers der Kirche auf Gottes eigenen Willen gründet (*divina auctoritate—iubet Deus —de traditione divina*)[18] und daher in fast allen Kirchenprovinzen befolgt wird. Selbstverständlich werden daher die zukünftigen Mitarbeiter des Bischofs um ihre Meinung und ihr Urteil ersucht. Doch genauso wichtig und unverzichtbar ist beim Wahlverfahren das Einverständnis des Volkes, von dem zusammen mit dem Klerus *suffragium et iudicium* erwartet wird, um die Rechtmäßigkeit der Ernennung zu gewährleisten.

Cyprians Zeugnis über die Mitverantwortung und Mitbestimmung des Volkes bei der Wahl des Bischofs verdient, übrigens nicht nur im Blick auf Calvin, unser besonderes Interesse.

---

[16]Vgl. Num. 20:25–26.
[17]Ep. 67, 3.4.5. *CSEL* 3.2.738–39. Vgl. dazu auch die deutsche Übersetzung in Anlehnung an BKV 60, 293ff.: "Deshalb muß sich auch eine Gemeinde, die den Geboten des Herrn gehorcht und Gott fürchtet, von einem sündigen Vorsteher trennen und darf nicht an den Opfern des gottlosen Bischofs teilnehmen, da ihr vor allem die Macht zusteht, würdige Bischöfe auszuwählen und unwürdige abzulehnen. Auch diese Sitte geht, wie wir sehen, auf eine göttliche Weisung zurück, daß der Bischof in Gegenwart des Volkes vor aller Augen erwählt und durch öffentliches Urteil und Zeugnis als würdig und geeignet anerkannt wird. Denn so gebietet im Buche Numeri.... Vor der ganzen Gemeinde, so befiehlt der Herr, soll der Hohepriester aufgestellt werden, das heißt: er lehrt und zeigt, daß die Einsetzung von Bischöfen nur im Einverständnis mit dem dabei anwesenden Volk erfolgen darf, damit in Gegenwart der Gemeinde die Missetaten der Bösen aufgedeckt oder die Verdienste der Guten gepriesen werden und die rechtmäßige und gesetzliche Ernennung zustande kommt, die durch Abstimmung und Urteil der Gesamtheit geprüft ist.... Deshalb muß man auf Grund der göttlichen Überlieferung und der apostolischen Gepflogenheit sorgfältig die Regel beobachten und befolgen, die auch bei uns und in fast allen Provinzen eingehalten wird."
[18]Neben der Schriftstelle aus dem alttestamentlichen Buch Numeri erinnert der Autor an die Wahl des Apostels Matthias (in Apg. 1:15–26), den die elf Apostel gemeinsam mit den 120 Brüdern durch Gebet und Los bestimmten.

Im folgenden werden wir nun untersuchen, wie Calvin sich zu diesem Problem stellt. Dazu werden wir uns die von ihm rezipierten Texte Cyprians in den Ausführungen zum Wahlverfahren des Bischofs bzw. des Hirten genauer ansehen.[19]

2. Calvins Ansicht zum Wahlverfahren

Im Rahmen seiner Darlegung zu den Fragen, von wem und wie ein Amtsträger der Kirche gewählt werden soll, führt Calvin an drei Stellen seiner *Institutio* neben Stellen aus der Heiligen Schrift auch die beiden oben bereits behandelten Briefe 14 und 67 des afrikanischen Bischofs an. Da er den oben zitierten Satz aus Brief 14 als Zeugnis für die Demut Cyprians und die große Bedeutung des Volkes für die Rechtsprechung einbringt, muß hier nicht näher auf ihn eingegangen werden.[20] Es bleiben also zwei Zitate aus Brief 67 für unsere Zwecke übrig.

Im ersten rezipierten Text aus der *Institutio*, der für unser Thema relevant ist, gibt Calvin Antwort auf die Frage, ob der Diener von der ganzen Kirche gewählt werden soll oder von seinen Amtskollegen und den Ältesten, die der Zucht vorstehen, oder ob er auch durch die Autorität eines einzelnen eingesetzt werden kann.[21] Im zweiten Text wird etwas später die Handhabung der Wahl zur Zeit der Alten Kirche mit Hilfe dieses Textes illustriert.[22]

Zunächst zeigt Calvin die nach seiner Meinung mißbräuchlichen Wahlverfahren auf, wie sie von Rom bzw. von den Anabaptisten gehandhabt werden. Deshalb bleibt für ihn nur die goldene Mitte übrig. Um aber zu seinem Vorschlag für die richtige Praxis kommen zu können, nimmt er sich die Freiheit, die entsprechende Passage aus dem 67. Brief Cyprians ein wenig nach seinem Sinn hin zu verändern, wenn er schreibt:

> Bene ergo Cyprianus, dum contendit, ex divina autoritate descendere, ut sacerdos, plebe praesente, sub omnium oculis deligatur, et dignus atque idoneus publico iudicio ac testimonio comprobetur. Siquidem hoc videmus iussu Domini in sacerdotibus leviticis fuisse observatum, ut ante consecrationem in conspectum populi producerentur (Lev. 8,6, Num.

---

[19]Wesentlich häufiger als dem Begriff *episcopus*, den Calvin nahezu ausschließlich in Schrift- und Väterzitaten verwendet, trifft man beim Lesen der *Institutio* auf das Wort *pastores*. Das Amt des Bischofs übernimmt Calvin in Abgrenzung gegen die römische Kirche bekanntlich nicht. Zu den, verglichen mit Cyprian, veränderten Bedeutungen der Begriffe *sacerdos, presbyter, pasteur* und *prestre* vgl. A. Zillenbiller, 107.

[20]Zur besonderen Rezeptionsweise von Ep. 14, 4, vgl. meine Ausführungen zu Calvins Verwendung des Florilegium Patristicum Martin Bucers in: *Die Einheit der katholischen Kirche*, S. 92–93, und 99–100. Mit ähnlichem Tenor zitiert Calvin in c. viii(60) der dritten *Institutio* Brief 38.

[21]Vgl. *CO* 1:570: "Quaeritur nunc a totane Ecclesia eligi debeat minister, an a collegis tantum et senioribus qui censurae praesunt, an vero unius authoritate constitui possit."

[22]Vgl. *CO* 1:581.

20,26). Non aliter ascribitur Matthias apostolorum collegio; nec aliter septem diaconi creantur, quam populo vidente et approbante. Haec exempla, inquit Cyprianus, ostendunt sacerdotis ordinationem non nisi sub populi assistentis conscientia fieri oportere: ut sit ordinatio iusta et legitima, quae omnium *testimonio* fuerit examinata.[23]

Calvin vermeidet in seinen Zitaten dieses Textes nach 1541 den Gebrauch der Wendung *suffragium et iudicium*, die sich im Original findet.[24] Und so kann er denn auch als Fazit ziehen, daß die Berufung eines Dieners dann rechtmäßig sei, wenn sie in einhelliger Übereinstimmung und mit Billigung des Volkes, aber vor allem unter der Leitung anderer Hirten stattfindet. Dem Volk traut Calvin zu, daß es sich, wie er selbst schreibt, ohne eine Leitung bei der Wahl durch Leichtfertigkeit, böse Umtriebe oder durch Aufruhr versündigen würde.[25]

Auch in dem, diesen Ausführungen folgenden Abschnitt über den Ordinationsritus findet sich übrigens noch einmal ein Hinweis auf die zweitrangige Rolle, die das Volk bei diesem Vorgang spielen soll.

Im Rahmen seiner Darlegung der Entwicklung des Wahlverfahrens im Laufe der Kirchengeschichte betont Calvin immerhin ausdrücklich, daß es eine Zeit gegeben habe, in der das Volk sogar seine Zustimmung zur Aufnahme eines neuen Klerikers geben mußte.

Schließlich aber sei dem Volk, so weist der Reformator anhand von Konzilsbeschlüssen nach, das Wahlrecht mehr und mehr aus der Hand genommen worden. Doch dafür zeigt er sehr viel Verständnis, wenn er mit Vergil seiner Grundüberzeugung Ausdruck verleiht: "Die Menge ist unbestimmt und spaltet sich in einander widersprechende Bestrebungen auf."[26]

Die darauf folgenden Ausführungen stehen bedauerlicherweise ganz im Schatten des Anliegens, die im Vergleich zur frühen Kirche große Macht des Volkes gut begründet einzuschränken. Dabei interpretiert Calvin die beiden von ihm in diesem Zusammenhang zitierten Abschnitte aus Cyprians 67. Brief wiederum ganz auf sein Anliegen hin und schenkt dadurch der eigentlichen Aussage keine Beachtung, wenn er schreibt:

---

[23]Vgl. *CO* 1:571.

[24]24. Vgl. dazu auch A. Zillenbiller, *Einheit*, 89–91.

[25]Vgl. ebd.: "Habemus ergo, esse hanc ex verbo Dei legitimam ministri vocationem, ubi ex populi consensu et approbatione creantur qui visi fuerint idonei. Praeesse autem electioni debere alios pastores, nequid vel per levitatem, vel per mala studia, vel per tumultum a multitudine peccetur."

[26]Vgl. Otto Weber, *Institutio* [dt.], 732 bzw. *CO* 1, 571: "Incertum scindi studia in contraria vulgus." Dieses Zitat aus Vergils *Aeneis*, 2:39: "scinditur incertum studia in contraria volgus") hatte Calvin allerdings bereits in seiner ersten Ausgabe der Institutio verwendet. Zur Rolle des Volkes vgl. die Bibliographie von R. C. Hancock, *Calvin and the Foundation of Modern Politics* (Ithaca, N.Y.: Cornell University Press, 1989) und sein Kapitel "Government and the People," 62–81.

Auch geht aus den Worten Cyprians hervor, daß diese Bischöfe nicht erst nach der Wahl herbeigerufen wurden, sondern daß sie in alter Zeit gewöhnlich auch bei der Wahl selbst zugegen waren, und das hatte den Zweck, daß sie gleichsam als Leiter (*moderatores*) wirkten, damit bei der Menge kein Durcheinander entstünde.[27]

Der karthagische Bischof ist weit davon entfernt, den Anschein zu erwecken, daß er ein Durcheinander seitens der Menge befürchtet. In Wirklichkeit beabsichtigt er, mit diesen Worten sicherzustellen, daß der Bischof rechtmäßig innerhalb der Kirche stehend, also nicht als Verursacher eines Schismas, gewählt und dann ordiniert wird. Die Rolle des Volkes steht für ihn hier überhaupt nicht in Frage.

Calvin fährt mit seiner Rezeption fort:

Ubi enim dixit plebi esse potestatem vel dignos eligendi sacerdotes, vel indignos recusandi: aliquanto post subiungit, Propter quod diligenter de traditione divina atque Apostolica servandum est et tenendum (quod apud nos quoque et fere per provincias universas tenetur) ut ad ordinationes rite celebrandas, ad eam plebem cui praepositos ordinatur, Episcopi eiusdem provinciae proximi quique conveniant, et Episcopus deligatur plebe praesente.[28]

An diesem Beispiel kann man einerseits erkennen, daß Calvin den Quellentext nahezu wortgetreu in seinen Text aufnimmt, andererseits aber durch die unterschiedliche Gewichtung und Akzentuierung in dem von ihm geschaffenen Kontext zugunsten des von ihm verfolgten Anliegens den Zugang zur wirklichen Auffassung Cyprians verstellt.

Aus diesem Grund kann man auch bei Calvin von einer Uminterpretation der von ihm so geschätzten Quelle sprechen. Dies verbindet ihn, wie anfangs erwähnt, mit den meisten seiner Zeitgenossen. Die Treue zum Quellentext behält er nur solange bei, wie dies seinen Argumenten zu größerem Gewicht verhilft. Greift er in die ursprüngliche Aussage durch eine Veränderung des Textes oder des

---

[27]Vgl. *CO* 1:581: "Et apparet ex Cypriani verbis, non post electionem vocari, sed electioni interesse olim solitos. Atque in eum finem, ut essent quasi moderatores, ne quid in ipsa turba fieret turbulenti."

[28]Vgl. *CO* 1:581. Die Übersetzung O. Webers, 734, lautet: "Cyprian erklärt nämlich zunächst, das Volk habe die Vollmacht, würdige Priester (sacerdotes) zu erwählen und unwürdige ablehnen; dann aber fügt er kurz nachher zu: Deshalb muß—wie das auch bei uns und in fast allen Provinzen geschieht—auf Grund der göttlichen und apostolischen Überlieferung fleißig darauf geachtet und gehalten werden, daß zum gehörigen Vollzug der Ordinationen die Bischöfe der betreffenden Provinz alle in der Gemeinde zusammenkommen, für welche man den Vorsteher ordiniert, und daß der Bischof in Gegenwart des Volkes erwählt wird."

Kontextes ein, so erfolgt dies stillschweigend. Dadurch bleibt der Eindruck bestehen, daß ein Kontinuum zwischen der Kirche des Cyprian und der des Reformators existiert.

History
Source Legacy

Substance Idea
substance evolution/expression

IBM ThinkPad 380
1 800 426 7255 ext. 4651